MONTROSE

Praise for Kill the Messenger

"This is an important piece of work that has been exhaustively researched and written with humility and assurance. Maria Armoudian plunges in beyond the headlines and the mind-numbing television images and the celebrity pundits shouting at one another—what suffices for 'mainstream journalism' today. Instead, she takes us on an eye-opening journey into the struggles of people around the world. From Mexico, Nazi Germany, and Northern Ireland to Taiwan and Rwanda, Senegal and Yugoslavia, she provides the painful history, the deep background, and the authentic understanding most of us have been sorely missing for too long. Her book is both a moving documentary exploration of the darker side of our humanity and a hopeful prescription for our future. She has taken the media, the history, and the culture of these countries and woven it all into a cautionary tale that one won't soon forget."

—Michael Paradies Shoob, filmmaker of *Driven* and *Bush's Brain*

"Maria Armoudian has written a fascinating book that combines the rigors of academic scholarship with the lucidity of journalistic writing at its finest. In today's world the media plays an increasingly important role on all sides of a conflict. It can foment fear and resentment against another group or nation that leads to widespread carnage, terrorism, and genocide; it can also mobilize people against entrenched authorities and empower the oppressed. It is therefore of little surprise that the messengers are at once embraced as heroes and targeted for violent retribution. Armoudian's penetrating insights into the role of the media are sure to enhance our knowledge in the academic community and make compelling reading for a much wider audience. I congratulate Maria Armoudian for her exemplary effort."

—Dipak K. Gupta, Fred J. Hansen Professor of Peace Studies
and Distinguished Professor in Political Science,
San Diego State University

"Maria Armoudian wisely and insightfully inspires us to look at the character of the messenger who delivers today's news. This book should be read by anyone concerned with the fate of the world, which should be everyone."

—Thomas M. Kostigen, Dow Jones MarketWatch *Ethics Monitor*
columnist and *New York Times* bestselling author

KILL THE MESSENGER

THE MEDIA'S ROLE
IN THE FATE OF THE WORLD

MARIA ARMOUDIAN
Foreword by Tom Hayden

Prometheus Books
59 John Glenn Drive
Amherst, New York 14228-2119

Published 2011 by Prometheus Books

Cover image © 2011, Media Bakery, Inc.
Cover design by Nicole Sommer-Lecht

Inquiries should be addressed to
Prometheus Books
59 John Glenn Drive
Amherst, New York 14228–2119
VOICE: 716–691–0133
FAX: 716–691–0137
WWW.PROMETHEUSBOOKS.COM

15 14 13 12 11   5 4 3 2 1

Library of Congress Cataloging-in-Publication Data

Armoudian, Maria.
    Kill the messenger : the media's role in the fate of the world / by Maria Armoudian.
        p. cm.
    Includes bibliographical references.
    ISBN 978–1–61614–387–9 (hardcover : alk. paper)
    ISBN 978–1–61614–388–6 (ebook)
    1. Mass media—Political aspects. 2. Mass media—Social aspects. 3. Mass media—Moral and ethical aspects. 4. Journalism—Political aspects. 5. Journalism—Social aspects. 6. Journalism—Moral and ethical aspects. I. Title.

P95.8.A76 2011
302.23—dc22

2010053122

Printed in the United States of America on acid-free paper

Dedicated to the journalists, leaders, scholars, activists, and members of civil society who work to make the world a kinder, gentler, more peaceful, and healthier place for everyone . . . and to my family, friends, mentors, and champions, to whom I owe my continued existence.

Thank you.

Contents

PART 4. MEDIA AND SOCIAL CHANGE

PART 5. MEDIA'S ROLE IN THE FATE
OF THE WORLD

Acknowledgments

I t is impossible to acknowledge and thank everyone who has contributed directly and indirectly to this book. But I certainly could never have done this if it were not for the people who carried me through the most difficult times: my parents, Aghavni and Garabed Armoudian (my unofficial consultants and copy editors), Bruce Haring, Dan Stormer, Wyatt Underwood, Anna Krajec, Dikran and Rouben Tourian, Jim Provenza, Ron Levy, Senator Richard Polanco, Charles (Kit) and Chris Crittenden, Lance Childers, Jay Levin, Dutch Stowe, Rod Hull, Assemblyman Scott Wildman.

My agent, Paul Levine; our introducer, Tad Daley; my editor, Steven L. Mitchell, and the rest of the Prometheus Books staff.

My academic mentors: Ann Crigler, Pat James, Sheldon Kamieniecki, Ricardo Ramirez, Richard Hrair Dekmejian, Ernest Wilson, Robert English, Daniel Lynch, Abraham Lowenthal, Nora Hamilton, Bryan Rathbun, Howard Gillman, Dan Mazmanian, Janelle Wong, Anthony Kammas, Nick Weller, Art Auerbach, Wayne Glass.

The experts for their time, review, wisdom, comments, and guidance: For South Africa: Albie Sachs, Allister Sparks, James Zug. For the Six Counties/Northern Ireland: Eamonn Mallie, David McKittrick, Desi Murray, Tom Hayden, Alasdair McDonnell, Mari Fitzduff, Martin McGinley, Eamonn McCann, Kelly Candaele, Martina Purdy, Terry McLaughlin, Kevin McCafferty, Sean Brennan, Tom Hartley, Danny and Ciaran Morrison, Sir "Reg" Empey, Brian Rowan, Bill Rolston, Billy Hutchinson, Brendan McCourt, Máirtín Ó Muilleoir, the Loyalists, Unionists, and Republicans who talked with me but have not agreed to be identified. For Chile: John Dinges, Abraham Lowenthal, Marc Cooper. For the Holocaust: Randall Bytwork, Rabbi Haim Dov Beliak. For Bosnia: Robert English, Rudy Baker, Judge Phil Weiner, Mirsad Abazović, Goran Kovačević, Zlatiborka Popov-Momčinović, Vladimir Andrić, Nedim Hogic, Emil Pinkas. For Taiwan: Daniel Lynch, Stanley Rosen, Jeanine Yutani. For Mexico: Nora Hamilton. For climate change: Erik Conway, Naomi Oreskes, Elliott Negin. For the tipping point and Senegal: Cody Donahue, Ganon Gillespie, Molly Melching. For Burundi: Alexis Sinduhije, Bryan Rich, John Marks, Samantha Nduwimana. For the introduction and theoretical chapters: Ann Crigler, Rick Gelm, Charles (Kit) Crittenden, Jack Fong, Phil Seib. For help navigating the research: the VKC librarians, especially Robert Labaree, Mary Clark, Katharin Peter, Rita Romero.

My Armoudian family: Ohan, Rosemary, Adam, Kara, Anto (Nick), Marion, Sophia, Nicholas, Annig and Moushegh Tourian, Dan and Rob Zeytoonian. My grandfather, Megerditch Megerditchian, my late grandparents, and my Megerditchian, Franjeskou, Elmayan, and extended Armoudian family members.

My amazing friends: Ankine Aghassian, Josif and Ani Kahraman, Loucin Mekhjian, Vatche Mankerian, Paul Karon, Joe Dunn, Robert Davidian, Mark Levy, Jenny Kildjian, Spencer Downing, Stephen Barbara, Tom Camarella, Dennis Davis, Adrin Nazarian, Michael Shoob, Hrag Yedalian, Cliff Stewart, Dennis Arnold, Erin Wafer, Jeff Harris, Phil Appleton, David McClure, Garen Yegparian, Emanuela Cariolagian, Eric and Christina Hacopian, Joe Zefran, Denise Robb, Pamela Koslyn, Silva Sevlian, Jeff Kalousdian, Bob Jimenez, Jim Clarke, Sarkis Ghazarian, Sudd Dongre, Bob Benenson, the Sookiasian family, Jim Vaught, Lynn Ruch, Debbie Haring, Gary Simonian, Crystal Shepheard, Kevin Acebo, Rodger Dillan, my LALCV family—especially Jonathan Parfrey, David Allgood, Mitchell Schwartz, Moe Stavnezer, John Fentis, Jessica Hall, Mary Nemick, Joan Satt. My KPFK family, including Maureen Milledge, Alan Minsky, Sonali Kolhatkar, Jon Wiener, Lila Garrett, Ian Masters, Terrance McNally, Jan Goodman and Jerry Manpearl, Stan Misraje, Mark Maxwell, Jee, Tamika, Bob Conger, Jonathan Alexander, Ali Lexa, Jennifer Kiser, Ric Allen, Matt Perez, Leilani Albano, Maggie LePique, Terry Guy, Zuberry Fields. My USC cohort, including Nukhet Sandal, Kate Svyatets, Jenifer Whitten-Woodring, Adrian Felix, Denise Gonzales, Jesse Mills, Dave Walker, Dave Bridge, Jamie Simcox, Katherine Chu, Christina Faegri, Linda Cole, Cathy Ballard, Aurora Ramirez, Jody Battles. My family away from family—the LA Armenian community. My fellow commissioners: Alina Bokde, Joyce Perkins, Irma Munoz, Teresa Villegas.

Foreword

by Tom Hayden

Karl Marx was not a militant on the barricades but a journalist who wrote frequently for the *New York Herald Tribune* on great issues of the day, like the American Civil War. But when he retired to the London Library to write of capitalism and history, he seemed to forget the power of the pen, instead conceiving of murky "material contradictions" as the key origin of consciousness and historical cycles. Nearly a century later, my sociological hero C. Wright Mills commented that it was easy to overlook the role of mass media because "in Marx's day, there was no radio, no movies, no television; only printed matter, which . . . was in such shape that it was possible for an enterprising individual to start up a newspaper or magazine."[1]

Given the times in which he lived, Marx can be forgiven for thinking the essential struggle was over the means of material production, even if he himself was a working journalist and not a factory producer. As late as the early 1960s, as an ambitious young university newspaper editor, I was hardly aware of the power residing in the media either. The Student Nonviolent Coordinating Committee (SNCC) made us aware of the power of photos of beaten protesters and the practical urgency of press releases bringing northern media attention to southern injustice.

But it was not until Marshall McLuhan's *Understanding Media* (1964) and *The Medium Is the Message* (1967) that Marxism became completely inverted, that is, the media that had been considered mere "superstructure" for Marx now became the material basis of consciousness itself. In a typical observation, McLuhan merrily announced that "Heidegger surf-boards along on the electronic wave as triumphantly as Descartes rode the mechanical waves." A historical shift toward digital cognition, from the printing press to the computer, was unleashed. The endless struggle of the many against the few changed from a battle over the means of material production to one over who controls the production of information. The new corporate serfs surfed the Web. The Canon became more powerful than the cannon. Something called media studies all but replaced Marxism and coexists now alongside gender, racial, and environmental studies in the core university curriculum.

This environment is the setting for this book on the media's role in a number of the world's bloodiest and most persistent conflicts, including those in the former Yugoslavia, South Africa, Rwanda, Nazi Germany, Bosnia, Northern Ireland, Chile, Mexico, and Taiwan, and addressing violence against young girls and the debate over global warming. The author, Maria Armoudian, is an Armenian by background, which might explain her personal engagement in these long and painful struggles over identity. She is the host of a weekly talk show on KPFK, the Pacifica radio station in Los Angeles, and a fellow in political science and international relations at the Center for International Studies at the University of Southern California.

Armoudian tells each of these horror stories with a fine journalist's eye for drama and narrative, as well as the unique ability that certain journalists have to focus on unspeakable episodes that most people prefer not to know or pass on to their children. In fastening her attention to so much pain, she also finds threads of redemption in the bravery of so many journalists. Hundreds of journalists (to be exact, 850 since 1992, and 72 in 2009 alone) have been killed as eyewitnesses to violence. These people were not detached and neutral bystanders; given the growth of secrecy, journalists are an enemy to the institutions they cover.

This work is a survey of media patterns in conflict and crisis situations. But it is clear from Armoudian's account that the "mainstream media," whether state or corporate controlled, have largely acted as an instrument for shielding government, corporate, or military interests. There are exceptions—for example, in the case of special investigative reporters, or for media that find niche markets with a countercultural bias—but in general, the "mainstream media" reflect the status quo. We lack a new C. Wright Mills to take this question further and reveal whether there are interlocking directorates, for example, that connect the supposedly independent media with the interests of the state or corporations.

Take the case of Iraq and Afghanistan. Are there top journalists today who are "assets" of the Central Intelligence Agency (CIA) as there were in the 1950s? The matter is shrouded in secrecy. Or are there social connections that produce a common mind-set, as in the case of the *New York Times*' Judith Miller, who wrote the misleading front-page articles about mysterious aluminum tubes that shaped the official justification for the 2003 Iraq invasion? Is it only accidental that in a "free media in our free society," virtually no mainstream editorials have appeared to urge the withdrawal of all our troops from Iraq and Afghanistan—an opinion shared by as many as 25 to 50 percent of the American people, depending on how the survey questions are asked?

If the media fail their critical function in the run-up to wars, it is also true that the media sometimes serve to interrupt the war makers when doubt has spread into key institutions, as in the case of the 1971 Pentagon Papers disclosures by the *New York Times* or the 2010 publication of the WikiLeaks documents by the *Times, Guardian*, and *Der Spiegel*. Are papers like the *Times* capable of intellectual growth on their own, are they responsive to complaints from the reader market, or do their editors and publishers represent particular viewpoints within the national elites? How are individuals chosen to be on their editorial boards? What are the roles of their publishers? Who decides to delay a story at the request of the White House or the Pentagon? We simply don't understand the internal processes, which are kept opaque by the same journalists who demand transparency of others. But obviously the mainstream media is not a monolith, though it moves in mysterious ways.

But Armoudian does suggest the cutting-edge role of an "independent media," the underground press, and more recently the blogosphere, in reporting important news far ahead of the mainstream. This is not a new phenomenon, as she notes. The story of the My Lai Massacre in Vietnam was reported first by a passionate young reporter for the Pacific News Service, Seymour Hersh, who soon after became one of the country's leading investigative journalists at the *New York Times*.

When I began writing and reporting, the concept of an "investigative reporter" was unknown—or at least unmentioned—in the schools of journalism and among budding writers. The niche of investigative journalism grew in the default of mainstream journalism and was incorporated (along with the editorial-opinion page) as a response to the rapid growth of the counterculture and so-called underground papers in every city and on every campus in the country. Publications like *Ramparts* went further, not only scooping the mainstream media but becoming glossy and successful in their time.

Armoudian gets it right that social movements invent their own media and propaganda organs, shedding light on conditions that other-wise go unreported but that, in time, gain the attention of the main-stream media and the wider public. They also reflect an alternative com-munity of meaning to the media narratives that typically reduce the news of protests to fringe or violent behavior. The alternative media wrests control of the all-important naming process from the elite media and hands it to writers and spokespersons who represent the authentic voices of protest. They provide vital information, a sense of belonging, and direction for those at the current margins. They do not wait for the mainstream media to catch up. They begin to embody a new ethic: We write ourselves into history. We write, therefore we exist. (Or is it, per-haps, we exist, therefore we write?)

I am not sure that media studies, as an analytic framework, can see that "all the news that is fit to print" is itself a wholly inadequate descrip-tion of the journalistic mission. The very phrase "fit to print" suggests a censorial and elitist standard. Real news—like the four North Carolina students who began the sit-in movement in February 1960—is not really news as conventionally defined when it is most important, at the moment of its inception. There is a response to McLuhan that says the revolution will *not* be televised—at least not at its birth.

Mills believed that the differences separating a "community of publics" from a "mass society" were fourfold: (1) in the ratio between givers of opinion and recipients; (2) in the possibility of answering back; (3) whether there were possibilities of acting on information; and (4) whether people have "genuine autonomy from instituted authority."[2] In a "public," he wrote, "virtually as many people express opinions as receive them," "public communications are so organized that there is a chance immediately and effectively to answer back," there are "ready outlets for effective action," and "authoritative institutions do not pene-trate the public, which is thus more or less *autonomous* in its operations."

How far we are from the autonomous public, one might say, espe-cially after reading Armoudian's accounts. But Mills too was a journalist, though describing himself professionally as an academic sociologist. Through his opinionated works, he became more than an objective observer but was participatory observer as well. He realized that through his writings and criticisms he could alter the subject matter at hand. The "subject matter" included his own role.

Where Mills was very much a loner, a whole generation of Maria Armoudians has become media reformers, a collective presence inside and outside the media world representing a journalistic community of conscience.[3] Instead of viewing media as an objective institution, she sees herself and her peers as inescapably part of its dynamics. Her most interesting chapter, I believe, is the final one, in which she conceives of building a better media as part of building a better society, complete with a concrete and international code of conduct for all journalists. Her closing image, drawn from the Quaker tradition, is one of journalists who are "holding candles to the darkness." May more be drawn to this moral core of a profession at risk.

Preface

History can be recounted in many ways and seen through many lenses. This book looks at some of the last century's most profound historical developments through the lens of media and their contributions. But as with any such approach, when one focuses on a particular aspect, or "frame," of a history, one is bound to lose some other facets. That is the essence of "framing," a key concept in this book that pertains to selecting, organizing, and distilling massive quantities of information into something more understandable and meaningful. We make decisions largely based on frames—decisions that collectively affect the fate of the world.

Each of the following chapters first takes you squarely into the lives of a few men and women who experienced—and often helped shape—some of the most dramatic and excruciating developments of the last century. Through their lives and experiences, the chapters explore how such developments—genocides, vicious wars, peace agreements, bloody coups, democratization, social change, and environmental policy failures—came to be, with emphasis on the vital role of media. Sometimes, due to the sheer brutality of the events, these stories are hard to bear, even long after they have occurred. But revisiting them—unsanitized—is perhaps critical toward understanding what is really at stake as well as the forces that shaped the outcomes.

Through these stories and the analysis in this book, I hope to show the profound role that the media play in people's lives and to stimulate new thought about how to approach our future media—as media professionals, as policymakers, and as a humanity. But I do not intend to rehash a "media effects" debate or tackle the so-called CNN effect about whether broadcasting humanitarian crises catalyzes public policy.[1] Rather, mine is a "constructionist" approach, recognizing that the media are one of many integral forces that shape the present and future and which are, in turn, shaped by social and political forces. And while this book predominantly focuses on journalism, it also includes other types of media—books, comedy, radio drama, and film—as they also contribute to the construction of social and political reality.

19

While there were numerous other histories that could have been included in these pages, I chose those that I believed collectively demonstrated a picture of media's role in the fate of the world. The research is based on peer-reviewed literature, available news articles, books, transcripts, and interviews.

Every book has inherent limitations, and this one is no exception. It was simply impossible, for example, to include all the important factors and developments in a project of this size. Each chapter rightfully deserves volumes of its own books and years of exploration. And learning the disparate histories of powerful world events alongside the theoretical literature in a short period of time has been a daunting task.

I am deeply indebted to the subject and regional experts as well as to family and friends who took the time to read and comment on the respective chapters. Ultimately, I hope to have shown two things: first, how deeply media can affect our lives—for good and bad—and second, that now, more than ever, it is vital to create, empower, and support responsible media that educate, explain, and elevate, and to discard those approaches that merely blame, deprecate, and divide.

Introduction

It was a lovely July morning in Knoxville, Tennessee. The sun shone down on the lush green valley where two hundred proud parents and other churchgoers filled church pews in the local Unitarian Universalist church. Sitting shoulder to shoulder, they smiled happily, captivated by the children's performance of *Annie Junior*. Outside the church, fifty-eight-year-old Jim David Adkisson was infuriated. "Liberals are evil," he wrote after he purchased a semiautomatic shotgun, sawed off the barrel, and placed it inside a guitar case.[1]

When the door to the church hall swung open, the stout man with a mustache and wavy, gray locks casually entered. Members thought nothing of him; he could have been any child's uncle. He might have been a musician. After all, he carried a guitar case. But Adkisson was armed with more than the twelve-gauge shotgun in the guitar case, more than the rounds of shells crammed into his fanny pack. He was armed with long-steeped beliefs that liberals had "ruined" America and an intense motivation to save the country that he loved from the grip of the "left-wing conspiracy."[2]

Adkisson walked past the children who were awaiting their turn on stage and into the church sanctuary. He casually reached into his guitar case, drew out his shotgun, and opened fire, killing two church members and injuring eight before he was tackled by a small group of parishioners.[3]

His ultimate desire, Adkisson wrote, was to kill "every Democrat in the Senate and House, the one hundred people in Bernard Goldberg's book," and "everyone in the mainstream media," which included the major networks CNN and PBS. But because his true targets were "inaccessible" to him, the former US Army private instead aimed for those who voted for Democrats—members of the Knoxville Unitarian Universalist Church, which declared that it was "transforming the world through love and justice." Adkisson admitted, "This was a hate crime: I hate the damn left-wing liberals."[4]

What drove Adkisson's rage? The out-of-work truck driver felt hopeless about his own life and the state of the country for which he had served. An avid reader of books by radio commentators Michael Savage,

Bill O'Reilly, and Sean Hannity, he had come to believe that "liberals are evil." They are, in his own words, "traitors," a "cancerous pestilence," and "like termites." Liberals, he said, had "ruined every institution in America." It was his duty, he wrote, calling for "like-minded" people to join him in taking matters into their own hands. They must "go and kill . . . liberals" and "Democrats. . . . Kill them in the streets. Kill them wherever they gather."[5]

Adkisson truly believed he was on a mission. Proud of his pernicious act, he pleaded "guilty as charged" at his trial and declared that he would do it again if he could.[6] Why?

The books found in Adkisson's home give us a clue. It seems that Adkisson took literally what he had read or heard in mass media, material that may have been meant as dramatization and entertainment. Cast as "more dangerous than Hitler," liberals and their philosophies, according to radio host Michael Savage, are "the HIV virus [sic] that weakens the defense cells of a nation."[7] "The left wing," Savage said, "is on the side of the terrorists. . . . They're actually glad the World Trade Centers went down."[8]

Savage, whose program is heard on three hundred fifty radio stations and reaches some 8.25 million listeners weekly, is among a clique of broadcasters and authors who have, for years, used hateful language toward "liberals."[9] Broadcaster Rush Limbaugh called liberals a "scourge" and argued that "liberals are destroying virtually everything they touch."[10] Author and media personality Ann Coulter claimed, "Liberals are always rooting for savages against civilization." That included, in her estimation, rooting for "Nazis."[11] They are "treasonous," she argued, both on The O'Reilly Factor on Fox News and in her latest book, Treason: Liberal Treachery from the Cold War to the War on Terrorism. "Whenever the nation is under attack . . . liberals side with the enemy."[12]

Liberals, according to these broadcasters, are "raping" Americans.[13] "Get ready to get gang-raped again," said Limbaugh on his syndicated program. "People in the private sector are getting raped by this administration."[14] "[President] Obama is raping America," according to Savage. "Obama is raping our values. Obama is raping our democracy."[15] And Limbaugh warned of "gang rape by a Democratic Party, the American left and the drive-by media to finally take us out."[16]

Throughout the "shock jock" circuit, broadcasters sling malevolent slurs at "liberals," Democratic leaders, and other targets. In these media, US president Barack Obama was called a thug, a vampire, a dictator, a mobster, a racist, an agent of voter fraud, an anti-Semite, an associate of terrorists, a liar, and the Antichrist; his agenda has been vilified as anti-American.[17]

Just how truly evil are liberals and Democrats? According to many of these broadcasters, they are comparable to mass killer Adolf Hitler and the Nazis. President Obama "wants to gas the Jews, like the PLO [Palestine Liberation Organization] wants to gas the Jews, like the Nazis gassed the Jews," said Bill Cunningham on his syndicated radio program. Savage argued that Obama planned to intern American citizens into camps and called his policies "Hitler-like executive orders." He called a speech by then-senator Hillary Clinton "Hitler dialogue" and labeled Congressman Maurice Hinchey a "Nazi" seeking "the final solution for conservatives on talk radio" for his position on media reform.[18] On Fox News Channel's *Hannity and Colmes* program, Fox commentator Ann Coulter called Obama a "two-bit Hitler" and his memoir a "dime store *Mein Kampf*." Limbaugh compared the Democratic Party to the Nazi Party and cheered protesters carrying "Obama-as-Hitler posters and the Nazi stuff," calling them "fabulous and fantastic." Even on the more mainstream ABC network, broadcaster Mark Levin called President Obama's healthcare plan "Hitleresque."[19] And while liberal media also feature outrage, incivility, mockery, and sarcasm, scholars have found that the conservative media are considerably "nastier," and they occupy much more of the airwaves, particularly on radio.[20]

Harmless fodder? Entertainment? Perhaps. But many Americans came to believe the comparisons made in the media. In early 2010, a Harris Poll showed that 20 percent of Americans believed that President Obama was pursuing "many of the same things that Hitler did." Those with either a high school education or less were even more likely to believe the Obama–Hitler comparison (24 percent). Divided by party, the numbers are particularly striking, with more than one-third of Republicans believing the Hitler statement.[21]

In the same poll, some responded with more outlandish beliefs. Among Republicans, for example, nearly 25 percent believed that President Obama "may be the Antichrist."[22] Across all American adults, 14 percent believed in a possible Obama–Antichrist connection.[23] More than one-quarter of American adults (29 percent) believed that President

Obama "wants to turn over US sovereignty to a one-world government," that he "resents America's heritage," that "he is a domestic enemy that the US constitution speaks of" (25 percent), and that "he is anti-American" (23 percent). Less-educated Americans and Republicans held these beliefs at much higher rates.[24]

Might these beliefs have consequences? They might. While a causal relationship has not been established, in the United States membership in conspiracy-rooted or antigovernment organizations has surged.[25] In 2009, some 363 new "patriot" groups emerged, reaching a total of 512, of which 127 have militias.[26] By the spring of 2010, these types of extreme groups numbered nearly one thousand, then surpassed one thousand by the spring of 2011.[27] Some of them believe that the "genocide" of the white race is under way and that the Federal Emergency Management Agency (FEMA) is secretly running concentration camps. This growth has also corresponded with an increase in sales of guns and ammunition.[28]

In 2010, threats to members of Congress surged 300 percent[29] and reached an all-time, historical high, according to the FBI records obtained by the Hill. Among some twenty-six threats of violence directed at representatives in both major parties, provocateurs warned lawmakers that they would "come after" them. At least two threatened to "put a bullet" in a congressperson's head or body, and several threatened to kill family members and staff. One letter said, "vote for progressive liberal programs and DIE in the near future. . . . Make no mistake we will come for you, take the wife out to dinner [and] risk getting shot, take the kids to soccer practice [and] risk getting shot." In one case, directed at Senate Finance Committee chairman Max Baucus, a caller said, please tell the senator that, like, he wants to redistribute my income, and I'm gonna redistribute his brain with a f—ing baseball bat and his head. . . . I'll kill that f—er." Another caller suggested that a congresswoman's "off-spring will pay" for her affirmative vote on healthcare reform.[30]

In addition to the threats, a flurry of politically motivated, small-scale violence surfaced, directed primarily at Democrats. Angry Americans hurled bricks and other objects through office windows of at least two Democratic lawmakers, spat at a Democratic congressman, and cut the gas lines to the home of another Democratic congressman's brother.[31] Months earlier, someone painted a swastika over a congressman's name-plate outside of his office and faxed him irate letters, one of which read,

"Death to all Marxists! Foreign and Domestic!"[32] In early January 2011, the violence turned deadly: A gunman opened fire, killing a federal judge and five other people and injuring another fourteen, including Arizona Congresswoman Gabrielle Giffords. One firefighter refused to respond to the shooting because of "political bantering" in which he "did not want to be involved," according to internal memoranda.[33]

Could the media's messages have had an impact on these developments? Scholars have been studying this question, and the answer is a resounding "maybe." Under certain conditions, media have exacerbated conflict and accelerated disintegration by reinforcing differences and divisions, focusing on the negative, and using divisive frames that portray realities as if they are "us-versus-them" or "blame frames," which condemn persons or groups for complex political problems that they alone did not create.[34] But although mass media have been used to fuel some of the world's worst atrocities, media have also been known to help build bridges between adversaries and build communities, educate publics, support the protection of human rights, and elevate human dignity.

MEDIA AND MASS VIOLENCE

Over the past century, the "major humanitarian crises and human rights conflicts . . . began with a propaganda phase, where extremists took control of the means of mass communication and used them to incite conflict," wrote political communication scholar Mark Thompson.[35] In these cases, extremists used mass media to incite fear, anger, and hatred for an "evil other" and to galvanize forces for violence and complicity in violence. Propagandists laid blame upon an "enemy" for socioeconomic and political problems, depicted "them" as either evil or subhuman, and disseminated messages to generate fear about the future and other negative emotions.[36] When people believed these frames—these hypercritical imagined realities—any hope of discussion, compromise, and agreement became virtually impossible.[37]

Wars "begin in the minds of men," often through submersion in vitriol, blame, and hate, which promotes the interpretation of sociopolitical or economic situations as so horribly unjust and unacceptable that the only recourse is to destroy the "other."[38] Violence, torture, and mass killing are justified by wrapping these acts in a "noble" cause that masks the ugliness and makes destruction an important part of a larger goal: exterminating the "others" is framed as vital for the "greater good." This combination of language and ideas makes "fighting words"—language that incites violence.[39]

In the most extreme cases, blame and hate frames have justified and fueled some of the world's greatest atrocities. In Rwanda, for example, after decades of intermarrying and living in relative harmony, Rwandan Hutus, en masse, mutilated, raped, tortured, and murdered their Tutsi neighbors, using clubs, machetes, acid, boiling water, and the spread of HIV. After just three months, the Hutu people had brutally and heinously exterminated three-quarters of the Tutsi population. Yet the violators were not hardened criminals with violent histories. Rather, they were ordinary people—farmers, active churchgoers, and teachers. But most were remorseless in the killings, believing that they were doing an important job, exterminating the "cockroaches" that were ruining their beloved country.[40]

While many factors combined to influence the Hutu people to commit these atrocities, among the most important was a powerful mass media, through which broadcasters persuaded and organized Hutus to carry out genocide against the Tutsis through messages of hate, fear, and "noble" lies: They must kill the Tutsis in order to establish a majoritarian democracy, aid development, emancipate the "victimized" Hutu race, and end Tutsi domination. Tutsis, they claimed, were rising to victimize Hutus as they had historically done and, therefore, the Hutus must kill "them" before they kill "us."[41]

In Nazi Germany and the former Yugoslavia, similar blame and hate frames made killing the "other" part of an important cause. In Nazi Germany, destroying Jews, Slavs, Poles, Gypsies, Serbs, homosexuals, and disabled people was portrayed as an important part of "purifying" and rescuing a great Germany from "infestation" and the throes of an international conspiracy that was poised to annihilate the Germans. Propagandists usurped control of the mass media and increasingly inundated audiences with framing that justified their cause and supported their ideology. In these narratives, their "enemies" were so pernicious that they had to be destroyed; they were "fleas," a "disease," groups that were hellbent on destroying Germany. It was again "kill or be killed."[42]

Similarly, in the former Yugoslavia, nationalist television programmers warned their respective communities that the "others" were raping and killing their people as part of a planned "genocide" or ethnic cleansing. Hundreds of newspapers and television stations channeled nationalist rhetoric, while journalists presented "evidence" that aroused fear, confusion, and hatred within the "kill or be killed" frame. Many were convinced of these atrocities and answered the call to rescue their own people, and some "retaliated" with horrific human rights abuses against innocent people.[43]

Even as far back as 1915, when media were considerably less technologically advanced, propaganda machines worked to blame an "enemy" for problems within the Ottoman Empire. Armenians, said the Young Turk government, were a treasonous threat to national security and plotting an uprising to kill the empire's Ittihadist leaders. Similar to the genocides that would follow later in the century, a designated department—in this case, the Turkish War Office—created the narrative and campaign, then propagated it through such media as the weekly magazine *Harb Mecmuasi* to justify annihilating an entire race of people.[44]

In each of these cases, members of the targeted groups were portrayed as so despicable, inferior, evil, or subhuman that destroying them was cast as an honorable duty toward the greater good, such as "rescuing" a country, a principle, or a culture. Although some people in the respective communities remained unconvinced, for many, lethal violence became *desirable*, not simply permissible.

But if wars and other violence "begin in the minds of men," then "they are not over until they have ended there, too."[45] Can media help to assuage years or even generations of extreme animosity? Once the demarcations, emotions, and experiences are firmly established, can media make a difference? It is a daunting task, but in some cases media have facilitated peacemaking.

In Burundi, Rwanda's "twin" nation with which it shares a border, a similar fratricidal war between the Hutus and Tutsis raged, leaving tens of thousands dead. While Burundi's traditional media exacerbated the conflict, new media emerged and eventually helped facilitate a turning point. Through media projects, including a radio production studio, Studio Ijambo, Hutus and Tutsis, once enemies, joined together to cooperatively produce news, features stories, and other programs to promote healthy and constructive dialogue, as well as mutual understanding and reconciliation among antagonistic groups. While multiple international efforts worked to secure peace accords, Ijambo's programs and their progeny helped end rumormongering and bridge the divide, leading numerous Hutus and Tutsis to make amends and reengage with each other. While the peace is fragile and tenuous, media were vital in helping diminish violence and deepen insights and cooperation between the warring communities.[46]

Instead of emphasizing differences and escalating violence, these media focused on common ground and sought to develop deeper understanding and empathy between those who might otherwise have remained enemies and escalated retaliatory violence. Such projects have emerged in Catalonia, Nicaragua, South Africa, and Colombia, where citizens of warring sides work together on media projects that might begin to resolve intractable political problems and quell the madness of tit-for-tat violence. In one of the most violent South African communities, mortal enemy commanders collaboratively produced a film seeking to understand the roots of mass violence. Over six months, they worked together documenting the impact of the destruction on their communities. The video spawned discussions and ultimately the realization that the chief division between them was political rhetoric. In the spirit of reconciliation, the community forged new projects to heal the discord.[47]

In Northern Ireland, after decades of internecine war, the international and domestic media helped usher in and encourage support for a historic peace agreement. Though it's an imperfect agreement, the cyclical pattern of sectarian violence has largely subsided. In an unlikely outcome, warring factions agreed to share power and resolve conflict through democratic means, and it might not have been possible without media recharacterizing the conflict, legitimizing the political actors and their grievances, and avoiding the "hate trap."[48]

Across the globe, media have impacted matters of life and death, human rights, health, and governance. A faction of Chilean media professionals actively participated in the destruction of Chile's once-pluralistic democracy and genteel culture. With wild accusations and antagonistic frames, these journalists intensified the societal disintegration that helped provoke the 1973 military coup. These same journalists hid the junta's atrocities and legitimized the regime while it tortured, killed, "disappeared," and exiled thousands of its own people. It took many years of life-risking work for another set of political leaders and journalists to rebuild Chile's democracy.[49]

In South Africa, many journalists in the Afrikaans-language domestic media ignored the brutalities that Africans faced and legitimized the apartheid system. But other journalists and leaders refused to accept the status quo and exposed the system's horrors. Over time, with international media on their side, these journalists and activists built an enormous global campaign that helped replace the apartheid government with a multiracial democracy.[50]

Under the new South African government, the mass media elevated the status of the Truth and Reconciliation Commission with live broadcasts and continual national coverage. Through the window of mass media, South Africans, long divided by race, collectively experienced their history, acquired shared concepts, and established new principles, ultimately helping bridge divisions and establish new laws and norms reflective of multiracial political equality.[51]

In both Mexico and Taiwan, a group of journalists helped expose corruption and systemic injustices in their respective governments, paving the way for greater transparency and democracy. They faced firings and prison sentences; some faced death, and some were killed. But with a relentless fight and support from the international community, they helped usher in a more transparent and less abusive government. While still imperfect and struggling, both systems are more open, and people are less inclined to accept the old authoritarian government practices.[52]

In Senegal, media helped thousands of young girls escape the excruciating pain of "the custom," a long-standing, sometimes deadly practice of cutting off girls' external genitals, usually with crude cutting tools and no anesthetic. When seen within the context of such larger social goals as health, human rights, and democracy, female genital cutting (FGC), once a social necessity, was no longer appropriate. Through an education and media campaign that combined local and national efforts, the once-sacred, "commonsense" custom became questionable and was ultimately abandoned across thousands of communities.[53]

How media help shape political outcomes is the subject of a later chapter, but in brief, media play a critical role in helping people understand and evaluate sociopolitical developments; they contribute to building culture and help define what is and what is not acceptable. When media get it wrong, and when people believe these inaccurate frameworks, it can set in motion some disasterous possibilities. Just as "wars begin in the minds of men" through "social construction," so do enemies, heroes, institutions, commonsense "truths," propriety, values, norms, and "the way we do things." Constructed "realities" that are disseminated through mass media become increasingly engrained. Media set agendas, and they prime or provoke thoughts and concerns. They disseminate frames that favor a particular ideological perspective and contribute to the shaping of identities and cultures. Collectively, these agendas, beliefs, emotions, identities, and cultures produce political outcomes. Of course, the construction is not one-directional. As media affect systems, cultures, and outcomes, the media are also affected by them in a dynamic process of social construction.[54]

There are some hard, persistent realities, however, that no amount of spin or reframing can change. In these cases, media can either elucidate, explain, and help publics understand, or they can distract, distort, and mislead, which can have dire consequences. Such is the case of climate change. By framing global warming as a debate when no meaningful debate exists in the scientific community, the public was left misinformed of the true nature of the threat, leaving a harrowing problem that affects the fate of the entire world unmitigated.[55]

Today, in the age of WikiLeaks and new forms of media, the media's impact is both magnified and diffused. It is magnified with its expanded reach and the enhanced speed of communication. It is diffused because new media have multiplied the potential voices, messages, and frames that enter the public sphere, creating a larger menu of perspectives from which people can choose. This process has expanded the number of power brokers and power wielders, allowing power to spread beyond government officials into the hands of nongovernmental organizations and actors who now share in making meaning and in explaining and constructing realities. While state actors scramble to maintain control over the flow of information, citizen journalists, hackers, and norm entrepreneurs are asserting themselves and seizing the reins to define what can and should be. With the aggregations of both new media and more traditional media, they are working to achieve those ends. Through multiple channels, including Qatar-based Al Jazeera and the Internet, for example, citizens of Tunisia and Egypt asserted their desires and demands for a more just society, generating a vast outpouring of world-wide sympathy as they toppled their dictators. Through media, citizens of the world joined in celebration with Tunisians and Egyptians as their revolutions inspired additional waves of defiance and determination toward creating more representative governments. And despite efforts to quash it, the revolutions were, indeed, televised.[56]

In many parts of the world, through media, rising classes of programmers, journalists, concerned citizens, and political entrepreneurs are creating new sources of information and understandings, some that may harm and some that may heal, raising the fundamental question of this book: Is it possible to use the channels of media to construct great societies and fulfill human potential? I assert that the highest and best use of media is yet to be explored. By providing vital information and important contexts, media can help their audiences understand the roots of sociopolitical issues, explore levelheaded solutions, and engage with their communities in more meaningful ways. With great content and framing, they can help build deeper understanding among people, help protect human rights, facilitate democratic processes, inspire excellence, and contribute to the highest fulfillment of human potential.

Each of the following chapters is a snapshot in time, gazing into a particular region where media have played a prominent role in a particular outcome. While the chapters strive to capture the key dynamics through the eyes and ears of media, each chapter truly warrants substantially more discussion than can be provided here. But through these pages, one can see the crucial roles media have played: building and destroying, exposing and hiding, withholding and disseminating vital information and perspectives from which social and political realities are made, realities that then shape the future of media. At the end, we delve into the questions of "how" and "why" media may have these effects and explore how we might "kill the messenger"—today's media paradigm—in the service of a new model that might help take humanity to its next level. As we say in radio, stay tuned.

PART 1

THE BAD NEWS:
MEDIA, GENOCIDE, AND WAR

Chapter 1

Hate as a Contagion: Media and the Rwandan Genocide

Jean's[1] brother Michel lay before him, battered, bleeding, and writhing in agony from the bludgeoning he had just endured by members of his ethnic group. Jean stood, machete in hand and gun at his head, confused about the decision he was being forced to make—decapitate his brother or face his own brutal demise. Both Jean and his brother were Hutus, one of three ethnic groups that occupy Rwanda. But his brother was married to a Tutsi woman, the group targeted for annihilation by the Hutu-led Rwandan government in the spring of 1994. When the Rwandan genocide began, Jean and Michel had offered food to Tutsi refugees who were driven from their homes through mass burning and pillaging. As penance for aiding the *imyenzi* (the Rwandan word for "cockroach"), Rwandan military reservists ordered Jean to behead his brother. He stood frozen, hesitant, distressed: Could he kill his own brother? As he agonized, reservists reminded him that he must either kill or be killed as an accomplice to the Tutsis. In a moment of fear and confusion, Jean thrust the machete into his brother's neck, severing his head from the rest of his body.

A local tavern owner and father of three, Jean was among the less extreme Hutus caught up in the mass-murder sprees and "made" to kill their loved ones. Others like him killed neighbors, family members, and friends under a similar "kill or be killed as an accomplice" threat. So they killed or helped kill to prevent being placed on the government's infamous hit list of recalcitrant Hutus who were also to be hunted down and destroyed. Some Hutus killed one group of Tutsis while simultaneously hiding and protecting others who were dear to them or who offered bribes for shelter.[2] Others anguished over "killing my neighbor; we used to drink together. . . . He was like a relative." Yet thousands of Hutus were more like Pierre, a father and subsistence-farmer-turned-killer. Pierre and his neighbors came to believe that the Tutsis had killed Rwandan President Juvénal Habyarimana and thus refused to "stand with their arms crossed [doing nothing]." Filled with rage, Pierre and thousands of regular Rwandan Hutus—farmers, teachers, parents, and active churchgoers—sought revenge, going on murderous rampages to eliminate those whom they believed were evil, criminal accomplices out to kill their Hutu brethren. They were on a mission to eradicate an infestation of vermin, infiltrators, and criminals who were coming to take their land and pile their dead bodies into "pits." They killed every Tutsi with whom they had ever been in contact—community members, neighbors, and friends. Children and infants were hacked up mercilessly because "if you kill a rat, you must also kill the rat in gestation; it will grow up to be a rat, like the others." To prolong their pain before death, victims were often physically and mentally tortured. One primary school teacher, Naasson, pounded a young child relentlessly with a hammer before finally killing him. Another, Jean Bosco, crushed an already-battered ten-year-old girl with a stone.[3]

Women were targeted for torture through rape. Told that they must rape the women before slaying them, men often sequentially raped women until their victims collapsed. They raped with farm tools, spears, gun barrels, and machetes, or mutilated their victims' genitals and breasts with acid or boiling water. One group of soldiers held a hatchet to a twelve-year-old boy's throat, forcing him to rape his mother, while his younger siblings were forced to hold her legs open. Some raped to intentionally spread HIV, killing their victims slowly and painfully. In fact, 70 percent of surviving rape victims contracted HIV.[4]

Some mothers killed their own children before others could slay them. Other mothers watched helplessly as mad killers slaughtered their children—one by one or two by two.[5] Children begged and screamed for mercy as they watched their parents and siblings butchered. After witnessing eight of her siblings be bludgeoned to death, one three-year-old child cried out, "Please don't kill me. I'll never be Tutsi again!" But without a second thought, killers clubbed her until her screaming faded to silence.[6]

Ultimately, "everywhere I went, I was a killer," admitted Pierre, who participated in multiple murders. Sometimes he and others used the rampage as a means of seeking revenge upon their Hutu rivals. By falsifying their foes' identities as Tutsis, their fellow Hutus were subjected to the same horrors.[7]

Although some impoverished Hutus participated in the murders for monetary gain or prestige, others were prominent members of society. Doctors, priests, teachers, and school principals all "rolled up their sleeves to get a good grip on their machetes," hacking up their colleagues, students, and patients. "They all killed with their own hands [and] . . . they had no trouble sleeping."[8]

Similarly disturbing was the slaying of people who had lived like brothers, such as the teammates on the local soccer team. When the slaughters began, star soccer player Evergiste, a Tutsi, fled to the home of his most trusted friend, a fellow Hutu teammate. To his horror, he found his friend, bloody machete in hand, had already slaughtered two children. At the moment of realization, Evergiste fled—in a full sprint—to the forest, burying himself deep in the vegetation to hide from his pursuers. He recalled passing "the ball back and forth" with those same teammates who now rabidly hunted him. Evergiste sank into the swampy vegetation, listening attentively to angry, taunting voices nearing him.

"Evergiste!" they called out. "We sorted through the piles of bodies; we have not seen your cockroach face!" they yelled. "We are going to sniff you out. . . . We shall get you!"[9]

For days, Evergiste remained buried in the swamps, rising only in the darkness of night to scrounge for food. As a Tutsi, he lives with the reality that "not one teammate gave a helping hand to another." Another surviving soccer player, Celestin, lamented, "We had lived as brother players" and "parted as enemy brothers." Ultimately, he noted, "Nothing survived the genocide. It cut down soccer with a casual swipe, like all the rest."[10]

Even the most vulnerable populations received no mercy. Hutu killers ripped the gates off of a maternity hospital, hacked up new mothers with machetes, and smashed their nursing infants against walls. Some tossed live infants into heaps of corpses to slowly die of starvation.[11] Others, to prolong the agony, "would call everyone to watch," then hack off their victims' limbs or crush their bones without killing them, leaving them to suffer until death.[12]

Acts of compassion were severely punished. A young woman, Mathilde, spotted a child left for dead after his head had been split with a machete. Day after day, Mathilde returned to his hiding place, delivering food, water, and medicine—until the day her deeds were discovered. In one slash, her husband slit her throat.[13]

After decades of living in relative harmony with each other, Rwandan Hutus from all walks of life rose to annihilate the Tutsis.[14] Using farm tools, knives, acid, or boiling water, they hacked, mutilated, and tortured their fellow Rwandans to their deaths. In search-and-destroy missions, they moved from house to house and scrutinized every crevice to be sure they had not missed someone in hiding.[15] If Tutsis were discovered, the killers dragged them out and publicly clubbed or stabbed them to death. Women pleaded for their lives, sometimes for twenty minutes or more, yet the Hutu killers hacked off their limbs or bludgeoned them to death while other Hutus walked by, going about their business.[16] To ensure they had not missed a hidden Tutsi, "workers" set houses and entire villages ablaze.

In droves, Tutsi families fled for their lives, seeking cover in churches or other public places, only to find these locales had become slaughterhouses, where killers mutilated hundreds at a time, sometimes by cutting off their genitalia to inflict the greatest possible pain.[17]

Roadblocks littered the land, guarded by townspeople who had become bloodthirsty warriors and ensured that no Tutsi escaped death. Mutilated bodies filled church aisles, pews, halls, city streets, and alleyways in the once-idyllic land. Pools of blood "turned black in the heat of the sun." Entire villages became heaps of dead bodies—so many that crews commissioned dump trucks to dispose of them.[18]

In just over three months, the Hutu people had brutally and heinously exterminated three-quarters of Rwanda's Tutsi population. Hutus were also killed—either because they resembled the Tutsis, had helped a Tutsi escape, or because they had refused to kill.[19] Most violators were ordinary people who had not committed violence in the past. Yet they were remorseless in the killings, believing that they were doing an important job by avenging the death of their president, defending themselves from what they believed was an oncoming slaughter, and exterminating the "cockroaches" that were causing all their political and economic troubles.[20]

What converted the Hutu people from good neighbors to savage murderers in such a short period of time? Although there had been periods of ethnic rivalries among extremists, most Tutsis and Hutus had lived side by side, intermarried, and attended the same schools and churches. Historically, they had banded together to fight common enemies.[21] And for centuries, they shared stories, lives, food, drink, and beds. Differences between them were minimal. Physically, one could hardly distinguish their respective traits, and they shared racial backgrounds, languages, customs, traditions, and territories. Most Rwandans had little ill will toward their own neighbors, teammates, fellow churchgoers, and friends. But in a matter of weeks, Hutus from all walks of life rose to destroy their neighboring Tutsis. How can we explain this?

THE BACKGROUND: SETTING THE STAGE FOR GENOCIDE

Although some observers attribute the Rwandan genocide to "ancient tribalism," that depiction is too simplistic to be accurate. For centuries, Hutus and Tutsis lived together in Central Africa, the region now divided into Burundi, Rwanda, and Uganda.[22] Substantive divisions between them arose during the late 1800s with European colonization. Belgian settlers devised a scheme to separate and distinguish the tribes from each other based on minor physical differences—Tutsis were somewhat taller, more slender, and had smaller noses. The distinctions were so slight that colonists instituted an identification system, requiring Rwandans to maintain papers so as not to confuse the groups.

Throughout the first few decades of colonization, the Belgians bestowed benefits onto the Tutsis—offering them better education, power, and prestigious social and political positions—in essence, making the Tutsis an upper class and the Hutus a lower class. However, in the 1950s, when Tutsis agitated for independence, Belgians shifted loyalties, slowly replacing the Tutsi chiefs with Hutus, who were the majority group. Hutu leaders seized the opportunity and, in a turbulent "revolution," they conquered the Tutsi rulers and took power. In the process, they killed an estimated one hundred thousand Tutsis and left several hundred thousand refugees.[23] The refugees fled to neighboring countries, such as Uganda, Burundi, and Zaire; but having lost their homes and with limited civil rights in their new host countries, they lived with

a deep sense of discomfort and injustice. By 1961, the Belgian colonization ended, but a new, oppressive Hutu regime had begun.[24]

In 1973, defense minister Major General Juvénal Habyarimana
deposed the sitting president and seized power in a coup, which killed
some fifty-five people by poison or beatings.[25] Although President Habyarimana ended targeted ethnic violence, his administration still
oppressed, jailed, and sometimes executed political opponents.

Through a tightly knit network of family and allies, Habyarimana
maintained power for more than twenty years.[26] Rwandans facing oppression fled, swelling the number of exiles and refugees in neighboring countries to nearly six hundred thousand by the 1980s. But other countries,
particularly Uganda, persecuted Rwandan refugees.[27] In Uganda, one
group of exiles formed the Rwandan Patriotic Front (RPF) with a stated
mission of ousting Habyarimana and establishing a more democratic government in Rwanda.[28] On October 1, 1990, the RPF crossed into Rwanda
and shot and killed the customs guards at their entry point.[29]

Rumors circulated throughout the nation about RPF attacks; Habyarimana rallied support for his regime and jailed political rivals.[30] With
the assistance of foreign troops from France and Zaire, the Rwandan
military pushed the RPF back toward the Ugandan border. In the
process, they summarily killed between five hundred thousand and one
million unarmed people, mostly for suspicion of aiding the RPF.[31]

Violence erupted throughout the land. Bombs were detonated on
buses, and land mines exploded in roads; unidentified assailants
attacked people, led death squads, raped, pillaged, murdered, and
threw grenades into homes.[32] Although the government blamed the
RPF for the violence, human rights groups assert that the Habyarimana government, the national police, and the Rwandan military perpetrated many of the attacks.[33] While opposition political leaders and
extremists attacked each other and members of the other ethnic group,
civilians from both groups continued living without overt animosity
toward each other. "We shared everything [among Tutsis and Hutus],"
said one farmer-turned-killer. But suspicions were growing.

In 1992, at the urging of the Organization of African Unity and France,
the Rwandan government and the RPF ceased fire and entered peace negotiations. On August 3, 1993, they signed the Arusha Accords, agreeing to
establish rule of law, share power, and repatriate refugees. But eight months

later, assailants shot down the plane carrying President Habyarimana and Burundian president Cyprien Ntaryamira, killing both leaders.

MEDIA AS A WEAPON

When you have been prepared the right way by the radios and the official advice, you obey more easily, even if the order is to kill your neighbors.

—Pancrace, one of the Hutu killers[34]

In one hand, they held their weapon of choice—a machete, a club, or a hatchet—in the other, a radio, most often tuned to Radio-Télévision Libre des Milles Collines (RTLM),[35] the privately run station that aired hip, popular music; vital political information; lively on-air hosts; and messages of mass murder.[36] Financed and controlled by what were known as the Akazu faction (and Hutu Power) of the Habyarimana government, the RTLM launched its broadcast programs just after the Arusha peace treaty was signed.[37] Led by a young intellectual and university professor, Ferdinand Nahimana, the radio station was designed to be the "voice of the people," luring listeners with exciting content, entertainment, breaking news, call-in requests, gossip, and quick wit.[38] It fast became the most popular station in Rwanda. But nestled between Rwandans' favorite songs and off-color jokes was an intense campaign designed to evoke passion, pride, hatred, and dedication for a murderous cause and to convert the annihilation of others into a noble act.[39]

How was this cause constructed? Broadcasters weaved together a passionate tale of good versus evil, in which the unmistakably evil forces—the RPF and its fellow Tutsi accomplices—were actively destroying all that was good. They were enemies of democracy, justice, the Hutu people, and, ultimately, Rwanda itself.[40] The radio hosts bolstered the story line with tales of horror that repeatedly depicted the antagonist Tutsis as irreconcilably evil. In one tale, the Tutsis from the RPF had allegedly tortured, castrated, and murdered the Burundian president alongside countless other victims.[41] In another, Tutsis had reportedly cut innocent Hutu people "into pieces with a machete [and] terrorized the population and the authorities."[42]

The stories consistently conveyed the *Inkotanyi Inyenzi* as savage and heartless. The descriptions and the cumulative narrative attacked the fundamental character of the Tutsi people, as if they were intrinsically detestable and driven to evil. They allegedly burned Hutu people alive, locked them in houses to die of hunger, and threw their dead bodies into Lake Muhazi.[43] The RPF "completely unscrupulous," asserted Valerie Bemeriki, the Rwandan socialite-turned-broadcaster.[44] "They mutilate the body and remove certain organs, such as the heart, liver, and stomach; they eat human flesh," she said.[45]

The Tutsis "always find a way of performing evil arts," added Kantano Habimana, Rwanda's most popular radio host.[46] At their core, the Tutsis' reason to exist was wicked, argued radio hosts. They were bloodthirsty scoundrels and terrorists,[47] "created to drink Rwandan blood and to kill," according to Bemeriki.[48]

The bimonthly newspaper *Kangura*, published by Hutu Power, corroborated this myth, asserting that Tutsis could never change their fundamentally evil nature. "Tutsis stay always exactly the same. . . . The malice, the evil are just as we knew them in the history of our country."[49]

Kangura's cartoons depicted RPF soldiers slicing up a Hutu baby for dinner as its mother looked on in horror. The caption read, "The RPF Democracy in full function: equal shares for all."[50] In the article THE APPEAL TO THE CONSCIENCE OF THE HUTU, *Kangura* writers insisted that all Tutsis, men and women alike, were dishonest, "seeking supremacy" and living "among us," waiting to "decimate us."[51]

Kangura advocated for a racially purified Rwanda, one that either segregated and closely monitored the Tutsi enemy or was entirely devoid of them.[52] Overall, these journalists blamed the Tutsis for Rwanda's misfortunes and political problems, whether real or imagined. Ultimately, they suggested that the Tutsis' heartlessness and cruelty was so intrinsic that it could "be cured only by their total extermination."[53]

In addition to deeming the Tutsi people to be fundamentally evil, Hutu Power journalists portrayed them not as people but as subhuman, repulsive vermin. Most often, they called them immutable cockroaches. "A cockroach cannot give birth to a butterfly," asserted one writer in *Kangura*.[54]

Broadcasters emphasized this static nature, in part, to prevent Tutsis from escaping by using false Hutu identity cards that they may have obtained through bribery or sexual favors. The Hutu identity cards could not "change anything," declared Habimana.[55] "If you are a cockroach, you must be killed. . . . No one can say that he has captured a cockroach and the latter gave him money as a price for his life!" he argued. "If someone has a false identity card, if he is *Inkotanyi*, a known accomplice of RPF, don't accept anything in exchange. He must be killed!"[56]

Although "cockroach" was the most frequent slur, broadcasters also called the Tutsi people cannibals and snakes, hyenas, and other animals—objects to be hated, feared, and destroyed.[57] In their depictions, Tutsis were so fundamentally different from Hutus that intermarriage would create "hybrid" offspring—"beings with two heads."[58]

These labels made the Tutsi people seem so despicable that many Hutus came to believe their "single job was to crush the cockroaches."[59] Through this desensitization, Hutus "forgot" that they were killing other human beings.[60] "We no longer saw a human being when we turned up a Tutsi," said Pio, one of the Hutu killers.[61] It "meant nothing" to slaughter neighbors and friends, concurred Ignace, another Hutu killer. "To think we were cutting up our neighbors down to the last one became a goes-without-saying," he said. "They no longer were what they had been. . . . They had become people to throw away."[62] Many Hutus compared their former friends to "an insect that chews up clothing and nests in it, so you have to squash them hard to get rid of them. We didn't want any more Tutsis on the land."[63]

As radio hosts transformed the Tutsi people into antagonists and enemies, they also manufactured protagonists and heroes. The Hutus, said radio hosts, were the only "true" Rwandans. They had inherited "the integrity, the truth" and stood for "the rejection of inequality, of the lie" that the Tutsi people represented.[64] As part of their patriotic duty to country and fellow Rwandans, Hutu people who "have faith in the republic" needed to "stand up, so we may continue to kill the *inyenzi*," announced Ananie Nkurunziza.[65] "Rise up as one man!"[66]

The "heroes" were those who "worked," a euphemism for murder. In the mornings, just as the sun rose, radio hosts greeted their listeners: "Hello, good day, have you started to work yet?"[67] Using deeply emotional appeals, the hosts offered a sense of heroism, nationalism, and admiration to Hutus who were brutalizing their fellow Rwandans and glorified them over the air, sometimes by name. "I seize this opportunity to thank the youths fighting at the front: Ruguyekera, Ntwali, Nzarora, and others, . . ." said Nkurunziza. Habimana lavished them with praise. "So, you killed five of them! Keep it up!" He bellowed. "Dear friends who are listening to us, you hear that people in town are still doing well in Kimicanga."[68]

As part of their encouragement, journalists called for special distinctions and to honor the "workers" with special medals and celebratory parties, for which the killers expressed deep appreciation. One of them, Alphonse, reported that "coming home from the massacre in the church, our welcome was very well put together. . . . It was the most terrific celebration."[69]

In contrast, the broadcasters shamed and threatened the Hutus who resisted killing. "Nobody loves a coward!" proclaimed Habimana. "It is evident that he will never be useful . . . neither to himself, neither to his country." In fact, he insisted that the "ignorant cowards" were dishonoring the entire Hutu population. Ultimately, he argued, "We have to stop these things because they dishonour us."[70]

"Every time that you cross a coward, throw stones at him," Habimana demanded. In time, conscientious objectors became targets of violent deaths similar to the Tutsi people. To prevent their escape, broadcasters urged listeners to "learn to be sly. . . . You can dig a pit for them to fall into . . . lay a trap for them . . . you can lay whatever snare for them, but you have to really fight against those people!"[71] At one point, they suggested compiling lists of conscientious objectors so that they could be systematically "eliminated . . . by the good workers who want to work."[72]

Alternating between insult and morale building, Habimana and his colleagues encouraged Hutus to continue the cause. "Those who are fleeing will regret," he insisted. Those who refuse to "die for your country [will] die like a dog." Instead, he argued they should work together to "fight . . . no matter how many years the war can take, provided we kill them all."[73]

Day after day, the Hutu Power media—RTLM, *Kangura*—and the government-sponsored Radio Rwanda inundated audiences with gory stories that demonized the Tutsis, exalted the Hutu fighters, and made the "war" more real and imminent. Like coaches and sportscasters, they cheered on their imagined team and detailed battles as if keeping score at a sporting events. Through building camaraderie and by equating extermination with an all-important cause, journalists abetted the slaughter and helped motivate their audiences to use axes, machetes, and clubs so not to waste bullets on "cockroaches."[74]

"Take heart," hosts frequently invoked, "we are together." And later, "Our wish for the Rwandans . . . that they work together . . . continue to listen to the songs supporting our armed forces and . . . support one another." Radio hosts assured listeners that they were winning. The Tutsi people, they said, "will all be exterminated and none will live to tell the disastrous story. Let them come. The Rwandans are waiting for them with machetes and other equipment . . . young men and women [are] burning with the desire to . . . fight the *Inkotanyi*, to finish and beat them pants down!"[75]

The Four Ends That Made Up the Grand Cause

Broadcasters portrayed the genocide as a grand cause, for which all walks of life, including children, teenagers, and the elderly, were recruited— either by joining in with the killing or by rooting out the *inyenzi* for others to destroy.[76] That grand cause, according to these journalists, was the permanent eradication of evil. Like Hitler's "final solution," this "final war" required them to "exterminate the Tutsi from the globe . . . make them disappear once and for all."[77] The cause contained four "righteous" ends: righting injustice through revenge and destruction, asserting self-defense, instilling a majoritarian democracy, and protecting their country.[78] With this crusade, Hutus could feel good about the savage deeds before them.

Righting Injustice and Asserting Self-Defense

Although the RTLM and *Kangura* had spewed hatred since the signing of the Arusha Accords, it was President Habyarimana's death and the related stories that triggered the intense emotions driving many massacres. When Habyarimana's plane was shot down, many Hutus simply waited, "listening to the radio," and watching droves of Tutsis reflexively flee.[79] But without court or jury, radio hosts issued a guilty verdict: The Rwandans "will never forget that those bandits killed their president, whom they loved very much," remarked Bemeriki.[80] And "now that they have killed him, what are they fighting for?" asked Hutu Power leader Frodouald Karamira.[81] This radio verdict of the plane crash catalyzed the Hutus. "We kept only one idea . . . suddenly Hutus of every kind were patriotic brothers," remarked one of the killers.[82] Another Hutu, Pancrace, agreed that before the president's death there was suspicion but not hatred: "The hatred came over us suddenly" after Hutu Power journalists and leaders "shouted, 'just look at these cockroaches—we told you so!' And we yelled, 'right, let's go hunting!'"[83]

Habyarimana's death, claimed Hutu Power journalists, was yet another in a long line of injustices perpetrated by the Tutsi people. Stirring historic resentments, radio hosts argued that the Tutsis had a "superiority complex," related to their past positions and privileges.[84] For too long, the Hutu people had endured a Tutsi-driven monarchy, slavery, and exploitation, argued broadcasters.[85] Tutsis had undeservedly held the upper classes and sent their children to exclusive schools while "enslaving" Hutus, argued broadcaster Georges Ruggiu. "According to feudal colonial legend," said Ruggiu, those schools were "meant for only those born to govern."[86]

Making the injustice more pronounced, journalists insisted that the land of Rwanda rightfully and exclusively belonged to the Hutus, the "true" Rwandans who had descended from Kanyarwanda. The Tutsis were "invaders" infesting the region to rob the Hutus of their rightful homes. "There is no proof to convince us that [the Tutsis] are Rwandans," declared Habimana.[87] They came to Rwanda to "attack our country . . . usurp power . . . plunder and grab everything the Rwandans have amassed in thirty years . . . the fruit of Rwandans' labor," he said.[88]

While the past was unbearable, according to broadcasters, the worst was yet to come—the ultimate injustice—the annihilation of the Hutu people. The RPF and their Tutsi accomplices were coming to "exterminate, exterminate, exterminate you until they are the only ones left in the country, so that they can keep for a thousand years the power that their fathers had kept for four hundred years," said Bemeriki.[89] But the true Rwandans are united in their fight against them, she insisted.[90]

The all-important cause made destroying the Tutsis a simultaneous fight against injustice and an act of self-defense, a preemptive strike to prevent the Tutsis from annihilating the Hutus and taking their land and property. "We have . . . to fight tooth and nail to defend our lives and property," demanded Habimana.[91] Many Hutus truly believed that they were doing the right thing, defending themselves, restoring what they believed justly belonged to their own ethnic group, and protecting their country.

Fighting for Majoritarian Democracy

Although the Habyarimana government and the subsequent military-controlled government oppressed suspected political opponents,[92] Hutu Power journalists asserted that theirs was a "government for the entire country, not for political parties."[93] Through the genocide, they would maintain democracy and prevent a Tutsi dictatorship, they argued.

Their tale created a dichotomy—democracy versus the "dictators of extremists"—in which the democrats were the Hutu Power's Coalition for the Defense of the Republic (CDR) who "defend the interests of the people . . . the masses and not those of this or that minority group," according to CDR chairman Stanislas Simbizi.[94] The others, particularly the RPF and their "accomplices," were dictators and "feudal-monarchists" who "rejected democracy . . . cast [it] . . . out the window" with hopes to "strangle it forever."[95] The RPF and the Tutsis "take and monopolize power . . . govern by force [and] oppress the Hutus," claimed Hutu Power journalists.[96]

As broadcasters proudly recalled the Hutu "democracy" revolution that overthrew the Tutsis,[97] they argued that because Tutsis were a minority, their "miniscule . . . clique should not decide the fate of Rwanda. . . . This Rwanda is mine. I am of the majority. It is I, first and foremost, who will decide . . . not you [the RPF]."[98]

Annihilating the Tutsis would therefore "help Rwandans . . . embark on a real democracy," according to RTLM broadcasters.[99] While calling for mass slaughter in the name of democracy, these journalists accused their enemies of doing just that. The "bloodthirsty *Inyenzi Inkotanyi* who are exterminating the Rwandans [are] lying that they are fighting for democracy," declared Hutu broadcasters. But they were instead attempting to establish "a killing and oppressive regime" and a "dictatorship [by] genocide, the elimination of the Hutu majority."[100]

The Hutu-controlled broadcasters criticized the RPF for refusing to "lay down their weapons unconditionally"[101] and "ask for forgiveness . . . promising not to resume hostilities again in Rwanda," remarked

RTLM editor in chief Gaspard Gahigi.[102] "Nobody should take power again through the barrel of the gun or . . . through war," argued Gahigi.[103] They claimed that the RPF "chases people from their homes" and indiscriminately "butchers people and rips open their bellies,"[104] while the Hutu journalists encouraged similar heinous acts.

Saving This God-Given Country

In the RTLM narrative, the massacres ensured that the Hutus would take their rightful place as inheritors of the sacred place known as Rwanda. "We are Rwandans. Let us fight for this Rwanda," they frequently invoked. It was their very own country, in which they should have great pride: "Rwanda is nowhere else in the world. Rwanda is here—in Central Africa—where God located it."[105] But their God-given country's survival was at stake, requiring Hutus to "Rise up!" and "Take up clubs, cudgels, and axes and confront them head on, in order to prevent them from continuing to destroy our country," according to Habimana.[106]

Beyond Incitement—Directing Genocide

In addition to provoking destructive emotions, Hutu Power journalists instructed and helped organize massacres. Hutu people listened intently to the radio for information, particularly about where victims might be hiding. In some programs, journalists directed the Hutus to search banana plantations, bushes, and marshes, where Tutsis frequently hid.[107] In other broadcasts, they directed listeners to scrutinize Tutsi homes, particularly abandoned houses, and in drains, ditches, water conduits, and gutters, "especially in the evening," when people in hiding might scrounge for food.[108]

RTLM hosts also announced specific locations where they had received tips that Tutsi people were hiding. In one broadcast, Habimana urged listeners in Nyakabanda to "be vigilant, search the footpaths thoroughly [and] ferret them out." In another, RTLM broadcaster Noel Hitimana called out to "the people living in Rugunga . . . Kanogo . . . Mburabuturo" to scrutinize hiding places within the woods.[109] Habimana also broadcast specific leads, such as one from "Bernard Ntushoboye's houseboy," who allegedly witnessed an escape toward the town of Kimisagara. "Two of them are going toward APACE premises while the other two are going towards Nyakabanda," declared Habimana. "Start looking for them within the APACE premises in Kabusunzu."[110] Later, Habimana advised, "Now, they have arrived in Bishenyi [and] in Kigese, in Runda."[111] He pinpointed the people "sleeping in Karamira's house . . . in Nyamirambo near Saint Andre. Others are lying in Rukebesha's house . . . [and] in Kavutse's house where they have installed a small clinic."[112] At another time, Karamira announced, "We know that some left Kimihurura" and suggested entrapping them when they were expected to return to find food.[113]

At roadblocks scattered throughout Rwanda, broadcasters urged heightened scrutiny to identify all who passed through while "checking particulars to avoid surprises."[114] If a Tutsi attempted to cross a checkpoint, "Look closely at his cute little nose and then break it!" urged Habimana.[115]

Journalists also encouraged division of labor and suggested the proper use of weapons. "What counts is cooperation among the people," said Gahigi over the RTLM airwaves. "Those with bows, spears, clubs, catapults must get ready. If one or two people are armed with guns, they must join this group. So if an *inyenzi* infiltrates in the night, shoot him with an arrow." And to dislodge Tutsis from their homes, use "a rocket launcher and grenades," he said.[116]

WHAT WAS THE EFFECT OF MEDIA?

Several conditions coalesced to facilitate disaster. First, with long-term hierarchical governance, Rwandans tended to obey authority. "When authorities say move to the left, we move to the left," admitted one Rwandan Hutu.[117] "If you are my authority and you tell me to kill . . . I could kill him even if I had no disagreement with him," admitted another.[118]

Second, by 1994, the sociopolitical atmosphere in Rwanda was already under intense pressure. A troubled economy rife with poverty and famine, tense political conditions, and the sudden death of President Habyarimana generated emotions that needed only a spark to cause an eruption. "Before the president's death, we had no problems. . . . There were no misunderstandings," said a thirty-five-year-old farmer who participated in several attacks.[119] Others iterated the same sentiment. One businessman and farmer "had a Tutsi wife [and] . . . was never interested . . . in the history of the Tutsis" until Habyarimana's death. "I did not know how to differentiate Hutu from Tutsi," he said.

Third, the Rwandan genocide was well orchestrated through the military and police channels that took advantage of Rwanda's ethnic divisions, which had been accentuated by the Europeans and the death of Rwanda's president.[120] Finally, the media connected historic injustices, current issues, meanings, and blame on the Tutsis for many Hutus. The RTLM broadcasts blamed the Tutsis for President Habyarimana's death and an array of sociopolitical problems in Rwanda. Until two days after the plane crash, the Hutus and Tutsis "continued to live together as usual," according to one teenager who participated in the genocide. "We heard on the radio, 'Look for the enemy no matter where he is; he is your neighbor!' . . . After [April] tenth, that is when people started to kill each other."[121]

Through these "blame frames," the media incited ethnically based resentment, fear, anger, pride, and hatred—intense emotions in a combination that was not widespread before in Rwanda—and used the frames to create new cultural values. Together, the emotions and cultural values guided behavior. Hutus' growing fear, resentment, anger, and hatred also emerged from the belief that their neighboring Tutsis were evil, were plotting genocide, and must be preemptively exterminated. As greater numbers of community members joined the cause, it became increasingly difficult to resist the ubiquitous forces of culture and intergroup emotions. "We had lived with Tutsi friends," explained one of the Hutus who participated in the killing. But soon, "We became contaminated by ethnic racism without noticing it."[122] Hutus really came to believe that "the Tutsis would kill us," they admitted. "Little by little . . . our hearts changed."[123]

Using the Hutu Power doctrines as their foundation, broadcasters consistently tied annihilation to existing values, calling the killings important, patriotic "work" for their country and a pathway to honor.[124] Through inundation, repetition, and passion, this juxtaposition aroused emotions, masked the heinousness of the crimes, and transformed the meaning of butchering other human beings into lofty, noble acts. With the new values, "working" Hutus were bestowed pride and glory, while nonworkers were shamed, humiliated, and often killed.[125]

Simultaneously, radio hosts generated an ultimatum of disaster, should the Hutus fail to annihilate the Tutsi people. In their battle of good Hutu versus bad Tutsi, their view was a choice of only two options: either the forces of "death and desolation" or "the people."[126] As this false dichotomy and the accompanying stories permeated the airwaves, Hutu listeners grew increasingly resentful of the Tutsi people for the litany of injustices they had allegedly perpetrated—particularly the death of their president. "Everyone was angry because the president had been killed," remarked one of the Hutu killers.

Because only about 50 percent of Rwandans were literate, radio's power was enhanced as a primary means of obtaining political and communal information. For some, radio was like "the voice of God."[127] Beginning in 1990, most other radio was muted, allowing the Hutu Power's RTLM to monopolize messaging to the public. Although the RPF broadcast on the AM band's Radio Mutubara, its broadcasts failed to reach many parts of Rwanda, and the government strictly forbade listening, frequently beating people caught tuning in to it.[128] In this media-oriented society, even some Tutsi people listened to RTLM—largely because of its popular music, entertainment, commentary, and what was believed to be breaking news.[129] Without competing sources of information and framing, and because of their connection to government, these messages were both homogenous and authoritative, ultimately making the Hutu Power's version of Rwandan politics and the Tutsi people ostensibly more and more plausible.

The media did not convince all listeners. Many Hutus worked alongside Tutsis to prevent intergroup warfare. But the media's "blame frames" reinforced the thinking of those who were already inclined toward hard-line attitudes and fostered an environment of fear, anger, and hatred.[130] Amid the trying circumstances and virulent messages, within one hundred days, ordinary people who had never before killed rose to collectively slay some eight hundred thousand of their fellow Rwandans.[131] It's an unbearable chapter of history that unfortunately does not stand alone.

Chapter 2

Conspiracy and Murder: Media and the Holocaust

“I have faith in my fellow Germans,” said Eve Soumerai’s grand-father on the night that Adolf Hitler became Germany’s chancellor. Streets were alive with drums, marching feet, and chants of “Heil Hitler! Heil Hitler!”[1] Although he acknowledged Hitler’s deep hatred of Jews, they should not be concerned, he said, and went on to list his many close German friends. “Remember, we live in the country of Goethe, Schiller, and Beethoven—the most civilized country in all of Europe.”[2]

The “most civilized country,” however, was in tatters, having its dreams of continental empire crushed in World War I.[3] Forced to pay war reparations by the Allies, Germany’s economy and morale sunk to an all-time low. By 1933, over six million people were unemployed, political unrest abounded, and masses of Germans faced a profound “crisis of the soul.” Things couldn’t be much worse. Many in Germany—hungry and desperate—welcomed a “savior” who promised to reinvigorate Germany’s grand aspirations and restore its place in the world.[4]

Everything was changing, even between the closest of relations: Over time, spouses sought government-sponsored divorces, citing their shame for marrying Jews. Best friends became ruthless enemies.[5]

“Our mothers were best friends too,” recalled Eve of her best friend, Adelheid. They “had known each other from before we were born.” But two years later, they were all bitter enemies. Adelheid had joined a Nazi youth group for girls. She and her fellow Nazi friends regularly spat at Eve. They waited and watched for her, chased her down, and pummeled her.[6]

What began as the pummeling of young Jewish girls eventually became a life of misery for all Jews in Germany. Mass rallies called for boycotting Jewish businesses; posters and signs appeared, warning, “Germans, defend yourselves. Don’t buy from Jews.” Although the boycott didn't last, it warned of approaching decay. Soon, laws prohibited Jews from participating in Germany's public life, stripped them of land ownership, and forbade them from engaging with media, labor unions, military service, and civic and cultural organizations. The Nazi government revoked Jews' citizenship, abolished their legal rights, and segregated them. It prohibited Jews from riding tram cars, owning pets, sitting on public benches, or moving about without wearing the infamous yellow Star of David that publicly identified them. Finding work became nearly futile. Signs warned Jews that they were not welcome: "Jews Enter This Town at Their Own Risk." Jewish children were forced to the backs of classrooms, and teachers were required to wear swastikas.[7]

Still, many Jews believed that maybe "things would turn around."[8] Instead, they worsened.

On November 9, 1938, to avenge his family's persecution, seventeen-year-old Herschel Grynszpan (or Gruenspan), a Jewish refugee of Polish descent, fatally shot a German diplomat in Germany's Paris embassy. The homicide, although a single act of one young man, became the perfect excuse to blame and terrorize the entire Jewish community.[9]

"Pull back the police," said Hitler. "This time, the Jews should feel the hatred of the people."[10]

"We will not allow this cowardly murder to go unanswered," added propaganda minister Joseph Goebbels.[11]

Flames lit up the night sky. Fires, sirens, screams, and drumbeats blended together into a terrifying cacophony. "Death to the Jews!" the crowds shouted on November 10, as they moved in on Jewish neighborhoods. "Death to the Jews!"

Within forty-eight hours, hundreds of synagogues were set ablaze; hospitals, schools, and businesses were destroyed; a thousand Jews were killed, and thirty thousand Jews were arrested and sent to concentration camps.[12]

The Grynszpan incident, according to the Nazi paper *Voelkischer Beobachter*, became an excuse for Germany to "protect itself by force" from what the publication called "the intention of a criminal parasitic minority" and the worldwide "anti-German agitators." The destruction, said *Voelkischer Beobachter*, was a justified response to the "international Jewish problem. . . . The exasperation of the whole German people over the murderous deed of the Jew Gruenspan gave itself vent." Although the Germans do "not begrudge the right to live to any people on earth,"

Gruenspan's vengeance was "evidence" that Germany must be "free of the Jews," claimed the Nazi paper.[13]

Under this guise of protecting Germany from a murderous people, Nazi officials rounded up Jews en masse and sent them to reservation-like regions, isolating them in tightly monitored, overcrowded ghettos. With no access to food, they relied upon government rations in exchange for hard labor. Thousands died of disease and starvation. People were "like skeletons," according to one witness. "They walked until they fell, and they were dead. . . . We couldn't keep up with burying the dead."[14]

With increasing ferocity, the Nazi government stepped up the destruction. Nazi gunmen gathered up hundreds of Jews at a time, lined them up, and shot them dead. At gunpoint, dozens of Jews were forced to climb into ravines that would soon become their collective graves. Others stood before massive ditches and fell, one by one, as the bullets pierced their already-weak bodies.[15]

In one lineup, sixteen-year-old Zia Michalowsky stood before the mass grave, holding his father's hand, counting seconds between the gunshots. A split second before the bullet penetrated his body, Michalowsky dropped into the ditch, faking his death. Dead bodies piled on top of him, pushing him into the bodies below. He waited silently until the gunfire and the celebratory laughter ended, then snuck out of the grave. Naked and covered in blood, Michalowsky walked to an acquaintance's home and knocked on the door.[16] But the response was shocking: "Jew, go back to the grave where you belong!"[17]

Michalowsky then approached an elderly widow and pursuaded her to shelter him; he later escaped into a forest where he hid with partisans until the end of the war.[18]

Using a race-based eugenics theory, the Nazis argued that they needed to remove weak, degenerate, and evil genes from the hereditary chain to prevent their reproduction. They first tried forced sterilization upon people considered weak—while claiming that Jews in New York were forcing German sterilization. Under the guise of therapy, Nazi officials rounded up the disabled, ill, and impaired into special centers where officials killed children with poisoned tea and doomed the adults by sealing them in chambers filled with carbon monoxide gas. The goal of eradicating roughly seventy thousand "weak" links was, in part, to make room for incoming German settlers from the Baltic regions. But the effort was met with resistance, particularly from the Catholic Church, which, along with numerous other protesters, managed to force Hitler to end to the "mercy killings."[19]

By the fall of 1941, Hitler and his reich intensified their pursuit of the "final solution." Germany, Europe's "foremost icon of high culture and education," now used its great talents to perpetrate a mass killing that surpassed any in modern history—the largest-scale genocide of the twentieth century.[20] But the "final solution" needed support, acceptance, or blind complacence from society—churches, academia, medicine, and education.

In the name of science, doctors and scientists experimented on people they came to believe were "subhuman." They tested poisons and diseases and attempted to prove eugenics by correlating criminality, illness, and social class with physical features such as skull size.[21] One Nazi doctor selected more than one hundred Jews for measurements. Nazi officials then killed them in gas chambers and defleshed them for the study. In other experiments, Nazi doctors and scientists infected subjects with typhus to experiment for a cure, froze others in ice water, shot their victims with poisoned bullets to measure the speed of death, or cut up their legs to test sulfanilamide as a treatment.[22] The list of atrocities continued.

By the end of the Holocaust, the Nazi government had exterminated more than eleven million people, including approximately six million Jews, two to three million Soviet prisoners of war, nearly two million Poles, more than a half-million Gypsies, two hundred and fifty thousand disabled or impaired people, eighty thousand Freemasons, more than five thousand homosexuals, and more than twenty-five hundred Jehovah's Witnesses.[23]

THE FOUR FACTORS OF GENOCIDE

How did this bastion of high culture become part of a ruthless killing machine that treated fellow human beings with such indifference and disdain? Scholars have grappled with the question, and a few key elements have become clearer. Alongside difficult socioeconomic and political conditions, a carefully implemented propaganda campaign convinced Germans that it was necessary to eliminate entire groups of people in order to save the "true humanity" and "transform the nation" into a new utopian state. Designed largely by the propaganda minister Joseph Goebbels, it was a so-called revolution of the spirit that built upon a festering racism in Europe. The propaganda campaign worked, in part, because of four factors: the dire social and economic conditions in Germany, a simple but corrosive web of misinformation, emotional appeals, and a pervasive and authoritarian message and ideology that blossomed and grew through control of mass media and public space.[24]

A Dire Country: The Losers and Their Salvation

Germany was in ruins after its crushing loss in World War I, which destroyed the once-aspiring empire. Politically, socially, and economically devastated, the once-proud country was beset with ruin, shame, and desperation, making many people more susceptible to a new nationalistic ideology and a leader who could make the people feel powerful again—one who offered to restore German pride and rebuild the nation's image and its shattered economy. Many in the audience, in essence, "desperately wanted to be converted," and Hitler's simple narrative and ideology would serve to rehabilitate morale and relieve angst by casting blame upon the "others."[25] The narrative contained essential elements, including a cast of characters, a powerful plot, a "noble" cause, and the stirring of deep emotions, all fitted together neatly into a tale of good versus evil.

Misinformation: The Narrative, Its Characters, and the Plot

In Hitler's simple tale, the "good guys" needed to vanquish the "bad guys," lest the bad guys continue to harm humanity, as they had allegedly done for decades. It was vital for the survival of humanity, which in this story were the pure, healthy, virtuous, and superior Germans. Germans were consistently described as the epitome of goodness, innately endowed with qualities such as courage, altruism, loyalty, and naturalness. But these "great" Germans and their homeland had been victimized by evil schemers, particularly "international Jewry" and the Bolshevik Communist sympathizers.[26]

The "bad guys" were, by their very nature, "poison" to "our people,"
said Hitler in a 1920 speech. They were like "fleas" that needed to be
cleansed from the home. Even if "alone in this world, they [Jews] would
stifle in filth and offal; they would try to get ahead of one another in
hate-filled struggle and exterminate one another," said Hitler. It was
rooted in their very biology, he asserted, for a Jewish person to be "a
sham, a parasite, a liar" that harmed society by mere existence. That
made it vital to "purify," he asserted. "Lost purity of the blood . . .
plunges man into the abyss for all time," Hitler warned.[27]

Jews were "to blame for everything," according to Goebbels. But
while Jews were the Nazis' primary target, the Nazis' "evil other"
included Poles, Slavs, Gypsies, Communists, Bolsheviks, and Freemasons, along with homosexuals and the disabled. They were all "enemies
of the people."[28]

Over time, the Nazis unfolded the narrative's plot—an international
conspiracy theory in which the powerful international Jewry was con-
spiring with other powers to destroy Germany, instigate a second world
war, and exterminate the Germans. In this simple story line, these nefarious groups worked to control the Soviet Union and, through their conspiracy to take over the world, drove Germany to ruins. They caused
Germany's World War I defeat and its 1929 economic crisis.[29] International Jewry, the source of German destruction, was the "problem" that
needed solving.

In this plot, the problem had a "natural" solution—elimination.
Because Hitler believed that evil was rooted in racial biology, the only
means of rescuing the "good" humanity—essentially, the light-skinned
Aryans—was through cleansing the "blood" of impurities, such as other
ethnicities, weaknesses, frailties, and evil. That, to him, meant genetically
purging the weak, criminal, and antisocial "genes" to prevent their recur-
rence and build a "pure" world free of evil. Because they were "tumors"
and "racial tuberculosis," Jews "had to be cut out" and "isolated." Otherwise, the "healthy body of German society" faced continued "infection"
from the "disease-carrying lice, vermin, or bedbugs."[30]

The good-versus-evil story transformed genocidal destruction into
an important cause that would eradicate the Jewish "pestilence" from the
earth and simultaneously rescue the great-yet-victimized Germany,
restore its superior place in the world, and rebuild the "Thousand-Year

Reich." In the end, the "people's" community would permanently triumph over evil, unless the people failed to destroy all Jews at their "roots" and "branches," in which case Europe would "die" of the "Jewish Disease." This left Germany only one choice: "kill or be killed." Gradually, German media, under the direction of Nazi officials, escalated warnings that the Germans were under threat of annihilation, making it imperative to completely destroy their enemies to rescue themselves.[31] Such a task would require Germans to unify, putting "the community before the individual." They were "One People! One Reich! One Führer!"[32]

Through media and word of mouth, Nazi officials reinforced this narrative and framing. Goebbels experimented with messages to maximize effectiveness, perfect his formula, and intensify the nation's fanaticism by the late 1930s.[33]

Emotional Appeals: Propagation, Repetition, Assimilation

Hitler and his propagandists understood persuasion. Through incrementalism and repetition, and by appealing to base emotions, such as hate, fear, and pride, they aimed to "reeducate" the German people into a "good society."[34] To maximize assimilation, Goebbels and Press Chief Otto Dietrich used bright colors and simple slogans along with emotional words, music, and images.[35]

Although Hitler's hatred for Jews was clear in his early writing, his rhetoric and plan to exterminate the Jews did not become clear to the average German until 1939; nor were Jews his sole target at that time. But after 1939, the Nazi anti-Jewish tone intensified, while Hitler and his reich suppressed the Holocaust's details. By 1941, propagandists focused their blame for Germany's woes squarely on the Jewish conspiracy to destroy Germany.[36]

The dichotomy of a heroic Nazi Party and Germany against a uniformly nefarious Jewry underlay Nazi media messages. Throughout public spaces, thousands of posters exalted Nazis with towering images of Hitler and the words "One people, one reich, one Führer." They blamed Germany's "enemies" for its economic and military woes and issued dire warnings of their foes' planned annihilation of Germany.[37]

Using simple slogans and degrading or terrorizing images, the "Word of the Week" posters filled public spaces, clearly articulating the conspiracy. One poster, "Behind the Enemy Powers: The Jew," featured a cartoon figure of an overweight, stereotyped Jewish man peering out from behind a curtain of US, British, and Soviet Russian flags. "He Bears the Guilt for the War!" read another, featuring a giant finger pointing at the caricature of a Jewish man. The "The Jew: Instigator of the War, Prolonger of the War" poster featured a curtain drawn back to expose another caricature.[38]

One Message, One Ideology

The Press

Germany's newspaper and magazine articles supported and elaborated on the reich's argument. Leading up to the war, newspapers featured Hitler's fiery attack speeches on the front pages.[39] And Goebbels, until 1940, published articles in the Nazi Party's *Voelkischer Beobachter*, after which he regularly penned the lead article in the prestigious weekly *Das Reich*. While all the articles Goebbels wrote reinforced Nazi ideology, 218 specifically denounced Germany's "enemies," which were predominantly Jews.[40] Prior to publication, Goebbel's essays were circulated to Nazi Party leaders; afterward, they were broadcast over the radio.[41]

CHURCHILL PROMISES GERMANY AS BOOTY TO JEWS, said one headline in *Voelkischer Beobachter*. The United States, Great Britain, and the Soviets were in SOLIDARITY WITH THE WORLD PARASITE, said another. In partnership with Jews, the United States was implementing an EXTERMINATION PROGRAM, claimed the paper, ROOSEVELT DEMANDS STERILIZATION OF GERMAN PEOPLE; GERMAN PEOPLE TO BE EXTERMINATED WITHIN TWO GENERATIONS.[42]

In *Das Reich*, Goebbels warned Germans to temper their "world-famed good nature. . . . Don't be too good-natured, since our enemies are not noble enough to overlook our mistakes." Instead, he argued, Germans should overcome their naïveté, to prevent falling for "Jewish tricks" and understand that there is "no distinction among Jews." It was a simple feature of their "birth and race" to be "part of an international conspiracy against National Socialist Germany." They were akin to "child rapists, thieves and pimps" who could not change their fundamental fabric. "Every Jew [is] our enemy in this historic struggle . . .

single-mindedly seeking one thing: to reward our foolishness with bloodshed and terror," requiring Germans to harden "against the destroyers of our people."[43]

Because Jews had so disguised their "true" nature, Goebbels expressed fear that Germans may forget that the "enemy was beside him," he wrote. This argument became justification for segregation and forced donning of the infamous yellow Star of David, which Goebbels called a "remarkably humane measure . . . a hygienic and prophylactic measure to be sure that the Jew cannot infiltrate our ranks . . . [and] sow discord."[44]

World War II was specifically referred to as the "Jewish War," according to Goebbels in *Das Reich*.[45] "The historic responsibility of world Jewry for the outbreak and widening of this war has been proven so clearly that it does not need to be talked about any further. . . . The Jews wanted war, and now they have it," he wrote.[46]

Another Goebbels article, "Mimickry," claimed that Jews were "secretly . . . planning to strangle us" as part of their plan to conquer the world and make the rest of humanity their slaves. Jews were the driving force behind Bolshevism and plutocracy, asserted Goebbels.[47]

From the early 1930s, the weekly newspaper *Der Stürmer* regularly ridiculed and denounced Jews in a quest for a "greater Germany without Jews." With sensational content, simple and blunt language, cartoons, and photographs, *Der Stürmer* appealed widely, selling hundreds of thousands of copies. Distributed throughout public bulletin boards in glass-covered cases, the newspaper lauded Hitler for "saving" Germany from Jewish plans to enslave the National Socialists.[48] From its first issues, editor Julius Streicher used *Der Stürmer* to sow fear about Jews, claiming, "As long as the Jew is in the German household, we will be Jewish slaves. Therefore he must go. Who? The Jew!"[49]

As Hitler took power in 1933, *Der Stürmer*'s lead article, SECRET PLANS AGAINST GERMANY REVEALED, offered terrifying, biblically justified plans by the "World Jewry" to annihilate its enemies. Using quotes from Deuteronomy, the article sought to convince readers that Jews were plotting to bring "Germany to its knees. They will stop at nothing," it warned. With simplicity, bluntness, and repetition, the paper offered ongoing "evidence" of the threat facing Germans and the "truths" about eugenics. "Racial science has incontrovertibly proven that the bastard, the half-breed, receives only the bad characteristics of the races, not the good, spiritual, or physical characteristics," according to the paper. "Therefore, the Jew possesses the lust of the Negro, the craftiness of the Mongol and the criminal drives of all the races, which have combined to produce his blood."[50]

By 1941, *Der Stürmer* articles blatantly called for annihilating all Jews as a last resort to eliminate the "Jewish danger." Because past efforts to "water down" the "Jewish race" through intermarriage and incorporation were "catastrophic," argued journalist Ernst Hiemer, they no longer had alternatives. "Jewry is organized world criminality," he wrote. "The Jew was a liar, a swindler, an exploiter, a troublemaker, a poisoner of the blood and a murderer from the beginning." *Der Stürmer* cartoons relentlessly portrayed Jews as vampires, toads, vultures, monsters, insects, or bacteria. At the bottom of nearly every page, Streicher printed his motto: "The Jews are our misfortune." The publication also intimidated the people who remained friendly with Jews by labeling them "disgraceful," "shady," or "notorious," then publishing their names and addresses.[51]

Special editions complemented the weekly *Der Stürmer* with thematic coverage about Jewish "ritual murder," criminality, world Jewish conspiracy, and sex crimes. In the 1934 "Ritual Murder" special, for example, the cover read, JEWISH MURDER PLAN AGAINST GENTILE HUMANITY EXPOSED. The articles described an alleged rite during which "murderous" Jews were "charged with torturing their victims, especially the children; and during this torture, they shout threats, [*sic*] curses and cast spells against the Gentiles."[52]

As evidence of the Jewish conspiracy, propagandists used Theodore Kaufman's book *Germany Must Perish!* The obscure book, penned by a thirty-one-year-old American Jew, argued for sterilizing German people as their "total penalty" for forcing a "total war" upon the world. Although the book had little significance in the United States where it was published, it was the perfect opportunity to demonstrate the nefarious plot hatched by the Jews. Goebbels ordered the book's main themes translated into an easily distributed pamphlet, which argued: "As monstrous as a plan to cold-bloodedly exterminate a people of eighty million is, and as much as one may be inclined to consider it impossible and unbelievable, World Jewry is serious. We would not be the first people to be murdered by the Jews."

Propagandists distributed five million copies of the pamphlet along with ration cards and directed editors to discuss the matter in each of their publications. Goebbels discussed Kaufman's book in his *Das Reich* articles while other publications reiterated "how clearly and realistically the [Jewish] plan has been thought out." A month later, they circulated a reminder flyer.[53]

Film

Film enlivened the narrative but also simultaneously acted as a diversion, disseminating particular topics in a "seemingly neutral fashion," popularizing programs such as euthanasia, reframing politics, rewriting history, and constructing heroes and enemies. While many films had no overt politics, the motion pictures were carefully censored to promote a particular German culture and politics through their simple story lines, their forcefulness, and their appeal to primal emotions. "Even entertainment sometimes has the task of arming the nation to fight for its existence, of providing it with the requisite spiritual uplift," said Goebbels.[54]

Through film, Nazis emerged as redeemers bringing to fruition a "new age" that would unite Germans into an "element of the mass" against their enemies. They linked optimism and positive images with swastika flags symbolizing the Nazi "utopia" for which all Germans should uniformly strive.[55]

Theaters featured films of Nazi Party rallies, depicting Hitler, the "invincible savior," and excoriating Jews as "agitators of conflict between people." *Triumph of the Will*, for example, exalted Hitler, while *Hitlerjunge Quex* told the "courageous" story of a young boy dying in Hitler's service.

Propaganda presented as "documentaries" and "historical" fictions, such as *The Eternal Jew* and *Jud Süss*, respectively, portrayed Jews as barbaric, cruel, soulless, and motivated solely by "lust for money." The latter narrated a story of Jewish financial adviser Joseph Süss-Oppenheimer, cast as a swindler and "race defiler" who received his just punishment when his victim triumphed in his hanging.[56]

Radio

Radio, declared Goebbels, must be in the "service of our [Nazi] ideology. . . . No other ideology will find expression here. The radio must subordinate itself to the goals that the government of the National Socialist Revolution has set itself." Through radio, Germans regularly received a dose of Nazi leaders' speeches and articles, particularly those of Hitler and Goebbels, which elevated and propagated the Nazi narrative, fomented fear, and denounced "enemies."As Hitler orated, restaurants and pubs throughout the cities turned on radios, expecting patrons to fastidiously attend to the words.[57]

Over the airwaves, Nazi leaders asserted Nazi resistance to the alleged Jewish intent to annihilate the German people.[58] Speaking "against the atrocity campaign of world Jewry," Goebbels railed against the Jewish "campaign of lies and tales of atrocity." And Hitler warned his radio audiences that Germany faced "complete extermination," even after Nazis killed some five million Jews.[59] Altogether, some 160 broadcasts specifically attacked Jews.[60]

In his daily broadcasts, *Hans Fritzsche Speaks*, radio star Fritzsche frequently invoked the claim that "like medieval bigots, they [Jews] would like to see anyone they regard as politically heterodox dragged to the stake." He contrasted that with Germany, "a nation that wants nothing more than to be allowed to get on with our work and put our house in order the way we like it."[61] As he railed against Jews, Fritzsche also used humor and sarcasm to counter Allied propaganda and diffuse its effects before German audiences received it.[62]

The Nazi press promoted and celebrated Fritzsche, solidifying his stardom and building his audience with biographical stories, books, and dedication poetry that cherished the "fifteen minutes . . . when Fritzsche talks . . . it becomes silent in every room." Fritzsche, the writings concluded, was like "light in the darkness. . . . Fritzsche speaks straight from the heart and without being pretentious."[63]

To stir even the "most apathetic citizens," broadcasters inundated listeners with German music, particularly the military march. Special thematic marches accompanied German offensives, including the "Prinz Eugen Marsch" when Hitler attacked the Balkans, and "We're Marching against England," a popular war theme. Non-German music, such as jazz, was eventually forbidden, and song lyrics sometimes reiterated Nazi ideology: [64] "That is the meaning of life, that God is astir in one's blood, but God is present only in pure blood," according to one obscure song.[65]

MORE ENEMIES

While Jews were the primary enemy, the Nazi media machine also targeted Poland, the Allies, Communists, Serbs, Czechs, and Soviets. To justify invading Poland, headlines warned of POLISH TERROR AGAINST GERMAN POPULATION and frightened readers with such headlines as GERMAN SCHOOL CHILDREN IN POLAND HUNTED DOWN. Consistently casting Germans as victims, the papers warned of "cruelties and acts of terror against ethnic Germans and extermination of ethnic Germans in Poland." The war itself was instigated by POLISH WAR MONGERING AGAINST GERMANY. Poles, like Jews, were described as "filth," and their land one of "slavery and disorder." [66]

In a similar campaign against Yugoslavia, headlines argued GERMAN VILLAGE BURNED BY SERBIAN SOLDIERS and SYSTEMATIC PERSECUTION OF ALL ETHNIC GERMANS HAS BEGUN: SERBIAN MOB BURNS DOWN VILLAGES AND WOODS. A few days later, German headlines claimed an UNHEARD-WAVE OF TERROR IN YUGOSLAVIA and a REGIME OF TERROR AGAINST ETHNIC GERMANS.[67] Each "enemy" received comparable treatment in Nazi media.

CONTROLLING THE MESSAGE BY CONTROLLING THE MEDIA

To influence "the mind of the nation," Hitler's propagandists sought hegemonic control and omnipresence of their messages. Through institutions such as the Reich Chamber of Culture, established in 1933 to regulate the content of literature, theater, music, radio, film, fine arts, and the press, they controlled media institutions and public spaces, inundating the public life with their narrative while silencing alternatives and dissent.[68] To salvage Germany from "degeneracy," Nazi officials burned and banned "decadent" books, literature, and music that did not conform to Nazi ideology and in turn infused literature, even poetry and fairy tales, with Nazism. They rewrote educational materials, incorporated Nazi ideology into classroom teaching methods, and introduced Nazi films into the schools. Drama and cabaret broadcast over radio used pro-Nazi humor and themes to drive and support their ideologies and politics.[69]

Knowing that propaganda "does not have anything to do with the truth," Goebbels pursued a "total war" strategy that included what he called "mind-bombing," by inundating Germany with the Nazi ideology to accompany regular warfare.[70] To achieve broad penetration, Goebbels sought widespread radio listening through the production of affordable radios, then he controlled radio content through his ministry and consolidated the film industry under a giant holding company, Universal Film AG (UFA).[71]

As head of Hitler's press office, Otto Dietrich eliminated 235 newspapers. Reich Press Chamber president Max Amann purchased 1,500 publishing houses and more than 2,000 newspapers. Officials enacted the Editorial Control Law, which placed remaining media, including some 2,200 privately held newspapers, under government control. By 1939, circulation of Nazi-controlled newspapers grew from 2 million to 13.2 million. Through 3,000 newspapers, 4,000 periodicals, and other media, they reached roughly 30 million readers.[72]

Once the media were under their control, Nazi officials purged them of all "non-Aryan" staff, personnel married to non-Aryans, and those who simply refused to carry the party line. The remaining employees were forced to abide by the reich's orders. Dietrich regularly dictated content to the press—the subjects to be covered, the material to omit, and the framing of issues and events—and compliance was compulsory. In Dietrich's frame, World War II must be reported as "instigated by world Jewry" and "directed by a Jewish group." The press must be "emphatic" about the war's roots—"British war-mongers and agents of world Jewry"—in order to maintain to their "true theme." Anything that might damage the government's image was off-limits.[73]

Because the Nazis crushed political opposition, a growing consensus emerged among public officials. The academy fared no better. Because the reich awarded financial support and accolades to scholars and research projects that advanced Nazi ideology, academic presses and institutes also focused on "the Jewish War" and eugenics. Throughout science, medicine, and education, research about "racial hygiene" flourished, and those studying eugenics won prestigious professorships and awards. Some academics bragged that the Nazi regime was "biology in action."[74]

Nazi officials supplemented the mass media, posters, film, arts, and institutions with leaflets and word-of-mouth campaigns through church groups, club meetings, even rumors planted through astrologers and psychics, such that the Nazi narrative and race-based explanations saturated public life. Counterarguments largely came from the "enemies," leaflets dropped by Allied forces and broadcasts coming from the United States and Britain.[75]

THE ELEMENTS COME TOGETHER

A ruined state of Germany and an existing, sometimes latent racism toward Jewish people made for a mostly receptive audience for the Nazi Party's narrative.[76] Rooted in eugenics with a simple good-versus-evil frame, that narrative was emotional and polarizing, generating feelings of pride, exaltation, and a unified community among Germans, and defraying their sense of humiliation.[77] The story of the all-evil "others" who were planning Germany's annihilation aroused intense fear, disgust, hatred, and indifference toward the targeted bad guys, which increasingly meant Jews. Nazis blamed Jews for all of Germany's problems—for which they had a "final solution."

In the Nazis' pseudoscientific ideology, because evil was embedded in genetics, Jews and other "undesirables" were biologically predisposed to be evil; purging was therefore the only means of rescuing humanity and remaining free from the "chains of slavery." By eliminating the bad genes through mass annihilation of the "others," Nazi leaders claimed that they were creating a utopia.[78]

The "genocidal frame" contained four parts: a good-versus-evil narrative with a cast of protagonists (the good Germans) and antagonists (the bad Jews) in a conspiratorial plot; dehumanization of the "others"; a "noble" cause that masked the ugliness of Nazi atrocities and made them part of a mission to achieve a greater good; and a fear-provoking urgency to "kill or be killed." The "grand" cause of eradicating the Jewish race was made every German's duty, requiring unity, sacrifice, and transcendence of individualism. In fact, Hitler claimed that life on Earth depended on defeating the Jews.[79]

Propagandists developed their key message and gradually inundated German society with it, so much so that it was inescapable in daily life. Through control of mass media, political and social institutions, and public space, Nazi officials silenced counternarratives, hid their ghastly deeds, and created a totalitarian, hegemonic message that touted only their "positive" achievements, such as higher German quality of life, while denouncing evil enemies.

Although the Nazi message frame became ubiquitous and hegemonic, the messages did not affect all Germans equally. For some, it merely reinforced or intensified already-festering hostilities toward Jews and other targeted groups. For others, it generated enough indifference, fear, or helplessness for them to fall silent. For dissenters, including some Catholics, working-class Germans, and the White Rose underground student movement, rejection of the Nazi ideology drew serious consequences; Nazi officials silenced, eliminated, ruined, or terrorized them.[80]

Nazi propagandists were assiduous in their efforts to persuade and were consistently concerned about stoking sufficient anti-Semitism. Through their collective management of media and public space, the Third Reich built upon existing resentments and provoked new, destructive emotions.[81] By muting other perspectives, they gave exclusive voice to their framework and ideology, creating a spiral of silence that made the ideology appear unanimous. Then, bit by bit, propagandists intensified their anti-Semitic campaign, rationalizing a "just" cause of destroying the Jews to save Germany and life itself. As they gradually targeted the Jewish "threat," greater numbers of Germans came to either accept, desire, or turn a blind eye to the fate of the Jews. While some Germans desired punishing or eliminating Jews, others were not particularly enthusiastic; but in the face of a hegemonic discourse and the harsh sociopolitical and economic reality, many went numb or distracted themselves by thinking of "other things."[82] The success of the Nazi propagandists in fueling emotions, silencing dissent, and shoring up public support and ignorance about the Holocaust would serve as a model for disasters to come.

Chapter 3

Killing in the Name Of . . . : Media and the Bosnian War

At 9:30 a.m., Djemo, a local writer who lived in Prijedor, Bosnia-Herzegovina, awoke to the sound of gunfire. He had recently moved into his cousin Fadil's home after finding a bullet hole in his bedroom window, likely shot by the Serb gunmen who had occupied the town. But still, Djemo—and his family and friends—thought little about ethnic or religious differences. The only time ethnicity or religion meant anything in Prijedor was during their community soccer games, which always ended in an evening of beer, barbecue, and song—funded by the losing team. And although war raged in Bosnia's capital city of Sarajevo, in Prijedor, "People have been living together here for ages." It can't happen here, they thought. That was until last month's takeover of the town. Ostensibly overnight, Muslims, en masse, were stripped of their jobs; schools were closed; and media were commandeered by Serb forces.[1] Soldiers wearing camouflage uniforms with weapons and ammo draped over their chests, arms, backs, and waists patrolled the streets and perched on buildings. Djemo's Serb friends had seemingly metamorphosed into "crazed servants of the new authority."[2]

An intense anxiety rested heavily on the town, and Serbian flags flitted above the city from buildings and hotels.[3] Non-Serbs—Croats and Muslims—could no longer participate in the same everyday life, especially after 10:00 p.m., when the curfew was enforced. Buses, food purchases, and other services were now segregated—one area for Serbs, one for non-Serbs. Signs, such as the one at the local flour silo, were erected to remind them of their lesser status: "No Flour for Muslims or Croats."[4] Djemo sipped his morning coffee amid intermittent sounds of gunfire, shelling, and fires that swallowed up homes, churches, and mosques. When thuds sounded on the front door, Fadil answered to the barrel of a rifle pointed at him. The masked soldier demanded Fadil turn over his weapons.[5]

"No, brother," Fadil said, "we have no weapons."[6]

"I'm not your brother, we can't be brothers, ever!" Exclaimed the soldier, he then turned to Djemo, who iterated, "I don't have any. I never have!"[7]

From that point forward, Djemo and his fellow Bosniaks' lives became a cruel chaos—forcibly moved at gunpoint, tossed into the back of a "paddy wagon," then restrained against a wall under the blazing sun, enduring body searches and the crash of rifle butts on their backs. An exhausted and helpless Djemo collapsed. Soldiers bludgeoned them with clubs, fists, and feet, then piled Djemo and his group into a bus that was being sent out of their old city, which was now engulfed in wild flames.[8]

"That's how all your houses will burn," remarked one soldier. Djemo didn't dare look toward his own home, but memories flooded his mind, reminding him of what Prijedor had meant to him—where he first fell in love, swam in cool night waters of the Sana River, smoked his first cigarette, and attended outdoor dance performances. The grief formed into a hard lump in his throat.[9]

They reached Omarska, where thousands of fellow Bosnian Muslims and Croats—teachers, intellectuals, engineers, police officers, actors, even the mayor of Prijedor—were crammed into tiny rooms with hard tile floors and no sanitation, to be left starving for four days—at least that was the fate of those who had not already been executed. But starvation was perhaps an easier aspect of prison life. Day after day, they suffered from disease, dehydration, lice infestations, and routine bludgeoning—the latter as prisoners attempted to reach the latrine or canteen—and often during efforts to extract "confessions" about terrorist activities—which then justified their extermination. To avoid beatings, the men remained in the confines of their tightly crammed dorm and urinated in plastic buckets. For the painfully parched, their fellow prisoners' urine became a prized commodity. Any moisture offered temporary relief from extreme dehydration.[10]

Forced confessions were cruel and absurd. Serb forces tortured a blind man until he confessed to being a sniper. A local doctor admitted to hiding smuggled medicine in his cellar—even though he had no cellar.[11]

Upstairs, women were incarcerated. Most of them were Muslim or Croat, but Djemo knew at least two Serbs imprisoned for protesting soldiers' behavior. One woman was Djemo's neighbor before the occupation.[12]

In fits of drunkenness, power-crazed machismo, revenge, and hate, guards routinely tortured the incarcerated men. Djemo watched drunken guards gather ten prisoners outside and order them to strip to their bare, emaciated bodies. All complied, except for one tall, bearded man who stood stoically, head bowed—even after a guard settled a rifle barrel into his neck. Enraged by his quiet defiance, the guards slammed him to the ground with multiple blows of their rifle butts to his head and body. Then, with knives, they cut away his clothes—but without sparing his genitalia or buttocks. The tall, bearded man let out a piercing scream as his blood splattered onto the guards and the ground. They reportedly finished him by dousing his bleeding body with gasoline, lighting him on fire, then dumping his charred remains into a garbage bin.[13]

Among the most infamous guards was Zoka, the self-proclaimed strongman of the Serbian military. Zoka taunted his victims before lashing them with his weapon—a strip of lath with a nail protruding from one end: "Which of your eyes do you like better?" or "Which ball?"[14]

Every day, Djemo and his cell mates cringed from the bloodcurdling sounds of cracking skulls and bones, screams of terror and pain, and the unbearable sights of cruelty and humiliation. As more prisoners were crammed into the cells, more were called to the "white house," a room where Serbian guards bludgeoned male prisoners for hours or days at a time until they collapsed or died.[15]

Djemo heard a drunken guard call his name. He knew it was his turn in the white house. He peeled himself from the arms of Ari, his sobbing, teenage son, and assured him that he would return. As Djemo stepped out of the crowded dorm, a club landed on his neck. He stumbled but caught himself. It was easier to take a truncheon while standing than a boot while on the ground.[16]

In the white house, the notorious Zoran Žigić, rumored to have killed more than two hundred people in Prijedor, demanded, "On all fours, like a dog!"[17] Djemo and the others complied. Clubs, boots, metal, and wire bashed their faces, heads, and bodies. Djemo intermittently lost consciousness but clung to the promise he had made to Ari: to survive, so not to leave him alone in the camp.

Others' bodies failed, sometimes at the hands of people they knew, either professionally or personally. Djemo overheard a student declare to his former professor, "I'm gonna beat the math out of you or die trying!"[18]

Intense hatred, expressed openly, fueled the violence. "Today is my twenty-fifth birthday, and I've only killed twenty-three Muslims," proclaimed one guard with a proud chuckle. Another declared, "The only good Muslim is a dead Muslim." To many in the Serb forces, Croatians and Muslims were collectively "Ustasha motherfuckers."[19]

Although not comparable in scale, some observers called Omarska the "Auschwitz of Bosnia," where "Serbian military and volunteers carried out by hand, with clubs, guns, and revolvers, the work that at Nazi Germany's Auschwitz was largely entrusted to gas chambers and crematoriums." But unlike the dispassionate destruction that marked Auschwitz, Omarska was fueled by intense emotions, a *desire* to inflict pain on others.[20] Like Auschwitz, the perpetrators ostensibly believed that their "enemy" was evil or less than human. "We won't waste our bullets on them," said one soldier of the Omarska victims. "We give them no food and no water . . . sun and rain, cold nights and beatings two times a day . . . they will starve like animals."[21]

Omarska was one of several Bosnian concentration camps where Serb forces imprisoned and tortured the Bosniak Muslims and Croatians who had not yet been killed. In other parts of Bosnia-Herzegovina were the similar Keraterm, Luka Breco (also Luka Brčko), and Manjača camps. While camp prisoners endured their bodies being burned with cigarettes, their fingernails pulled out, and their ears cut off, the worst agony was saved for the "uncooperative"—like Hadzic Ilijaz, local chairman of the Muslim SDA Party.[22] He refused to disclose the names of "all Muslim activists." Military men reportedly bore into his and his wife's chests with an electric drill and impaled his three toddler children "on spikes," witnesses told journalist Roy Gutman.[23]

In other parts of Bosnia-Herzegovina, Croats imprisoned Muslim Bosniaks and Serbs in their own camps, such as Dretelj, where prisoners were crammed into "stinking putrid spaces" of underground storage hangars and where drunken Croatian guards fired indiscriminately into sheds packed with prisoners. They routinely bludgeoned prisoners, rained gunfire into their dorms, and dehydrated or humiliated them. In one account, prisoners were stripped naked and sent running over rocky terrain while Croats fired at them.[24]

Women, children, and the elderly were more frequently sent to camps like Trnopolje, often called a "rape camp." Systematically, each day and night, Serb guards seized a set of Bosniak women and girls, as young as nine and as old as seventy, whisked them into separate quarters to "make" them into "Serb women," and forced them to "experience everything: sex and pain and humiliation."[25]

Because families were frequently imprisoned together, soldiers often serially gang-raped family members, usually in each other's presence or close enough to torment the family. Guards seized eleven-year-old Amina from her mother's arms and tossed her into a "rape room." Her helpless mother, unable to reach her, tried to muffle the sounds of her daughter "screaming in the next room."[26]

En route to a prison camp, a Serbian guard slugged a young Bosniak girl's face for resisting sexual assault. Her sobbing mother begged for their mercy, but three men, instead, threw the mother to the floor of the bus, taking turns raping her while the others held her down. Then, they returned to the daughter for the same abuse—in front of her younger sister and grandmother. As she lay half-conscious and bloody on the bus floor, exhausted and in pain, one assailant landed a fierce kick to the girl's ribs. "Haven't you had enough, you Turkish whore?"[27]

Another assailant kicked her body again. "On your feet, you dirty Turk, and give us a kiss for making a Serb woman out of you."[28]

Some women submitted to the soldiers' sexual demands "with great disgust" under threat: "If you go on resisting . . . we'll slaughter your little girl." Others complied but still couldn't escape the torture. One guard bludgeoned a woman until she fell to the floor, then plopped his sweaty body upon her, wielding a large knife. With the blade, he ripped her clothing away without sparing the skin on her breasts, neck, and thighs. After finishing, he gripped her bloody, bruised, and near-naked body, and shoved her back into the camp.[29]

Some women were tied and beaten until they passed out, raped dozens of times in a day or sold and never seen again. One woman was given the choice between "having her face carved with a knife" or her body tattooed with her assailant's name. She still bears his name on her arms and legs. Others were battered internally with foreign objects thrust into their vaginas.[30]

"*Balinkura*, you disgust me!" shouted Zoran, while repeatedly shoving a bottle into a woman's vagina. Then he forced himself into her.[31]

As part of the ethnic warfare, some twenty thousand women endured violent rapes, some up to one hundred fifty times. It was partly cruelty and partly an effort to impregnate the "others" with their "own" in a kind of "ethnic cleansing." Some one thousand impregnated women gave birth to babies conceived from rape.[32]

The camps and the rapes were only one aspect of a vicious war thrust upon civilians whose guilt was merely being one of the "other" ethnicities. With thousands of mortar shells and regular machine-gun blasts, Serb forces crumbled giant swaths of Sarajevo to rubble. They torched a maternity clinic where seventy pregnant women prepared to give birth and 173 newborns slept. Others shelled a group of children—one as young as four—while the kids played in an enclosed courtyard. During a so-called cease-fire, ostensibly to draw people out of hiding, soldiers opened fire on a queue of people at one of the last remaining banks, killing twenty-one people, three of whom were children. They shelled hungry Bosnians in line to buy bread. Survivors watched severed body parts—human hands and feet—flying from the force of the explosions.[33]

In an effort to oust Muslims and Croats from predominantly Serb-inhabited regions, Serb forces set villages, neighborhoods, and whole sections of cities ablaze. In house-to-house campaigns, they appeared at doorsteps with automatic rifles or hand grenades, confiscating family valuables, summarily executing the men, or killing entire families indiscriminately. Those still alive were arrested and forcibly removed from the area, or lined up and gunned down on the spot.[34]

Revenge begot revenge in a vicious all-out war.[35] Croat forces and, to a lesser extent, Muslim Bosniaks captured and savagely beat, electrocuted, or burned alive Serbs. Some carved up Serb captives or crammed them into tiny tunnels.[36] In acts of retaliation or mutual aggression, each of the forces brutalized the others. Like a terror mirror, Croat and Muslim forces raided and pillaged, set fire to the homes of "the other," and massacred those who failed to escape.[37] Serb forces argued they were reacting to "treatment of our people" in previous conflicts while fighters on all sides of the war questioned what they had become. "We [are] becoming them—or rather what they wanted us to become," lamented one soldier.[38]

Countless families were destroyed, and surviving children were orphaned. Take the case of a teenaged Bosniak named Elvir. His family scrambled to escape from Croat soldiers who surrounded their house. Grenades blasted his twelve-year-old brother to death and blew his mother's hand off. His mother, after a gunshot pierced her abdomen, curled up next to her oldest son's lifeless body in a stable behind the burning house and died, leaving Elvir and his four-year-old sister alone in the throes of the war.[39]

In a most devastating massacre, after the United Nations had declared Srebrenica a "safe" zone, Serb forces overran the city. Firing squads tied the hands of some eight thousand Muslim men and boys and executed them. Surviving women, the elderly, and children were expelled from their longtime homes in an effort to "ethnically cleanse" non-Serbs from the region.[40]

More than one hundred thousand people were killed in the Bosnian war between 1992 and 1995. Another million were displaced and left homeless from the devastation and forced deportations. The dead were often dumped into mass graves, thrown into a river, or burned.[41]

While many perpetrators were militants, others were regular people who became violators as media frames and circumstances changed. The wars converted "good and faithful friends" into ruthless killers, some of whom bragged about killing "more than a hundred prisoners in eighteen days." Many had been neighbors, former friends, colleagues, or "teachers who had taught our children"—people who had for more than forty years lived in harmony like a "multi-ornamented carpet"[42] and experienced much shared history together.

"Yugoslavia seemed so safe," wrote Slavenka Drakulic. "Brotherhood and unity seemed so real. We grew up together, went to school together—Serbs and Croats and Muslims—befriended each other, got married, had children, never thinking that nationality could be something that would split us apart."[43]

In Sarajevo, the sentiment was particularly strong. "Nobody can divide us," insisted one resident. But attitudes were similar in other parts of Yugoslavia: "We never thought of nationality before the war. Yugoslavia was my country," said Zlatiborka Popov-Momčinović, who grew up in Vojvodina. "I didn't even know my nationality growing up. I identified as a Yugoslav."[44]

But in short order, Serbs sought "revenge" for their 1389 "defeat at Kosovo" in the conflict with the Ottomans and for "the murdered Serbs at the hands of Croat Ustashas" and "Muslims" during World War II. Croats sought to destroy "Chetniks," the name for "royalist" Serb forces during the World War II, the worst of times among the Yugoslavs. At that time, during the German/Axis invasion of Yugoslavia, one group of Croatians, led by Ante Pavelic—the Ustashas—sided with Nazi Germany and the Axis powers. In efforts to annihilate Serbs, the Ustashas massacred and imprisoned them en masse in concentration camps, killing some three hundred thousand. In Fascist-occupied Kosovo, another seventy to one hundred thousand Serbs and Montenegrins faced expulsion and incarceration, and some ten thousand were killed. Although one group of Serbs, the Zbor, led by Dimitrije Ljotic, allied with the Germans, Serbs largely joined resistance movements, either the Royalist Chetniks, which collaborated with Fascists, or the Communist-led, multiethnic Yugoslav Partisans.[45]

With the help of the Red Army, the Partisans, headed by Josip Broz Tito, ultimately ousted the Axis, first from Serbia and eventually from the rest of Yugoslavia. Although other ethnic groups filled the ranks of the Partisans, many Serbs felt that they had rescued Yugoslavia yet again, this time from the Nazis' grip, and sacrificed their young and their own interests to defend, liberate, and preserve Yugoslavia's "unity and integrity."[46]

Although the two world wars were times of great division among the Balkan people, ethnicity was not the primary driver of hostilities before the wars, when the region had more "cooperative ties than conflict." Even in the 1389 Battle of Kosovo, heralded by Serb leaders as the defining nationalist war, ethnic groups including Serbs, Croats, and Albanians fought on both sides of the conflict.[47]

HOW DID WE GET HERE? EARLY HISTORY

Historically, after the South Slavs (Yugo-Slavs) migrated to the region during the sixth century, each established individual dynasties in medieval times. For the most part, those dynasties were short-lived, falling, at various times, to other kingdoms, such as Hungary, Bulgaria, or the Habsburg and Ottoman Empires. Religiously, Serbs and Croatians had converted to Christianity (Orthodox and Catholic), while those who became known as Bosniaks converted to Islam. Among Albanians, all three religions were practiced.[48]

Ideas about statehood either based on language and ethnicity or a larger Yugoslav state emerged during the eighteenth century from an amalgam of thinkers connected to the French Revolution, German Romanticists, and writers. Intellectuals in each ethnic group developed the concept of their own individual nationhood, while political leaders and small national movements built upon the notion of their "great" historical nations—the Great Serbia, Croatia, and Bosnia.[49]

Serbs were particularly determined to wrest the South Slavs from the Ottoman Empire. Some sought a "Greater Serbia" devoid of Croats while others desired an inclusive state for all Yugo-Slavs.[50] Their dreams were thwarted again when the Austro-Hungarian Empire annexed regions of the Balkans—at least until June 28, 1914, the anniversary of the Battle of Kosovo. On that day, a nineteen-year-old Bosnian Serb, Gavrilo Princip, assassinated Austrian Archduke Franz Ferdinand and his wife, Sophie, throwing Europe into political chaos and the horror of World War I.

From the ashes of that war, the first Yugoslavia was born. But the new country, rife with dysfunction and inner turmoil, was again torn apart during World War II, then spliced back together by warrior-turned-president Tito. In his reconstruction of the newly established Yugoslavia, Tito compiled a federation of more than eight disparate peoples into six republics.[51] It was, by some accounts, the "most successful experiment in building a multinational federation in Europe" since the end of World War II.[52]

In Tito's formula, each of the six republics maintained a degree of autonomy and culture under a central socialist authority that cracked down hard on ultranationalism. Ethnically, most republics were relatively homogenous with a few pockets of the other ethnic groups, but many people increasingly began identifying as Yugoslavs more than as Serbs, Croats, or Bosniaks.[53] Bosnia, aptly nicknamed "little Yugoslavia" for its tapestry of peoples, was more diverse. In its cities, particularly the capital city of Sarajevo, many Serbs, Croats, and Bosniak Muslims lived harmoniously without strong, national-identity-based animosities.[54]

Under Tito's strictly enforced ideology of "brotherhood and unity," ethnically driven wounds from the world wars were gradually healing, particularly in Bosnia, the state nestled between Croatia and Serbia.[55] By the late 1980s, one-third of Bosnia's urban marriages were interethnic;

nearly all Bosnian families had relatives from one of the other ethnicities or religions, and only 17 percent of urbanites considered themselves to be particularly religious.[56] In the capital city, Sarajevo, 40 percent of marriages were mixed.[57] Most people hardly knew the religious or ethnic backgrounds of their friends, and incidents of ethnic violence were rare.[58] They lived together in the same buildings, attended the same schools, and worked side by side for the same employers.[59] How, then, did neighbors, friends, and colleagues morph into hostile enemies who raped, killed, or tortured those who might have been "best men at their weddings," members of the family, or "godfathers to their children"?[60] A sequence of events created a simmering tension: Across the federation, Yugoslavia faced looming financial crises, corruption, and power struggles, particularly in the wake of Tito's death in 1980. Soaring debt and unemployment sent Yugoslavs demonstrating in the streets against austerity measures and led to inter-republic finger-pointing with leaders feuding over political and economic benefits. Richer republics resented supporting the "black hole" of poorer republics, while poorer republics resented the richer republics' quality of life. Yugoslavia's governance structure compounded the leadership power struggles. The one-year, rotating presidents in a decentralized federation were relatively ineffectual in the face of the growing chaos. Meanwhile, in Kosovo, Albanians agitated for greater equality and control over their own affairs, railing against local Serbs. Serb-led law enforcement cracked down on the dissident Albanians, and resentment toward Albanians grew across Serbia.[61]

While the federation's circumstances were increasingly trying, on their own the events do not explain the rabid nationalism and vicious cruelty that emerged. Yugoslavia could have still traversed another path and resolved its issues nonviolently. But together, the crises and the void in leadership set the stage for the rise of nationalist leaders and their quests for a "Greater Serbia" and later a "Greater Croatia." National parties heightened divisions between the ethnic groups and the sense of "us" and "them." Ethnic distinctions became more pronounced, and stereotypes gained greater expression.[62] But the catalysts came through the airwaves and publications in a frenzy of blame, rage, fury, fear, and hatred toward the "others," ultimately shattering any semblance of Tito's dream of "unity and brotherhood." In its place, leaders such as Serbian leader Slobodan Milošović and later Croatian leader Franjo Tudjman brought to life—through their respective media—the once-dead historic narratives of abuse and injustice that the groups had perpetrated on one another during the world wars.[63] The reawakened fear and bitterness was met with tales of twisted histories and modern fabrications to make it seem necessary to obliterate all the "others"—men, women, the elderly, children—even when they had no role in the conflicts. Some sought "revenge," some "justice," and some merely killed out of a belief that they must destroy the enemy lest they themselves be destroyed. Conditioned by a story line about a righteous "us" versus a monstrous "them," many committed heinous acts while drunk with power and numbed by alcohol.

The onslaughts and horrors occurred first in mass media—in the form of accusations, blame, name-calling, stereotyping, and making "monsters" out of people they had known personally. As tales of horror and injustice, many untrue, traveled through airwaves and headlines, the real acts of abhorrent destruction followed, as if media foreshadowed what was to come. People came to believe these depictions and narratives in the media, then acted on those beliefs with violence, morphing their worst fears into an even worse reality, one that was hardly plausible before the long media campaign. It became a self-fulfilling prophecy.[64]

By the time the republics began seceding—Slovenia then Croatia in 1991, followed by Bosnia in 1992—many Yugoslavs were sufficiently primed with the fear and blame in broadcasts and publications, and they were willing to follow their nationalist leaders to help perpetrate heinous acts against the evil "others" and "save" their own. Serb leaders, in their call to "defend" Serbs living in Croatia and Bosnia, sent forces on a city-by-city, village-by-village rampage, killing, incarcerating, and deporting non-Serbs.[65] Yugoslavia had experienced this pattern of a media war evolving into real violence before: during the late 1980s, this same progression occurred in Kosovo.

LEADING UP TO THE BOSNIAN WAR: THE SERBIAN MEDIA, KOSOVO, AND THE RISE OF SLOBODAN MILOŠEVIĆ

"Republic, Kosovo-Republic!" chanted Albanian students in the streets of Pristina, crying out to place Kosovo, an autonomous region that was home to a majority of Albanians and a minority of Serbs and Montene-grins, on equal footing with the six Yugoslav republics.[66] The atmosphere was tense and, at times, hopeless in Kosovo. Kosovars of all ethnicities faced trying conditions: crippling poverty, underdevelopment, corruption, the federation's lowest average wages, and the highest unemployment and illiteracy.[67] But the region's discontents also grew from interethnic disputes. For one, both Serbs and Albanians laid claim to the region that had been conquered by Serbs in 1912–13. After World War II, Tito gave Kosovo autonomy, but his security chief and other Serb officials ruled the region with a "rod of iron." Albanians revolted with anti-Serb riots that sent thousands of Serbs fleeing into Serbia.[68]

By the early 1980s, Albanians, under police occupation, agitated for full autonomy. They rebelled with mass demonstrations, periodic riots, the burning of cars, and sporadic attacks on Serbs. Law enforcement punished them severely with long imprisonments, beatings, and broken limbs.[69]

The "steady stream of horror stories" from Kosovo fueled a growing discontent among Serb leaders. In 1985, a group of Serb intellectuals coauthored a memorandum decrying the Serbs' regional losses and victimization.[70] In 1986, the leaked memorandum appeared in a Belgrade newspaper, *Večernje novosti*. Their people had long sacrificed themselves for the rest of the federation, they wrote. Now they faced a coming "genocide" by "racist" Albanians who were waging "total war" upon Serbs to drive them out of Kosovo via high birth rates and other means of domination. The memorandum resonated with many Serbs and served as a catalyst among key leaders, including Slobodan Milošević.[71]

At Milošević's encouragement, Kosovo Serbs launched their own demonstrations, "emphasizing the mythic significance of Kosovo in the construction of Serbian nationhood." They rallied against Albanians and the Communist league, and asserted their rights to Kosovo.[72]

By the late 1980s, through extensive exaggeration and stereotyping, media and political elites cast all Albanians as public enemy number one. In headlines and in broadcasts, they racialized individual crimes, blaming isolated incidents on the entire Albanian population: A single rape equaled, "They are raping our mothers and sisters." A single murder was "anti-Serbian," a product of "Albanian terror."[73] Accusations that Albanians were "poisoning wells and slitting the throats of children" soared across Serb television airwaves.[74]

Nationalist activists boosted the media campaign when on April 24, 1987, they prepared the perfect, made-for-TV provocation: an angry mob and a truck full of stones to throw at local police just outside the location where Serb leader Milošević was attending a meeting. Just before the event came the call: Milošević's "safety" was at risk, said Mirjana Marković, Milošević's wife, to Dušan Mitević, the Belgrade Radio and Television executive and one of many high-level journalists befriended by Milošević through "behind-the-scenes" information during his rise through party ranks. Although Milošević told Mitević that he would be okay, Mitević understood the opportunity.[75]

Before a prepared camera crew, approximately fifteen thousand Serbs and Montenegrins tried to force their way into the hall where Milošević attended his meeting. Police forcibly blocked the entrance, and demonstrators pelted the officers with stones until the police responded with clubs. The mood shifted: "Murderers! They are beating us!" the crowd cried out.[76]

In the perfect setting for a hero's emergence, Milošević, stern and confident, stepped into the crowds and faced television cameras.[77] He signaled police with his hand to allow the Serbs entry and declared, "From now on, no one has the right to beat you! No one should dare beat you!" Later he insisted, "This is your land!"[78] Instantly, Milošević emerged as the "defender of Serbs," as his images spread across Serb television screens. TV Belgrade repeated the scene over and over, showing only the police response and Milošević's stand, not the stone throwers. Milošević was catapulted to the unquestioned position of leader for the Serbs.[79]

"This is what launched him," admitted Mitević. "We showed Milošević's promise over and over again."[80]

The following September, a mentally ill Albanian soldier serving in the Yugoslav army, in a crazed rampage, opened fire on ten of his comrades—five were Muslims, the other five were Serbs and Croats. Of the four who died, one was a Serb. Although the soldier ostensibly fired indiscriminately, without making ethnic or religious distinctions, the incident was "made-to-order," according to Živorad Minović, chief editor of the influential newspaper *Politika*.[81]

Generate "huge publicity" about "an Albanian soldier killing four Serbs!" he said to his staff before realizing only one Serb had died. Nonetheless, the framing and publicity turned the tragedy into an issue of nationalism, another victimization of Serbs. In a show of national solidarity, approximately twenty thousand Serbs appeared at the Serb victim's memorial.[82]

It was prototypical of the emerging stories in Serbian media—stories about innocent Serbs being slaughtered and a fast-approaching genocide—what many Serbs began to believe was really being organized. THE SAVAGERY OF ALBANIAN NATIONALISTS AGAINST EVERYTHING THAT'S SERB: THEY ARE BURNING, RAPING, STONING, WRECKING, BREAKING, VANDALIZING, read one headline in the Serb magazine *Duga*.[83] They are preparing an "armed rebellion with hellish plans to conquer" the Serbs and create an "'ethnically pure Kosovo,'" stated another article in the newspaper *Politika*.[84]

High rates of childbirth, in particular, were labeled a sinister "demographic war," some of the Albanians' "immoral and inhuman" acts that were "being boosted by Albanian separatists . . . to conquer foreign territories," according to one newspaper article.[85] Their "numerical superiority . . . [is] not a natural consequence . . . but rather a result of their political will. . . . It is essential that we understand this as an act of violence . . . and handle it accordingly, using violent means." In some Serb media, Albanians were "megalomaniac . . . demographic conqueror[s]"[86] who had launched an "unprecedented campaign for their wretched and pitiful women to bear children."[87]

In order to black out dissenting views throughout Serbia and Kosovo, Milošević carefully controlled the story that the public would hear, using four methods. He personally chose the correspondent who would report from Pristina, then regularly phoned the reporter to shape the story.[88] He and his team then toppled publishers, directors, and editors from their positions and purged their newsrooms. By seizing television transmitters, they silenced or controlled entire networks.[89] Finally, they discredited anyone with the courage to voice another perspective.

The practices served them well in Kosovo. Serb forces seized the Kosovo broadcasting service, Radio-Television Pristina, fired more than thirteen hundred staff, including the editor in chief, and proceeded to shut down the six Albanian-language radio stations and three Kosovar newspapers, including the only one in the Albanian language. Staff who refused to sign a loyalty oath were summarily dismissed. With the Albanian-language media under Serb government control, Albanian news coverage was suddenly silent.[90]

Altogether, this four-pronged strategy left only one dominant, hegemonic narrative: "The savage Albanian terrorists are now running amok in Kosovo . . . breaking into the homes of Serbs and terrorizing the few people who have stayed behind. Kosovo and Metohija are gripped by the fear of terrorists armed to the teeth."[91]

In 1989, Serb officials quashed another Albanian demonstration and punished participants, dismissing them from their schools, colleges, and workplaces. Fourteen of the young organizers and demonstrators received prison sentences; at least one was for twenty years.[92] Serb authorities reacted perhaps less to the demonstrations themselves and more to their attrition of power in a region that they long held as their historic and spiritual homeland. Serbs were gradually losing power to Albanians, who had become the majority ethnic group, a development that for nationalist Serb leaders amounted to "physical, political, legal and cultural genocide," against which they would fight with all their might. Kosovo, to them, unquestioningly belonged to Serbs, not to those they called Albanian "terrorist-separatists" in Serb media during the mid-1980s.[93]

The depictions, believed by many Serbs, became the justification for mass civil rights violations; by 1989, nearly six hundred thousand Kosovars were either arrested, interrogated, reprimanded, or interned. Albanian public employees were systematically fired for refusing to sign loyalty pledges; schools that refused the "programme of Serbia" were closed; finally, Kosovo's autonomy was struck from the constitution.[94]

Emboldened by successes in Kosovo, nationalist Serbs easily turned their frightened and angry audiences against other non-Serbs. Using the Kosovo "success" as a model, they turned to the next enemy on their list—the "Vojvodina autonomists."

Politika's pages were flooded with demands to dismiss all Vojvodina representatives who had called for discussion before making drastic constitutional changes. Weeks of headlines argued, THEY LOST THEIR REPUTATIONS.

Milošević supporters bused thousands of protesters into Vojvodina, the multiethnic autonomous region, for mass rallies in a campaign to oust Vojvodina representatives. To support the "threatened Serbs and Montenegrins from Kosovo," protesters threw stones and yogurt-filled plastic bags at government buildings and flaunted signs calling for the hanging of non-Serb politicians. Milošević suggested a solution: "Submit your resignations and you will be saved," he said to Vojvodina politicians.[95]

Vojvodina's autonomy crumbled next.[96]

The Secessions in Succession

By 1989, Milošović and his team controlled 90 percent of "all information available to Serbs." They could now "restore Serbia's dignity" and make it "whole," they said.[97] Milošević's party unified Serbian radio and television under its control. And by the summer of 1991, media restrictions were so tight that even music by non-Serbs was forbidden on Serbian Radio-Television (Radio-Televizija Srbije or RTS).[98]

After a series of failed negotiations to compromise with Milošević, the republics began to secede—first Slovenia, then Croatia, and later Bosnia. The Serb media's enemy list grew to include "Shiptar separatists," the "anti-Orthodox Catholic alliance," "vampirical Ustasha," the Bosnian "Muslim mujahideen," and "Jihad warriors"—all of whom were intent on "destroying Serbia."[99] Serb headlines and broadcasts told heartbreaking yet unverified stories of massacred Serb children in an elementary school,[100] of Muslim extremists tossing "Serb children to the lions in the local zoo,"[101] children's "eyes and bones" being made into "necklaces," and Serbs being held hostage and made into orphans by a "Muslim offensive."[102]

The era of "searching for understanding and consensus" had ended.[103] It was time instead to arm Serbs so they could "defend" themselves against Slovenians, Croatians, and Bosnian Muslims, according to *Politika*. GENOCIDE MUSTN'T BE REPEATED! warned headlines. Through posters reprinted from World War I and Serb media, Serbs were called to take up arms and help "save Serbia."[104]

Although tens of thousands of Serbs expressed dissent by protesting in the streets, Milošević's team blocked the independent stations' transmissions to prevent the larger population of Serbs from hearing alternative views. Dissenters, whether citizens, government officials, or journalists, were quickly punished as traitors of Serbia. The disobedient faced the wrath of government officials, who rapidly passed new media laws and obtained judicial support to oust them and shut down entire media operations.[105]

Slovenia fell off the Serb media's active enemy list, having freed itself from the onslaught of the federal army in just ten days. With Slovenia lost, Serb media focused on the remaining enemies—Croatians and Muslim Bosniaks—since there were significant numbers of Serbs in both states. Milošević and his media allies easily justified their offensive thrusts into Croatia, then Bosnia, by claiming they were "saving" Serbs from these enemies.

As Serb forces entered Serb-inhabited regions of Croatia, Croatian authorities and media responded with their own nationalistic, anti-Serb rhetoric, showing "beady-eyed Serbian generals, wrecked Croatian churches and resolute Croatian soldiers." Like Milošević's campaign to buy and control newspapers, Croatian president Franjo Tudjman required journalists' loyalty, even when Croatian forces abused non-Croats. Tudjman's team fired some one thousand media staff for disloyalty and converted Croatia's "finest" daily newspaper into a nationalist organ.[106] Newspaper articles and broadcast stories frequently called all Serbs "terrorists," showed "images of dead bodies," and claimed that Croatian police were tortured and mutilated by the "bestial hands" of "Chetniks." Croatian public opinion grew virulently anti-Serb.[107]

The message from both sides amounted to this: "We are the victims, and they are the culprits. We must annihilate them to save ourselves." This narrative was easily integrated for people who had historically suffered some form of injustice.[108]

Serbia and Croatia fought a vicious war. By January 1992, the Croatians had fended off Serb forces—but only after the Serbs had lopped off a quarter of Croatia's territory.[109] Bosnia, however, sandwiched between the two powerful feuding states, suffered for much longer. With no army, no military tradition, and no substantial artillery, the landlocked country was doomed from the start. After Bosnian leaders declared independence, both Serb and Croatian forces foisted their aggressions onto the weaker Muslim Bosniaks and began divvying up the territories of Bosnia-Herzegovina, where large numbers of Serbs and Croats lived.[110]

"This might lead Bosnia into hell and [cause] one people to disappear," warned Radovan Karadžić, the poet-psychiatrist-turned-leader of the Bosnian Serbs.[111]

Hell on Bosnia

The Bosnian declaration of independence was "a fatal mistake!" said Serb leaders in newspapers and broadcasts. The referendum was days away, and if Bosnians voted to affirm secession from rump Yugoslavia, Serbs could not "accept responsibility for what might happen," they warned.[112]

Bosnia's president, Muslim Alija Izetbegović, publicly declared his refusal to fight: "There will be no war in Bosnia and Herzegovina. It takes two sides for war." He was willing, however, to "sacrifice peace for a sovereign Bosnia-Herzegovina."[113]

Bosnian journalists encouraged audiences to "resist going to war against their neighbors."[114] As barricades were erected throughout the country, a Yugoslav National Broadcast News (YUTEL) television editor persuaded rival leaders to talk to one another in a live broadcast. Sarajevo Television likewise asked viewers to signal their wish for peace by powering down their lights for two minutes.[115] Sarajevo city, for two minutes, went dark.

Although most Bosnian Serbs boycotted the referendum, 64 percent of Bosnians outside of Herzegovina voted to support an independent "state of equal citizens and nations of Muslims, Serbs, and Croats and others who live in it."[116] Rejecting both Croatian and Serbian nationalism, most sought instead to continue what they saw as their tradition of "inter-ethnic tolerance."

One month later, tens of thousands of Bosnians—Bosniak Muslims, Serbs, Croats, and Jews—filled the streets of Sarajevo, chanting, "Bosnia is a community of brotherhood." The mass of people marched toward the Holiday Inn, where Karadžić's Serbian Democratic Party maintained their offices, hoping to "plead with them not to fight," according to one red-haired English student. But what seemed impossible to Bosnians became a cruel reality: a sniper atop the hotel opened fire on the crowd, killing a medical student and a clerk who worked in the Bosnian Parliament.[117]

The Sarajevo siege had begun, to the surprise of most Sarajevans, but the war on media had begun months earlier. That war awakened old fears, memories, and feelings of revenge that had long been laid to rest, ripped apart communities, and turned long-standing friends into enemies. The shredding of Bosnian communities would take hard, concerted efforts, but the men behind the task were dedicated to the job.[118]

The War on Journalism

Months before the first bullet was fired, the media war had begun. Using a successful model in Kosovo as their prototype, Serb forces, on August 1, 1991, seized one of eleven transmitters that broadcast TV Sarajevo into the living rooms of ethnically mixed communities in Bosnia. One by one, they forcibly snatched another eight, reducing TV Sarajevo's reach to less than half of the Bosnian territory. In one transmitter battle, on the mountain above the Vlasic meadows and pasturelands, Serb forces arrested and imprisoned the entire crew and shot dead the television engineer.[119]

By the end of 1991, Serbian paramilitary forces controlled most of Bosnia's transmitters. They turned most transmitters to receive Serbian television and destroyed the rest. The "media blockade" was soon followed by the closing down of Bosnia's postal services, telecommunications, roads, and rail links.[120]

In northern Bosnian communities such as Prijedor, Serb forces confiscated the entire media apparatus and placed the town under high alert. The military-run mass media then warned residents of purported attacks on them by Muslim "extremists," and disseminated descriptions of "good" Serbs—those who were armed and loyal to the occupiers—even among children.[121]

The messages emanating from Serbia were largely under the control of Milošević and his allies, including commander and extremist Vojislav Šešelj who called for the "cleansing" of "tainted" journalists in Serb-controlled media. En masse, hundreds were dismissed. In one January 1993 purge alone, at Radio Television Belgrade (RTB) and RTS, some two hundred journalists and more than one thousand staff were summarily fired. As some journalists arrived at work, snipers and armed police awaited them, preventing their entry into the building.[122]

Once they controlled the channels, Serb forces created a "systemic instigation of hatred toward anyone who could possibly be thought of, or felt to be, non-Serb." Local broadcasts were particularly "nationalistic and problematic," according to sociology professor Mirsad Abazović: "They blamed the 'others' for their own atrocities as an effort to motivate their people, showing brutalities committed by Serbs while blaming Muslims for them. Local people came to believe the messages," he said.[123] Repeatedly, these broadcasters alarmed the community about attacks on them by "Muslim extremists," even when no such attack had occurred. In an ostensible effort to generate more fear, they implored people to "remain in their homes and apartments" for their own safety and to display white flags to signal their loyalty.[124]

While highlighting offenses committed by the other warring parties, Serb media refused to cover the Serb forces' destruction, leaving Serb audiences to feel victimized without understanding the dynamics of the war. "They were completely silent on their own offenses, such as the destruction of thirteen mosques in Banja Luka," said Abazović. Worst of all, "these media accused Muslims of bombing themselves as a means to blame Serbs."[125]

Meanwhile, Serbs watched their painful past literally excavated from the ground. Bones of World War II Serb victims were exhumed from mass graves in order to give them "proper" burials and blessings by church leaders. Television cameras zoomed in on dozens of small coffins, broadcasting their images throughout Serb homes.[126] Serb radio and television aired programs such as *Red Is the Sky* and *The Consecration of the Kupresko Polje Grave* about the past war crimes committed against Serbs, packaged with new warnings about the coming genocide and the necessity to fight. Should they fail, they would again face "concentration camps and the pits used as collective tombs," wrote Jovan Rašković.[127] Their fellow Serbs, according to television and radio reports, were already being slaughtered.[128]

In many Serb media, Bosniak Muslims were degraded, called "genetically spoiled material" that was "reinforced generation after generation."[129] Mixed marriages, which were quite prevalent in urban Bosnia, were causing "degeneration of [the] Serb nationality," according to Serb leaders in Bosnian papers.[130] Bosnia-Herzegovina had already perished, according to the media; it was consistently called a "former republic."

Serbs who questioned these depictions and narratives were quickly labeled "against their Serb republic" and disgraced.[131]

The War on Journalists

In the capital city of Sarajevo, journalists faced a barrage of attacks and harassment. Because printing presses and distribution networks were controlled by Bosnia's ruling party and because advertisers only purchased space in media that followed the party line, the few independent media, such as daily newspaper *Oslobojenje*, struggled to survive. Television and radio stations that refused orders to split their coverage into three ethnically oriented channels found their bank accounts locked.[132] But worse than the attacks on the media organizations were the attacks on the journalists themselves. Journalists who tried to remain neutral faced death threats, arrests, beatings, sniper fire, destroyed equipment, shelling of their operations, humiliation, and hate letters containing human excrement. Confronted with death, disappearance, intimidation, or financial ruin, most independent-minded journalism went silent.[133]

While assaulted by a tidal wave of terror and constant shelling and machine-gun fire, some journalists continued reporting vitally needed information to the Bosnian communities. In April 1992, Serb forces launched twenty mortar shells into TV Sarajevo, blasting the building and filling it with plumes of thick, black smoke.[134] They repeated the blasts daily, knocking reporters, staff, and equipment to the floor. Amid gunfire and shelling, TV Sarajevo journalists continued to defy attempts to silence them. In June, they aired a tape capturing a disturbing order: "Burn it all!" ordered Serbian general Ratko Mladić, calling on his forces to burn down even the Serb-inhabited regions of Sarajevo.[135]

Another defiant operation, *Oslobojenje* also operated under a barrage of regular gunfire and shelling. The multiethnic staff cooperated to deliver news to a public that was desperate for information about the fate of their families, town services, and other key occurrences. But their dedication was costly. Serb forces dragged one of the paper's reporters, Kjasif Smajlovic, from his Zvornik office, feet first, and executed him on the sidewalk.[136] They shot dead the paper's accountant, Zuhra Besic, and killed photographer Salko Hondo in a rain of shell attacks. Hondo had just photographed a spring discovered in a local backyard, big news for a water-deprived city. "The only thing left was Hondo's camera, flung some distance away by the force of the blast."[137] Serb forces also shot directly into editor Mehmed Husic's home, forcibly entered the building, tossed in a hand grenade, and arrested him and his entire family, including his two children.[138] Finally, they set fire to the newspaper's stately glass and steel building with incendiary bullets. Firefighters rushed to the scene to save the building, but snipers opened fire on the firefighters; one was shot dead.[139]

The journalist "death list" was long. Near the top of the list was news anchor Mirsada Sakic-Hatibovic of Radio Televizija Bosne i Hercegovine (RT-BiH). After she spent months working under shelling and gunfire in a building deprived of heat and water, Serb forces bombed her home. Sakic finally fled to Paris.[140] On national television, Karadžić called for the assassination of Nenad Pejic, editor in chief of Sarajevo Television, and Goran Milić, director of pan-Yugoslav YUTEL in Sarajevo. Pejic fled the country in fear. YUTEL, a prime target of paramilitary groups, eventually shuttered its operation.[141]

In just two months, twelve members of the Bosnia and Herzegovina Television Network and five reporters from the principal newspaper *Oslobojenje* were killed in shelling or sniper attacks.[142] One year into the war, assailants had attacked a total of 68 journalists, killing 30 and wounding 33. At least one wounded journalist died when Serbian forces refused him medical attention. Still dozens more faced death threats, property confiscations, and arrests.[143] The numbers grew as the war continued.

International journalists in Sarajevo fared no better. Snipers shot forty-year-old CNN camerawoman Margaret Moth through the window of a minivan as she and fifty-nine-year-old CNN correspondent Mark Dulmage drove toward the Sarajevo airport. Dulmage sustained injuries from shattered glass during the assault. Both survived but were among the lucky ones. Snipers shot dead Spanish photographer Jaime Pujol and ABC television producer David Kaplan. Shrapnel explosions also wounded an Associated Press photographer and BBC reporter Martin Bell, and Serb forces convicted then *Christian Science Monitor* reporter David Rohde of illegal entry and tossed him into prison.[144]

A number of Serb journalists who refused to toe the line were spared death but still faced public humiliation. They were denounced as "Serb-

haters" and public disgraces, according to Šešelj on the news. One journalist working in the multiethnic Bosnian TV was forced to "publicly . . . spit on himself for serving 'Muslim television.'"[145]

The Whole World Was Watching

Karadžić stood, stout and defiant, with his giant stature, at yet another
press conference where he would again deny that there were concentration camps. He challenged journalists to come see for themselves.

Breaking stories in Britain's ITN, the *Guardian* of London, and
Newsday in the United States finally exposed the prison camps. Just after
Newsday's exposé, titled THE DEATH CAMPS OF BOSNIA, Bosnian Serbs
closed Omarska, though they continued operating others that had not
yet been discovered. Initially, the US government attempted to
"manage" the news, claiming it had no real evidence. But as television
pictures of emaciated camp survivors appeared across viewers' screens,
officials finally sent in the International Red Cross, which helped to
rescue surviving prisoners.[146]

From the window of their television screens, the Western world
watched a "never-ending stream of heart-rending stories and images."[147]
Western journalists exposed the indiscriminate killing of civilians
standing in line for bread or to withdraw a few dollars from their bank.
Throughout the Western world, viewers helplessly watched Serb forces
shelling Sarajevo, limbs flying through the air, "dismembered bodies of
the dead and not-quite dead lining alleyways in pools of blood," reducing
a once-elegant city to a blood-stained lump on the map.[148] Yet even two
years into the slaughter, none of this rose "to the level of massacre";
standing on the sidelines, the United Nations and most Western states
held steadfast to "neutrality," and many in their media remained in virtual lockstep with them—all while the besieged state of Bosnia crumbled
and tens of thousands of innocent people died horrible, unnecessary
deaths.[149]

With no clear understanding of the conflict, the slaughters became
understood, inaccurately, as a "spontaneous outburst of ancient ethnic
hatreds" for which there was little solution. Rather than an impetus to
act, media audiences' doubts, confusion, and ostensible hopelessness sent
them into the "security of home."[150] This portrayal obscured the real

nature of the war as well as its underlying motivations, justifying nonintervention and leaving the horrors unmitigated.[151]

BLAME ON THEM

"They had ice in their ears," said the six-foot-four towering leader Karadžić to *New Yorker* journalist Mark Danner, just before he bit into his stew. "The Muslims took bodies from the morgue and they put them there, in the market," he insisted. "Even when they shell themselves like this, no one shell kills that many. So they went to the morgue."[152]

"I was there, the bodies were real. You can't be serious," Danner responded. He had personally witnessed the devastation, seen the dead bodies, and counted them one by one. He couldn't fathom Karadžić's response.[153]

"Yes but, did you check their ears? You didn't? So how can you be sure?" asked Karadžić.[154]

With Milošević's control of mass media, Serb audiences could hardly understand the realities of war. While Serb forces demolished entire towns and executed thousands, Serb leaders and journalists blamed the Muslims. In efforts to get "international sympathy," said the Serb media, the Bosniaks were "killing themselves" and "holding Sarajevo from within."[155] Serb leaders and parroting journalists explained each incident away: The bread queue massacre, said a Pale Television reporter, was the result of "Muslims killing their own people." A young girl killed by Serb-launched shrapnel, said journalists, was killed by Muslims who "raped her, killed her, and threw her out on the plaza in front of the stadium . . . as she was trying to escape to the Serb part of Sarajevo."[156] Thousands of Muslims lay dead, and still Serb media asserted that Muslims were perpetrating "genocide against the Serbian people," who were the "Jews . . . of modern times, victimized throughout history and never understood."[157] The Serb paramilitary attack on Bijeljina was characterized as a "rescue of innocent Serbs threatened with genocide" on TV Belgrade.[158] In account after account, Serbs were the victims. Even after the Srebrenica slaughter, state television aired reports of investigations for war crimes but asserted that they found "no evidence" of executions.[159]

Blame for the war and the thousands dead was placed on "so-called independent journalists" and peace advocates who "want to sell our brother Serbs . . . just to help our enemies destroy Serbia and Serbs," according to Belgrade television. "If there is anybody to be blamed for war in Bosnia, it is the so-called independent newspapers," asserted self-proclaimed religion expert Milan Jevtic. "By campaigning for peace, they actually prevented Serbs from being properly prepared for fighting with Muslims. So they are responsible for so many dead Serbs."[160]

WHAT HAPPENED?

"Goebbels was kindergarten compared to the media here," asserted Abazović. "Media didn't directly kill people, but while bullets may kill one man, ideas kill thousands."[161]

Political and socioeconomic hardships alongside excruciating histories made Yugoslavia like a blazing hot, dry day that needed only a series of matches to engulf an entire region in flames. It was a time of struggle and suffering across the Yugoslav federation. But the hardships could have been resolved, as they had been for years, through dialogue and without the intense blame that shredded the federation.

Slobodan Milošević lit the first fires. He rose to power by blaming other ethnic groups for Serbia's woes, by exploiting the Serbs' historic pain, anger, and fear, and by playing the role of the Serbs' protector.[162] Beginning in Kosovo, Milošević and his allies consolidated the media and political apparatus to excoriate Albanians and silence dissent. In their story, Albanians were the cause of Kosovo Serbs' woes. They were committing cultural "genocide" on Serbs and taking what rightly belonged to them. If the Albanians were not stopped, conditions for Serbs would only worsen, according to the narrative. Ultimately, they had no choice but to respond with force.

The crises in Yugoslavia—both economic and sociopolitical—along with Milošević's attack on Albanians drove other Yugoslav states to secede. Milošević's response was to repeat the successful Kosovo strategy against the others: first Vojvodina, then Slovenia, then Croatia, and finally Bosnia. Once Serb media was largely under the direction of Milošević and his allies, they generated messages that destroyed the decades-long "brotherhood and unity" among Yugoslavs, divided them based on minute ethnic or religious differences, and vilified the "others." In reality, there were more similarities among them than differences. Once Milošević launched his strategic attacks on the others, Tudjman installed similar controls and patterns in Croatia.

Like in Rwanda and Nazi Germany, media professionals generated a simple narrative that their own group was under threat of extinction by "perpetrators" who, in many cases, had been their neighbors and friends. This theme, combined with real historical atrocities and horrific images in media, fueled intense emotions and generated an immutable sense of national identity. Because Serbs had faced mass slaughters during World War II, the narrative was not particularly far-fetched in their minds. Suspicions grew, and many Serbs grew deeply fearful, resentful, and in some cases hateful toward the alleged "perpetrators." Simultaneously, media emphasized the intense need for "Serbian unity."[163]

With these media depictions, Yugoslavs increasingly divided and sought shelter in their own respective ethnic groups, which stripped many of their individual autonomy. Many Serbs, in particular, transformed "into warriors, defenders, or at least silent supporters of the wars." It became their mission to save their fellow Serbs from the murderous others and to right these purported wrongs.[164]

A significant number of people dissented from the dominant framing. But because Milošević and his allies consolidated and controlled so much of the media, the nationalist narrative became so dominant that other perspectives had little chance for consideration among the masses. Dissenters and their views were silenced, ridiculed, or otherwise destroyed. Decent people and their activities were completely expelled from the public sphere, in essence, aiding "the bad guys."[165] With a "spiral of silence," a culture of hatred replaced a culture of tolerance and neighborliness.[166]

Western media depictions of the war as resurgent "ancient hatreds" oversimplified the causes of the war and ostensibly suppressed intervention. This framing and scarce coverage of the efforts of peacemakers and other decent people made peace in the region appear a lost cause.[167]

Although the Bosnian war ended with the Dayton Accords in 1995, the atrocities that were committed and the ongoing narratives about them have shredded a once close-knit people such that reconciliation and restoration may take decades.

PART 2

THE GOOD NEWS:
MEDIA, GLOBAL COMMUNITY,
AND PEACE

Chapter 4

Averting Genocide:
Media in Burundi

The words were etched in Alexis Sinduhije's mind: "You Tutsis, why are you so arrogant?" It was an innocent question posed by his Hutu childhood friend—but simultaneously loaded with assumptions and stereotypes about him and his ethnic group.

"We elected our president, and your soldiers killed him," continued his friend.

Although some of Sinduhije's relatives served in Burundi's military, he himself was not military affiliated, and he didn't support such an action. Sinduhije was troubled that his friend assumed his guilt merely because of his Tutsi ethnicity.[1] Although Sinduhije was ethnically Tutsi, he grew up in a Hutu neighborhood—the other main ethnic group in Burundi.

Throughout much of Sinduhije's life, Burundi had been embroiled in cycles of murderous violence that destroyed lives and families. Similar to neighboring Rwanda, Tutsis, while in the minority, had for years held political power and dominated political institutions. In 1959, Hutus seized power in Rwanda; three years later, Burundi declared independence from Rwanda, maintaining Tutsi power, and suppressed its Hutu population.[2] By 1988, when Sinduhije reached age twenty-two, two communes in the small, landlocked country were ripped apart in turbulent ethnic warfare. Hutus attacked, and the Tutsi-controlled army retaliated.[3]

In 1992, under international political pressure, Burundi's new constitution was born, stipulating the "right to freedom of opinion and expression." The Burundi government permitted privately owned media to emerge, but the new publications only exacerbated ethnic tensions. Extremist newspapers with inflammatory editorials flourished, accusing the "other" of "inciting ethnic tensions." By some accounts, these publi-

cations tried to "rival each other over calls to kill," advanced "their mutually macabre ideologies," and generated "mutual terror and distrust
based on historical fears."[4]

Egged on by incendiary articles in newspapers loyal to the factions,
violence raged for years. Rumormongering filled the pages and the radio
airwaves, triggering preemptive slayings that were nearly always followed
by retaliatory slaughters. In 1988, for example, after one "warning" about
a coming Tutsi attack, Hutus struck first, slaughtering their Tutsi neighbors with machetes. Tutsis retaliated, generating another vicious cycle of
vengeance.[5] Based on a rumor, five thousand people were mercilessly
slain.[6]

Mired in years of interethnic massacres, animosities between the two
groups hardened, making peaceful coexistence ostensibly impossible. In
fact, intergroup acts of kindness were considered betrayals, marking
those who may have saved the life of the "other" as traitors by their own
ethnic group.[7]

The conflict intensified one night in October 1993 when, at 2:00
a.m., mortar shells and automatic rifle fire awoke Bujumbura, the
sleeping capital city.[8] Sinduhije, then a reporter for a local newspaper and
the government-run Radio Burundi, rose from slumber. Quickly, he
checked his home radio for the news. Static. Outside, soldiers and tanks
filled the streets.

What happened? he wondered as he stepped outside. That's when his
friend posed the question: "You Tutsis, why are you so arrogant? We
elected our president, and your soldiers killed him!"

Was the president dead?

Melchior Ndadaye, Burundi's first democratically elected president, was
the first Hutu to hold the post. His election instigated a rabid faction-
alism led by ethnic party leaders and their associated media.[9] It was
"vulgar tribalism" that was "reviving divisions," the new president had
declared.[10]

Over the next few days, Sinduhije began investigating to determine
what had actually happened. He found that "everywhere, emotion took
hold of reason." So he headed directly to the presidential palace. With
the help of a soldier he knew, Sinduhije slipped onto the palace grounds.

One wall south of the palace had been blasted down by tank fire; palace windows were shattered, the roof pockmarked with bullet holes. Inside, soldiers gleefully celebrated, toasting one another with champagne they had looted from the dead president's stash.[11]

"Would you like some champagne?" asked one soldier upon catching sight of Sinduhije.

"I never drink before sundown, and it isn't yet midday," he replied.

Sinduhije realized what had happened: Tutsi soldiers had assassinated Ndadaye because he was Hutu. To Hutus, like his childhood friend, blame fell beyond the soldiers who committed the act and onto the entire Tutsi community.

Mayhem rained down on Burundi:[12] Hutus on Tutsis, Tutsis on Hutus. Safety existed only within one's own community, driving both groups to seek protection within their own ethnic enclaves.

Because his own safety was at risk, Sinduhije left his predominantly Hutu neighborhood to shelter in a small Tutsi-dominated area outside of the capital city. He was devastated by the sights: Bodies of dead children lay scattered on the roads. Children were particularly vulnerable. Because they were Hutus, Tutsi police refused to protect them, and unlike adults, they were too slow to escape their pursuers.[13]

Sinduhije's eyes fell upon a grisly sight. A group of Tutsi boys gripped two Hutu girls who were six or seven years old. The girls begged for their lives—to no avail. With machetes, the boys mercilessly hacked the girls' throats, as if they were "cutting down a tree trunk."[14]

"We had to kill them because their parents killed our parents, our brothers, our sisters," the boys said to Sinduhije, laughing. "But you must not broadcast it on the radio, and you shouldn't write about it either," they insisted.[15]

Particularly striking was "how happy" many of the killers seemed to be, some of whom Sinduhije knew from college. Because they believed the Hutus were "criminals," they were pleased with their actions. "They [Hutus] killed thousands of Tutsis since the death of President Ndadaye, and we must do the same," explained the slayers.[16]

Each act of violence justified another act of retaliatory violence. Like the Rwandan genocide, many killers had previously been friends, neighbors, acquaintances, and colleagues to those they later slaughtered. Take the case of one Hutu schoolmaster. He called upon the local peasants to burn to death his eighty Tutsi students. Many joined in to help destroy the schoolchildren, despite having been friends with their families.

"I shared a beer yesterday evening [with] Mpawenimana," said one survivor whose children perished in the fire. "[Today, he] was with the people who killed my children."[17]

No one was untouched by the homicidal violence. Scores of Sinduhije's own relatives were massacred—aunts, uncles, nephews, cousins—a total of 102 of his own blood now lay dead, mostly at the hands of Hutus, avenging the death of their president and on a mission to "kill them before they kill us."

Sinduhije returned to the radio station where he worked, ready to report the conflict as "an endless tragedy of violence" with an intent to call upon "political leaders of all persuasions," the police, and the military, "to cut short the rumors . . . and give very clear orders to their men to stop the violence."[18]

This would not work, insisted both his Hutu and his Tutsi colleagues, and for vastly different reasons. Each side justified its own group's positions and wanted to report the war according to its own perspectives. "My parents always told me that the Hutus dream only of exterminating the Tutsis," said one Tutsi colleague. "It's true. Don't be naïve."[19]

Sinduhije's report never made it onto the airwaves. Instead, the state-run Radio Burundi journalists continued covering the conflict by reading the statements provided to them by the warring factions, perpetuating a culture of bitterness, suspicion, rumor, and hatred. This, Sinduhije realized, was the "disease of my society," which he believed was incompatible with his duty as a journalist.[20]

Tutsi-controlled media rarely mentioned Tutsi-perpetrated killings or Hutu deaths.[21] They called the Hutus "genocidal killers," while referring to Tutsi government officials as "forces of order."[22]

Privately held media fueled the fire. The Tutsi paper *Crossroads of Ideas* belittled the Hutu, insulting their physical features, and repeatedly warned readers of the "Hutus' dream"—to exterminate the Tutsis. "All Tutsis must be very clearheaded about confronting the Hutus, using their methods, because they are not the only ones who know how to use a machete," the paper said. "If not, they will roast us all on the spit."[23]

Hutus were portrayed as soulless cannibals, eating their Tutsi victims so that the remains could not be found, according to Tutsi media's portrayals. "The Tutsi are threatened with cannibalism," wrote the publication *Le Carrefour des Idées*. "The Hutu are totally capable of putting this plan into practice, if they can. . . . They will kabob us." *Le Carrefour des Idées* offered remuneration for assassinations: "one million [Burundian francs] to the person who brings [Hutu leaders] on a spear."[24] And it lambasted the election as having similar legitimacy as the Nazi Party's political achievement. "After the Holocaust, did the Nazi regime's constitutional legality still have any meaning?" asked the publication.[25]

In the Hutu-controlled media, such as Radio Democracy, journalists argued that the Tutsi-led government was a genocide purveyor: "Genocide" is a practice "dear to Burundi's bloodthirsty army," they said. The government soldiers, according to broadcasters, were "vampires" and "Nazis" that slaughter "Hutus in hillside villages."[26] Similarly, their publications, such as *Le Temoin*, reminded readers of atrocities committed by Tutsi extremists and warned them that the "Tutsi army is determined to exterminate the Hutu."[27]

Both sides targeted journalists and their organizations, raiding and ransacking their offices and arresting and attacking the journalists themselves.[28] The Tutsi military either assassinated or sent into exile "disloyal" Hutu journalists. The exiled jornalists often broadcast hate messages from Congolese radio station Radio Voice of the People.[29] Many journalists complied with the official demands, accepting bribes by generals or politicians to change "facts" and to release their statements uncritically.[30]

In April 1994, gunmen shot down the plane carrying Ndadaye's successor, President Cyprien Ntaryamira, also a Hutu. Hutus rose once more to avenge the death of their president, killing Tutsi people. And again the Tutsi retaliated by attacking the Hutu. Already two hundred thousand Burundians lay dead from the conflict, of which sixty thousand were in the two years before March 1995.[31]

Burundi's media never reached the heights of the Radio-Télévision Libre des Milles Collines (RTLM) that fueled the Rwandan genocide, but for years Burundi's media fanned the flames of hatred between the Hutus and the Tutsis. After media attacked the "other" in their pages and broadcasts, their audiences attacked these same "others" on the ground.[32]

Like its neighbor Rwanda, Burundi sat on the edge of genocidal violence.[33] But unlike its "twin country," Burundi did not plunge into the abyss that swallowed Rwanda. Instead, after years of on-again, off-again internecine war, Hutus and Tutsis gradually began to engage with and relate to each other again and heal the ethnic divide. Slowly, the vernacular changed, as did their understandings about the "others," the war's causes, and its humanitarian costs. Incrementally, "traitors"—those who had saved the lives of the "others"—became known instead as heroes.[34] It seemed impossible, but through repetitive broadcasts of new perspectives, humanizing stories, and deeper contexts to better understand the conflict and each other, the intense hatreds began to melt way, making room for new meanings, empathies, relationships, and the rebuilding of their lives. The transformation was painfully slow, beginning in a small studio known as Ijambo, meaning "wise words" in the Kirundi language.

IJAMBO'S WISE WORDS

They knew that the actions of media could rile suspicions and incite madness, as they had done in both Rwanda and Burundi. But could media instead be used to help diminish entrenched hatreds and stop future violence? Through mass media, could media professionals help heal the great ethnic divide, facilitate greater understanding among people, and help construct a new future—one that replaced killing with dialogue and problem solving? These were the questions posed during Sinduhije's first meeting with Bryan Rich of the Washington, DC–based nongovernmental organization (NGO) Search for Common Ground (SFCG) in March 1995.

The wholesale slaughters were subsiding, but trouble still brewed throughout Burundi, and both Sinduhije and Rich knew that the political environment was hostile to their ideas.[35] But with a seed of hope for a peaceful future, Studio Ijambo was born. It would become a place where Hutu and Tutsi journalists, writers, producers, and broadcasters would together create programs to dispel the rumors, stereotypes, and hate messages that had permeated the Burundian public sphere. Through a variety of programs—news, drama, and discussion forums— they might spark new ideas, approaches, relationships, and solutions for the seemingly intractable political mess.[36]

Trained to investigate, seek deeper understandings, and resolve conflict, the journalists retired their antagonisms in favor of finding common ground, dissipating antagonisms, building relationships, and changing meanings in their society. Ultimately, the team aimed to offer a "neutral and independent voice" that was "inclusive of all sides," including communities ignored by other media, and—in the face of factional leaders' attempts to provoke more brutality—to promote reconciliation.[37] As reporters and producers reached for new, inclusive, lofty goals, their own dispositions, attitudes, and language shifted to reflect a commitment to inclusive human rights and integrity. In the Studio Ijambo world, Hutus protected Tutsis and Tutsis protected Hutus, a microcosm of what might be possible in the larger community of Burundi.[38]

Initially, Rich and Sinduhije convinced Burundi National Radio and Television (RTNB) to give Studio Ijambo two forty-five-minute time slots per week to air "public" media that reached directly into the community for sources and served the community's needs, rather than those of the ruling elite or the military—an "inversion" of Burundi's media since independence.[39] Sinduhije and the small, fledgling team of journalists—in pairs of one Hutu and one Tutsi—cooperated to produce news, magazine-style talk shows, and radio dramas, eventually fifteen hours of programming per week.

What began in Ijambo's studio grew into multiple projects, including documentaries and new radio stations. Through the news, Burundians heard balanced, corroborated, verified information. Through magazine-style discussion shows, they heard new ideas, perspectives, and ways of interpreting the conflict. Through radio dramas and their fictional characters, they experienced their enemies as empathetic human beings who found ways to transcend intergroup differences.[40]

THE IJAMBO NEWS

While most media reported atrocities committed by the "other" side, Ijambo journalists covered them all. In their teams, one Tutsi and one Hutu journalist ventured together into conflict zones, refugee camps, and devastated lives, seeking to make sense of events and share their knowledge with their fellow Burundians. Together, their access to sources and information doubled, as they could communicate with both sides, hear both perspectives, and reach a cross-cultural balance. In a society of secrets, these journalists developed trust, interfacing with people throughout Burundi—in hospitals, markets, and communities—and verifying information across factions and sectors. They sorted out their own biases and ultimately delivered only the material that was both documented and agreed upon by the pair.[41]

"A key rule was that their stories needed at least three sources and that they represented at least two ethnic groups," explained Bryan Rich. "We used statistical methods to measure and ensure this."[42]

Using these guidelines, Ijambo reporters exposed corruption, gave voice to victims, and treated the conflicting parties evenhandedly. Beyond reporting news, the teams also probed for solutions and aspired to "break the circle of violence, promote accountable leadership, and improve the lives of the people."[43]

The endeavor was not without consequences. Two months after Ijambo's launch, a military patrol stopped Pamphile Simbizi, a twenty-five-year-old Hutu journalist.

"I'm a journalist," not a combatant, said Simbizi, as he raised his hands into the air. The military patrol shot Simbizi in the back, chopped his body into pieces, and dumped his remains into a latrine.[44]

"We can do the same thing to you," threatened a soldier in a call to the Ijambo studio.[45]

It was like "tightrope walking in a hurricane," said Rich.[46]

Life seemed immutably bleak. Amid ongoing slaughters and threats, Ijambo journalists worried, "Maybe we just can't live together anymore." But in the face of the situation's gloom and their own hopelessness, journalists plowed forward, exposing the humanitarian consequences of the violence, demonstrating that nobody was winning, and openly seeking solutions.[47]

"We have to carry on. Maybe sometime, things will get better," said Sindayigaya, a twenty-nine-year-old Ijambo broadcaster.[48]

Reporting humanitarian consequences was the easy part, as pain and suffering surrounded everyone. "I have no more tears," said one Tutsi woman whose children had been burned alive. "It is too much for one person to bear." She had lost her husband and two other children in a previous slaughter.[49]

Reporters traveled to the refugee camps, called "places of death" by those forced into them. Beyond the despair, journalists recorded and disseminated refugees' wisdom and their hopes to return to the time "when life was good, people lived together and helped each other. . . . Can't we live like that again?" asked one widow. It was a shared desire, echoed by a Hutu man reminiscing of life with his "old Tutsi neighbors . . . We are all the same," he said. "These problems have been imposed on us. . . . [The warring leaders] should let us live in peace."[50]

Sinduhije played the recorded voices to political leaders and publicly pressed them for answers: Why had they neglected the refugees? Why hadn't they sent delegations to the camps? And even more important: "How to stop the violence?"[51]

Even bolder, Sinduhije openly rejected the official statements arriving from the factions. Instead, he phoned each of the parties and called on them to take a public stand to "stop the violence . . . call for peace" and "condemn the crime[s]." They agreed, and Sinduhije was on to the next call.[52]

The calls worked. Political leaders vowed to visit the camps. They stopped dissuading refugees from returning home and began calling for an end to the violence—a complete reversal of pre-Ijambo messages. Gradually, Burundians returned home and were able to reclaim their lost and stolen land.

By 1996, studio news agencies Agence France-Presse, Reuters, and the Associated Press began calling on Ijambo journalists for reports. By 1997, the studio had produced roughly twenty-five hundred programs, news, and wire service reports that often served as the "sole documentation of historical events, many of which would have been conveniently displaced by political interests."[53]

INSPIRATION

Ijambo's news programs became highly respected in Burundi. After Studio Ijambo's launch, existing media followed suit, working to dispel disinformation, disseminate stories about reconciliation, and promote good citizenship. One station, Radio Bonesha, dedicated many hours toward helping its audiences understand the Arusha Accords, the peace agreement signed by the warring factions in 2000.[54]

In 2001, Sinduhije launched an independent radio station, Radio Publique Africaine (RPA). From the ranks of the Tutsi soldiers and Hutu rebels, Sinduhije recruited and trained new journalists who would now, instead of destroying each other, work together to uncover the roots of violence and seek avenues toward peace. "We had to convince these soldiers to take this job instead of fighting each other," said Sinduhije. "The hard part . . . was making them believe they could work together and fight for [all] people's rights by using a microphone instead of an AK-47."

No longer having to rely on other networks, Sinduhije and his RPA team broke the "codes" of the power interests on both sides of the conflict. Through their work, they reminded the president that the "people of Burundi are citizens, not his subjects," led the quest for "justice," and aired voices of the once "voiceless."[55]

In 2002, other journalists launched Radio Isanganiro, which remained affiliated with Ijambo. Like RPA, the station empowered local citizens to report news from their own communities. And through public affairs programs, the radio station explored causes and effects of violence.[56]

Together, these stations facilitated dialogue and exposed numerous injustices, including the time that government officials pillaged several houses and killed ten Hutus because a soldier's weapon had been stolen. RPA and Radio Isanganiro covered the events extensively, which ultimately resulted in the army returning the pillaged property to the owners.[57]

PUBLIC-AFFAIRS PROGRAMS

Do bystanders play a role in lethal conflicts? That was one of many questions posed in roundtable discussions, call-in shows, and debates in which broadcasters debated key issues and their causes and sought new ideas, perspectives, and solutions to big political questions related to lethal conflict.

"This program is based on searching for the origin of conflicts, the causes of conflict," said host Aloys, over the air. She introduced the day's issue: Can bystanders impact conflict?[58]

A culture of silence had settled over Burundi, and witnesses shrunk away in fear for their own lives and for fear of being considered traitors by their communities. Most believed the myth that bystanders had no impact, a fact acknowledged over the air: Very few "dare to denounce" the violence, said Beatrice, a guest on the show. Most people, she said, have accepted the "evil" as "normal." This acceptance, she implied, was making violence the status quo.

"Anyone who tries to denounce the killings is killed," added Pie, a student in Burundi.

Pie was right, added Claver, another student. People had been beheaded for opposing the violence. Still, a few "good people" were courageous enough to "inform the others" and warn students and teachers of a coming onslaught, which saved numerous lives. Another of the brave "others" hid his mother from assailants, which ultimately saved her life.

Often, bystanders "emotionally distanced" themselves from victims to reduce their own pain and prevent empathy, explained a radio host. By blaming the victims, these bystanders justified their passivity—as if the victims deserved the horror that had befallen them, said broadcasters. This psychological phenomenon occurred when people felt hopeless or afraid, they said. But inaction had serious consequences, the broadcasters explained. Seen as an endorsement of the violence, silence enabled perpetrators to continue, ultimately "supporting" continued killing. So while he or she may not have "killed by a rifle or a machete . . . [the bystander] kills by words [and] ideas."[59]

The consequences were bad for witnesses too, added another radio guest, because taking sides stripped them of their humanity. "We . . . changed . . . we were like animals," explained Jeanne.

Ultimately, the roundtable agreed that bystanders had *real power* to affect the outcome of the situation. Their responses could both "define what is happening and engage people in compassion for . . . the victims." Through their actions, witnesses had the power to alter the fate of their fellow Burundians and the future of the country itself, they said: "If observers do react against violent actions, perpetrators may question the validity of their actions and decrease their commitment to pursuing and intensifying violence," explained a narrator. "Questioning allows perpetrators to change their behavior, thereby saving human lives."[60]

As they publicly grappled to understand why so many had accepted the divisions and violence, possible answers emerged: "Long periods of devaluation . . . stigmatizing and dehumanizing the others." The devaluations "justified" inaction, but they could not "lead to the peace and the social justice of everybody," concluded a narrator.[61]

Could Burundians change the culture of killing, of stigma, and their justifications? Yes, they could, concluded Pie. But it would require "all people" to "refute the evils." In the throes of the conflict, however, such a position could be life threatening. "I escaped from being killed four times," said Laurent, another guest. "As I saved people, they threw a grenade at me."

That was what defined "heroes," concluded Aloys.[62]

Pie agreed. People like Laurent are "heroes who fought for peace. . . . They risked their own lives to save people."

It was a new and perhaps shocking idea that someone could be a "hero" for saving the life of an "enemy." The concept grew into a 150-episode program known as *Heroes*, featuring stories of Hutus or Tutsis who risked their own lives to save the lives of the "others," an act that had long been considered betrayal.[63] The program instigated those listeners who had long been silent for fear of being outcast and marked as a traitor to call into the program with their own rescue stories. Some publicly "admitted" to rescuing the "others," while others called to apologize for killing. Meanings were shifting: "Traitors" were becoming "heroes," and "warriors" were becoming "perpetrators."[64] For the first time, radio forums publicly explored and discussed such concepts and stories, and people were changing—both their beliefs and behaviors—as a result.[65]

RADIO DRAMAS

She was a young Juliet, and he was her Romeo. From opposite sides of the conflict, Natalie and Mbazumutima fell in love, but the war ripped their relationship apart. Members of her tribe killed Mbazumutima's father, then ambushed and abducted Mbazumutima. After a long captivity, Mbazumutima finally escaped to find his way back to his bride, only to discover that she had resigned herself to wedding someone of her own ethnicity. The romantic tragedy was one of many episodes in the radio drama *Our Neighbors, Ourselves*.[66]

In another episode, refugee Cassilda, with the help of her neighbors, returned home to her banana farm. She was rich with friends who helped rebuild her home, feed her children, and cultivate the land. In her appreciation, Cassilda invited the community to share her beer, considered the country's best. But one bitter neighbor provoked suspicion.[67]

"Those people never change," he said.[68] In a whisper campaign, the suspicious neighbor convinced other community members that Cassilda, a member of the "other" ethnicity, was "sent to take revenge on you and your children." In her plan to "poison" them, he said, "she bought a large quantity of acid."[69]

The rumor reawakened fears from the recent history of violence and triggered rage among neighbors. "We helped her . . . while she was planning our deaths!" they protested. Perhaps they should "take revenge on her."[70]

In the end, a local wise man questioned the prevarications, and humanity prevailed. The rumormonger was banished, and the community reunited while imbibing an awesome stash of banana beer.[71]

Twice each week, millions of Burundians—85 percent of the population—tuned in to hear the dramas unfold between Hutu and Tutsi families together solving problems of drought, hunger, and disputes in the throes of violent conflict. Through fictional characters, Burundians reengaged with the "other" ethnicity and learned of their humanity, fears, hopes, trials, and tribulations. Through stories and humor—burlesque characterizations and wordplays—radio dramas like the six hundred–plus episodes of *Our Neighbors, Ourselves* revealed underlying causes of conflict and demonstrated the foolishness of ethnically based violence."[72] In programs that transcended age, gender, profession, and ethnicity, producers pummeled the morally challenged and prejudicial-thinking characters with jokes, offering listeners a chance to laugh at their own foibles and cheer for conflict resolution.[73]

The project emerged after Ijambo reporters covered threats against a group of Mennonites. To express their appreciation for the coverage, the Mennonite group sent seed money to Rich for the development of a drama.[74]

BREAKING THE CODE

In the midst of the internecine war, Claude and his fellow Tutsi men found a bus full of Hutus, a "real opportunity." But among the Hutus aboard the bus was Claude's best friend, whom the Tutsis dragged onto Sixth Avenue.

Astonished, his best friend asked him, "Even you, Claude? Even you?"

For Claude, the friendship was long past. He could no longer "conceive of him as my friend." Within moments, Claude thrust a knife into his old friend's abdomen. "It was like a tire deflating," he said to Sinduhije and other journalists who interviewed killers in a quest to uncover the "roots of violence."[75]

These men were "breaking the code" of silence in hopes of ending the war by openly confessing, first one on one with journalists, then in a roundtable discussion with killers from the other side. In the documentary produced by Rich and Sinduhije, Burundians recounted how they learned to fear and hate the "other" through the framing of history and the rumors about coming massacres. They finally realized: "You never see rich Hutu and Tutsi fighting. . . . The people fighting each other are poor Hutu and Tutsi. That's why I decided to tell the truth."

"The solution is to communicate," Celestine, one of the Tutsi killers, told the journalists. "If we talk the truth to each other, that can be the example for our children."[76] From warring sides that had committed ghastly deeds, these men dialogued, coming to understand and relate to each other. "You get hate when someone is not open with you," Celestine explained. "But once you talk openly, you don't have any hate for each other."[77]

THE OUTCOMES

Burundian media were one vital part of many efforts to end the vicious war. The international community invested tremendous resources into efforts to end antagonisms.[78] Western nations, the United Nations, the African Union, and several African heads of state, including South

African leader Nelson Mandela, facilitated the Arusha and Pretoria peace agreements, which set the terms for coexistence, ethnic parity, and democratic participation in a healing nation. Simultaneously, NGOs worked to establish active dialogue, peacemaking groups, and activities to reestablish relationships between Hutus and Tutsis.

But these encouraging outcomes would have been very unlikely without the active work of the journalists who successfully changed people's beliefs about one another and reframed the meanings of such key concepts as "hero," "perpetrator," and "traitor." Beginning in March 1995, with the support of international NGOs and private donations, journalists relentlessly challenged status-quo rumor mills and erroneous beliefs about the "others," and actively sought solutions to Burundi's political problems.

Broadcasters also created radio dramas and discussion forums that revealed new understandings about the conflict and societal roles. Their programs uncovered a shared humanity and struggle for all Burundians, eliciting the empathy and understanding that ultimately helped quell long-entrenched hatreds.[79]

Part of what enabled the change was giving journalists the resources and training they needed, according to Rich. "Because people didn't have enough money to get the story—no equipment, no bullet-proof vests, vehicles, or technological equipment—only the elite interests could run the media and control the narrative. That doesn't favor good reporting."[80]

Over time, after repetitive themes broadcast on radio, disinformation and subsequent violence subsided, and the language and culture began to change. After decades in which communication was forbidden between the groups, the programs made "ideas like reconciliation and negotiation acceptable."[81] Other media followed suit, offering more neutral and fact-based news. Hatred subsided, and listeners increasingly engaged with the "others," reestablishing trust and vowing to resolve conflicts through dialogue.[82]

Even the soldiers' long antagonisms toward independent media had changed: "As I left Burundi, I received a note from the head of the military that acknowledged our work," said Rich. "He said, 'the work of the studio lowered the number of civilian deaths during the war, and for that I thank you.' That came from an institution that had been targeting us from the beginning."[83]

In many ways, the results in Burundi outshone those in neighboring

Rwanda. The small, landlocked country established a struggling democracy with ethnic parity, a relatively free press, and a "vibrant civil society." Burundians reintegrated hundreds of thousands of displaced persons and set up a unique, cooperative system.[84] But Burundi still faces considerable strife. Over the years, the government has threatened the independent RPA, periodically shut it down, and oppressed the political leaders that oppose them. Sinduhije has been among the ruling party's targets. After receiving prestigious awards, including the 2004 International Press Freedom Award and recognition by *Time* magazine as one of the one hundred most influential people in the world, authorities arrested Sinduhije for "insulting the president" and for holding an "unauthorized meeting."[85] In 2010, Sinduhije ran for president and, like other opposition leaders, was forced into exile.[86]

Chapter 5

Peace at the Edge: Media and the Belfast Peace Agreement

The pounding on the front door came much too early. The sun hadn't yet risen, and Patrick[1] and his family were still fast asleep in their small apartment. The pounding grew louder, and the British soldiers outside the door yelled at full volume. With a final thud, the front door swung open. Soldiers barged in, aiming guns at Patrick and his family.

Patrick's early morning fogginess made it difficult to comprehend what the soldiers were saying, but it was something about membership in the Irish Republican Army (IRA). Five soldiers seized his still-undressed body, handcuffed him tightly, and tossed him into the back of an armored vehicle where more than a dozen other Irish Catholic men—in similar states of confusion—were huddled on the floorboards. The morning raid was part of the British government's Operation Demetrius. In an effort to capture suspected "terrorists," the overzealous dragnet internment program ultimately captured and detained 1,874 Irish Catholics, some of whom were part of the IRA paramilitary and some of whom were not.[2]

Soldiers piled into the vehicle, wielding batons, and slugged the men's heads, shoulders, and stomachs during the journey to the detention facility. "Run!" ordered the soldiers, when they finally stopped. The men staggered out of the vehicle and ran, in their bare feet and over the broken-glass-laden, rocky ground. Alsatian guard dogs snapped at them as they ran. One dog bit the man running beside Patrick. Patrick stumbled over a stone, catching the rough ground with his hands. Soldiers were quickly upon him with another slug of the baton, ordering him to get up and run again.[3]

When Patrick entered the detention hall, which was filled with blaring, high-pitched sounds, two soldiers hooded him with a heavy cloth and forced him to stand in a "spread-eagle" position on his fingers and toes.[4] He held the stance—for hours—while soldiers demanded information about the IRA.

"I don't know," Patrick responded repeatedly to each of their questions. Finally, he collapsed. Officers clubbed him again and ordered him to resume the stance. For a week, Patrick endured this treatment—and was refused food and water. He lost thirteen pounds.[5]

These events culminated from a long history of strife between the "native Irish" and the settlers from England and Scotland who arrived in waves over the centuries. While the conflict's origin traces to the twelfth century, it escalated during the Plantation of Ulster, which followed the attempts by Irish clan chiefs to regain control of the island. Beginning in 1609, Britain made a concerted effort to confiscate the remaining tracts of land and forbade the settlers from employing or housing Irish natives. Religious differences—the settlers practiced Protestantism while the indigenous practiced Catholicism—also contributed to the continuation of segregation.[6]

The Irish rose repeatedly to overthrow British rule of the island, but the British suppressed their insurrections—until the War of Independence, which followed the Easter Rising of 1916. Using guerrilla warfare, a sophisticated spy network, civil disobedience, large-scale worker strikes, and electoral activities, the Irish forces proved formidable to the British. As both sides reached the point of uncertainty for victory, they entered negotiations, creating both a twenty-six-county Free State in the "South" that later became a republic, and a six-county region, Northern Ireland. Catholics and Catholicism dominated the south while Protestant descendants of the British and Scottish settlers dominated the "North." But the long conflict heightened suspicion and mistrust between the groups, and the partition fueled bitterness between supporters of island unity (mostly Catholics)—often called Nationalists or Republicans—and those in the six counties who desired to remain a part of Britain (mostly Protestants)—the Unionists and Loyalists.[7]

In Northern Ireland, Unionists discriminated against the minority Irish Catholic population, which faced glaring inequalities in housing, education, jobs, and political representation, and they justified the system based on their belief that the Nationalists were a subversive minority and disloyal to the state:[8] "The Nationalist majority in the county . . . stands at 3,684. We must ultimately reduce and liquidate that majority," said one Unionist Member of Parliament (MP) in 1948. "This county . . . is a Unionist county. The atmosphere is Unionist. The boards and properties are nearly all controlled by Unionists. But this is still a millstone around our necks. . . . I would ask the meeting to take whatever steps, however drastic, to wipe out this Nationalist majority."[9]

Animosities hardened between the so-called Nationalists and Unionists. But the Irish Catholics were relatively powerless to make substantive change. They generally had fewer resources, and the intense mistrust led the government to consistently harass them.[10] In some communities, such as Derry (Londonderry to Unionists), disenfranchisement and gerrymandering ensured Unionist control.[11] Police perceived Catholics as troublemakers, enforced a discriminatory system, and generally protected Protestants, not Catholics.[12] They frequently interrogated Catholics, demanding identification and other personal information—sometimes when the officers already knew the answers to their questions.[13]

During the 1960s, pressure on the system mounted. The introduction of free higher education and the inspiration of the US civil rights movement produced dynamic new leaders in the Catholic community and fueled demands for fair treatment. After failing to secure change through political channels, the community turned to public demonstrations. But they faced a major obstacle: the government declared demonstrations illegal, and police used force to ensure the law was upheld. Wielding batons, police cracked down on Catholic demonstrators' skulls and bodies, injuring swarms of people, including elected officials. In contrast, the constabulary protected those participating in Unionist marches, such as the annual celebration of Protestant King William's 1690 defeat of the Catholic King James II in the Battle of the Boyne.[14]

Catholics felt antagonized by the celebratory parades because of their symbolism and the harsh reality: Law enforcement officers escorted parading Unionists into Catholic neighborhoods where they flaunted their historic triumphs over Catholics. During the 1969 demonstration, Catholics rose to prevent the police and parade from entering their "turf." In efforts to force a detour, Catholics lobbed petrol bombs and bricks into the marchers' paths. Riots erupted in the Derry streets and continued for four days. The violence spread to Belfast, where hundreds of homes were set ablaze, gunfire filled the air, people hurled rocks at one another, and law enforcement officers charged into crowds, swinging batons at body after body. When the violence subsided, nearly two thousand families were displaced, 180 homes and other buildings had burned to the ground, 750 people were injured, and 8 were killed, with Catholics bearing the brunt of the casualties.[15]

"The Troubles" of Northern Ireland were under way. By 1972, this region of six counties was in the grip of violence, with shootings, bombings, and rioting. Catholic families were feeling despair—until January 30. Something was different on that day. The air was crisp, the sun shone brightly, and the atmosphere was jubilant. Arm in arm and dressed in their Sunday best, some twenty thousand hopeful Irish Catholics marched together through the streets of Derry, chanting and singing their signature song: "We shall overcome!" It was the biggest turnout for a demonstration in years, and demonstrators truly believed they could advance equality, fairness, and political change without violence.[16]

Organized by the Northern Ireland Civil Rights Association (NICRA), demonstrators called for political equality and an end to internment without trial.[17] Following a flatbed truck of local leaders, marchers detoured away from the army barricade and toward the corner known as Free Derry for a rally led by their young, fiery leader, Bernadette Devlin, who, at twenty-one, was the youngest elected MP.[18]

A group of angry youth ignored the organizers' commands and faced off against British soldiers. They jeered and hurled stones and bottles into the ranks of soldiers. Frustrated soldiers blasted a water cannon of purple-colored dye onto the crowd, then sprayed tear gas and shot rubber bullets at the protestors.[19] Drenched and gasping for breath, the young men raced back toward the rally to escape.[20] But their confrontation had triggered an onslaught.

The British Army advanced toward the crowd gathered before Devlin, who stood atop a platform on the back of a truck. She pushed her long hair back, pressed the megaphone to her mouth, and announced, "We will now have our meeting here peacefully if the British Army will allow us."[21]

But the army continued to advance on the crowd. "Disperse or we shall use CS Gas [tear gas]," ordered a soldier.

"Stand your ground!" Devlin insisted. "We outnumber the army fifteen to one! They can't possibly jail all of us!" But after she uttered her defiant words, soldiers in machine-gun-armed Saracen vehicles rammed through the barricade. Leaping from armored vehicles, soldiers opened fire on the crowd.[22] Singing and cheering turned to screaming and hysteria; thousands fled in panic. Saracen vehicles plowed into fleeing people, striking one person who landed hard on the cold ground.[23] Other officers slugged fallen demonstrators with cudgels, butts of rifles, fists, helmets, and boots.[24]

"Jesus! They're going to kill us!" someone shouted. "For fuck sake, get out of the way!"[25]

Bullets rained down on protesters who raced to escape. Eighteen-year-old John "Jackie" Duddy initially laughed at the sight of the local priest, Father Daly, running from soldiers—before fleeing alongside him.[26] Seconds later, the young man's smile became a deadly gasp as a bullet ripped into his back. Father Daly stopped in his tracks and dropped down to assist Duddy, who had fallen face-first to the ground. The shooting intensified around Daly as he hovered over the bleeding young man.

"Am I going to die?" Duddy asked. Amid another shower of bullets, Daly gave Duddy his last rites.[27]

Nearby, a twenty-seven-year-old printer and amateur photographer, William McKinney, focused his camera in efforts to document the chaos when Gerald McKinney raised his arms high in surrender and pleaded with soldiers, "Don't shoot! Don't shoot!" A bullet pierced Gerald's chest, and he fell to the ground. William dropped to Gerald's aid when another bullet tore into his own back. [28]

Forty-one-year-old peace activist Bernard McGuigan heard Patrick Doherty cry out, "I don't want to die!" after a bullet penetrated his backside. Huddled against a wall, McGuigan and dozens of fellow Catholics braced for the next round of bullets. But McGuigan was emotionally torn. "I can't let [Doherty] die by himself," he whispered to his neighbor. So he stepped out from behind the wall, waving a white handkerchief high above his head, certain that he could safely reach Doherty if soldiers knew he was unarmed and nonthreatening. More shots rang out. One landed squarely in McGuigan's head, killing him instantly.[29]

In total, on what became known as Bloody Sunday, British soldiers shot twenty-seven unarmed people who were publicly standing for civil rights and challenging internment. Of those shot, thirteen died on the scene. Seven were teenagers.[30]

Irish Catholics developed greater solidarity and international sympathy. Many who had not previously supported the Republicans'[31] armed struggle expressed a growing sentiment: "We are all IRA now."[32] Tens of thousands attended the victims' funerals; 90 percent of workers in Dublin halted work, and more than fifty thousand people marched to the British embassy carrying coffins and black flags.[33] By the end of the day, protestors had burned the British embassy to the ground.[34]

"After the civil rights movement was frustrated, there was resolve in people's minds that these issues would be dealt with—come hell or high water," said Member of Parliament Alaisdair McDonnell, of the Social Democratic and Labor Party (SDLP). "People were abused and treated very badly by the British Army, and people who had been previously passive and neutral became more enraged. It all fed into a movement that kept [growing]."[35]

The IRA, which had agreed to avoid the January 30 demonstrations, had a renewed sense of anger and purpose. Over the next two months, their members shot and killed more than a dozen soldiers and detonated a series of bombs. One bomb blasted through the barracks of the British Army's Parachute Regime, whose soldiers had carried out the Bloody Sunday massacre. The bomb killed five custodial staff, a gardener, and a Catholic priest.[36] Another bomb obliterated the Abercorn Restaurant in Belfast on a busy Saturday afternoon, blowing the limbs off of two young women, one of whom was preparing for her wedding. Two sisters died, and another seventy people were badly mutilated.[37] A third bomb, detonated on Donegal Street in Belfast's city center, killed three soldiers, one Loyalist,[38] and three civilian trash collectors. One body, blown to pieces, was unrecognizable. A total of 150 people sustained serious injuries, including an elderly man who lost part of his leg.[39]

In this "poisoned" atmosphere, the British government considered its options. On March 24, 1972, in efforts for a "fresh start," Conservative prime minister Edward Heath announced the suspension of Northern Ireland's Stormont government. Great Britain would directly rule over Northern Ireland.[40]

"Now is your chance," Prime Minister Heath said, primarily addressing the Catholic community. "A chance for fairness, a chance for prosperity, a chance for peace, a chance at last to bring the bombings and killings to an end."[41]

The announcement enraged Loyalists and Unionists, who rose to protest their loss. The IRA, they believed, was forcing their destiny through violence. Roughly one hundred thousand Protestants poured into the streets, waving British flags. For two days, they waged massive industrial strikes, bringing to a halt the public transportation system, parts of the power supply, and many businesses. Thousands of young men enlisted into Loyalist paramilitary groups.[42]

In contrast, the IRA believed the move signified a potential truce. As political efforts to resolve the conflict continued, IRA leaders stipulated two conditions for negotiations: (1) the IRA could choose its own delegation, including then-imprisoned Republican Gerry Adams, and (2) Republican prisoners would be given "political" status, effectively making them prisoners of war. British secretary of state William Whitelaw agreed to the conditions, and the parties entered into talks. On June 22, 1972, the IRA declared a "suspension of offensive operations."[43]

The roots of the conflict were far from resolved, and the peace was precarious. To prevent being "bullied" into a "united Ireland" and to counter the IRA's earlier violence, Loyalists waged their own paramilitary war.[44] Weeks after an IRA cease-fire, in the predominantly Protestant Rathcoole Estate neighborhood, they launched petrol bombs into the few Catholic homes in efforts to force them out. The families found vacant homes in a mixed neighborhood, of West Belfast and prepared to move there. But the Loyalist paramilitary organization, Ulster Defense Association (UDA), "threatened mayhem" should the Catholic families move into the neighborhood. A fragile IRA cease-fire hinged on the British government's decision. It could support the families, which would betray Loyalists; it could prevent the move, thereby supporting Loyalists; or it could do nothing.[45]

The IRA and an entourage of supportive Catholic families escorted one family and their moving truck toward what they believed was going to be their new home. When the group reached the army's barbed-wire line, a soldier ordered them to stop and confronted the procession's leader, Seamus Twomey. Twomey refused to back down, asserting the rights of the Catholic family to move into the vacant home. The army rammed the family's moving truck with a Saracen armored vehicle, triggering an enraged mob that swarmed the army. The army opened fire into the crowd, as Protestants cheered them on.[46] The IRA returned fire—by some accounts, more than three hundred rounds. Gunfighting spread throughout West Belfast into the night. When the chaos subsided, five people were dead, including a thirteen-year-old schoolgirl, Margaret Gargan, who was walking home, and the Catholic priest who went to her aid.[47]

The cease-fire was over. Efforts to resume talks faltered, and the region spiraled into a civil war. Twelve days later, on July 21, 1972, the IRA detonated twenty-two bombs throughout the city of Belfast, all within seventy-five minutes. Homes, hotels, rail stations, businesses, bus stations, and bridges were reduced to rubble. Although the IRA reportedly issued thirty-minute warnings detailing the bombs' locations to the media, many people never received the warnings and were not properly evacuated. Two of the bombs—at the Oxford Bus Depot and in a mixed North Belfast neighborhood—killed nine people, obliterating their bodies. Three teenagers were among the victims; one hundred thirty people sustained serious injuries.[48] Television crews and newspapers showed the stark reality as rescue workers scraped human remains into plastic bags.[49]

Loyalists, meanwhile, targeted Irish Catholics and killed them during unsuspecting times—at their jobs, near their homes, or, in one case, while kissing a loved one good night.[50] Britain launched Operation Motorman, deploying an additional four thousand troops in an effort to take control of IRA territories. Soldiers intensified their search for weapons, kicking in doors of Catholic homes and arresting suspected Republicans. In efforts to extract secret information about the IRA, soldiers beat and tormented detainees.[51]

Simmering disdain toward the "other" turned to boiling hate, and the war escalated to new levels. By the end of the year, Northern Ireland had lost five hundred people and witnessed two thousand explosions, more than ten thousand shootings, and five thousand serious injuries.[52] Some victims were soldiers and members of paramilitaries. Others were innocent civilians—either caught in gun-battle crossfire or in the vicinity of an IRA bomb, or specifically, targeted by Loyalists as revenge on the IRA.[53]

Coordinated campaigns between the British and Irish governments at year's end found more than two hundred IRA leaders, including Martin McGuinness and Chief of Staff Sean MacStiofain, imprisoned. The IRA answered by shifting its bombing campaign to London.

Talks between the British government and the IRA continued intermittently. But to Loyalists, change and compromise were essentially conceding to the IRA. IRA cease-fires became opportunities to strike without recourse—in the short term.[54] The IRA eventually struck back, and tit-for-tat killing between the groups mounted.

Negotiations between several parties produced the Sunningdale Agreement, which worked to accommodate a number of the Nationalist community's demands. But Loyalists rejected the power-sharing agreement and vowed to wreck the process. Loyalist paramilitary groups coalesced to form an umbrella group, the Ulster Army Council, while the Ulster Workers' Council organized another mass protest with power cuts, factory closures, and work strikes. Sunningdale was abandoned.[55]

In 1976, a change in British leadership hardened the British government's approach. "[I will] roll up the IRA like 'a tube of toothpaste," remarked new secretary of state Roy Mason. Mason pursued "Ulsterization, criminalization, and normalization." Marked by a "conveyor-belt" process, the government routinely captured "suspected" Republicans and Loyalists, used torture to extract "confessions," and locked them up as common criminals, not prisoners of war.[56] Among Loyalists, Mason captured Lenny Murphy, leader of the Shankill Butchers, who were known to mercilessly mutilate Catholics with butcher knives.[57]

Though temporarily deterred, the IRA was far from defeated. Outside the prison, Republicans targeted strategic locations and people, particularly prison guards, nineteen of whom were killed between 1976 and 1980. Inside prison cells, Republicans strategized on tiny shreds of toilet paper and cigarette paper, which they transported through bodily orifices, and launched a series of protests. In the "blanket" protest, they refused prison uniforms and prison labor, symbols of their "criminal" rather than "political" status. Guards punished them by leaving them naked in cold cells, then stripped them of furniture, family visits, and remissions, and periodically beat them or extinguished cigarettes on their bodies. Rather than concede their status, Republicans wore nothing but prison blankets.

Prison conditions led to the "dirty" protest: Republicans refused to wash, exercise, or leave their cells. They smeared their feces and urine on prison walls and doors.[58] In the darkest and dirtiest of hours, another group of prisoners began the protest that would ultimately catapult the Republican cause and give birth to the long war—the hunger strike.

As part of their "long war," Republicans ran twenty-seven-year-old hunger striker Bobby Sands for Parliament, challenging Unionist candidate Harry West. Sands, on the fortieth day of his hunger strike, without ever leaving his prison cell, defeated West by approximately fifteen hundred votes.[59] His tenure as an MP was short-lived, however. Sands and nine other hunger strikers died of starvation just weeks later, after the British refused to grant their "five demands."[60]

Sands's electoral victory kick-started the Republican movement's new political strategy, articulated by senior Republican Danny Morrison at an annual conference: "Will anyone here object if, with a ballot paper in one hand and the ArmaLite in the other, we take power in Ireland?"[61]

As the hunger strikes hoisted Republicans into the international spotlight, British prime minister Margaret Thatcher declared that the IRA had played its "last card" with the strike. But support for Sinn Fein, the Republicans' political party, grew. In 1982, the BBC estimated Sinn Fein's support at 3 percent of the electorate. But the party won 10.1 percent of the vote and five parliamentary seats. In the next year, the party's support reached nearly 13.4 percent of the vote.[62] Newly elected Sinn Fein parliamentarians, however, refusing to recognize the government, abstained from taking their seats.

For more than two decades, Sinn Fein and the IRA pursued their dual strategy, and Northern Ireland remained a war zone of gun battles, bombs, random killings, barricades, and curfews. But in the mid-1990s, something remarkable happened. Republican and some Loyalist leaders increasingly began to argue for peace and for peaceful solutions. Ceasefires became peace talks; soon peace talks became peace agreements, power-sharing arrangements, and, finally meaningful political change.

How did this come about? Political observers suggest five key factors: First, both the IRA and the British army realized they could not militarily defeat the other.[63] Second, political leaders, particularly MP John Hume and US president Bill Clinton, escorted Sinn Fein leaders such as Gerry Adams "from the sidewalks to the corridors of power."[64] Third, dedicated negotiators, including Hume, George Mitchell, Brendan Duddy, Harold Goode, and Father Alec Reid, worked tirelessly to find agreement among disputing parties.[65] The British and Irish governments together issued the Downing Street Declaration to "foster agreement and reconciliation" for a "consent" process to resolve the issues of the six counties. The paramilitary leaders, including Republicans Adams and McGuinness and Loyalist Billy Hutchinson, convinced their members to lay down arms and choose political solutions. (Hutchinson reportedly received thirty-two death threats for his support of peace.)[66] Finally, SDLP's MP Hume and Unionist David Trimble persuaded their respective parties to dialogue with people they had long considered "terrorists."

Woven within these factors was another vital force: Neither party could defeat the other in the communications war—the war of words. Bolstered by active, relentless media campaigns, the British, the Unionists, and the Republicans had each amassed an arsenal of support from their respective communities. And a shift in the mainstream media allowed for two essential transformations: the transformation of "terrorists" into peacemakers and the transmutation of an untenable, violent reality into an agreement to resolve differences through dialogue and political channels rather than through war. Ultimately, the media helped the leaders create a new reality in which political actors and situations were complex and dynamic, not fixed and one-dimensional.

THE SEVEN STAGES OF MEDIA

Stage One: The Media War Begins

"The IRA is waging a war, not only of bullets and bombs but [also] of words," uttered Britain's minister of state for defense.[67] In reality, the Northern Ireland civil rights movement alongside the IRA alerted the local and international media of their strife and the injustices they were enduring. Journalists flocked to the north, and most media condemned the Unionist government.[68] But after British soldiers arrived on Northern Ireland soil, this near-uniformity changed. Suddenly a split vision of reality emerged—one in the Catholic and international press, the other in the British media.

Reports of torture and the events of Bloody Sunday spread across Catholic and international headlines, unleashing "a wave of fury and exasperation."[69] Newspapers around the world carried images of dead civil rights demonstrators in bloody streets. IT WAS WILLFUL MURDER, SAY PRIESTS, read the *Derry Journal*'s lead article.[70] The *New York Times* featured statements from MPs Devlin and Hume calling the acts "mass murder" and "cold-blooded murder," respectively.[71] Radio stations broadcast sounds of gunfire, thousands of footsteps fleeing, screams of panic and terror, and British soldiers muttering, "We want some kills here."[72]

Most of the British coverage, however, used another frame. Blame for the Bloody Sunday massacre was directed at demonstrators, who created "conditions favorable to the murders," wrote the *Daily Telegraph*. March organizers provoked violence "by defying the ban on processions," asserted the *Daily Express*.[73] Less establishment-based media, such as the *Guardian*, remained somewhat tentative, suggesting that "men of the 1st Battalion, the Parachute Regiment . . . *may have* fired needlessly into the huge crowd."[74] Portrayals of Catholic leaders also changed. Once a media darling, twenty-one-year-old MP Devlin was now called the leader of a "sinister army of revolutionary extremists."[75]

The media wars were on, and Britain's defense minister argued it was time to fight: "If the IRA is allowed to win this war [of words], I shudder to think what will be the future of the people living in Northern Ireland."[76] Britain—with the help of the Irish Republic—had the upper hand. They had the institutional and military power to corner, jail, kill, outlaw, and sequester Republicans and their allies.

Stage Two: The Clamp—Soft Censorship

With its Bloody Sunday black mark, the British government intensified efforts to crush the IRA's public support while sequestering the group militarily, institutionally, and legally.[77] The media must not "provide propaganda platforms" for terrorist leaders, argued Britain's Lord Gardiner. Such an act, he said, should be "made a summary offense for editors, printers, or publishers of newspapers." The Press Council "should closely examine the reconciliation of the reporting of terrorist activities with the public interest," he argued.[78]

Government officials clamped down, especially on the BBC, which "is not and cannot be impartial," argued Independent Television Authority's Lord Ayelestone. "Britain is at war with the IRA . . . and the IRA will get no more coverage than the Nazis would have done in the last war."[79]

Using terrorism laws and a concerted campaign, British officials censored journalists and portrayed Republicans as one-dimensional "terrorists," "criminals," and "godfathers" who could not be reformed. Without explaining the complexities of the political situation, the British government placed the cause of "the Troubles" squarely on "terrorism."[80] In 1974, the BBC and Ireland's ITV broadcast their last IRA interviews, according to one observer.[81] Another counted a total of six interviews for the entire decade of the 1970s for both the Independent Television News (ITN) and the BBC. Stark realities of bombings, devastation, and mutilated bodies appeared on screens with little explanation.[82]

The Republic of Ireland was similarly forceful with its censorship. Beginning in 1971, senior minister Gerry Collins introduced blanket censorship to block the broadcast of any IRA or Sinn Fein members. Disobedient journalists were relegated to the children's, religious, or agriculture departments. Authors, artists, intellectuals, and elected officials were omitted from the airwaves—as if they, and their work, did not exist—because of their political affiliation.[83]

Within Northern Ireland, the print media remained highly polarized. Most local papers reflected either a Unionist or a Catholic perspective. While Catholic papers covered Republicans' activities, they were critical of the IRA's violent campaign. Unionist papers, perhaps harsher than the British press, portrayed Republicans as evil and depthless terrorists. Republicans and Loyalists, meanwhile, disseminated their respective messages through their own media. With dramatic language and imagery, these publications highlighted the horrors committed by the other side and declared the righteousness of their own causes.

Stage Three: The Turning Tide

By 1978, Secretary Mason was no longer worried, he said.[84] With the clampdowns, they were closing in on the IRA from all sides. They had militarily pummeled them, imprisoned their leaders, and severely limited their media exposure in both the south and the north.[85] In his "normalization" campaign, Mason and his communications staff flooded the region through mainstream media and advertisement with the message that all was "normal"—except for this small group of prisoners—unworthy, common criminals who wanted only to destroy society and terrorize the population.[86] "There will be less and less sympathy for prisoners," Mason asserted with great confidence. They will be "quietly forgotten about."[87]

The war of words, however, was far from over. The prisoners' wives and mothers and media-savvy Republicans refused to be silenced.[88] The women organized forums, speeches, tours, and press conferences. Communicating through symbols, they wrapped their bare bodies in blankets and displayed "conveyor belt" murals. Female family members traveled across Europe, addressed parliaments, and appeared at British embassies at the Hague, Brussels, Geneva, and the United States[89]

Republicans escalated a multilayered communications campaign—community forums, demonstrations, murals, and alerts to the international press.[90] They inundated the media with statements and generated their own "mosquito" media—newspapers, documentaries, posters, pamphlets, and pirate radio.[91] They polished their messages and professionalized their images.[92]

With a shoestring budget, Republicans published from an office so derelict that mushrooms were growing on the walls. But their rich content—thrilling insider stories of prison escapes, assassinations, prison beatings, hunger strikers' writings, and the much-coveted, exclusive Sands interviews—all smuggled from prison on scraps of toilet paper—caused readership to soar, by some estimates, to eighty thousand weekly copies.[93]

Short of banning their publications, the British government attempted to force down their operation. Armed officers burst into their small publishing office, confiscated thousands of papers, office equipment, and the paper's photo library, effectively destroying their publishing apparatus. In a final effort to wreck the Republican media enterprise, officers threw the Republicans' highly prized Telex machine out an upstairs window and imprisoned the managing staff—for conspiracy to pervert justice or membership in the IRA.[94]

Several international media outlets embraced the Republican messages, especially those from the women's groups. The *Washington Post* published details of the H-Block torture program, imploring President Carter to act on behalf of the "hundreds of Irish prisoners" who were living "in conditions of indescribable filth and physical deprivation." One *Washington Post* columnist wrote, "75 percent of the political prisoners in

Long Kesh" were "convicted by uncorroborated statements or forced confessions made in Stalin-like kangaroo court procedures." Public and religious officials issued statements and letters, calling prison conditions "worse than Saigon in 1968."[95] Times Square illuminated the words "Stop the H-Block Torture" in bright lights.[96]

The British government's Northern Ireland office defended its program, blaming the prisoners for their own conditions as they were "smearing the excreta on the walls and pouring urine through cell doors." The IRA members, they said, were "convicted of murder or attempted murder [and] . . . responsible for the deaths of hundreds of innocent people."[97]

Loyalists issued their own periodicals that presented their case, denounced the Republican campaign, depicted Catholic priests as "thugs with guns," and sometimes advocated the need to "eliminate" Catholics and other rivals.[98] Although Loyalist media boasted a circulation of up to sixty-five thousand the Loyalist cause rarely achieved mainstream media support.[100] And they, too, faced British raids and terrorist charges.[101]

Stage Four: The Tide Turns

The dramatic election of hunger-striking prisoner Bobby Sands to Parliament on April 9 catapulted him to international fame. Newspapers tracked the daily unfolding of the hunger strikes, and Sands's name and attractive face appeared in newspapers and on television screens. "The Irish population welcomed Bobby Sands' election to the parliament as a great victory of the forces that oppose the British occupation of Northern Ireland," said an editorial carried on the BBC's World Service broadcast.[102] "[Britain is] running a concentration camp in Northern Ireland," wrote the *Washington Post*, quoting *Irish Press* editor Tim Pat Coogan. *Newsweek* quoted former MP Bernadette Devlin-McAliskey, arguing, "I cannot see how even Margaret Thatcher could stand by and watch a legally elected Member of Parliament starve to death," and, prophetically, "If he starves himself to death—the result is likely to be more trouble for bloodstained Ulster."[103]

Many media abandoned "terrorist" or "guerilla" monikers that had previously been attached to Republicans. IRISH HUNGER STRIKER "VERY NOBLE PERSON," BELFAST PRIEST FOUND, read the *Globe and Mail* headline.[104]

Thousands of people marched through Belfast, pleading with the British government to grant the hunger strikers' "five demands." Marches turned to riots that extended for days, as demonstrators grew frustrated at Britain's refusal to save the lives of the starving prisoners.

Day after day, international media monitored Sands's deteriorating condition and the preparations for an "Irish bloodbath," should Sands die.[105] Criticism mounted against Britain for its hard-line response. The *Economist* found HOPE STARVED IN ULSTER and warned of a "violent protest if IRA hunger striker Mr. Bobby Sands dies."[106] Great Britain's *BBC Summary of World Broadcasts* reported commentary about a "surging tide of anti-British feeling . . . sweeping through new areas of Ulster. . . . [Sands] is . . . accused, nobody knows by whom, of terrorism and incarcerated without the observance of universally recognized rules of judicial procedure."[107] It condemned the British government for its "rigid posture" and "refusal even to consider the matter that is responsible for the growth of violence and the renewed death and destruction in Northern Ireland."[108]

But Thatcher was steadfast in her response: "Crime is crime is crime," she maintained. "Murder and bombing and terrorism are crimes. They are not acts of politics. These people will never be granted political status. Never!"[109]

At 1:17 a.m., on the sixty-sixth day of his strike, before an anxious world, Sands passed into his final sleep. In street-filling riots, youth hurled rocks and fire bombs, and police shot rubber bullets at rioters. Some one hundred thousand people marched four miles in the rain to mourn the loss of their martyr.[110] Throughout the world, mourners expressed anger and grief, passing resolutions in legislatures, blocking British ships, and issuing massive letter-writing campaigns. Protests flourished in Ireland, Switzerland, West Germany, Belgium, Holland, Norway, Australia, Greece, and Italy, where five thousand students burned the Union Jack.[111] *Radio Peace and Progress* compared Northern Ireland to apartheid South Africa.[112]

Some media exalted Sands as "a rare one," a young man who "thought enough of the place where he lived to want to die for it."[113] His decision was the "high road" when "Britain narrowed his options . . . [to] live as a criminal or die for an ideal," wrote Ireland's *Irish Press*. "His choice will be long remembered."[114]

Stage Five: Thatcher's Broadcasting Ban

Bruised by media criticism and fed up with the IRA's public justifications for violence, Thatcher decided to squeeze the "oxygen of publicity" out of the Republican movement. In October 1988, Thatcher's government issued a blanket broadcasting ban.

Already, many journalists were practicing self-censorship. On Independent Television, for example, self-censorship limited Republicans to a total of four mostly hostile minutes of airtime. But now, broadcasters were expressly prohibited from airing the voices of paramilitary groups, their supporters, or members of affiliated, legally constituted political parties, including bona fide elected officials, except when they spoke about specific matters unrelated to "the Troubles."[115]

BBC's local chief Collin Morris and some journalists sought to lift the ban—through official channels and courts. Those efforts ultimately failed, and most journalists, afraid of Thatcher's wrath, honored the ban. The Republic of Ireland, likewise, renewed its ban on both the IRA and Sinn Fein, despite the party's representation of nearly one hundred thousand citizens.[116] The ban's effects trickled to newspapers, and coverage of Republicans shrunk considerably.[117]

A handful of reporters creatively circumvented the ban: They broadcast Sinn Fein leaders' images without their voices while actors read their words over the air. In one segment, an actor perfected a lip-sync of Adams's statement. Lip-syncs were subsequently banned.[118] But despite the efforts to include the Republican point of view, the IRA and their supporters were still collectively branded as "a killing machine with no off switch."[119]

Many political leaders refused to work with them, even in their official capacities as elected leaders, locking them out and further straining relationships. Under these conditions, no peaceful resolution seemed possible.

Stage Six: Behind the Curtain

Journalists wrestled to convey the predominant story within the given restrictions. But behind the curtain, a transformation had begun that was initially missed by the entire media establishment. "The government had been lying to us," said journalist and author David McKittrick upon discovering the revelations.[120] For one, Thatcher, while publicly refusing to speak with "terrorists under any circumstances"[121] and forbidding journalists to do the same, had been secretly negotiating with the IRA through intermediaries.[122] In a second revelation, civil rights leader, peace advocate, and MP Hume was also talking with "terrorists." Hume, the power behind the leading Catholic political party and the New Ireland Forum, had been secretly meeting with Adams since 1986.[123]

The media establishment was rattled. "All started to shake. . . . There was no precedent for this," remarked McKittrick. What journalists "knew" as consensus and all certainties evaporated. "Terrorists" were talking "peace" with government officials.[124] It all seemed bizarre.

Out from the shroud of secrecy, Hume endured attacks from all corners. Unionists bashed him; media denounced him; Loyalists threatened his life.[125] Leaders in the very party Hume had founded shunned him, called him a "laughingstock," and accused him of "killing the party."[126]

Strong and steadfast, Hume stood his ground: "People are being killed every day," he retorted, a reality that far outweighed "killing the party."[127] About the criticism, "[I don't care] two balls of roasted snow," he remarked.[128]

Meanwhile, inside the Republican movement, Adams argued at the 1989 annual Sinn Fein conference for Republicans to focus on "the real needs of real people [such that] people increasingly participate in [the movement] and in their own liberation."[129] Still shunned by many Northern Ireland leaders, Adams took his campaign abroad and particularly to the United States, where the Irish-American community embraced and supported him and his new efforts.[130] He also spoke at length with Catholic priests, particularly Father Reid, who facilitated the meetings with Hume.

In 1993, Hume and Adams released a joint statement: "We accept that the Irish people as a whole have a right to national self-determination. The exercise of self-determination is a matter for agreement between the people of Ireland." The two continued to dialogue for the possibility of establishing "justice and peace in Ireland."[131]

"Was this real?" journalists wondered. Could it be the "killing machine's" potential "off switch"? In the midst of the talks, bombs exploded and violence continued to plague the community, creating doubt. Many reporters still mistrusted Adams, who said "peace" amid IRA violence, but Hume's engagement lent credibility to the process.[132]

A momentous 1994 began. In the first month alone, the Republic of Ireland lifted its broadcasting ban; Sinn Fein launched a "peace commission," and the United States granted Adams a limited visa—all allowing Sinn Fein leaders greater access and acceptance in the public sphere. But the biggest news of all arrived at the end of August when the IRA announced a "complete cessation" of military activities in order to "enhance the democratic process" and "our definitive commitment to its success." The Catholic community's newspaper, the *Irish News*, celebrated, declaring A NEW ERA and calling it "not the end of something" but "the beginning. From today the future of Ireland is in the hands of its people. . . . We must seize the day and build for peace."[133]

Unionist papers remained skeptical, questioning the cease-fire's motives and focusing on criticism of Republican leaders. Nonetheless, increased media coverage signified the group's growing relevance. Vacillating between antagonistic language and recognition, these media allowed Republicans to slowly remake their public image through their own words, in which they asked people to look "forward rather than at history."[134]

Stage Seven: A Giant on the Stage

Although many leaders vitally contributed to bringing peace to Northern Ireland, perhaps the most significant figure was US president Bill Clinton. In November 1995, Clinton made history as the first sitting US president to visit Belfast. With the weight of Clinton behind the process and with the appointment of George Mitchell to lead the process, political leaders and journalists realized peace was possible. For some Unionist leaders, Mitchell's appointment signaled a sense of fairness that they had not previously felt, according to Unionist MP Sir "Reg" Empey.[135]

Adams greeted Clinton on the Falls Road, in West Belfast, the heart of the Republican constituency. In a symbolic moment, the US president clasped the hand of the Sinn Fein president. That image and the words that followed, transmitted throughout both Northern Ireland and international media, expedited the transformation of Adams into a statesman with whom to negotiate, as well as the communities' expectations for peace. Bold headlines, BLESSED ARE THE PEACEMAKERS, filled the front pages of Belfast's *Irish News*. And inside: A TALE OF TWO LEADERS: BILL CLINTON AND GERRY ADAMS SHAKE HANDS ON THE FALLS. The paper celebrated the event and dedicated its entire issue to promoting peaceful resolution of the conflict.[136]

Other media were equally jubilant. CLINTON KINDLES HOPE IN NORTHERN IRELAND, declared the BBC. The *Evening Standard* announced, THE TARGET: LASTING PEACE; PRESIDENT USES HISTORIC VISIT TO PLAY HONEST BROKER. The city of Derry, the site of Bloody Sunday, was now A CITY SET ALIGHT BY HOPE AND NOT BOMBS, declared the *Daily Mirror*. It was, indeed, a new era.[137]

THE JOURNALISTS

During the Troubles and the peace process, journalists played an important role. Many of them dug deep into the conflict's root causes, "trying to understand why the IRA or the UDF or the UDA were doing what they were doing," according to veteran reporter Eamonn Mallie. Some took considerable risks and faced precarious conditions in pursuit of their stories. To obtain statements from the IRA, for example, both BBC journalist Brian Rowan and Mallie were blindfolded by masked escorts and driven to an undisclosed location.[138]

When the possibility of a peace agreement seemed increasingly real, most journalists focused on the positive without neglecting their duties to cover and report reality. By highlighting positive developments, they helped usher in an environment that was much more conducive to peacemaking. Emotionally exhausted from covering anguish and trauma and feeling the "moral tug in us all," reporters personally wished for an "end to the 'Troubles,'" said *Derry Journal* editor Martin McGinley, who worked for the BBC during the Troubles.[139]

"We're war correspondents but we're also citizens," explained veteran journalist McKittrick. "People were dying. These are human beings."

"I was preoccupied with the preservation of life," added Mallie. "I hated the violence."[140]

"Journalists who live in this society covered this process," remarked another reporter who requested anonymity. "We covered the conflict, and we had it up to the teeth with attending funerals and [hearing] the vicious cycle of 'he said, she said.' We wanted a better society. I would say that journalists were being rational."[141]

With the terror and trauma that reporters encountered when inter-viewing survivors and the family members of the fallen, many dreaded working on particular days when most bombings and shootings would occur.[142] The dread created an internal struggle. With "deep roots in the community, some [journalists] lost close relatives," explained BBC reporter Martina Purdy in a conference paper. "Can you really, one won-ders, be an impartial fly on wall when the society in which you live is being torn apart from within?" Ultimately, it was a "struggle" between journalists' own beliefs and emotions and "the need for impartial reporting," she wrote.[143]

That balancing act was consistently present: "Yes, we have a stake in the place," said Rowan. "But as journalists, we have a responsibility to report developments within the peace process accurately—both good and bad."[144]

Similarly important was that several reporters recognized authentic changes in the leaders of the paramilitary groups, which came through in their stories: "We saw the change in them and saw that they wanted to make peace. We could see a genuine effort to get a settlement and knew there was something to this. It was not a trick or a con, as some were saying."[145] The new framing allowed audiences to see and accept the changes as beneficial developments.

Still, there were concerns in the press corps. Veteran journalists Eamonn McCann and Terry McLaughlin both observed contradictions during the talks and called for more critical analysis of the process and the agreement that ultimately surfaced. "I spoke against [the agreement] because I saw that it guaranteed sectarianism," said McCann. "I see this as a problem."[146]

As political leaders negotiated, headlines and articles shed antago-nistic language and encouraged the peace process, ultimately allowing a transformation to occur. In 1998, after long, arduous negotiations, the parties finally agreed on the accords. Most of Belfast's media supported the agreement and requested that their readers vote for it. In total, the

Irish News ran sixty-four editorials that supported the peace process, five that were ambivalent, and one that was in opposition. Similarly, the *Belfast Telegraph* published sixty-two in favor, eighteen ambivalent, and one in opposition. Even the more hard-line Unionist paper, the *Ulster Newsletter*, published editorials favoring the peace process.[147]

MEDIA AND PEACE

Clearly, media alone do not bring about peace or justice, but they play a vital role, either contributing to resolution or exacerbating conflict by their portrayals of the political parties and situations. Media call attention to important issues, and they can help facilitate understanding of the conflicting points of view so that they might be resolved. In Northern Ireland, the media were diverse and, at times, intensely divided, which sometimes heightened antagonisms. But the combined media—local, national, international, and mosquito press—provided a greater palette of perspectives and prevented a hegemonic narrative, ensuring that no perspective was completely silenced at all times.

Perhaps more important, when political leaders across the spectrum finally made it possible to bridge the divide, most media embraced them—even if slowly. Instead of holding steadfast to historic narratives about the "others," journalists allowed the leaders to shed past personas and develop into legitimate statespersons with resolvable grievances. But neither did they accept the leaders blindly. When violent acts resumed, journalists "challenged the morality" of the violence.[148] Once the process was fully in place, Catholic and Protestant newspapers intentionally hired reporters of the other religion to ensure those positions were heard by their respective audiences.[149]

Although Northern Ireland continues to face deep, divisive issues in its six counties, the violence has drastically subsided, with some splinter violence remaining, largely from the emergence of new paramilitary groups. For the most part, in the place of bombs, stabbings, and shootings, rivals fight with political ideas within a shared government chamber. Leaders who once referred to one another as hatemongers and terrorists now sometimes share a laugh in the assembly chambers. One such duo has been labeled, appropriately, the "chuckle brothers."[150]

PART 3

MEDIA, HUMAN RIGHTS, AND DEMOCRACY

Chapter 6

In Black and White: Media and the Struggle against Apartheid

"**I** never realized it would be this bad," wrote Albie Sachs in his prison journal. He sat alone in the confines of his dark, barren prison cell surrounded by smooth gray walls—an "empty, concrete cube."[1]

"I'm not going to break down," he tried to convince himself.

It was only the first day of Sachs's initial ninety-day prison sentence. Although he had not been charged for any crimes, under South Africa's ninety-day detention law, the state could incarcerate anyone, based on a suspicion that the arrestee might have information about "terrorists."[2] Then they could be, and often were, rearrested for another ninety days, and another, and so on.

Sachs certainly had information. As a white human rights lawyer in apartheid South Africa, many of those deemed "terrorists" were his clients—members of the African National Congress (ANC) who would later become members of South Africa's Parliament, members of the Constitutional Court, and the country's president. Sachs was more than their lawyer; he was their friend, their comrade, their partner in efforts to overturn South Africa's apartheid regime.

In that regime, skin color determined everything: where and how one lived, what kind of work one did, with whom one could associate, and what sorts of legal rights one had. It dictated every aspect of life. Through institutions, laws, media, and brute force, the white Afrikaner government controlled the destiny of Africans, Indians, and "colored" people.[3]

Conditions were literally black and white—"white affluence and black poverty," white privilege and black powerlessness. Africans suffered from the overzealous hand of a government that evicted them from their homes and forced them into shanty towns with no fresh water, adequate shelter, access to healthcare, or means to make a living. Having been pushed off their land and forced into menial jobs and labor camps, they usually lived in perpetual poverty.[4] Entire families died from malnutrition, starvation, or disease. And they were forbidden from stepping foot into many of South Africa's public spaces.[5]

Every institution in South Africa prevented change. Africans could not legally vote, assemble, own land, elect representation, or communicate through most mass media. Their leaders wasted away in prison as a result of a perverse legal system in which apartheid was intertwined, concluded Sachs. Prison guards, police, and the bureaucracy were merely carrying out the law, while the law acted as "a façade" that hid tyranny and enabled the brutality, he realized.[6]

In 1955, the ANC and other antiapartheid activists organized a multiracial Congress of the People campaign and coalition, the Congress Alliance, from which the Freedom Charter was born. "South Africa belongs to all who live in it, black and white, and no government can justly claim authority unless it is based on the will of all the people," declared the charter, which called for equal rights, peace, and friendship across all sectors of society.[7]

Inspired by the success of India's Mahatma Gandhi, antiapartheid groups organized strikes, boycotts, and demonstrations to collectively and peacefully disobey apartheid laws in an effort to call attention to their injustice. But the Afrikaans government crushed their nonviolent protests—with beatings, shootings, and long, abusive prison sentences.[8]

In one demonstration, organized by the ANC breakaway group, the Pan-Africanist Congress (PAC), Africans challenged "pass" laws that required them to carry passbooks containing details about their lives. Without proper information and signatures—usually by their employers—Africans were arrested, herded to reservations, imprisoned without notice to their families, fined, or disappeared altogether.

On March 21, 1960, tens of thousands of Africans arrived at local police stations without passes, offering their arrest. At several stations, overwhelmed officers simply arrested some demonstrators. But at Langa, near Cape Town, officers shot dead two Africans and wounded forty-nine. And at Sharpeville, southwest of Johannesburg, some ten thousand unarmed Africans barricaded themselves behind a wire-mesh fence, bewildering officers inside the station who called for help. By midday, three hundred policemen, plus armored vehicles, Sabre jets, and Harvard Trainers moved in on the crowd. As the vehicles drew near, demonstrators hurled stones at them, reportedly hitting three officers. At the gate of the police compound, security officers arrested a few protesters. A scuffle broke out, and the crowd moved in closer.[9]

"Load five rounds!" ordered Lieutenant Colonel Pienaar to the officers. But the officers did more than load rounds. They barraged the demonstrators with gunfire, shooting dead sixty-nine Africans, wounding two hundred, and detaining another two thousand people. Ten of the dead were children.[10]

"They must learn their lesson the hard way!" insisted the police commander, who complained that stones had struck his car.[11]

The Sharpeville massacre was one example in a long list of the government's abuses, justified as protecting their system. Shortly after the massacre, the government declared martial law. It shut down townships, imposed curfews, turned off electricity, water, and telephone service, and drove workers back into the factories.[12] "We are building a nation for whites only," Prime Minister John Vorster said. "We have a right to our national identity."[13]

Believing they had exhausted all peaceful means to achieve democracy and equality, the ANC and the Congress Alliance turned to "armed resistance"—a violent uprising to overthrow the government. In a sabotage campaign, the ANC's military arm, Umkhonto we Sizwe ("Spear of the Nation"), blew up electrical power pylons in three cities.[14]

The government hardened, declared a "state of emergency," and granted itself more power to incarcerate, violate, torture, and kill "terrorists." It banned books, newspapers, people, and political organizations; outlawed their meetings; and imprisoned, tortured, and killed their political leaders.[15] Using the ninety-day detention law, officials detained and interrogated numerous people to force disclosure about "terrorists."

Sachs knew why he was detained: He had publicly advocated electing ANC President Albert Lutuli, winner of the Nobel Peace Prize, as prime minister; participated in civil disobedience against apartheid laws; and wrote antiapartheid articles in the resistance media. During the days, Sachs defended black activists in court; at night, as a member of the ANC, he worked with the "underground resistance . . . to overturn the entire unjust apartheid order."[16]

In solitary confinement, Sachs contemplated how he might appeal to the white population to "lay down arms and negotiate" in an effort to build a system that would benefit all races. He slid out of the suit that he was still wearing from the time of arrest, hung it up alongside a colorful beach towel, and listened to the silence, then a train, then motor traffic, and then a church chime—but no voices. Nobody.[17]

Sachs sustained himself by whistling, alone, until another detainee joined in. They whistled familiar tunes in call-and-response, neither knowing who the other was. "Whoever you are, oh whistler, thank you," wrote Sachs. "I love you for your loyalty, for your concern. You give me strength and remind me of beauty. Human beings are greater than walls. May we both have courage enough to see this through."[18]

He recalled the officers who seized him in his office and rummaged through his clients' files. "Those briefs are privileged!" Sachs protested, but to no avail. The officers chuckled at his protests. Now, these same agents had arrived to interrogate him. Sachs refused to answer their questions, but he understood why many prisoners talked. Solitary confinement created an irresistible need to communicate—with anyone.[19]

A sergeant slapped handcuffs onto Sachs' wrists and carted him to a harsher prison. The sounds of silence, trains, and whistles disappeared, replaced by the persistent clamor of doors slamming, shouting, cursing, shuffling, and engines roaring. The weight of the cacophony crushed Sachs's nerves and senses. "Gust after gust of misery" blew through him. "My nerves are exposed like electric wires pulled out of their sockets," he wrote. "My emotions have fallen apart, disintegrated." He reminisced and longed for the anonymous whistler's sweet sound, lamenting, "I'm sorry I couldn't whistle you a farewell."[20]

Weeks of solitary confinement and sleep deprivation that were intended to break him thinned Sachs's emotions. But he could live with neither disclosing the information demanded by interrogators nor the idea of repeated ninety-day solitary sentences. Perhaps he should hang himself, he thought. Yet in the depths of his prison and misery, Sachs was still attuned to his white privilege. "If they treat me . . . like this, how terrible it must be for the Africans," he wrote. He recalled other ninety-day detention law prisoners. One was found hanging in his cell. Another leapt from a seventh-floor window to his death; many endured beatings, broken bones, battered faces, electric shocks, and having their hair pulled out—torture that led some to acquiesce and give statements.[21] To compel Phila Ndwande to talk, officials stripped her, leaving her completely naked. To preserve a semblance of dignity, Ndwande constructed panties from a blue plastic bag. After several weeks, security forces shot her dead.[22]

From other parts of the jail, Sachs heard guards shouting, whipping, beating, and mocking African prisoners, some as young as eight years of age. As the bludgeoning tapered off, screams of agony subsided into a "piteous blubbering moan."[23]

In the Robben Island prison, guards thrust a wet bag over Indres Naidoo's head, then squeezed the knot, choking him. Naidoo gasped for air, but the wet bag blocked the air and prevented his lungs from working.[24]

"Coolie, today you're going to die," said one guard, laughing.

They shoved him into a chair and battered him with truncheons from the soles of his feet to the top his head, then attached electrical wires to his body. As volts of electricity shot through Naidoo, his body convulsed. He pleaded for mercy, but the officers continued with shot after shot of voltage.[25]

After months of solitary confinement and being inundated with the shrill sounds of torture, Sachs decided that once released he would flee South Africa, even though the "right thing to do" was to "stay and fight to the end." The reality was, "I can barely hold out."[26]

The time finally arrived, and the words were delicious: "You can go now." Sachs bolted out of prison, ran six miles from the prison to the sea, plunged into the waters, then left South Africa and fled into exile. He would do what he could from afar to assist the ANC in its quest to overturn apartheid.[27]

Things would get worse before they would get better for South Africa. The country was mired in economic crises, violence, and turmoil while facing increasing international isolation, boycotts, and sanctions. But in the midst of mayhem, in 1985, South African justice minister Kobie Coetsee secretly visited Nelson Mandela in the hospital. Mandela had repeatedly requested such a meeting, but it was the first time a conversation occurred. More clandestine meetings followed, in prisons, back rooms, and guest homes.[28]

Under growing international pressures and local chaos, the government proposed piecemeal reforms and offered a new constitution that still excluded Africans but gave Indians and "coloreds" representation in a trilateral parliament.[29] The exclusion and token reforms prompted another uprising that spiraled South Africa into more chaos.

Although still engaged part time in the ANC struggle, Sachs had been working abroad in England and Mozambique until April 7, 1988. That day, Sachs tossed his briefcase into the passenger side of his car, then circled to the driver side, pausing to wave to a neighbor. He gripped the driver-side door handle and clicked the latch open. As Sachs swung the door open, his world went black. With a loud explosion, the car bomb hurled him into the air, blew off his arm, and destroyed half of his eyesight and hearing.[30]

The bomb permanently injured Sachs, but it didn't kill him. Rather, it blew away the "schism" that had divided his life and became the impetus to thrust him to full-time dedication toward a nonracial, democratic South Africa. For that, he began penning the instrument that would serve as a new vision for the state, one that would give South Africans something grand for which to aim, rather than something to despise and fight. It was the seeds of the new South African Constitution.[31]

By 1989, domestic and international pressures were devastating South Africa. Its currency crashed, the economy was crippled, and much of the country was mired in violence. White support for apartheid waned; scores of young men refused to serve in the military. By the end of the year, Prime Minister Pieter Willem (P. W.) Botha suffered a stroke and, under internal pressure, resigned from his post.[32]

Botha's successor, Frederick Willem (F. W.) de Klerk, met and conferred with Mandela. But no one was prepared for de Klerk's unexpected action. On February 2, 1990, de Klerk delivered the speech that would, in essence, end apartheid.[33] In South Africa's first free election, voters elected Mandela as their president. And Mandela appointed Sachs as one of eleven justices in South Africa's new Constitutional Court.

Mandela's win was only a beginning. Mending a long-divided, deeply wounded society would take a concerted effort to heal the scars of the past and forge a new beginning. Chief among the new government's instruments were the Truth and Reconciliation Commission hearings, which engaged all of South Africa via live broadcasts and daily reporting. Together, South Africans watched the unearthing of the hidden parts of their collective past. The deeply transformative event laid the ground-work for constructing a new, egalitarian state and "the basis for common citizenship and for the joint efforts to improve the lives of everybody."[34]

"We saw the tears, heard the voices, the lamentations, the sometimes stilted apologies . . . our people on television, the radio, in the press," said Sachs. "It was the humanizing and personalizing of what had hap-pened that captured people's spirits."[35]

Long, painful histories, deep chasms, and festering hostilities are always difficult to erase. The transformation from an intensely oppressive, divided state to a multiracial democracy was hard-won by antiapartheid activists who engaged in a multidimensional fight. Key in their war chest was an arsenal of words—the information, framing, perspective, and channels of dissemination. The antiapartheid activists decisively won that war, particularly in the international media—through press, television, radio, books, theater, and music. But the seeds of the world media victory were born from the struggles in the pages and broadcasts at home, where journalists and advocates risked their freedom and lives to tell their truths for the world to hear. And it did.[36]

MEDIA UNDER APARTHEID: A "TOTAL ONSLAUGHT"

"I want you to approve . . . a propaganda war in which no rules or regula-tions count," said Department of Information secretary Eschel Rhoodie to Prime Minister Vorster. "If it is necessary for me to bribe someone . . . to purchase, for example a sable mink coat for an editor's wife . . . send somebody on a holiday to the Hawaiian Islands with his mistress for a month, then I should be able to do so."[37]

Inside South Africa, the mass media were a battleground mostly divided by language and ethnicity that "overwhelmingly reflected the social situation." Though not monolithic and while evolving over time, most Afrikaans-language media hid the ugly realities and upheld the apartheid system as natural and legitimate, particularly the South African Broadcasting Corporation (SABC) and especially during the early strug-gles against apartheid.[38]

"Speaking of my perspective as one who was disenfranchised . . . the Afrikaans and electronic media . . . supported apartheid . . . largely [acted as] mouthpieces of the ruling elite, hardly ever [as] the watchdogs," remarked Archbishop Desmond Tutu at the Truth and Reconciliation Commission media hearings.[39]

For many years, through omissions and commissions, these media facilitated ignorance, excluded vital coverage of white-instigated violence, headlined black-instigated violence, and denounced many antiapartheid leaders as "terrorists" and "undesirables." Behind the scenes, some reporters colluded with officials to oppress Africans.[40]

But through the cracks of the wall of silence erected by the apartheid government, another reality seeped out, first through the staunchly antiapartheid media; later, through the more established English-language and church media; and by the late 1980s, through some of the Afrikaans-language press. The alternative Afrikaans-language publication *Vrye Weekblad* became one of the more "outspoken, vigorous, and courageous antiapartheid publications in the country," according to Allister Sparks, veteran South African journalist.[41] Even *Beeld*, the long-nationalist Afrikaans-language newspaper, urged the government to release Mandela from prison and end petty apartheid.[42]

Throughout the media struggle, the government clamped down on activists, journalists, and media institutions that tried to expose and denounce the injustices; it succeeded in destroying many of them. But the words and images trickled through the fissures and engaged broader audiences throughout the world, winning hearts, minds, policies, and collective actions that coalesced to overturn apartheid.[43]

The Early Antiapartheid Alternatives

"This is the African National Congress, the voice of freedom," said the broadcaster over the outlawed Radio Freedom in 1969. "The ANC speaks to you! Afrika! Afrika! Mayibuye! The time has come. This government of slavery, this government of oppression, this apartheid monster must be removed from power and crushed by the people!" declared the host, calling for "all people" to take up arms and meet force with force. "They will never stop the pass raids, the arrests, the beatings, the killings—they will continue to drive us out of our homes like dogs and send us to rot in the so-called

Bantu homelands . . . until the day we . . . crush white rule. . . . Never submit to white oppression; never give up the freedom struggle."[44]

Radio Freedom was one of several resistance media piercing holes in the ideological wall of apartheid. Born from the "protest" press of 1880, the resistance media challenged apartheid's legitimacy, exposed ugly realities, helped build morale and cohesion among activists, and offered alternative frameworks from leaders such as Mandela and Oliver Tambo.[45]

With "pennies in the bank and policemen at the door," the national, radical *Guardian*, consistently faced closure—from the day it opened its doors in 1937. Ideologically, the paper opposed Fascism/Nazism, colonialism, and apartheid, and supported trade unions. But while facing multiple roadblocks—including charges of sedition and high treason—the *Guardian* team relentlessly broke news, uncovered scandals, and published unabashed criticism every week for twenty-six years, making it the longest-running "left-wing newspaper in South African history."[46]

Journalist Ruth First exposed forced labor camps on which farm owners chained, whipped, beat, and released attack dogs on laborers. She witnessed "large [welts] and scars whipped on [the] backs, shoulders, and arms" of workers, and she uncovered the state's role as "a recruiting force for bad farmers who cannot attract labor by normal means."[47]

First's investigation worked hand in hand with farmworker turned-ANC-activist Gert Sibande to free the semiforced laborers. Through their crusade, courts convicted one farmer, Max Mann, of thirty-nine counts of assault and battery—he had beaten farm workers with whips and pick handles. Mann was sentenced to five years in prison with hard labor.[48]

While global issues abounded, "the real fight for democracy is on the home front," argued an editorial in the *Guardian*. The South African system had condemned "four-fifths of our population to remain unskilled laborers," it explained. "Let us admit it—as regards [to South Africa's] attitude to eight million citizens of this country, the European section of the population is Fascist."[49]

Even after it was banned—twice—and finally collapsed, the *Guardian* reemerged, twice under a different name. Its staff launched the *New Age*, which continued the *Guardian's* tradition of exposing vast schemes of abuse, including the abduction and "sale" of children into forced labor. Through the government's "youth camp," traffickers sold children as young as eleven years old into slavery, according to the article.[50]

Another *New Age* article uncovered barbarous acts of farm owners. With hoes, they hacked workers' feet to prevent them from fleeing and bludgeoned laborers with such ferocity that some died from the beatings. Upon publication of this information, the ANC launched additional actions, including a successful potato boycott. As uneaten potatoes piled up, the *New Age* sarcastically noted, POTATOES: SUPPLY GOOD, DEMAND POOR.[51]

The *New Age* called for government investigations, which ultimately corroborated First's findings. FARM SLAVE SCHEME CRACKS, said the next headline. On June 17, after the state suspended the forced labor scheme, the *New Age* announced: *NEW AGE* DID THIS! WITHOUT *NEW AGE*, YOU WOULD NEVER HAVE KNOWN![52]

Issue after issue, First, Sachs, Brian Bunting, Govan Mbeki, and their colleagues tackled injustices and connected societal problems to their roots: crime and desperate levels of poverty. "A man must eat," wrote First. "The crime wave in Alexandra . . . is one of the by-products of this throttled community."[53]

After the 1960 martial law declaration, the government raided the *New Age* and arrested its entire editorial staff, except for Sachs, leaving him on his own to produce the publication. He delivered the issue, featuring articles on the Treason Trial, Tambo's escape, and the Langa March, to Pioneer Press for printing. But the minister of justice stopped the printing and confiscated all but a single, hidden copy of the paper.[54]

After five months and with fifty-five staffers in jail, the *New Age* reemerged, featuring the banned ANC leaders on its front pages with full, unedited statements. Juxtaposed with photographs of Mandela and Duma Nukwe walking home, one headline read, FREEDOM IS WITHIN OUR GRASP. Inside the paper, columnist Alex La Guma rated the prison wardens whom he encountered while incarcerated alongside exposés, such as one story that detailed "attractive, nice-time girls who attend house-parties in an apparent mood of gaity"—the women were ostensibly spies "hired to entrap ANC men."[55]

New Age journalists followed the plight of harassed Africans. For one article, as officials carted away twenty-five-year-old ANC member Anderson Khumani Ganyile on a prison train, the reporter managed a "shouting" interview. Ganyile escaped and fled to neighboring Basutoland. The South African government followed him, crossing the international border in violation of international law, to apprehend him. Ganyile scrawled a note onto scrap paper, which appeared in the *New Age*: "Kidnapped in Basutoland . . . by six policemen from the Union. We are three . . . and we appeal to our friends. We know and can identify our kidnappers." The *New Age*'s publication led to demonstrations outside of Parliament and eventually to a debate in London's House of Commons. The government released Ganyile from its custody, and he returned to Basutoland.[56]

With close ties to the ANC, the *New Age* regularly featured the organization's breaking news—including photos of exploded towers from the sabotage campaign and details of Mandela's departure from South Africa. When police arrested Mandela, the paper published, for the first time, the two words spray-painted on a fence that would decades later become an international, household phrase: "Free Mandela."[57]

Through an act of Parliament, the government finally destroyed the *New Age*. Balthazar Johannes Vorster waved an issue of the *New Age* before a session of Parliament. "One of the newspapers which ought to be forbidden is this paper, *New Age*, which is the propaganda organ of the Communist Party!" he insisted.[58] By the end of session, Parliament had legally engineered the paper's demise.

THIS IS A POLICE STATE, responded the paper in a four-inch headline. *New Age* stands "for equal rights . . . an end to apartheid . . . peace and harmony . . . and the rights of all people to be free from exploitation in any shape or form . . . and now we are to be silenced."[59]

Political leaders, including Dr. Martin Luther King Jr., and other publications protested the banning. One newspaper, the *Evening Post*, noted, "The government is creating the impression . . . that the people chiefly interested in the difficulties created by apartheid are Communists."[60]

"The political opposition of *New Age* becomes Communism because Mr. Vorster chooses to call it Communism," added the *Cape Times*. "He does so without hearing argument, without having to produce evidence, without having to give reason, subject to no appeal to any impartial authority."[61]

Just before the *New Age* shuttered, its writers launched *Spark*, with content that was essentially identical to that of *New Age*. But it was futile. The government had also prohibited the journalists' freedom to publish or to even be on the premises of a publication.[62]

WE SAY GOODBYE, BUT WE'LL BE BACK, said *Spark's* headline. But it never returned.

In 1963, using the ninety-day detention law, the government arrested First and placed her in solitary confinement for interrogation. To prevent breaking down and disclosing information, she attempted suicide. She survived long enough to be released and flee South Africa. Agents later killed her with a letter bomb.[63]

Other, less overt alternative publications survived a bit longer, some of which were connected to the trade union movement and the Congress Alliance and some of which were simply more subtle in their politics and criticism.[64] Both *Drum* magazine and the *Golden City Post* used sensational photos and stories to attract readers; both criticized the government without challenging apartheid itself. In *Drum*, the largest circulation magazine in South Africa, pinup girl photos ran alongside important journalism and literature, while *Golden City Post's* stories of "bad girls" or adultery shared a page with "soft" criticism. But *Drum* stood largely alone in documenting integrated communities and multiracial alliances.[65]

In 1966, the government used an amended anticommunist law and regular harassment to silence the remaining resistance media and journalists and to eliminate traces of their ideas. Security police tortured journalist Nat Serache for eleven successive days before he fled into exile. Some journalists, including Serache and First (until she was killed), continued their work from abroad, which ultimately expanded their audiences. And their work still penetrated into South Africa, often through illegal channels.[66]

Radio Freedom was one such medium. Through Radio Madagascar, Ethiopian Radio (VORE), and other supportive African countries' radio stations, the ANC broadcast Radio Freedom, lambasting the apartheid government and imploring its members to continue the "struggle." Throughout the 1980s, the outlaw radio station railed against "shameful acts, scandals, and atrocities" and "poisonous propaganda . . . racist lies," and it reported deaths resulting from "trigger-happy police" who killed "miners . . . during strikes against starvation wages," as well as "banishments, beatings, torture, . . . hangings, and shootings." The oppression, said broadcasters, "reinforced our determination to pursue the cause of liberation."[67]

Although antiapartheid media's reach was limited, their articles informed an important readership. And along the way, they received some help from the more mainstream, English-language press, which carried the battle one step further.

THE MAINSTREAM MEDIA WAR

A thorn in the side of the apartheid government, the English-language press frequently reported the dark underbellies of the system. The *Rand Daily Mail* joined the *Guardian* to report forced labor and bludgeoned workers with the headline NEAR SLAVERY IN BETHAL DISTRICT. The *Cape Times* lashed out at officials for banning the radical *New Age*. But under pressures from an overzealous government that infiltrated their organizations, spied on journalists, raided their offices, harassed reporters, and spread misinformation, most media refrained from challenges that might imperil their operation. While English-language press assailed the apartheid government, they often treated ANC leaders as "terrorists" and ignored considerable matters important to Africans. Internally, some also practiced "petty apartheid"—hired few Africans, paid them less than white journalists, restricted their topics of coverage, and segregated their canteens and restrooms.[68]

Among the most defiant English-language journalists was Laurence Gandar, editor of the *Rand Daily Mail*. What started as editorials analyzing and opposing apartheid under Gandar's pseudonym Owen Vine grew into loud exposés. Gandar connected the African uprisings to insufferable conditions—poverty, malnutrition, institutional oppression—and called for a new, just future for South Africa. In 1965, using eyewitness sources, Gandar and reporter Benjamin Pogrund exposed gruesome details of eleven African detainees who were bludgeoned to death in custody.[69]

Using laws such as the Prison Act, which outlawed criticizing army or prison officials without permission, government officials cracked down on the journalists. Police dogged Gandar with threats and raids, serially prosecuted his sources, and, using perjured evidence, convicted him and Pogrund of violating the Prison Act.[70]

South Africa has "lost its way," wrote Gandar, calling for racial integration and freedom of the press. Gandar's board eventually removed him from his position for fear of losing advertisers, but his work left an indelible mark, including incremental but meaningful changes, such as the use of "African" rather than "native" to identify the black population.[71]

Other English-language newspapers joined the fray with periodic exposés. The *Johannesburg Star* alerted readers to the government's sub-human treatment of Africans and criticized its "pathetic faith in the power of machine guns to settle basic human problems." In 1969, the paper exposed savagery in the prisons and called for judicial investigations to determine the extent of the abuses.[72]

In 1974, the *Durban Daily News* reported an upcoming rally in support of the Liberation Front of Mozambique (FRELIMO). Under the Riotous Assemblies Act, the government arrested its editor for printing "illegal advertising." The arrest, however, infuriated even the proapartheid Afrikaans media.[73]

At each turn, the government diminished media freedom, passing some seventy-five restrictive laws, which it justified by its call for a "responsible" media that promotes "our values and our interests." Censorship committees reviewed films, books, and plays to ensure "public morals, religion [and] the safety of the state." In reality, though, the results were clearly race driven: It banned African plays for being "harmful for race relations" but approved an extremist Afrikaner book claiming that Africans "smell like stale biltong [dried meat] which is unfit for human consumption" and that "murder and robbery are inherent characteristics of Africans."[74]

Black Is Beautiful

Black is beautiful. It was a simple sentence, coined by Black Consciousness (BC) leader Steve Biko, a founder of the Black Peoples' Convention and an initiator of self-help projects such as healthcare clinics and small-scale industries. BC leaders called for a multiracial South Africa through the "ridding" of the "shackles that bind us to perpetual servitude." They rejected white ideology and language and sought to create community strength from the inside. That included rejecting the use of the phrase *nonwhite* to describe several populations in South Africa. Black people were not "non-anything," which suggested negation. They—African, Indian, and "colored" people—were *positively* "black."[75] "We are merely refusing to be regarded as nonpersons and claim the right to be called positively," said the BC's *SASO Newsletter* in 1970. "Adopting a collectively positive outlook leads to the creation of a broader base which may be useful in time."[76]

BC ideas filled the pages of such publications as the *SASO Newsletter* and *Creativity and Development* and annuals such as *Black Review* and *Black Viewpoint*. Its advocates recruited black journalists, sought black-owned newspapers, and launched letter-writing campaigns to dissuade white-owned publications from using the negative language. When papers persisted in using such terms as *nonwhite*, BC groups expelled their reporters from meetings.[77]

The BC campaign altered the language and the political landscape. Both the *East London Daily Dispatch* and the *Rand Daily Mail* eliminated terms such as *nonwhite*. And white-owned, African-read publications, including the *World*, after long avoiding apartheid politics, finally denounced racist policies.[78]

The BC movement produced a new wave of political resistance, culture, literature, and art that reinvigorated the African community, which had been despondent after the Sharpeville massacre. But it also fueled the Afrikaans apartheid arguments for segregation in newspapers such as *Die Burger*, which claimed that South African Students' Association (SASO) supporters don't "want to be objects of white politics any longer, but desire to determine their future themselves as people in their own right. In South Africa we can be thankful that certain opportunities have been created in advance for the realities of the new ideas. It has been done among other things by the development of the Bantu Homelands."[79]

In 1976, thousands of energized African youth marched from their schools to Orlando Stadium, protesting the forced use of Afrikaans to learn mathematics and social studies. When they approached police barricades, most students continued peacefully, but some picked up nearby stones and lobbed them at the security forces. Police opened fire and sprayed tear gas, sparking riots that ultimately killed more than 661 people over the course of eleven months; nearly all the dead were black. But because foreign and white journalists had been "sealed off," only African journalists reported what became known as the Soweto Uprising. Police pummeled the reporters and arrested them, detained them, and charged them with terrorism and incitement of riots. But their stories still appeared in the *Rand Daily Mail* and the *World*, without which "the world would never have known what really happened."[80]

These published reports ultimately informed the actions of world actors, including Jimmy Carter and the United Nations. That year, the UN Security Council adopted a mandatory arms embargo, which diminished South Africa's capacity to fight in neighboring conflicts.[81]

In efforts to silence the BC, apartheid government officials arrested nine SASO leaders, including Biko, and banned eighteen BC organizations.[82] Biko never emerged from prison, but his tragic death ignited a global movement against the apartheid government.[83]

English-language newspapers assailed the government. The *East London Daily Dispatch*, the *Rand Daily Mail*, the *Cape Times*, and the *Johannesburg Star* all demanded a full investigation into Biko's death, an explanation to his family and "the world at large," and the resignation of Prison Minister James Kruger.[84]

Government officials greeted Biko's death with indifference. "I am not glad and I am not sorry about Mr. Biko," said Kruger. "He leaves me cold." Claiming Biko died while on a hunger strike, Kruger added, it was his "democratic right" to starve himself to death.[85]

Kruger's frigid response produced another tide of disgust through papers such as the *World*, the *Johannesburg Star*, and the *Johannesburg Times*. "What ignominy," said the *World*. "What arrogance. What a convenient ducking of responsibility for the whole ghastly business." The *Johannesburg Star* added, "The civilized world will be more than left cold— it will be positively chilled by the callousness of yesterday's display." The *Johannesburg Times* accused Kruger of "unforgivable crimes," including damage to South Africa's race relations and its reputation abroad.[86]

"This is the big one, the one they can't get away with," said Donald Woods, editor of the *East London Daily Dispatch*, before a large crowd. "This is the death they will not be able to explain away." Woods knew of the "possibility that if Biko was detained, he might not come out alive," he said.[87]

For more than a month, Kruger maintained that Biko died of a hunger strike. But medical examiners found extensive brain injury, bruises, burns, severe damage to his rib cage, acute renal kidney failure, and partial paralysis. He was too overweight to have been starving himself, they said.[88]

No Signs of Hunger Strike—Biko Doctors, affirmed the *Rand Daily Mail* on its front page.[89]

Torture in South Africa? queried the headline of the Christian Institute's publication.[90]

Instead of a sober acknowledgment or corrective action, the government attacked its critics. It ordered retractions from the *Rand Daily Mail* through the regulating Press Council, raided and banned three publications, including the *World*, outlawed eighteen additional organizations, and arrested forty-seven black leaders and seven sympathetic whites. Among arrestees were three journalists—*East London Daily Dispatch*'s Woods, *World* editor Percy Qoboza, and *Weekend World*'s Aggrey Klaaste for having "contributed to a subversive situation."[91]

Kruger Explodes the Myth of South Africa's "Free" Press, responded the *World*.

The government "seems bent on transforming moderate black opinion into extremism," said the *Johannesburg Star*. The banned organizations "will simply multiply in the dark," it predicted.[92]

The government banned Woods, and agents anonymously mailed his five-year-old daughter a Biko T-shirt laced with acid, which burned her skin and eyes when she donned it. Realizing his entire family was under threat, Woods planned their escape. Disguised as a Catholic priest, Woods jumped his fence, hitchhiked three hundred miles, and fled to Britain through Lesotho, where his family would later meet him.[93]

To suppress news and promote their own framing, the government launched a massive, international propaganda campaign. The *Rand Daily Mail* discovered the plan, later deemed "Muldergate," including the government's secret and illegal seventy-four-million-dollar fund used to repair its tarnished image. In a front-page story, the *Rand Daily Mail* detailed millions of earmarked dollars to purchase international media influence and thirty-one million dollars to launch an English-language, proapartheid publication, the *Citizen*. The scandal led to other exposés, including possible links to the death of a National Party politician.[94]

The government charged the *Rand Daily Mail* editor Allister Sparks and reporter Hamish Fraser with contempt of an investigative commission. But now, even the progovernment, Afrikaans-language press protested: "The press will continue to differ with whomever necessary and however high," argued William de Klerk, editor of the Afrikaans-language, National Party publication *Die Transvaler*.[95]

Although most readers of papers like the *World* and the *Rand Daily Mail* had little power to make change, many in the international media relied on the English-language press to understand South African politics. And international coverage raised the ire against the South African government throughout the world.

Biko Is the World

Although the war at home was vicious, the South African government had an even greater battle abroad—a growing, global, antiapartheid movement on an uncontrollable world stage and a dogged corps of journalists that relentlessly covered it.[96] Internally, the government fought with deadly violence and harsh, oppressive laws, but internationally, it was armed with only the millions of persuasion dollars and words that might rescue its disgraced image. Unpersuaded by those efforts, international journalists regularly exposed the South African government's brutalities foisted onto Africans.

Antiapartheid sentiment had been growing in international media from the early 1950s, both through mainstream press and activist publications such as *Southern Africa*, *Anti-Apartheid News*, and *Africa Today*.[97] In 1960, news of the Sharpeville massacre spread through the prestige press, including the *New York Times*, *Time* magazine, the *Baltimore Sun*, the *Observer*, the *Chicago Tribune*, and the *Guardian*.

EVIL IN SOUTH AFRICA: A CONVINCING ACCOUNT, wrote Alfred C. Ames of the *Chicago Tribune* editorial board. The article hailed the book, *The Tragedy of Apartheid*, celebrated Zulu chief Luthuli, and concluded, "One needs to see . . . apartheid's evil work in government, church, school, business, press, agriculture, and private lives. . . . The apartheid government is as stupid as it is wicked."[98]

As the antiapartheid movement grew, so did headlines. In 1961 forty-four members of the British parliament staged a seventy-two-hour vigil to honor the seventy-two people who died in the Sharperville onslaught. The vigil captured press headlines in the United Kingdom, particularly those of the *Guardian*.[99]

WORLD ATTENTION TURNS ON APARTHEID, said a 1961 front-page headline of the *Christian Science Monitor*, finding "the breath of world opinion hot upon [South Africa's] neck." There was "evidence," claimed the *Christian Science Monitor*, that "some of the excesses of apartheid have been halted by the moral weight of international opinion and perhaps by the dispatches of the much pilloried foreign correspondents stationed in South Africa."[100]

Exiled South African journalists worked in British media and organizations, and their relentless exposition influenced British journalists. Learning from Ruth First, *Guardian* reporter Adam Raphael led the charge against British companies' "starvation wages" and dire working conditions in South Africa. His front-page coverage was followed by editorials asking, "What are we going to do about South Africa?" Raphael's reports prompted the *Times* (of London), the *Financial Times*, the *Observer*, and others to follow, albeit with less intense coverage.[101]

In the United States, Jim Hoagland's ten-part *Washington Post* series on apartheid in South Africa won a Pulitzer Prize in 1971. With great detail, Hoagland described the apartheid system, including the reservations where "blacks are supposed to find their freedoms. . . . But there is mounting evidence that many of them find nothing but wretched poverty, disease, and isolation," he wrote. Others called the settlements "stinkwater" and "a place for weeping."[102]

With human rights at the center of US president Jimmy Carter's agenda, international media increasingly focused on South Africa. But inside South Africa, many of the media revolted against the pressure. In its proapartheid newspaper, the *Citizen*, a ten-part series attacked the United States, asserting a SECRET US WAR AGAINST SA. The Afrikaans-language *Die Transvaler* called for the white community to stand up against "American pressures."[103] But a media revolution was under way, incited by the circumstances of Biko's death, which sparked an avalanche of bad press for the South African government.[104]

Biko was South Africa's "Martin Luther King . . . devoted . . . to healing South Africa's racial wounds," wrote *Newsweek*.[105] But as a "banned" person, Biko had been forbidden to travel, to have visitors, or to speak with the press without prior government permission, and therefore he was unknown in most of white South Africa, said the Associated Press.[106] "Widely regarded as a founder of the black consciousness movement in South Africa . . . [and] an honorary president of the Black People's Convention (BPC)," Biko was the "twenty-first black to die in South Africa's police detention in eighteen months," wrote the Associated Press.[107] Calls for investigations into his death and moments of silence in governmental chambers filled newspaper pages and generated wider condemnations. A scathing *Washington Post* editorial openly asked: "Is there an explanation other than a calculated official policy to physically destroy substantial segments of the country's black leadership, and in so doing to try to intimidate others who would offer South Africa's black majority alternatives to tranquil acceptance of apartheid?"[108]

The United States was "shocked and saddened," said US secretary of state Cyrus Vance to the *Washington Post*. Vance had "deep concern" about the circumstances surrounding Biko's death. "Evidence reveals that Biko died as a result of police brutality caused by torture," said a civil rights advocate to the *Washington Post*.[109] A steady stream of reports followed: Biko suffered "multiple brain and body injuries," said CBS News, escalating calls for Kruger's resignation. The government denied Biko hospitalization, reported Canada's *Globe and Mail*.[110]

In the wake of Biko's death, South African police cracked down on Africans gathering to mourn and protest. They opened fire on stone-tossing youth and arrested some twelve hundred students to prevent an assembly. But increasingly under an international spotlight, South Africa's overzealousness generated global scorn. Now an international household name, Biko (and his death) symbolized the ugly apartheid system and triggered even more scrutiny into South Africa.[111]

"The still unexplained death . . . has more than ever put the South African system of justice—with its provisions for unlimited detention without trial or charges . . . and its apparent use of brutal assault and torture—on international trial," wrote the *Washington Post*. "Steve Biko is casting a long shadow across this racially troubled land." The article detailed South Africa's torture techniques: "Bodily assault . . . long periods of standing, two days and more without sleep, food, or even permission to go to the bathroom. . . . Electric shock treatment applied to various parts of the body, including the penis, the tying of bricks to men's testicles . . . throwing the detainee high in the air and allowing him to land on the cement floor."[112]

US WILL SEND TOP DELEGATION TO SOUTH AFRICAN'S RITES, reported the *Washington Post*, indicating the seriousness with which the Carter administration held Biko's passing. It "[underscored] growing American pressure on South Africa to change its system of racial segregation." European nations followed suit, and twenty-thousand people gathered for Biko's funeral, where US ambassador Andrew Young's three-foot wreath bore the inscription, "No nation can afford to lose its most dedicated and creative leadership."[113]

Thrust into international martyrdom, Biko became the subject of books, plays, documentaries, songs, and paintings. Among them, recording artist and human rights activist Peter Gabriel released the song "Biko" which reached number thirty-eight on the British music charts.

International media increasingly turned against the South African government. The *Economist* called its policies "repugnant" and a "recipe for disaster." The government was now on "the edge of full-blooded dictatorship."[114] The *Washington Post* called it an "abomination" about which virtually "all Americans" agree.[115]

"The ferocious South African racist Vorster regime plunged South Africa into a white terror," wrote the Chinese news service Xinhua as it detailed a litany of government human rights violations against the "anti-atrocities struggle of the South African blacks." Its actions would "only speed up the doom of the white racist regime."[116]

In 1978, for the first time on US national television, broadcaster Bill Moyers referred to the ANC not as a "terrorist" group but a "liberation organization." During the CBS-aired documentary *Battle of South Africa*, Moyers explained an intense struggle for the soul of the country that produced most of the Western world's gold, diamonds, and metals. Other international media increasingly changed course, calling the ANC "liberation forces," instead of "terrorists."[117]

National and international institutions' punitive actions were double punishment because of the actions themselves and the coverage that followed. Apartheid is a "crime against humanity," and the struggle to eradicate it is "legitimate," declared the United Nations. The organization embargoed arms sales to South Africa and reviewed existing contracts "with a view to terminating them."[118] Citing Biko's death, the US House of Representatives overwhelmingly approved a resolution that strongly denounced South Africa's "repressive measures" and called on President Carter to "take effective measures" against the South African government. The United States threatened to initiate economic sanctions unless South Africa made "significant progress toward the elimination of apartheid." African nations, universities, and other institutions divested their South African holdings.[119]

The actions weren't enough, according to exiled South African journalist Woods on national British television. "The time has come for the nations of the West to realize that if they hope to have any credibility in the increasingly important continent of Africa, they must adopt stronger measures and relate more to this as a matter of international conscience," said Woods. Otherwise, they are merely "propping up the system." He implored the United States to terminate nuclear cooperation, impose sanctions, change visa policies, and end diplomatic relations with South Africa.[120]

FREE MANDELA!

Free Mandela! The words were like poetry, easily forming on the tongue. ANC leader Mandela had been imprisoned when he was convicted of conspiracy to overthrow the government in 1962.[121] At his trial, he confessed to planning sabotage "not . . . in a spirit of recklessness" or for "any love of violence. . . . I planned it as a result of a calm and sober assessment of the political situation that had arisen after years of tyranny, exploitation, and oppression of my people by whites."[122]

The Free Mandela campaign began as an ANC petition but catalyzed a relentless explosion of media attention that grew until the day Mandela was finally released. Although "banned" in South Africa and locked away for twenty-six years, Mandela was an international sensation—both at home and abroad. His letters smuggled from prison made international news, as he called on "democrats of all races" to oust apartheid and its leaders. "The guns that serve apartheid cannot render it unconquerable," Mandela wrote. "Those who live by the gun shall perish by the gun. Unite! Mobilize! Fight on! Between the anvil of united mass action and the hammer of the armed struggle, we shall crush apartheid and white-minority racist rule. . . . The whole world is on our side."[123]

Mandela was essentially right. Across the globe, political and religious leaders called for his release.[124] The United Nations created the Special Commission Against Apartheid; thirteen US congresspeople formally requested to see Mandela; 7,199 Britons voted for Mandela to succeed Queen Elizabeth as the chancellor of London University. In a country thousands of miles from his home, Mandela received the third highest number of votes, coming in third behind Princess Anne and a labor leader.[125]

Humanitarian organizations and universities bestowed awards and honorary degrees to the imprisoned leader, while cities such as Rome offered him citizenship.[126] The largest South African black union elected him honorary life president.[127] Twenty-six US congresspeople gifted his banned wife, Winnie, with a signed quilt in ANC colors to replace her confiscated bedspread.[128] Each declaration and each unique gift bore another headline, building a movement and Mandela's global profile as a hero. Major newsmagazines featured Mandela's story and his accomplishments, including his organizing—from prison—a large-scale education program for other prisoners and completing his own law degree through correspondence. And South Africa's ultimate irony: While Mandela's name, words, and image were prohibited in South Africa, "Free Mandela" was boldly displayed on walls throughout the country.[129]

Mandela became the worldwide symbol for the "struggle for freedom, human dignity, and resistance to apartheid," said Tambo to the Associated Press. He is the "undisputed leader of millions of enslaved people," wrote the *Washington Post*.[130] Mandela "is legendary," said an article titled CONSCIENCE OF SOUTH AFRICA.[131] "The name 'Mandela' is magic," said Helen Joseph, a white antiapartheid activist, to the press. She and others, including Archbishop Desmond Tutu, predicted Mandela's ascension to prime minister of South Africa. Black South Africans unquestionably held him as the most important leader in the nation. "Releasing Mandela . . . is the only way whites will avoid a bloodbath in this country," said Winnie Mandela to the Associated Press.[132]

The government cracked down harder on journalists and liberation organizations to silence scrutiny and criticism. Officials raided and arrested journalists. For interviewing a banned person—Winnie Mandela—they arrested Allister Sparks, Suzanne Sparks, and Bernard Simon, all reporters covering South Africa for publications such as the *Washington Post*, the *London Observer*, the *Economist*, and the *Financial Times* of London. Suzanne Sparks was charged with "defeating the ends of justice."[133] They also expelled foreign reporters, including a twenty-four-year-old correspondent for the *Nation* magazine, and prohibited the sale of publications, including *Newsweek*, because they featured or mentioned banned persons such as Mandela.[134] But each oppressive act wound up, again, ironically, in the news.

Try as it might, the South African government could not suppress the movement. With political developments, books, plays, and speaking tours, month after month South Africans' cruel existence appeared in the media. Sachs published his prison diary, which was staged as a play in England, Canada, and the United States; Naidoo exposed the vast torture in the Robben Island prison in his memoirs; First penned several books; Mary Benson published a biographical account of Nelson Mandela; and Winnie Mandela sanctioned her own story. Tutu penned two important books and was awarded the 1984 Nobel Peace Prize. Tambo, meanwhile, tirelessly organized and orated on behalf of the "struggle."[135]

The United Democratice Front (UDF) and the Rise of the Alternatives

South African prime minister Botha had a plan to get the world off his back—small-scale reforms and a new constitution. He offered the conditional release of jailed leader Mandela, eliminated pass laws and prohibitions on interracial marriage and sex, and increased funding for black education. In the new constitution, Indians and "colored" people gained new rights and representation in a tricameral parliament, but Africans were still excluded.[136]

Through Radio Freedom, broadcasting over Radio Madagascar and Ethiopian Radio (VORE), ANC leaders encouraged listeners to continue the "struggle" for "a democratic and free South Africa, which guarantees . . . freedom and equal rights for all its citizens."[137] They called for more strikes, boycotts, international sanctions, armed rebellion—an all-out "people's war. . . . We call upon the trade unions and civic organizations . . . students and professional organizations; we invite all people from all walks of life to unite in action against this new scheme intended to entrench apartheid."[138]

Both international and domestic media looked on as swaths of South Africa descended into a labyrinth of violence. In a wild revolt with increased sabotage, apartheid opponents strategically detonated bombs, burned buildings, and rioted in the streets.[139]

As a result of Botha's proposed constitution, a new coalition—the United Democratic Front (UDF)—formed.[140] With its large, internationally supported treasury and staff, the UDF devised a countrywide organizational strategy. Through multiple media, including its own publications, *UDF News* and later *Update* and *Isezwe*, plus pamphlets, posters, stickers, and a burgeoning alternative press, the UDF saturated much of South Africa with its message.[141]

In its strategy to prevent continued suppression of antiapartheid movements, the UDF sought to simultaneously bridge across race and to reach the liberal white communities. As it launched its campaign, the new coalition blanketed the regions with hundreds of thousands of newsletters, resulting in the largest mass protest in twenty-five years. Its message was simple: "It is not for us to sit back and merely dream of the day that the people shall govern. It is our task to realize that goal now. . . . The organs of people's power must be democratic and they must be under political discipline." The "power" was not an "either-or" of choosing between the "workerism" and "populism" but rather one that included both.[142]

MASS UDF RALLY IN CITY, said the English-language *Argus* headline, welcoming the UDF's launch as bringing "together voices . . . that need to be heard for the sake of peace and good government." Another *Argus* feature called the UDF "the beginning of a new political ball-game in South Africa." But while some English-language newspapers celebrated the UDF, other mainstream media—including the South African Broadcasting Corporation (SABC), the *Daily News*, and the *Sunday Times*—largely ignored the emergent group.[143]

In contrast, fledgling publications, including the Catholic *New Nation*, the nonprofit *Grassroots*, and the commercial *South*, openly supported the UDF. *Grassroots*'s pro-UDF coverage fueled a resurgent protest movement in the Western Cape. With a stated mission to "articulate the needs and aspirations of the oppressed and exploited in the Cape," *South* exposed more apartheid injustices—police brutality, corruption, and other intractable problems: CHILDREN STRIPPED AND CANED, said one headline. Another read, VIGILANTES "KILLED UNION MEN."[144]

It was time to "crush" the uprising, according to Botha. He waged a "total strategy" against the alleged spread of "Marxist, Soviet influence" and imposed regular, countrywide states of emergency, curfews, and tighter restrictions, while agents assassinated movement leaders.[145]

For South Africa's "national interest," the Botha regime demanded the media's full support, barred international journalists and photographers from covering uprisings or strikes, and forbade support for "activities of subversive or revolutionary elements."[146] Already largely under government control, broadcast media obeyed the Botha government's "orders." Under regular attack and facing charges of inciting revolution, several media shuttered operations. Among them was the *Rand Daily Mail*. After eighty-two years of award-winning coverage, the paper had lost over one hundred nineteen million dollars over ten years.[147]

When the *Rand Daily Mail* folded, the *Weekly Mail* emerged, featuring the "unsweetened truth" about the country, "painful or otherwise." Alongside coverage of boycotts, forced removals, deaths in detention, and the disappearance of African activists, the paper uncovered South Africa's covert operations to destabilize Mozambique. The *Weekly Mail* covered events neglected by other papers, including the unrest in African townships and vigilante attacks. It reported the "necklacing"[148] of suspected apartheid collaborators; victims were forced into gas-doused rubber tires and then lit on fire. And it covered the innerworkings of the notorious Robben Island prison; this article was written by a journalist who was imprisoned there for six years. Although the *Weekly Mail* remained independent of the antiapartheid movement, it gave generous coverage to the ANC, the unions, and the emerging protest culture.[149]

As the Botha regime tightened media restrictions, the *Weekly Mail* made censorship the news. Its front-page headline read, OUR LAWYER TELLS US WE CAN SAY ALMOST NOTHING CRITICAL ABOUT THE EMERGENCY. BUT WE'LL TRY. Beneath the headline, large redactions covered sentences and chunks of articles. The bottom of the page warned: "Restricted: Reports on these pages have been censored to comply with Emergency regulations."[150]

Intent on destroying the UDF movement, the government recruited young African men to help enforce apartheid rule alongside an "instant" police force, while allowing unemployed, vigilante, "self-defense" militias to run rampant. For two years, as parts of South Africa descended into near civil war, the government stood aside, allowing assailants to rape, assault, and kill fellow South Africans. Bombs exploded, fires raged, and officials called in the military to "occupy" the UDF-controlled townships and restrict the organization's movement.[151]

Instead of relenting, the UDF intensified its efforts, placing full-page advertisements that called to "unban the ANC" in sixteen newspapers. The police commissioner responded by outlawing ads or articles that "promoted" banned organizations. In February 1988, the government effectively banned the UDF. Unwilling to acquiesce, UDF members created another organization—the Mass Democratic Movement (MDM)—that continued the work of the UDF.[152]

Mandela, the Legend

Across the world, Mandela became legendary. His story was recounted in movies, books, and songs, reaching an ever-growing international audience. THE STRUGGLE IS MY LIFE included a large collection of Mandela's writings. In his Graceland tour, singer Paul Simon crooned "Bring Him Back Home," specifically calling for Mandela's release. Twenty-four television networks around the world aired the dramatic film *Mandela*, about which the *Sunday Mail* wrote, "If you can watch the Nelson Mandela film dispassionately, you have no soul."[153] In essence, Mandela had "imprisoned his white keepers," asserted the *Washington Post's* Howard Simons, for the government feared that his death could spawn a "rampage" and drive the state into even worse peril.[154]

In one of the world's largest media events, antiapartheid activists produced a ten-hour Wembley Stadium concert featuring superstar musicians, including Dire Straits, Whitney Houston, Simple Minds, George Michael, Phil Collins, the Bee Gees, Joe Cocker, the Eurythmics, Peter Gabriel, and Chrissie Hynde. In addition to the seventy-two-thousand-member live audience, artists performed to one billion television viewers in sixty countries.[155]

"Now, the whole world is watching, P. W. Botha," announced Archbishop Trevor Huddlestone, president of the antiapartheid movement, from the stage. "Tonight I appeal to him to unlock the doors of the apartheid jails. . . . The artists of the world have spoken with one voice: 'Free Nelson Mandela!'"[156]

South Africa was imploding, and its government was running out of options. The country plunged into deeper crisis, and as the white community's support for apartheid was waning. "We can't go on like this!" cried South Africans. But there was hope, suggested the *Weekly Mail*. After many secret meetings with ANC leaders, the *Weekly Mail*'s 1989 headline prepared readers: The government was QUIETLY THINKING THE UNTHINKABLE.[157]

At the end of 1989, after a stroke and internal cabinet pressure, President Botha resigned.[158] His successor, F. W. de Klerk, called for Mandela. Agents retrieved the ANC leader from his confines and smuggled him through the presidential office basement garage for their first meeting. Still, no one was prepared for what would take place.[159]

On February 2, 1990, the biggest names in mass media arrived in South Africa, ready for the big announcement of Mandela's release. For the entire week, Ted Koppel broadcast ABC's *Nightline* entirely from South Africa. But with no hints or foreshadowing, de Klerk shocked the world.

"Walk through the open door and take your place at the negotiating table," de Klerk said, unbanning the ANC and some thirty other political organizations, including the Communist Party, in a single breath. It is time for "a totally new and just constitutional dispensation in which every inhabitant will enjoy equal rights, treatment, and opportunity," he declared. South Africa was among the "historic" opportunities occurring in the world, acknowledging profound changes in the Soviet Union and Eastern Europe. Now South Africa was ready to "set aside its conflicts and ideological differences and draw up a joint program of reconstruction."[160]

In one afternoon, de Klerk unconditionally lifted the long-established bans, suspended the death penalty, lifted the state of emergency, freed the media and trade unions from cumbersome restrictions, released all political prisoners, and relaxed exile laws. The country would now engage in "a new democratic constitution, universal franchise, equality before an independent judiciary, the protection of minorities as well as of individual rights, freedom of religion . . . [and] dynamic programs directed at better education, health services, housing, and social conditions for all."[161]

Nine days later, through the window of mass media, the world watched the unconditional release of Nelson Mandela. The ANC laid down its arms, and the parties began constructing the new South African constitution. But even after negotiations, a new constitution, and the election of Mandela to president, the hard reconciliation work was far from over. As stated by ANC leaders over Radio Freedom, "We [South Africans] must be one people. Our communities must be united and not at war with each other." It was time for a "peace" in which "communities do not see each other as enemies."[162] That would take an extraordinary event and a so-called media moment.

Truth and Reconciliation: The Media Moment

The cameras were on, broadcasting live on television sets in South Africa.

"Show the Commission how you would smother us until we thought we were drowning, that we would suffocate and die," said Tony Yengeni to Sergeant Jeffrey Benzien, who had tortured Yengeni in detention.

Benzien, one of several people asking for amnesty, walked to a person lying on the floor and placed a bag over his head.

"Now please show us how you held it there—how long you held it there."

Benzien knelt, holding the bag as time passed.

"Can you explain how one human being can do this to another human being?" asked Yengeni.

Benzien's eyes puffed up and filled with tears. A man who, in his role as a hard, tough officer, had tortured people now wept before all of South Africa when confronted with the very real, human question: "How can one person do this to another person?"[163]

The Truth and Reconciliation Commission (TRC) set out to heal a deeply divided and injured South Africa. It sought to "repair and lay the basis for common citizenship and for joint efforts to improve the lives of everybody."[164]

"We knew terrible things had happened," explained Sachs. "But facts can be cold and lacking the [human] dimension. The Truth [and Reconcilation] Commission brought these experiences into the public. We saw the tears; we heard the voices; we heard the lamentations, the sometimes stilted apologies. We saw on television, heard on radio, [read] in press; and it was that humanizing of what had happened that captured the minds and spirits and healed. It didn't heal the iniquities, but until we got rid of these hidden and denied examples of atrocious conduct and behavior, we couldn't secure forward-looking government."[165]

While initially vilified in some Afrikaans-language media as a "witch hunt" and "Tutu's Commission on Confessing and Lying," as the hearings began even the more skeptical media covered the testimony.[166] The live daily broadcasts in television and radio plus weekly television summaries and daily newspaper articles made the TRC hearings the most important and unifying event in South Africa. With mass media focused on the singular event, a fractured South Africa experienced a common, transcendent moment, a "common national history of the apartheid era," and generated a shared use of language, such as the phrase "gross violations of human rights."[167]

"The TRC process largely succeeded to lay bare South Africa's past to many ordinary Afrikaners who, for a very long time, had no idea what was done by agents of the apartheid government to maintain white minority rule," wrote journalist Tim du Plessis. "Had it not been for the TRC, many Afrikaners (and other White South Africans) would have never known" about the misdeeds.[168]

Through mass media, the TRC was everywhere, signaling to audiences its seriousness and legitimacy as it reshaped society's understandings of itself and its government and offered new norms for acceptable behaviors.[169] "The impact was enormous," acknowledged Sachs. "You just had to acknowledge what was going on."

The TRC marked the end of one society and government and the birth of a new one—one that was embedded in an entirely different set of values and principles. "It created a common mold platform that there are some things people just can't and mustn't do to other people," according to Sachs. "And in the new country, [there would be] no secrets, no lies."[170]

MASS MEDIA AND SOUTH AFRICA'S POLITICAL TRANSFORMATION

For decades, South Africa's Afrikaans-language establishment media held the apartheid system as legitimate and normal, helping to create a "climate in which gross human rights violations occurred," according to Archbishop Tutu and journalists' own admissions.[171] With multiple tools, the antiapartheid movement fought that system. In their arsenal was mass media that exposed, organized, and encouraged world partners to assist in their struggle for a multiracial democracy. Within South Africa, a small group of journalists and advocates risked their lives and livelihoods to expose injustices and atrocities and challenge the legitimacy of apartheid. Their work fed the international media, and word spread, making the antiapartheid movement a global phenomenon. The seed planted by struggling publications eventually grew into an international phenomenon that engaged massive numbers of people and leaders. Although the government sought to silence the media and perpetuate its own illusion, it could not control the international forces, which grew into a juggernaut.[172]

Ultimately, South Africa's transformation was the result of multiple factors, including visionary leadership in the churches and antiapartheid organizations. But media played a crucial role, informing and denouncing the injustices of the system, which spread internationally and helped build multilayered pressure on the South African government. Through mass media, the stand of a few dedicated leaders for multiracial democracy became the accepted truth. Finally, through its live broadcast of the Truth and Reconciliation Commission hearings, mass media helped close the doors on the old South Africa and give birth to a new South African government and society.[173] While that government still struggles with countless sociopolitical issues, in some ways it was ahead of its time in addressing issues of social equality.

Chapter 7

One Nation, Ripped Apart: Chile's Fall and the Rise of Democracy

THE ORIGINAL 9/11

P resident Salvador Allende Gossens was surrounded. Tanks and armed military men created an impenetrable circle around the presidential palace. His foes—his own military—were determined to seize power in a coup d'état. If they succeeded, they would achieve the "impossible" in Chile: topple the democratic rule that had stood for more than one hundred years.

"Unconditional surrender!" barked General Augusto Pinochet to Admiral Carvajal for delivery to Allende, the physician-turned-president.[1] "No negotiations. You hear? Unconditional surrender!"[2]

The admiral delivered the offer to the besieged president: surrender and be safely flown into exile or die at the hands of his own armed forces. But the admiral knew there was no safety for Allende. His plane would crash midflight.[3]

Allende consulted with his advisors and came to realize, "I will repay the loyalty of the people with my life." But he wanted no "pointless victims" and thus sent his ministers, officials, colleagues, and daughters out of the palace for safety. The presidential guard, too, could leave without their weapons.[4] Allende settled before the special emergency telephone to deliver his last radio address to the people of Chile, knowing that the coup forces had already blasted two radio station transmitters into oblivion. Only Radio Magallanes remained of the left-oriented stations to broadcast his final words.[5]

"Surely, Radio Magallanes will be silenced, and the calm metal instrument of my voice will no longer reach you. It does not matter," he said to his constituents. "You will continue to hear me. I will always be with you. . . . Long live Chile! Long live the people! And long live the workers!"[6]

Just three years before the military's siege, Allende won the presidency in a tight, three-way race after three unsuccessful previous attempts. Upon his election, he initiated an economic revolution, one in which vast discrepancies in opportunity and wealth might slowly fade. It was a new day for those who eschewed class divisions. Students, workers, and other professionals celebrated—they taught janitors to read, renamed maids "home advisers," and helped factory workers take over manufacturing companies.[7] But their glory was short-circuited, culminating in the bloody military coup and its reign of terror that wrecked their dreams, families, and lives.[8]

Allende acknowledged his unfinished work but implored Chileans to build the dream without him, knowing that his end was near. "I am prepared to die, if necessary, but I will not resign," said Allende over Radio Magallanes. "They have the force; they can subjugate us. . . . But social processes cannot be detained by crime or by force. History . . . is made by the people. . . . I have faith in Chile and its destiny. . . . Men and women will overcome this dark and bitter moment in which treason seeks to take power. Know that sooner, rather than later, the great avenues will once again open where free [men] can walk through them to build a better society. . . . These are my last words."[9]

Tanks plowed forward; airplanes roared overhead, dropping bombs, firing rockets, and releasing tear gas into the eighteenth-century-style building that had long represented Chilean culture, access, and democracy. The windows shattered, the curtains ignited, the palace was ablaze. On the ground, some one hundred infantry leapt from buses and darted to the now smoke-filled palace.[10]

"Allende will never surrender!" announced the president shortly before he placed the butt of an automatic rifle between his knees, its barrel beneath his chin.[11] In the next moment, Allende, at sixty-five, along with his grand experiment and the long-standing, ever-resilient democracy in Chile, was dead.

Midway through broadcasters' condemnation of the coup, Radio Magallanes, too, went silent.[12] While a small number of students and workers fought back against the military coup, most resistance crumbled in the face of an overpowering military.[13] The junta took control of the nation and swore itself into power by nightfall, with General Pinochet at its head.

It was our "'moral duty' to overthrow the 'illegitimate' government," said junta officials over the radio. They swore to uphold the constitution, "salvage" the country, protect the workers, and unite Chileans in the "'brotherly task' of rebuilding the nation."[14]

Reality, however, looked nothing like the grand ideas the junta espoused over the airwaves: Using an emergency valve in the constitution, Pinochet's regime declared the entire country an "emergency zone" and placed all civilian activities under military control. It banned political parties, labor unions, and civic organizations, shut down Congress, expanded military courts, confiscated media, froze bank accounts, and eliminated countless civil rights. Tens of thousands of Chileans suspected of opposing the regime were fired from their jobs and expelled from schools and universities. Anyone who remained "belligerent"(bearing arms and fighting), said the junta, would be "executed on the spot."[15]

The nation became a blood-soaked battleground ruled by a military dictator. In a house-by-house search-and-destroy campaign, military men, using lists of suspected Allende supporters—labor leaders, students, and peasants—busted down doors and summarily shot everyone inside, killing entire families. The bodies of Allende officials turned up floating in the Mapocho River. Soldiers, indoctrinated to hate Allende supporters, humiliated, tortured, raped, and killed at will. Masked guards beat prisoners until they lost consciousness, and they forced others to lick the ground or to run naked until they fell from exhaustion. They submerged victims into the "submarine," a tank filled with excrement and ammonia, until they neared death, hung others by their extremities until their bones broke, administered electrical shocks to their genitals, and inserted rats into women's vaginas. Guards whipped one prisoner until he bled, then ground salt into his open wounds.[16]

The freezing Dawson Island served as the prison for left-leaning elected officials, academics, and dignitaries. There, the once-respected elite performed hard labor under the watch of guards carrying machine guns and spouting political vitriol. "God, how I hate you all," exclaimed a guard. During the initial roundup, one senator narrowly escaped. An

East German diplomat, disguised as a traveling salesman, smuggled him out by hiding him beneath a pile of suitcases and pharmaceutical samples in his car.[17]

Many Chileans were shocked to see South America's most stable democracy completely dismantled. Although Chile's neighboring democracies had fallen to coups, it seemed unimaginable in Chile. The nation's long-steeped culture of deep respect for the rule of law, civility, and the democratic process distinguished Chile from other parts of Latin America. Even among ideological opponents, "everything could be negotiated between gentlemen." Political differences were reconciled through democratic processes and competitive elections. In fact, before the coup, public officials who virulently opposed Allende's policies had declined large bribes from the Central Intelligence Agency (CIA) of the United States. After all, they said, Allende had won the election fairly.[18]

Unfortunately, Chilean "exceptionalism"—that it can't happen here—proved a myth. Pinochet's regime disappeared or killed either by torture or by gunfire more than thirty-five hundred people. It tortured tens of thousands more, detained more than one hundred thousand, and forced more than two hundred thousand into exile, based mostly on their ideologies.[19] Its wrath destroyed people, families, democracy, the rule of law, and the once-genteel nature of an elegant country.

For more than fifteen years Pinochet reigned over Chile, the first four with brutal military force, arresting, imprisoning, disappearing, and killing anyone suspected of opposing his rule. But after a long period of bloodletting and iron-fisted rule, under the radar, small groups of committed citizens moved to rebuild a democratic Chile.

At each phase of Chile's turbulent history, media were key players, instigating, supporting, denouncing, comforting, or revitalizing. Media contributed to the nation's vibrant democracy, and media helped to instigate democracy's downfall. Media helped to destroy human rights, and media helped to restore them.

Through the dissemination of lies and the withholding of truths, Chile's postcoup mainstream media created mythical realities, provoked chaos, and hid and thus enabled the dictator's dark designs. But with relentless strife, determination, and tenacity, advocates for human rights and democracy built and expanded an alternative media to finally expose and topple the dictator and return their government to a democratic form.

THE FIVE STAGES OF MEDIA

Stage One: Before the Coup—Weaving the Revolution

In the years before the coup, Chilean press and television largely reflected the nation's diverse political views.[20] Parties across the political spectrum maintained active publications and contributed to a wide-ranging public debate.[21] Each of two university television stations mirrored the left and right ideologies, and the national television station generally delivered its mandate to air all political parties' views in proportion to the votes they received. Although most radio stations were owned and dominated by large agricultural and mining companies, under Allende, left perspectives were no longer locked out of the radio dial.[22] Left-leaning parties and coalitions purchased a series of radio stations, enhancing their radio power from one station to six, most of which were held by separate political parties: Radio Magallanes, Radio Corporación, Radio Candelaria, Radio Luis Emilio Recabarren, Radio Nacional, and Radio Portales.[23]

Over time, Allende and his ideas gained traction, particularly among poor people and workers who had suffered from the country's disparate wealth and power gaps.[24] But these same ideas embraced by the poor sent chills through the ranks of the rich, whose power and vast empires were at stake. To a handful of the wealthiest, democracy was a poor excuse for losing their privilege and their large corporate holdings. Among the most vehement was publishing magnate Agustin Edwards Eastman, known to his friends as "Doonie."[25] Because Edwards's media empire was threatened by Allende's effort to nationalize Chilean newsprint,[26] he led the campaign to vanquish Allende. But by destroying Allende, the junta would also crumble Chile's democracy, culture, and social fabric, alongside the dreams and aspirations of the working poor who had struggled with the president. The chaos that ensued, the dictatorship that emerged, the torture, death, and disappearances—all followed Edwards's relentless public and private campaigning: through his media empire to convince Chileans of his point of view, and behind the scenes to persuade US president Richard Nixon to unleash the CIA on Chile.[27]

Stage Two: Doonie

Doonie Edwards was distraught. The heir to a vast media empire, Edwards published Chile's paper of record, *El Mercurio*, alongside numerous other media. As one of the country's wealthiest men, Edwards had much to lose should Allende win the election and succeed with his plans—especially his plans to nationalize *El Mercurio*'s newsprint supply.[28]

"The United States must prevent Allende's election," Edwards implored David Rockefeller on a March 1970 trip to Washington, DC.[29]

If Allende were not stopped, Edwards would "be ruined," he said to then US ambassador to Chile, Edward Korry. But Korry reminded Edwards that the United States had already funded propaganda to tarnish Allende and backed opposition candidates. In its efforts to secure "anybody but Allende" for president, the CIA had spent millions of dollars on an anti-Allende campaign.[30]

Undeterred and backed by his "lunch crowd" of elite media managers, Edwards returned to Washington.[31] Through Donald Kendall, chairman of PepsiCo, he relayed a message to the very top—President Richard Nixon himself. A September 15, 1970, breakfast meeting with National Security Advisor Henry Kissinger, Attorney General John Mitchell, and Edwards prompted a call to CIA Director Richard Helms. The men hatched their plans to ruin Allende: First, mass propaganda would tarnish Allende; bribery would prevent his inauguration; economic ruin would foment chaos throughout Chile. If all else failed, a military coup would finish Allende. President Nixon was prepared to spend ten million dollars to "Bring [Allende] down," "smash" that "SOB . . . bastard Allende," according to declassified documents and witness testimony.[32]

The agency placed *El Mercurio* on its payroll to defame Allende, and the paper filled the public sphere with outlandish claims and hyperbole. But despite the million-dollar propaganda campaign, Allende emerged as victor—narrowly—of the three-way race, as the leader of a coalition of left-leaning parties.[33]

Bribery was the next effort. CIA officials offered money to members of the Chilean Congress and to the outgoing president, Eduardo Frei Montalva, to stage an institutional coup in which they would shun Allende and instead ratify the runner-up, Jorge Allesandri Rodríguez.

Allesandri would resign, call for new elections, and allow Frei to be reelected. They wired telegrams to Frei's wife and mailed international "CIA-planted news articles" about Chile's coming demise directly to Frei—a total of 726 stories against an Allende presidency. But the plan was dead at its inception, as the officials refused the bribes—Allende had legally and fairly won the election.[34]

In the so-called Track II, CIA-supported rightist groups, one led by retired general Roberto Viaux, and one led by General Carnilo Valenzuela of the Chilean army, sought extreme means to sabotage Allende. The Viaux-related Fatherland and Liberty ("Patria y Libertad"), armed with US-supplied machine guns and tear gas, plotted Allende's assassination and provoked chaos throughout Chile.[35] Their assignment was to kidnap the devout constitutionalist chief of the Chilean army, General René Schneider, and blame the abduction on leftists in hopes of generating enough mayhem to derail Allende's inauguration. Schneider, said Ambassador Korry, was "the main barrier" to a military takeover. But the plan went awry in October 1970 when the group instead shot Schneider to death. The Chilean public responded with a wave of support for the constitution, which included a continued Allende presidency.[36]

"Make the economy scream," demanded a frustrated US President Richard Nixon.[37] His administration called US companies and financial institutions to withdraw all resources and shipments from Chile, arranged trade blocks, slashed aid from $260.4 million to $3.8 million, and encouraged Chilean corporation owners to "strike": Investors withdrew their funds, and trucking companies and agribusiness owners halted operations, leaving fields unplanted and food and basic necessities undelivered and unavailable. The monthlong business-class strike cost the country more than one hundred million dollars and ninety thousand construction jobs.[38]

They failed to prevent Allende's ascension through the election and inauguration. And to the horror of Edwards and his allies, the new president initiated economic transformations in efforts to empower and provide property to the poor. He accelerated agrarian reform, began nationalizing industries and financial institutions, began initiating acquisition of foreign-owned industries, and supported workers in securing better work conditions.[39]

To publicize his vision for an expanded democracy and peaceful socialism,[40] Allende had also initiated a communications revolution, supporting grassroots media. He increased public ownership of publishing, film, and record companies; and helped establish new, leftist radio stations, a medium long dominated by giant capitalists.[41]

Pandemonium erupted: In a quest to destabilize Chile and provoke a coup, CIA-supported rightist groups detonated bombs every night, blowing up electrical towers, railroads, oil pipelines, and other key infrastructure. They sabotaged industrial machinery, vandalized factories, and cut phone lines.[42] Leftists in the MIR (Leftist Independent Movement) agitated for a popular uprising. Police and strikers violently clashed. The Chilean Congress censured the troubled president,[43] and a renegade army tank opened fire on the presidential palace and the Ministry of Defense. Despite the chaos, General Carlos Prats, with the trademark graciousness of Chilean culture, approached the rogue soldiers and convinced them to surrender.[44] But the tumult and strikes left Chileans across the country unsettled, afraid, and without basic food and necessities.[45]

As he was central in the instigation and planning of the chaos, Edwards and his team knew that the destruction was orchestrated. Yet, through his media, including *El Mercurio*, Edwards deliberately misled the public and engendered more turmoil.[46] With more than $1.95 million in direct financial aid,[47] the CIA ensured the newspapers' reach and stability such that *El Mercurio* could relentlessly hammer Allende, blame him for the country's economic and social woes, and generate panic.[48] Another $1.24 million paid for ads and campaigns of the oppositional municipal candidates, and an additional $1.5 million funded the ads and campaigns of opposition congressional candidates.[49]

While publicly supporting the real saboteurs—including the Fatherland and Liberty groups—Edwards's media claimed that it was Allende's supporters causing the destruction.[50] The "out-of-control Marxists" were attempting to "achieve total power" through "extralegal or de facto" means, according to his media.[51]

Day after day, *El Mercurio* headlines bred fear about "Marxists" causing "terror" in schools, slaughtering dogs, beating handicapped veterans, and planning to execute members of the middle class and armed forces. But there was one problem: The stories were untrue.[52]

Allende was depicted as a deadly dictator and an "irresponsible drunk."[53] Alongside attack articles, *El Mercurio* juxtaposed Allende's photographs with those of slaughtered animals[54] and blamed Allende for the violence.[55]

La Segunda fabricated an Allende interview in which it claimed he admitted plans to expropriate small businesses such as candy stores and lollipop stands.[56]

Tribuna lampooned threats on Allende's life: YANKEE AGENT DISCOVERED HERE ON MISSION TO KILL ALLENDE: HIS NAME IS JOHNNY WALKER.[57]

Rightist media flooded readers with terrifying warnings of a coming "leftist" coup. "Leftist guerilla groups" were stockpiling arms, creating guerilla schools, infiltrating the military, and converting factories into fortresses for organizing their paramilitaries, they said. They alarmed readers with a coming "totalitarian nightmare." The wild claims raised the ire of the already-suspicious rank-and-file soldiers.[58]

A sensational media grew increasingly high-pitched, inflammatory, and divided, depicting a once-great Chilean society as spiraling out of control, descending into a wild abyss, and headed for destruction. While the rightist newspapers blamed BLOODY MARXISTS SHOOTING and "the government" for the chaos, claiming that they had "gravely broken the constitution," the leftist media called for rescuing Chile from the "Fascist coup"[59] and asserted that the militant right wing was promoting "a climate of fear and chaos." Leftist publications could not compete against the well-funded, powerful voice of *El Mercurio* and its sister media. It was no contest.[60]

Across sectors of Chile, the strategy worked. Chileans grew enraged—not toward the instigators of chaos but toward Allende and his supporters. "[I had to] stand all night in the cold to get milk for the baby," said Carmen Garcia, "[and go from] store to store trying to find a bit of cooking oil or sugar. I will never, ever forgive the Communists for that." Others grew afraid. "My dad put up bars on the house because he was afraid the Communists would come and rape us," said a young advertising executive.[61]

As media hardened into extreme positions, so, too, did the Chilean people. Like a shadow to the media framing, Chile's atmosphere grew so vitriolic that Allende's long-cultivated negotiating skills were useless. Friendships disintegrated, and social gatherings erupted into rabid arguments. Violent riots broke out in the streets, and enraged people vandalized and destroyed property.[62] The once-civil Chilean society in which people "addressed each other as 'madam' and 'gentleman'" degenerated into an ugly bedlam.[63]

Middle- and upper-class women—a key audience of the coup planners—added to the military woes. They taunted soldiers, flicked corn kernels at them, and declared, "You are a bunch of chickens. You are not defending the honor of the women of Chile." They demonstrated at the home of General Prats, demanding his resignation for his loyalty to the constitution and the president. Prats resigned a few days later.[64]

Military men grew convinced that leftist guerillas had infiltrated their ranks. Rumors emerged that Allende was plotting to assassinate senior officials, leaving an already-suspicious military increasingly unsettled. The ranks polarized between those dedicated to upholding a democratically elected presidency and those who wanted a coup at any cost. Coup-favoring officers won and imprisoned the soldiers and sailors opposing the military takeover.[65]

El Mercurio editor Arturo Fontaine admitted to "doing everything we could to provoke a coup."[66] In July 1973, *El Mercurio* publicly called for the coup and to end democracy. "Renounce all political parties, the masquerade of elections, the poisoned and deceitful propaganda, and turn over to a few select military men the task of putting an end to political anarchy," wrote the paper.[67] On its front page in huge letters, it featured a leading senator calling for "the armed forces of the Fatherland to clean out the workers from the illegally occupied factories and smash the Red Army being trained inside them."[68]

Chile was fast going dark. A rightist group gunned down Arturo Araya, Allende's naval aide-de-camp; and the Chilean Air Force, "on its own authority," raided one of the largest worker-owned factories in a quest to find "illegal weapons."[69]

President Allende acknowledged the chaos and demands for the coup but vowed that Chile's constitutional democracy would win. "Some people say we need a coup to avert a civil war," he said on September 10, 1973. "But in Chile there will be neither a coup, nor a civil war!"[70]

Stage Three: From Public Debate to Hegemony— "Rescuing" Chile

The day after Allende spoke his defiant words, Pinochet's military ambushed the presidential palace. With bombs, guns, and tear gas, it seized the palace and usurped the power long vested through democratic means. But Pinochet's job was not over until the military also destroyed the coalition that had elected Allende.

In Operation Silence, Pinochet muted all media except for those supporting him. His military knocked out and confiscated radio transmitters for both Radio Portales and Radio Corporación.[71] It seized forty broadcast stations and converted them into junta propaganda machines, either by channeling them through the favored Radio Nacional or by selling them off to other rightist organizations. For the left, the lone Radio Magallanes remained, and only briefly, due to a mistake—the military bombed the wrong tower. Shortly thereafter, soldiers gunned down the last standing leftist radio station.[72]

The junta then destroyed all "politically incorrect" newspapers, magazines, books, and movies, mostly through violent destruction or confiscation.[73] In a matter of days, a once-diverse mass media lay dead, leaving only a narrative of loyalty, justification, and subservience to the junta.[74] To be sure, the junta established censors and police officers inside each newsroom and radio station and forbade entry of foreign films, even films like *Fiddler on the Roof*.[75]

The once-free press now contained four national newspapers, including Edwards's *El Mercurio*, as well as *La Tercera*, and *Cronica*, two weekly magazines, and Pinochet's co-opted television and radio.[76] Only one independent journal remained—a small-circulation Jesuit publication, *Mensaje*.[77]

The military then turned its guns and bombs onto civil society and civilians themselves. With the coup's takeover, genteel Chile morphed into an unrecognizable country. Gone was the pluralistic society, diverse communication, and the workers' aspirations for a better life. In the place of the old gallant Chile, Pinochet installed an iron-fisted, intolerant military dictatorship that destroyed anyone who was suspected of opposing him. We will "exterminate Marxism," he declared, and expel "left-wingers who were given asylum by Allende."[78]

As Pinochet unleashed deadly fury onto civil society, the remaining media cheered what they called the "Wagnerian finale" of the Popular Unity coalition behind Allende. "To open a new door, the country had to pay its quota of blood," opined the conservative *Que Pasa* magazine.[79] These media channeled Pinochet's justification for the mass violence and ruined social fabric into Chileans' homes through television, radio, and newsprint. It was wholly necessary, said Pinochet to the last remaining media. Had they not acted with lethality, the leftists would have imposed a dictatorship, he asserted.

To convince Chileans, the media blanketed the nation with lurid tales about the now-dead Allende and his supporters. Under headlines such as Scandals of Allendismo, publications reported vast storage rooms filled to capacity with liquor, food, imported clothes, thousands of dollars, pornography, and sexual paraphernalia that could "fill a super-market. . . . The pueblo has been groped and deceived," said General Gustavo Leigh in *Ercilla* magazine. The "true" Allende, they wrote, was hypocritical, arrogant, and morally weak, his allies opulent and excessive.[80]

Pinochet, on the other hand, was "His Excellency" and a "fair liber-ator" committed to process and the rule of law, according to *El Mercurio* articles. His military government had rescued Chile from leftists plotting to violently overthrow Chile, massacre military men, assassinate leaders, and eliminate political opponents by force. Without them, Chile would have fallen to the "savage orbit" of "political cannibalism" that had plagued Russia.[81] As evidence, newspapers claimed to have uncovered "Plan Z" and the "White Book," both of which were largely fabrications of CIA agents and ultraconservative Chileans, including Gonzalo Vial, cofounder of *Que Pasa*. Plan Z, said Pinochet's regime, was "proof of Chile's rendezvous with political genocide."[82]

For weeks, media built up a plot like a "horror movie," escalating the terror with a "cascade of revelations" with increasing "new layers of per-versity." These "chiefs feed themselves [by] devouring other chiefs," according to *La Estrella del Norte*, which, along with *Cronica* and *El Mer-curio*, published a flurry of conspiratorial articles, complete with lists of people allegedly targeted for death by leftist "cannibals." Hundreds were slated for "the death sentence," wrote *Cronica*. "[They] would be elimi-nated without any thought or mercy, whether old people, children, or even infants," ultimately sending Chile into the "Moscow orbit."[83]

As evidence of the alleged conspiracy, newspapers published photos of a vast range of weaponry, reportedly uncovered by the military. "An abundant arsenal of weapons, of great firepower, was found in the Interior of La Moneda Palace . . . [firepower] of Russian and Czechoslovakian manufacturers," said one caption. Military press conferences displayed their "uncovered" arms in dramatic "field settings,"[84] ultimately accusing leftists of plotting exactly what Pinochet was doing: overthrowing the government and imprisoning, disappearing, torturing, and killing innocent people.

It was no time to relent or relax, warned *La Tercera* and *El Mercurio*, as "bloodthirsty" leftists and "fanatic assassins" still planned to unleash mass violence and civil war through "Plan Leopardo" and "Plan Boomerang Rojo." They were organizing "diabolic and macabre conspiracies" and spreading "hatred" that "scattered about like the metastasis of cancer among the incurably ill."[85]

"Foreign countries sent weapons and mercenaries of hate to fight us," claimed Pinochet in his national address. "There continues the state of internal war and the state of siege. . . . Our soldiers are still fighting against armed extremist groups that wound or kill in the dark." These hysterical claims became the impetus and justification for beating, torturing, executing, and incarcerating thousands of innocent people.[86]

"Denounce them," decried *El Mercurio*. "Contribute to cleansing your homeland of undesirables."[87] As the regime touted its justifications for continued repression, Chilean mass media disseminated Pinochet's narrative, without questioning the veracity or highlighting the hypocrisy. *La Tercera* and *El Mercurio* reported gun battles with Communists wielding automatic weapons and bombs, when in reality the alleged fighters died in detention. *Cronica* claimed that Isidoro Carillo, a local official and the administrator of a nationalized coal-mining company, confessed to his leadership in Plan Z and to gathering "antipersonnel bombs and grenades intended to massacre whole families." In truth, dynamite was a necessary part of the mining operation and was properly stored. Nonetheless, Carillo was executed.[88]

In Operation Colombo, one of the regime's most disturbing fabrications, the junta attempted to falsify the fates of missing Chileans. It planted Chilean identification cards on the bodies of two badly charred, unrecognizable Argentines, victims of the Argentine Anticommunist

Alliance (AAA) death squads. The Chilean ID cards were meant to suggest that the bodies belonged to disappeared Chileans. Regime agents then planted stories and photographs of the bodies along with lists of 119 disappeared Chileans in two obscure publications in efforts to propagate the false story that they had perished at the hands of guerillas and infighting.[89]

Citing "government sources," papers like *El Mercurio* continued the fabrication. It published articles claiming that in the WAR BETWEEN MIRISTAS, the "Chileans" were "victims of their own methods, exterminated by their own comrades, every one of them demonstrates with tragic eloquence that violent people end up falling victims to the blind and implacable terror they provoke."[90] The victims were EXTERMINATED LIKE RATS.[91]

Under Pinochet, national television's mission was to "'serenify spirits' and unite citizens behind the regime." Political debate was banished, and most programs featured only soccer games, soap operas, and a steady rotation of procoup events alongside fear-inducing exposés about "violent" leftists.[92] They featured women's groups, usually headed by military and official wives, thanking the regime for "rescuing" them from the throes of a leftist scourge. As symbols of gratitude, the women donated their personal jewelry to the Fund for National Restoration, trading their gold wedding bands for copper rings inscribed with "Eleventh of September 1973."[93]

While thousands of Chileans disappeared from their homes and workplaces, most media ignored their fates. The bodies turning up in Mapocho River seldom received even a blurb. Although some reporters filmed the bodies, they never dared defy the government by airing the footage, particularly knowing the fates of journalists who questioned the military government: those journalists were fired, arrested, and tortured, their homes raided and/or burned down, their media operations shuttered—or any combination of these punishments. In all, the Pinochet government killed at least ten professional journalists (one account claims forty), forced three hundred into exile, and fired another one thousand.[94] Even procoup media faced closure for publishing seemingly innocuous articles.[95] *La Segunda*, for example, faced a temporary closure when censors determined its article about rising cigarette prices had "altered people's tranquility."[96]

The military campaign and Chile's media complicity built an environment that stifled resistance and created a faux legitimacy for coup leaders through an impenetrable wall that fabricated information and hid realities. Chileans reported believing the military's story. Convinced that Communists were attempting a "Soviet-style revolution," Chileans said they were "all in favor" of the coup.[97] In one 1974 poll, 80 percent of Chileans said they supported the junta—although some assurances of support were likely elicited under intimidation.[98]

The International Stage: Dissent Abroad

While the Chilean media acquiesced under junta control, the international community rose in protest against the junta's mass tortures and killings. Tens of thousands of demonstrators filled the streets of such European cities as Rome, Paris, Hamburg, and Frankfurt, raising the international reporting bar.[99] "Down with the murderers and the CIA!" shouted demonstrators in Paris.[100] Religious and human rights organizations banded together to support beleaguered Chileans. They crossed borders, released damning reports, and lobbied extensively throughout the world.[101] Chilean exiles formed investigative organizations and launched high-profile forums and publications. The efforts garnered international publicity, exposing the junta's torture and killing machines.[102]

In the United States, the silent partner of the military coup, initially many media didn't report their own government's role in the siege.[103] The *Wall Street Journal* blamed Allende for failing "to control leftists."[104] The *New York Times* faulted Allende's transformations with "no electoral mandate"[105] but also reported on a large demonstration, featuring Angela Davis, who blamed the United States for the coup.[106] Some journalists were more suspicious. *Time* magazine hinted at the US role, noting that while "anti-imperialists everywhere immediately assumed that Washington was behind [Allende's] downfall . . . one country was conspicuously silent: The U.S. The Nixon Administration had been antagonistic to Allende ever since he emerged as the likely winner."[107] A number of reporters tried to but could not verify the connection. "I reported everything I could nail down, but it wasn't much," said *Washington Post* correspondent Louis Diuguid.[108]

Chilean solidarity groups built awareness through newspapers, radio, televison, magazines, newsletters, and film. Pacifica Radio and other community radio stations featured Chilean exiles as frequent guests, while smaller circulation publications publicized both the regime's abuses and the solidarity community's efforts.[109] Growing revelations of Chile's torture and homicide expanded US media coverage. Comparing Chile to the terror of *The Exorcist*, *Newsweek*'s James Pringle accused Pinochet of making "fear and torture almost a way of life. . . . The junta's terrorist campaign" is not aimed solely at revolutionary groups, wrote Pringle, DINA agents "have arrested ordinary Chileans after over-hearing them complain about the nation's runaway inflation—or for no apparent reason." They even arrested a three-year-old girl in effort to "induce the surrender of her fugitive father."[110] Two years postcoup, wrote the *New York Times*, forty-one thousand Chileans, including forty clergy, still languished in prison for "political reasons."[111] As human rights reports increasingly revealed death by torture, the *New York Times* reported the executions of clergy, trade union officials, and people who simply disagreed with the government.[112]

After a 1975 congressional investigation exposed the Nixon adminis-tration's role in Chile's coup d'état, the US media unleashed another ava-lanche of news, detailing torture, lies, and cover-ups. In 1976, the Chilean death machine reached Embassy Row in the United States. Chilean agents planted a remote-control bomb in the car of exiled Chilean foreign min-ister Orlando Letelier in Washington, DC. It blew off his legs, killing him and his twenty-five-year-old passenger, Ronni Moffit, who drowned in her own blood before the ambulance arrived. News of the assassination peppered US and Chilean headlines. Although US journalist John Dinges identified the incident's similarity with other Chilean assassinations, Chilean media did not publicly acknowledge the connection.[113]

Pinochet steeled his position, issuing new bans on "the existence, organization, activities, and propaganda" of parties, and threatening them with fines, prison, and exile. Alongside new powers to censor mail and prohibit foreign publications, Pinochet attacked his detractors abroad with advertisements in newspapers such as the *Washington Post*.[114] The problem was "terrorism" rooted in "international communism . . . which threatens innocent victims and often sows chaos," said Pinochet supporter Jamie Guzman over Chilean airwaves. The accusations leveled by human rights organizations were merely efforts to "sling mud at the

fatherland and join in on the foreign conspiracy." It was "political mean-
ness" and "an extreme of blindness."[115]

Jimmy Carter's election to the US presidency raised the human
rights bar and prompted another sea change in US media coverage.[116]
Under Carter's leadership, the United States cosponsored the UN
Human Rights Commission's resolution condemning Chile's "constant
and flagrant violations of human rights," withheld Chilean aid due to
their "human rights situation," and investigated Chilean officials in Letelier's assassination.[117]

Each new development led to another "publicity avalanche" in
Chilean media, which reported US findings alongside the junta government's response.[118] Previously taboo subjects reached across Chilean
headlines, slowly unraveling the official Chilean story.[119]

General Pinochet acknowledged international pressure in an interview published in *Ercilla*: "The problem [of political opposition] cannot
be seen only inside Chile," he said. "This is a chessboard. And the players
are outside. We are inside and try to place ourselves outside the
board."[120] While Pinochet replaced the hard-line direct censorship with
monitoring and periodical closures of noncompliant media,[121] the dictator blacklisted select journalists, forbade publication of damaging news,
sent thirty officers to physically shut down Radio Balmaceda, and
flooded media with his pro-Pinochet message.[122]

To date, only *Mensaje*, the Jesuit magazine, could legally publish criticism.[123] But Pinochet relented and permitted a handful of independent
publications to emerge. At the same time, to show the world that Chileans
supported his continued leadership, Pinochet appeared on broadcast
media and announced a plebiscite.[124]

Stage Four: Ripples and Awakenings

In the undercurrents beneath the radar, through the careful work of committed advocates and journalists, critical information seeped through the
walls of censorship and media control. They quietly circumvented censors
by distributing "resistance" publications and underground documentaries
through their own networks—churches, community groups and labor
union centers. They launched community radio programs and built a
movement with alternative information, frames, humor, and socially con-

scious music. Carefully, these journalists and advocates disseminated forbidden information; helped find missing loved ones; addressed broad issues of hunger, disease, injustice, and exploitation; reaffirmed community-oriented values; and generated a sense of cohesion.[125]

Exiled journalists daily broadcast uncensored radio programs from abroad—through Moscow, Prague, Berlin, and Havana—on shortwave radio, alerting Chileans of dissenters' views and activities.[126] "We worked fourteen hours a day, maintaining contact with Chile, checking on the fate of prisoners, building links with human rights groups, denouncing the crimes of the junta and reflecting on our past mistakes," said Ricardo Núñez about their broadcasts.[127]

Internally, defiant journalists used indirect communication to bypass government censors. Humor, code, suggestive remarks, music, speeches, and interviewees might broach forbidden words and subjects that journalists themselves could not utter.[128] Radio Balmaceda was particularly defiant. To ridicule government-sponsored news, broadcaster Ignacio Gonzalez Camus reported irrelevant news items, such as the price of peanuts in Mexico and the Pittsburgh Pirates' latest wins, alongside the required government's press releases. Using code, the station also slipped in coverage about disappearances and played forbidden political music. But they paid a price. Censors eventually came to understand the "code" in their absurdist news. They ordered its termination, threatened journalists, deported the director, and finally shut the station down permanently in 1977.[129]

The junta permitted the intellectual magazine *Apsi* to publish, as long as it refrained from covering Chilean politics.[130] To pass through censors, *Apsi*'s editorial team published analysis and reports about "parallel" developments as a means of dropping hints to their readers about what could happen in Chile. "[Our audience] could read between the lines to see what we were saying about Chile" by coverage about other "movements to democracy," said *Apsi* cofounder Dinges.[131]

Occasionally, during the course of mandated reporting, slivers of truth slipped into the public sphere. In 1975, as required, reporter Patricia Politzer covered the annual September 11 celebration on live television. Attendees invariably declared their gratitude to the junta for liberating Chile—except for one man who was just "walking around," he said. "I have no reason to go to this meeting of assassins of who knows what." Because it was live television, Politzer could not edit his remarks before they were broadcast throughout Chile.[132]

Chilean families of the disappeared organized public protests, demanding information about their loved ones. Hundreds of bereaved family members filled the Supreme Court chambers with a mass petition, and hunger strikers occupied the Economic Commission for Latin America (CEPAL) offices, churches, and the International Red Cross, spawning breakaway coverage both domestically and abroad.[133] While sympathetic publications such as *Solidaridad*, Chile's Vicaria publication, gave the families front-page coverage, even the conservative *Que Pasa* reported on the hunger strikers.[134]

Another wave of negative publicity plagued Pinochet when a US grand jury indicted three Chilean officers for conspiracy to murder Letelier. Chile's subsequent arrest of the officers and extradition standoff with the United States unfolded in the pages of Chilean press, including *Que Pasa*, *La Segunda*, and *Ercilla*.[135] Even with the coverage, most Chileans saw no connection to Pinochet.[136]

In acts of defiance, journalists gradually founded new outlets. Emilio Filippi, former editor of *Ercilla*, launched *Hoy* magazine to reveal "truth without compromises."[137] With its investigative research and analysis, *Hoy* frequently embarrassed Pinochet and fast became the leading magazine.[138] From the ranks of frustrated television reporters, Radio Cooperativa launched a news program offering political information, interviews, and upcoming demonstration plans. By interviewing dissenters, journalists broadcast forbidden words and subjects without ever uttering them.[139]

Both Radio Cooperativa and *Hoy* faced crackdowns and suspension. Cooperativa lost its press privileges and seven of its affiliates, but it formed coalitions with other stations, workers, students, and *pobladores* ("residents").[140] With "no money [and] no ads," Cooperativa grew to have the "largest listening audience in Chile."[141]

After *Hoy* argued for the return of democracy and interviewed a socialist, the military suspended the publication.[142] *Hoy* fought the suspension in court and received broad support from the community. With growing political opposition, dissenters—including former president Frei—publicly lashed out at the government's oppression. *Hoy*'s suspension, said Frei, "was to silence an organ of expression that was both independent and objective." Even *El Mercurio* came to *Hoy*'s defense.[143] Two months after the shutdown, *Hoy* appeared back on newsstands with pages full of multinational advertisers.[144]

Artists and cultural groups used theater, paintings, and music to express their discontent. Their growing reach led Chile's secret police to argue against direct closure of dissenting media and artistic organizations. Instead, police called on the interior minister to use "indirect pressure" against them, and to persuade media to ignore and denounce them and support countermessage cultural groups that espoused "traditional values."[145] The struggle for the truth in Chile continued, but perhaps Pinochet's most formidable opponent came from the Catholic Church.

The Catholic Church

"You can't stop the Vicaria," said Cardinal Silva directly to Pinochet, referring to the Church's human rights organization. "And if you try, I'll put all the refugees under my bed, if that's necessary."[146]

Silva and other Catholic Church leaders were unwavering in their work to restore human rights protections in Chile. Junta officials had already imprisoned scores of clergy. They reportedly tortured one church worker and shot a priest then chopped his hands off.[147]

Silva personally confronted Pinochet about the "defense of human rights" and delivered the Chilean bishops' declaration in opposition of the junta's "climate of insecurity and fear." He and other Catholic leaders built a movement through Church radio stations, publications, and direct actions.[148] Seeking to be the "voice of the voiceless," they vowed to counter the "oppressive system that affects the whole of Chilean society . . . systematically destroying consciousness, terrorizing, exploiting, isolating, and repressing."[149]

While Church broadcasters personally obeyed the junta's censorship laws forbidding particular words and subjects like torture, disappearances, and rampant poverty, they aired others' speeches, sermons, and forums that broached both. Church radio stations broadcast human rights leaders, Brazilian bishop Dom Helder Camera, international fact-finding commissions, and the hunger-striking Families of the Disappeared.[150] With a growing audience, pockets of Chileans awakened to the plight of their fellow countrymen and countrywomen.[151]

The relatives have a "right to know" what happened to their loved ones, declared Silva over the airwaves.[152] He led the painstaking process of documenting disappearances, abuses, and extra legal activities; distributed the report; and submitted it to Chile's Supreme Court.[153] Prompted by a secret confession, Silva led a team of human rights lawyers and journalists to find missing persons and ultimately peeled back another layer of the government's cover. In the mining community of Lonquen, the ad hoc investigation found the human remains of twenty-five or more missing persons stuffed and sealed inside a mining oven.[154]

Four radio stations and Catholic University's television broke the silence, broadcasting the findings in a series of reports. *Hoy* and *Solidaridad* published details of the discovery in print. And once the courts released a damning report connecting the atrocities to Chile's national police, even the pro-state media covered the findings.[155]

Chileans in the region were astounded. More than fifteen hundred trekked to Lonquen and built shrines of candles and flowers to honor the dead, gradually increasing awareness in the country's mass consciousness, but not quickly enough to counter Pinochet's next move: to institutionalize his reign through the plebiscite and a new constitutional charter.[156] Already, in January 1978, 75 percent of Chileans had voted in favor of the statement, "Before the international aggression unleashed against the government of our country, I back President Pinochet in his defense of the dignity of Chile, and I reaffirm the legitimacy of the government of the republic to sovereignly lead the process of institutionalization of the country."[157] Gallup polls suggested that 65 percent of Chileans supported Pinochet's government.[158] But now Pinochet planned to demonstrate his legitimacy through a vote on his new charter.

Stage Five: The Fight for Restoration

Posters, fliers, and a flurry of media flooded the Chilean public sphere, supporting Pinochet's proposed constitutional order. Pinochet's new charter, the campaign claimed, would maintain tranquility and order and prevent the "return of the Communists . . . who took us to the edge of civil war, sowing hate."[159] Ads supporting Pinochet filled radio, television, newspapers, and electrified signs, urging voters to vote "*Sí* for the Freedom Constitution." But opposing parties, banned by the junta and prohibited from appearing on television, relied on meager alternative media, such as leaflets and public forums, which were frequently broken up by police.[160]

Pinochet's media management worked. With an absence of opposing views in mass media and a strategically set election day of September 11, voters affirmed the new charter.[161] "Look, Pinochet's no saint, but he's the best thing for this country now, and the people know it," said one highway contractor to an Associated Press reporter.[162] Pinochet's power was "legitimized." But legitimacy would only go so far in the face of the country's growing woes.

SLOW TURNING

Chile was beset with trouble, giving rise to a growing discontent. Economic hardships plagued the country with skyrocketing inflation and unemployment.[163] Disputes arose among high-level Pinochet officials. Students and dissidents rose in demonstration against the government, and Pinochet's control of media was slipping.[164]

In 1983 the twenty-one-thousand-member Copper Workers Federation began organizing for the first day of national protest that would recur every month.[165] Organizers distributed instructions for the mass demonstration through media such as *Hoy*, and through labor unions, educational institutions, human rights organizations, and political groups. When the moment arrived, masses of Chileans across social classes throughout both urban and rural communities simultaneously honked horns, banged pots, chanted, sang songs, and created human barricades in the streets.[166] Awareness was growing, and the tide was slowly turning. Each month, en masse, Chileans filled the streets, demonstrating against the military regime, and they faced arbitrary beatings and shootings. To turn up the heat, the unions, for the first time in ten years, called a general strike; but most media, fearing shutdowns, refrained from reporting them—except for the Catholic radio station that regularly defied the Pinochet government.[167]

Progovernment media was divided in its coverage. *El Mercurio* called the demonstrators "delinquents and extremists" but warned the government that it faced a "most serious challenge."[168] The conservative *Que Pasa*, however, argued that the government had alienated many Chileans.[169]

"[We are again facing] a problem of international character, guided and led by Russia," Pinochet said on national television. It was justification for his resurgence of attacks—including arrests, house raids, beatings, death threats, and shootings—and for heightened prohibitions on media. Media were forbidden from interviewing organizers or miners and from using the phrase "national protest."[170] Instead, journalists were required to use the terms *"disorders, disturbances,* or *incidents"* to describe the mass protests.[171]

Desperate parents took drastic action in efforts to save their arrested children before they could be tortured or killed. Sebastian Acevedo was among them. He doused himself with kerosene and threatened to publicly immolate himself if his children were not returned. As he set himself ablaze, the government finally released his daughter. She reached him by telephone just before he died.[172]

Acevedo's dramatic suicide was "too spectacular to suffocate," making the front page of both *Hoy* and *La Tercera. El Sur* and *Cronica* ran testimonials, while Radio Cooperativa discussed the event as part of a broader discourse about government torture. With the broad response to Acevedo's plight, even *El Mercurio* and *Que Pasa* could not avoid coverage.[173]

As documentation of torture emerged from investigative commissions, two priests, inspired by the Academy Award–winning film *Gandhi,* formed the Anti-Torture Movement. Dozens followed them to a secret National Center of Information (CNI) jail in downtown Santiago and the Supreme Court, where they distributed leaflets about the continued use of torture while unfurling banners: "Here People Are Tortured" and "People Are Tortured in Chile and Justice Is Silent," respectively.[174]

Thousands of Chileans appeared in strategic locations, communicating through compelling imagery and poignant attire, such as the group of women wearing black mourning dresses and gags over their mouths. Human rights groups gave advance notice to sympathetic journalists, who gradually stopped using code and instead directly referred to torture and disappearances. Even *El Mercurio* reported on these issues.[175]

The military used violence to silence demonstrators: In one incident, they bludgeoned Carmen Gloria Quintana and Rodrigo Rojas, soaked them with gasoline, lit them on fire, and dumped them into a ditch to die. Quintana survived only to find that most national media blamed her and her fellow demonstrators, calling them violent criminals and terrorists.[176] But outside of the mainstream media, a different picture was emerging.

"[Please see me not] as a symbol of the repression" but as a symbol "for young people . . . to move forward," said Quintana to the live radio audience of the Methodist Church's Radio Umbral. She was one of many "terrorists" and "criminals" to whom Radio Umbral offered voice during the 1980s. Their broadcasters scooped mainstream news through their community connections and smuggled recording equipment into women's prisons to broadcast prison conditions and prisoners' coping means: For example, incarcerated women donated clothing and toiletries to incoming prisoners, particularly on visitation days, "to let [their children] know [they] were OK." The in-prison broadcasts continued secretly for two years, until the government finally discovered the equipment.[177]

Radio Umbral also aired forbidden political music, such as "Todo Cambia" ("Everything Changes"), unleashing intense emotions in listeners who called radio hotlines crying and thanking radio staff. The "New Songs" broadcasts developed into large concerts that supplemented radio funds to maintain their programs. The station finally shut its doors in 1993 when the Methodist Church stopped its subsidization.[178]

After near silencing, Radio Cooperativa emerged as one of the most important media with the largest radio audience and a 41 percent top credibility share.[179] Their daily news program aided the movement by alerting listeners to upcoming demonstrations and other key information.

Magazines grew even bolder. *Cauce* decided to "shatter the news frame altogether," to name names, and to show its news as "irrefutable." *Cauce* reporters exposed Pinochet's opulence and corruption and challenged the official narrative. Through its strict, independent standards, the magazine won wide respect and prompted other publications to open investigations.[180]

Cauce's first volume, published November 1983, declared the "year of protest." Reporters interviewed disgruntled military officers and soldiers who disavowed Pinochet's "power by force." Its choice of cover imagery also spoke volumes. One cover featured Pinochet before the national seal and motto, "By Reason or by Force," but because his chair blocked the middle words, the cover read, "By . . . Force." After Pinochet's government attacked journalists and again prohibited coverage of either protests or the regime's opponents, *Cauce* resorted to sarcasm, placing a "giant blank" on its cover. Censorship was now the cover story.[181]

Like *Cauce*, *Analisis* broke numerous rules, featuring Quintana's story, in which she recounted her experience of being burned alive. "I sincerely pleaded with the [policeman] . . . to put a bullet in me to end the suffering," she said. "I realized that the dictatorship had filled the soldiers' heads with the idea that the people who struggle for freedom are their enemies."[182] In September 1983, *Analisis* printed the "irrevocable objective" of the Chilean people—"putting an end to the current regime." The military, according to the article, was "one of the few in the world that can claim many more victims among its own people than among its enemies on the battlefield." The cover featured the country's last democratically elected president—Allende.[183] The new boldness came at a cost. The military government arrested and jailed editor Juan Pablo Cardenas for criticizing the military.[184] It would be the first of several incarcerations. Cardenas faced jail again when he published an opinion poll that suggested 80 percent of Chileans wanted Pinochet to step down.[185] Officials also dragged *Analisis*'s international editor, Jose Carrasco, from his house and shot him thirteen times.[186]

The illusions were gradually melting away, and the regime resorted to renewed ferocity, raids, gunfire, and mass roundups. The war for the soul and the truth of Chile was alive—in the streets and in the media.[187] Alongside protesting military abuses, priests, nuns, and other Chileans demonstrated against *El Mercurio* for "complicity" through hiding the truth about secret jails and torture.[188]

Pinochet reinstated a state of emergency along with harsh restrictions, particularly on the investigative press, such as *Hoy, Cauce, Analisis*, and *Apsi*.[189] But rather than quietly complying, two hundred journalists staged a demonstration, twenty of whom went on hunger strike.[190] Times had changed: No longer did community members quietly accede. Not even the military supported the ongoing brutality, as evidenced when Pinochet's agents executed three Communist leaders. A "changed nation" revolted—with a public outcry far exceeding the one that took place after the disappearance of the entire Communist Party Central Committee a decade earlier.[191]

Encouraged by the growing dissent, journalists grew bolder, challenging the official story. *Apsi* serialized the Dinges and Saul Landau–authored book, *Assassinations on Embassy Row*, detailing the plot to assassinate Letelier.[192] On May 1, 1984, the Catholic Church's Radio

Chilena broadcast the entire speech of union leader Rodolfo Seguel, which described Pinochet's financial scandals at great length.[193]

To promote pluralism and greater expression, former congressman Jorge Lavandero launched another newspaper, *Fortin Mapocho*. The paper regularly exposed police abuses and corruption, and juxtaposed the living conditions of Chile's poor with Pinochet's lucrative land deals and luxurious mansion.[194] Just after he published the latter story, twelve men beat Lavandero until he was unconscious. It was one of twenty attempts on his life.[195] But as another sign of changing times, the beating became a story itself. *Cauce*'s cover featured photographs of the brutalized Lavandero lying on a stretcher, the details of the bludgeoning reported within.[196]

In 1987, *Apsi* published a THOUSAND FACES OF PINOCHET humor issue, satirizing the president through cartoons, stories, and photos in which Pinochet appeared as a vampire, a mummy, and a new Louis XIV. That same year, *Hoy*'s director, Emilio Filippi, attempted to launch a newspaper, *La Epoca*, which the Pinochet regime attempted to quash before it surfaced. But the courts sided with *La Epoca*, allowing it to commence publishing.[197] The paper offered counternarratives to official stories and reported the pope's remark about the Catholic Church's moral obligations to promote liberty in Chile. The next year, the paper published a serial exposé on the military rule's "hidden history."[198]

With new media voices, *El Mercurio*'s readership plummeted, tumbling to 13.1 percent and 33.5 percent of the upper strata, with the gain captured by *La Epoca* and *Fortin Mapocho*.[199] In an effort to regain readership, *El Mercurio* even published interviews with Pinochet's "enemies."[200]

To mobilize toward democracy, activists and journalists also established more than two dozen community radio stations, such as Radio Villa Francia, and set up media associations, including the National Organization of Popular Radio Stations.[201] Their boldness was met with more oppression. The regime arrested and indicted several journalists. A bomb blew up the offices of *Fortin Mapocho*, and mysterious threats arrived at radio stations.[202] The movement was still growing through radio and print, while television was still tightly controlled—but not for much longer.

The Pope

In anticipation of Pope John Paul II's 1987 arrival, Pinochet's regime attempted to placate Chileans with television spots, featuring a benevolent Pinochet signing peace documents and happy, "open-to-the-world" Chileans welcoming "visitors." The smoothing and soothing were temporary, as the pope's visit deepened the fissures in the regime's veneer even before his arrival, particularly when he publicly called Pinochet "a dictator."[203]

As television cameras followed his twenty-four public events, Pope John Paul II publicly acknowledged Chile's painful past. He embraced a badly scarred Carmen Gloria Quintana—twice—acknowledged her pain from being burned alive and publicly blessed her.[204] On live camera, the pope listened to excruciating details of Chileans' experiences, living conditions, and pleas. "[Please persuade the government] to stop killing us," implored Mario Mejias in one encounter. All we want is a "decent life for all without dictatorship," added Luisa Riveros. It was the first time such stories aired on national television. But again, the truth came with a price. Two months later, a bomb was detonated in a Catholic radio station, and abductors pummeled Mejias until he was unconscious.[205]

In efforts to obscure the glimpses of truth and restore the regime's image, the government saturated national television with promotional programs and advertisements. "Fourteen years ago . . . another Chile was born . . . from a labor, with tearing and suffering, with amazement and hope," announced narrators. "Today it serves not at all to relive those wounds, if not to remember that from them was born the new country—this country."[206] Perhaps it was too late. Chileans were ready for change, and democracy advocates were working tirelessly for the regime's ouster at the next plebiscite.[207]

THE TURNING POINT

For one month leading up to the 1988 plebiscite, the Pinochet regime allowed for a single daily, thirty-minute television slot of debate at 11:15 p.m., in which each side was permitted fifteen minutes to argue its positions.[208] In its fifteen minutes, the "No" campaign's creativity nourished a hungry Chilean public who, after being "force-fed nothing but official television for fifteen years," stayed awake late to see the broadcasts.[209] With humor and hope, the "No" campaign's argument was simple: "Without hatred, without fear, vote no."[210]

The long-closed television airwaves were cracking open. In 1988, each of three television stations, University of Chile Television, Catholic University Television, and Catholic University of Valparaiso Television, began airing new political discussion programs, opening up the airwaves just enough to allow a hint of dissent. Chileans tuned in to watch *Opinion Currents*, *Facing the Nation*, and *Right to Answers*.[211] That allowed for the turning point: On the first political television program since 1973, *de Cara al Pais* ("Facing the Nation"), Richard Lagos, representative for the Party for Democracy, faced Pinochet and pointed his index finger directly at him.[212]

Lagos admonished Pinochet for running again after promising in 1980 "not to run in 1989." "And now you promise the country eight more years—with torture, assassinations, and violations of human rights. To me, it seems incomprehensible that a Chilean would be so power-hungry as to presume to hold on to it for twenty-five years." It was live television, fully accompanied by a video clip of Pinochet making the 1980 promise and charts demonstrating a decreased quality of life for most Chileans.[213]

When the show's moderator attempted to redirect the forum, Lagos refused to relent. "You will excuse me. I speak after fifteen years of silence, and I believe it is essential that the country know it is at a cross-road. . . . Chile has never been like nowadays, and you [Pinochet] will have to respond. Our best chance to move forward is through the victory of the 'no.'"[214]

Lagos became an instant national leader.[215] And the day of reckoning arrived. On October 5, 1988, Chileans cast their votes again, but this time they were armed with better information and an unrigged election. The majority (54.7 percent) affirmed their desire for change.[216]

After seventeen years of hard-fisted dictatorship, democracy was on its way back in. Although Chile never returned to the pluralistic state that it once was, an elected civilian president and parliament eventually replaced the military dictatorship—a profound change.

Pinochet continued to serve in high roles, first as continuing commander in chief of the armed forces and then as senator for life—until 2004, when a Chilean judge issued a warrant for his arrest. Pinochet was eventually charged with approximately three hundred criminal counts, including human rights violations, tax evasion, and embezzlement. He died two years later. Agustin Edwards Eastman and *El Mercurio*, along with the rest of his media conglomerate, supported Pinochet until his death.[217]

THE CHILEAN STORY OF MEDIA AND DEMOCRACY

For 130 years, Chile's democracy stood: solid, unassailable, supported by institutions, leaders, media, and political culture. But even with strong roots and sound establishment, the democracy and culture could not withstand the overt distortions, lies, omissions, and direct meddling of the mass media, their owners, and the collaborators that worked to topple Chilean democracy and replace it with a violent, homicidal, totalitarian rule. Led by media owner Edwards, US president Nixon, and the CIA, Chile's mainstream media used psychological warfare to create the enemy within.[218]

Because most of what the public read and heard was shocking stories of "Marxist terror," while the truths of torture and mass killing were largely hidden, a hegemonic discourse of procoup propaganda emerged. Many Chileans believed the stories and voted their support time and again in polls and plebiscites for continuation of the dictatorship. Some who heard about the torture and killing still never believed it.

Despite the country's genteel culture and Chileans' record of expressing respect for one another, in a matter of a few years some citizens grew to support the torture and detention, based on mass media's argument that the "Russian rotos [rabble]" were trying to "take over." The "Communists," said one woman, "deserve to die."[219]

Chile could have been a model of plural, active participation and experimentation. But Edwards, his fellow media professionals, and the Nixon administration built a campaign to convince the military and Chilean masses that they were better off trading democracy for a military dictatorship. The return to democracy took a decade and a half of arduous, life-risking work, through international media and institutions and within Chile's alternative media. It was a slow construction. Although the movement restored Chile's democracy, in reality, Chile has never fully recovered. Its diverse politics has never fully returned, and its media today has largely been consolidated under large businesses, which regularly black out damaging information and contain little investigative journalism, dissenting opinions, or deep analysis.[220]

Chapter 8

Death of the Perfect Dictatorship: Media, Democracy, and Regime Change in Mexico

Rosario Ibarra de Piedra had no chance in the 1982 presidential race, but neither did the five other non-PRI candidates running for president in Mexico. The longtime human rights activist founded the Eureka Committee of the Disappeared and successfully campaigned for the release of 148 of 557 political prisoners.[1] But as an outsider to the one-party rule, she received no media coverage and no substantive political support, and she could not rise beyond a few percentage points of the electorate's votes. Neither could the other candidates, as the system was, in essence, rigged for the world's longest-reigning authoritarian regime—the Institutional Revolutionary Party (PRI). Since 1929, through "corporatist co-optation, electoral 'alchemy' (fraud) and selective repression," the party ruled over Mexico—for more than seven decades. At the end of each term, the outgoing president chose his successor. Then Mexico staged an "election." The PRI held the presidency and all thirty-one governorships, and it controlled the national congress.[2]

Ibarra was an accidental candidate. Years earlier, she moved to Mexico City in a quest to find her disappeared twenty-one-year-old son, Jesús Piedra, who, as a medical student, had joined the guerilla group known as The 23rd of September. Ibarra tirelessly traveled from prison to prison and from government agency to government agency, knocking on doors. She never found her son, but she did find that she wasn't alone: Hundreds of other women were also looking desperately for their own children, brothers, and husbands.[3]

Ibarra's search became a lifelong fight for human rights alongside other mothers whose children had been imprisoned, exiled, or disappeared, usually for their politics. She faced government harassment, and her husband was tortured. But Ibarra continued to carry the human-rights torch. After multiple demonstrations, hunger strikes, and speeches calling for political amnesty throughout Mexico, the United States, Canada, and Europe, President José López Portillo decreed a general amnesty law in 1978. Shortly after, Ibarra formed the National Front Against Repression and became a national figure. Through the process, though, something else was becoming evident to Ibarra: Mexican democracy was a sham.[4]

"Whoever thinks there is democracy in Mexico [does not know the truth]," she said. "I must speak that truth."[5]

A few years later, in 1982, the Revolutionary Workers Party (PRT) nominated her as its presidential candidate, a position for which she would receive forty anonymous death threats. It was the first time a woman had ever run for president in Mexico, but it wasn't the last: In 1988, at seventy-two years of age, Ibarra ran again. By then, she had been elected federal deputy for the PRT and twice had been nominated for the Nobel Peace Prize.[6]

That year, 1988, was a remarkable one in Mexico's electoral politics. After years in the PRI, Cuahtémoc Cárdenas ran against the party's chosen heir to president. But gunmen shot dead his chief strategist, Francisco Xavier Ovando Hernández, and his assistant as they were leaving Cárdenas's campaign office. Despite the double murder and emerging evidence of a vast electoral corruption scheme, voters still overwhelmingly supported the PRI—at least according to the official tally.[7] Deeply suspicious, both Cárdenas and Ibarra assailed widespread voter irregularities during the election.[8]

"The anticipated announcement of a supposed victory of the official party . . . long before the counting process was completed reaffirms our suspicions that a fraud of great proportions is being conjured," said Ibarra. Behind the irregularities, however, a truth was revealed: The PRI's support was slipping. It was the first time in the PRI's history that it received less than 70 percent of the vote. The political winds were changing.[9]

Over time, challenging parties toppled PRI incumbents in some mayoral and gubernatorial seats. By 1997, the PRI lost control of the Chamber of Deputies. And the big blow arrived in 2000: For the first time in seventy-one years, a non-PRI candidate, Vicente Fox of the National Action Party (PAN), won the presidency. The upset victory was hardly fathomable either within Mexico or among international communities. For most Mexicans, the PRI was the only system they had ever known.[10]

Three years after the monumental election, Mexico's Supreme Court ruled that the "dirty war" perpetrators behind the disappearances of the 1960s and 1970s, of whom Ibarra's son was a victim, could face prosecution. The accused included two top police officers and the official implicated in Piedra's disappearance. Newly uncovered documents finally revealed Piedra's fate: He had been tied up, shoved into a car, interrogated in a Mexico City military camp, and never seen again.[11]

Although Mexico was still riddled with problems and irregularities, a growing civic society and democracy was struggling to take root. Non-PRI candidates gained power, including Ibarra, who, in 2006, won a seat in the Mexican Senate through proportional representation. After so many decades of single-party control over government and elections, what changed? Multiple events rocked Mexico's political terrain.[12] Each event shored up a new kind of journalism—one that shed its allegiance to the PRI patronage and increasingly served the public. As a new civic journalism materialized, many among the public grew more informed and dissatisfied with the PRI's "perfect dictatorship."[13]

EARLY MEDIA UNDER THE PRI

Mexico was "a nation of secrets. Lies trumped facts, propaganda masqueraded as news, and government officials were accountable to no one."[14] The PRI's tentacles reached into most mass media through lucrative business deals that ensured its positive image and political dominance. Because the PRI allowed for some seemingly oppositional material—other ideological perspectives and some criticism—Mexico appeared to have a free press and free elections. But that kind of coverage was precisely what made it the "perfect dictatorship." By creating an illusion of free media and fair elections, the Mexican electorate remained largely unaware. But beneath the veneer, reality was that the PRI government prohibited media from covering particular topics, such as government corruption, fraud, or any serious challenge to the system.

And media were implicitly forbidden from giving voice to people like Ibarra. They were off-limits.[15]

Through a system of privileges, subsidies, concessions, and bribes, the PRI "captured" most mass media. By taking part in self-censorship and selective reporting, and by framing Mexican politics in ways that benefited the PRI, journalists reinforced the system. As "defenders of the government and right-wing business interests," they ignored government abuses and treated the PRI with great deference, particularly during election season.[16]

Since the 1950s, television had been Mexico's primary news source. Televisa, the dominant television network, commanded some 90 percent of audiences. But Televisa, though privately owned, largely acted as a publicity arm of the state and the PRI. Broadcasters read official press releases verbatim and ignored vital issues such as unrest, poverty, unemployment, disasters, bad economies, and election irregularities. Press conferences were largely scripted, with planted questions assigned to particular journalists. It was a failure of both words and silence.[17]

A minority of Mexicans tuned into radio, and another small percentage read newspapers for political information. But newspapers were, for years, an underdeveloped news source.[18] Universally, the mass media was failing their audiences, which led some young idealists to take communication matters into their own hands.

Massacre

It was the summer of 1968, and Mexico's students were brimming with idealism and hope. Together, they would stand for democracy, greater university autonomy, and the release of political prisoners. Knowing that "the newspapers wouldn't publish anything," they boarded buses to give speeches, gathered en masse at their schools in rallies and demonstrations, placed ads in newspapers, and distributed leaflets.[19]

In July, a scuffle between two high schoolers triggered a fight between students at two different schools. Truncheon-swinging grenadiers arrived to break up the fight. But after the students fled, the grenadiers didn't stop. Instead, they ran after the fleeing students, and bludgeoned the youth indiscriminately—even those who had not been involved. Students added police brutality to their list of grievances.[20]

Instead of considering their grievances, the Mexican government summoned the army to break up demonstrations. Using tear gas and guns, troops forcibly seized National University and the National Polytechnic Institute. At one school, soldiers fired a bazooka into a building. The use of force served to strengthen the movement.

In an effort to dispute the government's accusations against the movement, Professor Herbert Castillo appeared on television, asserting, "The student movement has no intentions of subverting the institutional order. The student leaders are prepared to initiate a dialogue with the highest authorities." Two days later, newspapers published ads attacking the students and warned readers about Soviets crushing the "Prague Spring."[21]

August 27 marked "the highest moment" of the movement, according to one former student, Marta Acevedo. It was the first time in Mexico's history that such vast numbers of people rose to challenge the president's authority. Amid music, dancing, and burning tires, students demanded release of their colleagues from prison and answers from the president.[22]

Armed soldiers surrounded the demonstrating youth. "You have been allowed to make your demonstration; now you have to leave," ordered the soldiers. Naïvely, the students held their ground, refusing to budge. Soldiers mounted bayonets on their rifles and moved toward the crowd of youth.[23]

THEY WERE EVICTED, said the headline in *El Universal*.[24]

Increasingly, students filled the jails, and with soldiers and army vehicles on guard throughout the public areas, the city resembled an occupied state. Still, the students believed that with unity they could break through.

On October 2, roughly ten thousand students gathered in Mexico City's famous Tlatelolco Plaza, the site of the Aztec Indians' last stand against Spanish soldiers. Restless youth played loud rock music, cheered rally leaders, and called for better housing, education, and food—and the resignation of President Díaz Ordaz.

Overhead, trouble was brewing. A helicopter dropped two flares into the crowd—one green, one red—while gunmen in helicopters and on rooftops opened fire on demonstrators. For a full sixty-two minutes, troops and tanks surrounded the plaza from all sides and barraged the crowd with gunfire. There was no escape. A total of fifteen thousand rounds flew, killing dozens and injuring hundreds. Among the injured were foreign journalists who had come to cover the Olympics. Troops stabbed a French journalist twice with a bayonet to teach him "order."[25] Italian journalist Oriana Fallaci took three bullets—in her thigh, knee, and back. "I have covered the Viet Nam war, but I have never seen anything similar to what happened last night," she remarked.[26]

Many newspapers worked directly with the president to cover up the day's events. Police ransacked the offices of a magazine that had published photos from the event.[27] Two things became clear for the students and their communities: the government was untrustworthy and unreasonable, and the Mexican press was not on their side. "*Prensa Vendida!*" they cried out at the press, "Sellout Press!"[28]

Slow Turning

In 1971, police vehicles arrived to break up another demonstration with "Falcons," government-sponsored ruffians. This time, however, newspapers reported the bludgeoning of demonstrators, marking the beginning of the press's awakening. The press also began exploring Mexico's previously hidden, dark underbelly of inequities and injustices, publishing articles about the plight of landless peasants, oppressed workers, government corruption, and fraud. At the lead of this new brand of journalism was Julio Scherer Garcia, editor of the cooperatively owned and managed newspaper, *Excelsior*.[29]

Scherer's willingness to expose the ugly realities in Mexico landed him into trouble with the PRI. In July 1976, the displeased PRI government unleashed its fury at him and began to organize his ouster. Using threats, bribes, and a discrediting campaign funneled through an internal "rebellious right-wing group" in *Excelsior*, it conjured and encouraged anti-Scherer sentiments and charged him with embezzlement. Mainstream media denounced Scherer as "unpatriotic," and PRI leader Humberto Serrano led roughly three hundred squatters onto *Excelsior* property. The large crowd settled in and refused to leave unless *Excelsior* agreed to change its political coverage. The fifty internal *Excelsior* rebels called for Scherer's ejection, referring to him and his support staff as "aristocrats" and "pseudo-intellectuals." They barged into the paper's print shop to prevent *Excelsior* from publishing an ad that was signed by forty-nine intellectuals supporting Scherer. Rather than face "armed thugs," Scherer walked out.[30]

Under the new, progovernment editor, *Excelsior*'s content changed. Like the bulk of Mexico's mass media, the paper avoided controversial topics that might embarrass the government and offered the PRI its unfettered support.[31] Frustrated with the censorship, roughly two hundred staff revolted and collectively resigned. Among them was celebrated Octavio Paz, editor of *Excelsior*'s literary monthly, *Plural*.[32]

Because most newspapers were either owned or sustained by government subsidies and advertisements, it was difficult to shun the government's demands. But Scherer, in his dedication to independent journalism, launched a new weekly magazine, *Proceso*, in which he continued revealing never-before-published information, including details of his ouster. *Proceso* soon became the most popular weekly publication in Mexico.[33]

"This publication appears amid distressing difficulties and in the heat of the battle for freedom of expression, a perennial battle between a press that aspires to be responsible and an authority that does not feel constricted by the law," wrote the editorial team in *Proceso*'s first issue. "*Proceso* is an act of confidence in the ability of our society to mature as a nation. Besieged by evidence to the contrary, the worst that Mexicans can do now is despair of the democratic possibilities of overcoming the present crisis."[34]

The PRI's battle with Scherer and its subsequent takeover of *Excelsior* fueled important changes in Mexican journalism. For one, the exodus of journalists from *Excelsior* resulted in a host of new publications, each one carrying some of *Excelsior*'s spirit. Among the new publications founded by former *Excelsior* staff were *Reforma*, *Vuelta*, and *Nexos*, which spawned another cooperatively operated daily newspaper, *Uno Mas Uno*. Internal rifts between journalists at *Uno Mas Uno* then gave birth to *La Jornada*, which soon became the "voice of Mexico's anti-regime left." A few other journalists carried the *Excelsior* lessons to their new jobs—at existing media outlets, including the government-run Channel 13 and publications such as *El Universal*, *El Diario de Mexico*.[35] The information dam had been breached, and Mexico's journalism would not be the same.

While independent journalism was emerging, other media were being consolidated under powerful operators. The government already owned Channel 13, but now President Echeverría and his colleagues purchased a thirty-seven-newspaper chain headed by *El Sol* and dismissed the top editorial staff. In the private sector, four television channels merged into Televisa SA, asserting that the merger would improve content and coordination.[36]

The Constitutional Right of Information

Public officials, including the then president, Jóse López Portillo, and L. J. Solana, the national coordinator of social communication, acknowledged media's inequalities. It hampered the "common good" that was born from objective information and free expression, said Solana. Information should be treated as a "right."[37]

The "right of information," a phrase from the Mexican Constitutional Reform of 1977, was the new buzz in Congress, too. In reality, such "rights" were still largely rhetorical, with no substantive signs of support for an independent and effective media.[38] In fact, despite the rhetoric, the president was the first to fire on the independent media.

"I won't pay them to beat me up!" declared President López Portillo just before the government ordered a radio magazine off the air and pulled all financial support from the "hostile" publications, *Proceso* and *Critica Politica*, both of which were struggling to survive. In his defense, López Portillo asked, "Do opposition news magazines have a right to receive a specific amount of money from the government?"[39] Although most publications continued to kowtow to the government, *Proceso* reorganized, culled together independent financing, and became a highly influential political journal.[40]

It wasn't a new phenomenon for media to pander to government. For years, government financial aid ensured supportive mass media coverage. By some estimates, 90 percent of Mexican reporters traded positive spin for personal "side" benefits. Some took direct payment from campaign organizers, police, businesspeople, or government officials. Others received commissions when they sold advertisements to the organizations in their "beats."[41]

Real journalism was a risky enterprise. During the early 1980s, roughly twenty-one journalists were killed. Journalist Ivan Menendez Macin was found in the trunk of his Chevrolet Nova, riddled with bullets. But because Menendez rarely challenged power, his slaying was more puzzling than the deaths of more aggressive journalists, like *El Popular*'s publisher Ernesto Flores and columnist Norma Moreno. They had relentlessly pursued and uncovered local corruption and suffered a "gangster-style" double killing. Similarly, *Excelsior* columnist Manuel Buendia regularly exposed the activities of drug traffickers, the Central Intelligence Agency (CIA), and corrupt government officials, which ostensibly made him a target and cost him his life.[42]

Despite the obstacles in independent journalism—the chilling effect from the slayings and lack of funding—a truly independent press was being born. The new civic journalism and a series of events shook up Mexico's establishment journalism, which would eventually shake up Mexico's power structure.

The Shake-Up

Early morning on September 20, 1985, the loud thundering began. Within two minutes of the earthquake, large swaths of Mexico City and three coastal states had crumbled. Amid thick clouds of dust that enveloped the city and with little assistance from an unprepared government, citizens scrambled to find their loved ones buried beneath the rubble.

The key mass media—broadcast television—also failed the citizens: it failed to hold government accountable for the carelessness, incompetence, and corruption that led to shoddy infrastructure; it failed to offer devastated citizens necessary information to help them rebuild their lives; and it failed to reveal the extent of the devastation—until its own tower collapsed and knocked it off the air, jolting them "from their slumber," according to Radio Red anchor José Gutiérrez-Vivó.[43]

With government and the go-to television network failing to provide necessary aid and information, civil society and radio stepped into the void. In the wake of the devastation, thousands of young men and boys pulled victims from the rubble; hundreds of private cars patrolled the city seeking trapped or injured people; and students organized food and water supplies. To fill the information vacuum, new independent radio networks disseminated vital information about relief effort that had been organized by the neighborhoods themselves and painted a more realistic picture of the PRI government and its failings.[44] As a result of the events and new-found access to critical information, Mexicans' displeasure with the government was building. But it wasn't enough to change guards—yet.

The 1988 Breakaway Challenge

Cuauhtémoc Cárdenas, the son of Mexico's most popular president, a former governor and high-ranking PRI official, may have been the candidate who could unseat the powerful PRI in 1988. After breaking with the PRI, the National Democratic Front (FDN) nominated Cárdenas to challenge the "shoo-in" PRI candidate, Carlos Salinas de Gortari.[45]

To many observers, Mexico needed a change in leadership. High inflation, mounting foreign debt, and plummeting real wages crippled the economy and sparked unrest.[46] But until 1988, there had not been a serious challenge to the PRI. Cárdenas's candidacy in particular changed that, but even with credible challengers, the media, particularly Televisa, still focused on and protected the PRI candidate, Salinas, who by some estimates received 80 percent of media coverage.[47] In fact, *La Jornada* stood virtually alone in covering Cárdenas's candidacy.[48] Even with lopsided coverage, however, polls showed Cárdenas slightly ahead of Salinas.[49]

On election day, poll watchers reported massive voting irregularities and foul play: polling places opened late; ballots arrived late; election judges were harassed and beaten; and ballot boxes were stuffed before voting began. The day before the election, gunmen shot to death Cárdenas's chief campaign strategist, Ovando Hernández, and his assistant, Roman Gil Heraldez.

As early results trickled in, Cárdenas was winning by "alarming" proportions. But mysteriously and suddenly, the computer system "crashed."[50] Carlos Salinas de Gortari was declared president.

"A fraud of great proportions [has been perpetrated]," declared three presidential candidates early on July 7. Without legal resolution, the candidates—Cárdenas, Manuel Clouthier, and Ibarra—refused to "accept" or "recognize the authorities that are produced by these fraudulent deeds."[51]

For many Mexican citizens, the computer failure was more than a technical flaw. To them, democracy itself and the Mexican system had crashed.[52] It was yet another incident in a series of developments transforming Mexico's media and, along with them, civil society.[53]

Explosions

For hours the explosions continued, crumbling parts of the ancient Mexican city Guadalajara into rubble. Houses collapsed. Stones, body parts, and chunks of cars flew into the air. The blasts killed more than two hundred people, injured hundreds more, and left thousands homeless.[54] But this time, it wasn't an earthquake. Nor was it the "cooking oil factory" on which the government laid blame. Rather, the explosions resulted from a gas leak in the state's own plant.[55]

Alejandra Xanic of the feisty tabloid *Siglo 21* was there when it happened. Suspicious of the government's claims and denials, she remained on site through the night. Mistaken for a technician sent from the United States, Xanic had great access to workers whom she followed and interviewed about the horrible smell. Her front-page report exposed a cover-up: the government had had advance knowledge that such an explosion could occur. She "woke us up, angered us, and made us ashamed of our so-called leaders," said Jorge Regelado, a Mexican political science professor.[56]

Although after the blast the local *Ocho Columnas* newspaper's headline demanded PUNISHMENT FOR THE GUILTY,[57] *Siglo 21* stood mostly alone in its comprehensive coverage. It connected the causes, contexts, and fallout from the explosions. The fledgling paper, which had faced bankruptcy just a few months before, was now catapulted into the front lines. Its readership soared from four thousand to thirty thousand, and its coverage forced several senior officials to resign. One year later, the paper scooped the other dailies in revealing the assassination of Cardinal Juan Jesús Posadas Ocampo. *Siglo 21* became Guadalajara's third-largest newspaper under a new name, *Publico*.[58]

After learning of the deception and neglect, Guadalajara's citizens expressed their discontent through the ballot box. In the next Guadalajara mayoral election, voters ousted the PRI.[59]

Across Mexico, an independent, civic journalism was being born from the destruction and devastation, and the patronage system was being abandoned. A small crop of journalists were leading the way. The next few years, however, challenged Mexico's journalists like never before. "Chiapas changed everything."[60]

Chiapas

Who are these people? Many had no idea, as they had been hidden from public view and forgotten for decades. They were left poor, landless, locked out of power, long trampled by the government, and ignored by media, other than *Proceso*. But the indigenous people from Chiapas's Lacandon Forest would be silenced no more. In one afternoon, they successfully seized the attention of the nation and world.[61]

At 4:30 a.m. on New Year's Day, 1994, hundreds of masked "Zapatistas," members of the Zapatista National Liberation Army, descended into the cities of Chiapas. They blocked the roads and seized four towns, including the Chiapas capital, San Cristóbal de las Casas. In San Cristóbal, Zapatistas occupied four government buildings, including the mayor's office, and a radio station. They broke into the penitentiary and freed more than one hundred political prisoners, then stood, wearing ski masks and bandanas, before the television cameras. Across Mexico, eyes were upon them, as they explained through their masks.[62]

"We came here because we couldn't take it, see? The army is persecuting us. We came to the war," said the leader into the cameras.[63] "We are the product of five hundred years of victimization. . . . We are dying of hunger and disease. . . . We have nothing, absolutely nothing: not a decent roof, nor land, nor work, nor education. Today, we say: Enough!"[64]

From the depths of the Lacandon Forest came one of the most sophisticated and well-organized communication campaigns ever seen by mass media—certainly the most impressive for one organized by poor, landless peasants. Within an hour of their takeover, the Zapatistas, named for the 1910 Mexican Revolutionary hero Emiliano Zapata, had delivered their messages across the international media via e-mail and fax.[65] "Yes, we are the people who are denied the most elementary education," said the communiqué. "For [the government] it doesn't matter that we possess nothing."[66]

The Zapatistas called for land, education, farm financing, and the release of political prisoners—in essence, the right to live their lives with dignity. Beyond their own struggles, they wanted "democracy, [and] that there not be inequality," and they demanded the "illegitimate" president's resignation.[67]

The uprising was long coming, according to presidential challenger

Cárdenas, who flatly blamed the government for the conditions behind the incursion. "The social, agricultural, and political problems of Chiapas have been ignored by local governments, which have sought to silence the demands through repression, intolerance, [and] violence, and by provoking confrontations . . . with the intent of defending the interests of a small oligarchy," said Cárdenas.[68]

Through their Internet campaign, the Zapatistas were an instant international phenomenon, eliciting worldwide sympathy for their cause. Within hours, the Zapatistas' declaration, translated into several languages, appeared across computer screens, bulletin boards, and conferences. The world press corps experienced the rise of its first Internet-made hero—the charismatic, poetic, masked man who called himself Subcomandante Marcos.[69]

As the government fought to regain control, mass media puzzled over Marcos's identity and reported the clashes and rarely heard information about the indigenous of Chiapas. In Television Azteca's "Good Morning from Mexico," correspondent Samuel Prieto announced his "journey to Ocosingo" in Chiapas, describing the Zapatistas and their conditions: "Roadblocks . . . stale biscuits," and "hardened tortillas." Many of the Zapatista Army of National Liberation (EZLN), he noted, were "very young, even children."[70]

Day after day, more news arose from the developments of the conflict. CHIAPAS GOVERNOR ACKNOWLEDGES CLIMATE OF TENSION, said one *Uno Mas Uno*'s headline in March 1994.[71] Even when broadcasters adopted the official government framing, the plight of the indigenous people was no longer hidden. In one radio broadcast, journalist Juan Carlos Santoya called Zapatistas "law violators" and reported the government's assertion that the rebels were "hiding in houses there and holding its occupants hostage to protect their own lives."[72]

Newspapers such as *La Jornada* and *Proceso* helped keep the Zapatista cause alive. *La Jornada* distributed its statements throughout Mexico. "We are the inheritors and the true builders of our nation," said one declaration. "The dispossessed, we are millions, and we thereby call upon our brothers and sisters to join this struggle as the only path, so that we will not die of hunger due to the insatiable ambition of a seventy-year dictatorship led by a gang of traitors that represents the most reactionary groups. . . . The war that we have declared is our last resort, but also a just one." In another communiqué, the EZLN announced, "Throughout the world, rural and urban workers celebrate their rebellion against exploitation and reaffirm their hope for a more just world."[73]

No journalist was left untouched. Many noted the stark contrast between the Zapatistas and the Mexican government. Zapatistas carefully waged their war to avoid harm to civilians while government forces targeted all in their path, including the journalists in clearly marked press vehicles. In the ten-day battle before the government declared a cease-fire, dozens lay dead and many more injured—among them were journalists, including *La Jornada*'s Ismael Romero, who was shot three times in the shoulder. The Zapatista plight, the obvious power discrepancies, and the deliberate firing on journalists affected reporters and changed their relationship to government.[74]

"Chiapas changed everything," admitted journalist Ismael Garcia, one of many journalists who increasingly sympathized with the guerillas.[75]

The Zapatistas' campaign enlivened Mexico. Throughout the country, tens of thousands gathered in public demonstrations, chanting for "peace yes, war no." In Mexico City, more than one hundred thousand demonstrators gathered, calling for the PRI's ouster.[76] A movement was taking shape.

The Zapatistas' sophisticated communication campaign persuaded even the progovernment Televisa to report the indigenous side of the story. In mid-March, the government attempted to muscle concessions by declaring that they had reached a peace agreement. But through their savvy electronic system, the Zapatistas transmitted a clarification: "There was only dialogue. Do not allow yourself to be taken in by lies. . . . How can there be peace if the causes of the war continue to cry out [*sic*] due to our perpetual misery?"[77]

A NEW KID ON THE BLOCK

For $641 million, Ricardo Salinas Pliego's consortium became the proud owner of the Azteca television network that had been held by the state. The 1993 sale spurred a new air war between Televisa, long the television monopoly, and the now privately held Television Azteca. Azteca's ratings crept up and horned in on Televisa's audience, forcing Televisa to review and change its pro-PRI political news.[78]

Those changes were evident during the 1994 presidential election. Although Televisa still portrayed PRI challengers as bland and boring, both channels balanced the candidates' time allotments. But neither adequately covered the widespread election "irregularities." In fact, the National Chamber of the Radio and Television Industry urged its members to avoid airing matters of fraud or coercion.[79] But after a few more shake-ups, broadcasters, too, became more inquisitive, particularly in the wake of a second high-level PRI official slaying.

On September 28, 1994, PRI secretary-general and former Guerrero governor José Francisco Ruiz Massieu climbed into his car after a breakfast at PRI headquarters. A gunman opened fire, shattering his car windows, and piercing Ruiz's his neck with bullets.[80] Ruiz was the second high-level PRI official killed in three years. The other was PRI presidential candidate Luis Donaldo Colosio, widely expected to be Mexico's next president. As Colosio left a campaign speech near Tijuana, a gunman shot him twice. Colosio died in a Tijuana hospital.[81]

Shortly after Ruiz's death, President Ernesto Zedillo held a press conference in which he uttered the phrase "bad guys." Clearly breaking out of their more compliant roles, journalists barraged him with questions. "Bad guys?" they asked. Who were the killers? Were they inside the PRI? Could this "cabal" really be responsible for the country's problems? Were they really "*malosos*"?[82]

AGUAS BLANCAS MASSACRE

Just outside of Acapulco, twelve police vehicles stopped an eighty-farmer caravan. In the deadliest clash since the Zapatista rising, police killed seventeen peasant farmers and a small girl. What prompted the shooting was unclear, but two newspapers—*La Jornada* and *Reforma*—relentlessly pursued the massacre's underpinnings and sought an explanation. Their extensive investigations revealed unarmed peasants, trigger-happy police who shot victims point-blank, and a deeply dishonest official story. The newspaper coverage planted the seeds for change, but real change came only after someone leaked a video of the bloody incident to Televisa.

Perhaps Televisa would never have aired the leaked videotape had its competitor not arrived on the airwaves. The network had routinely presented a picturesque Mexico and hidden the ugly, contradictory images. But with Azteca next door, Televisa was forced to reconsider its entire approach to the news.[83] And with Mexico's evolving journalism norms, audiences were asking for more—more depth, more honesty, and more inside stories.

Televisa's release of the video triggered a domino effect. Within a year, the governor, Ruben Figueroa Jr., was forced to resign, and two dozen other officials faced prosecution. Within the journalism profession, because the video raised Televisa's ratings, the network and other media professionals pursued additional stories with similar dramatic appeal. Every few months, journalists broke another scandal, exposing official corruption, repression, drug trafficking, fraud, murder, and high-level cover-ups.[84] The new dogged reporting offered Mexico's citizens an inside view of their political system. And increasingly, voters were fed up. That mood accelerated after Televisa's El Tigre died and passed the baton to his son.[85]

DEATH OF THE TIGER

El Tigre was among the richest men in Mexico. Emilio Azcárraga Milmo's Televisa SA was the largest producer of Spanish-language television programming in the world. The $1.45 billion empire held broadcast, publishing, radio, music, cable television, and satellite interests. But the man behind Mexico's largest media conglomerate was dying. When he learned of his cancer, Emilio Azcárraga turned the reigns over to his twenty-nine-year-old son, Azcárraga Jean. On April 16, 1997, after a months-long battle with cancer, Emilio Azcárraga Milmo died on his yacht off the coast of Miami. For Azcárraga Jr., the heir, politics were second to business. In pursuit of higher ratings, PRI-favored coverage fell by the wayside.[86]

"I don't think having a good relationship with political figures is going to benefit us in terms of what matters," said Azcárraga Jr., ending a decades-long unspoken policy of favoritism toward the PRI. "I am a business man. . . . I like to make television. . . . I care about getting the best rating possible. . . . I don't mix my ideology with the screen."[87]

Suddenly, Televisa was no longer PRI's "private ministry of truth" but an emerging channel of information. Along with the rest of the journalistic establishment—print, radio, and television—the mass media began to fully expose the PRI's incessant scandals.

During the next election, in 1997, Televisa and Azteca covered the political candidates equally, framing non-PRI parties as choices that were as legitimate as the PRI candidates. In that election, considered by many to be the fairest and freest in Mexico's history, the PRI lost its majority in the lower house of Congress, and Cárdenas won Mexico City's mayoral race.[88]

In the next presidential election, mass media continued their new trend—offering candidates roughly equal attention and more neutral framing. Voters went to the polls and finally ousted the PRI. In its place, they elected Vicente Fox.[89] The perfect dictatorship was dead. But the battle to tell the truth continues under a different kind of oppression.

Death of the Dictator

For decades the PRI ruled Mexico with impunity. But after years of controlling enough mass media to hide its "perfect dictatorship," the long-powerful PRI faced an independent media corps in Mexico. As independent publications refused to be the PRI's "official scribe," they awakened a growing awareness in Mexico that something was not right. Journalists scrutinized and exposed political scandals and blunders and fed a burgeoning civil society by offering them coverage and legitimacy in their pages. Although their individual reach was small, the collective work of the press cracked open the door that eventually produced "revelations that reverberated throughout the Mexican political system." What began in the press continued among radio journalists, feeding Mexican citizens' growing hunger for fairness and democracy until, finally, television, no longer faithful to the PRI regime, changed its tune.[90] With a series of mishandled crises and disasters in public view, the Mexican voters, particularly the younger, more sophisticated voters, rejected the PRI.

Although for now, Mexico has escaped the grip of the PRI's "perfect dictatorship," Mexico continues to struggle for an authentic democracy.

Its controversial 2006 election declared National Action Party (PAN) candidate Felipe Caldereón Hinojosa as president. But scholars and other candidates, including Andrés Manuel López Obrador of the Democratic Revolution Party (PRD), have asserted numerous election irregularities, which have colored Mexico's political system once more.[91]

Perhaps the worst battle for journalists to date is the unprecedented struggle to report news and information in the face of Mexico's drug wars. Since 2006, some sixty-six journalists have been killed and twelve have disappeared, creating a so-called media blackout on the drug wars, according to the National Human Rights Commissions. (This number climbed in 2011, but it unclear yet by how much.) Because of threats, bribery, and other pressures, many of Mexico's regional newspapers are censoring reports about murders and other drug-related violence. So while cartel gunmen are slaying hundreds of people every month, the media are refraining—many for reasons of personal safety—from covering the developments. Many citizen journalists are turning to blogging and using Twitter to report what Mexico's mainstream media, a key target of the drug lords, have been unable or too afraid to cover.[92]

Chapter 9

Regime Change: Media and Taiwan's Fight for Democracy

For more than two years before that frightening September morning, Lei Chen and his family had lived under government surveillance.[1] Lei, co-founder of *Free China Fortnightly* magazine, was an early advocate for democratizing Taiwan, which had been under martial law and single-party, authoritarian rule since 1949. But after the Kuomintang (KMT) party lost its battle to the Communists on mainland China, the KMT party that controlled Taiwan was deeply suspicious and not ready to share power. To KMT party leaders, Taiwan was the "last bastion" against the Communist forces. They hoped to eventually resume power in mainland China and reunite it with the island to make a "whole" Republic of China (ROC).[2]

Although KMT leaders professed to support democracy, they would permit it only after Taiwan's citizens had sufficiently advanced in their patriotism, respect for democratic institutions, material prosperity, and personal sacrifice for national goals. Until then, the KMT had little tolerance for democracy advocates. That included Lei, an early "troublemaker." Though once a high-ranking KMT member, Lei had become one of the party's chief critics. With his publication, Lei challenged Chiang Kai-shek's third presidential term and advocated for Western-style, pluralistic democracy, honest elections, individual liberties, a market-oriented economy, independent courts, and separation between the military and politics.[3]

"We have tolerated too much for the unity of the war against the Communists," wrote the *Free China Fortnightly* in February 1958. "This in turn has led to an embrace of one-party politics and hampers the path toward progress."[4]

Initially funded by the KMT, the *Free China Fortnightly* broke from the party, challenging the party's history of acting "selfishly, for the sake of its own interests," wrote Lei. Without demanding "conditions of equality . . . there is no hope for democratic government . . . in that case the only recourse is to wait for the next revolution! Let more blood flow!" he wrote.[5]

On September 4, 1960, Lei's family was still asleep. Morning had barely broken when government troops pounded open the door and barged into their home. They arrested Lei on grounds of sedition and participating in a Communist conspiracy.[6] *Communist* was the word officials attached to people they wished to marginalize, demonize, or criminalize.

For his crimes, Lei faced a military court without adequate counsel. Most lawyers, even those supportive of Lei's quest, feared government reprisals and hesitated to defend him. For ten years, Lei languished in prison while his life's work, the magazine of democratic ideas, folded. In prison, Lei continued to write, penning a four-million-word memoir. That too was seized and later burned.[7]

Lei's arrest was part of a long trend of repression against critics of the KMT's iron-fisted rule of Taiwan. Two years earlier, philosopher Hu Shih, a former student of political theorist John Dewey at Columbia University, also petitioned the government for permission to begin a new party. Police incessantly harassed Hu and his fellow petitioners, planting stories in media claiming they were Communist infiltrators.

Since February 28, 1947, the so-called February 28 Incident, mass media had been under KMT fire. On that day, a constable beat a widow for selling contraband cigarettes in the street. An angry crowd surrounded the officer, and police opened fire on them, killing at least one bystander. The watershed event created a "civil war within a civil war," marking the beginning of a "White Terror" that included a war on words. Ten newspapers folded, and several media professionals were either killed or disappeared.[8]

Indelibly intertwined with the government, the KMT controlled Taiwan through a combination of institutional power, physical repression, and a tight grip on mass media. Secret police or the Taiwan Garrison Command swept through Taiwan, arresting hundreds of "suspicious" people and detaining them without trial, charges, or recourse. Their chief targets included "unpatriotic" critics of the ruling Chiang family and advocates for either government reform or Taiwanese nationalism. In droves, arrestees were sent to a small, offshore island prison. In total, officials arrested, imprisoned, or executed some ninety thousand political reform advocates.[9]

After Lei's imprisonment, authorities arrested another one hundred activists, including a thirty-nine-year-old city councilman, Su Tung-chi, on four counts of treason and plotting rebellion. Su never emerged from prison. Officials executed him and sentenced his wife to life in prison.[10]

Writers, thinkers, and journalists were particularly vulnerable, should they publish "subversive" material. Writer Kuo Yi-tung (also known as Po Yang) learned the hard way. In the pages of the magazine *Wen Hsing*, he satirized the system, the government, and the president. In one cartoon, Kuo depicted Popeye and his son, marooned on a tiny island, holding a presidential election—despite only one candidate and one voter.[11] For insulting the president, authorities seized Kuo Yi-tung, held him for six months, then indicted and convicted him for Communist activities. His eighteen-year prison sentence was marked with such hardship that his daughter hardly recognized him; he became thin, frail, and gray.[12]

The KMT accumulated a rarely achieved level of power. The party dictated law and policy, selected officials, influenced the military, and infiltrated most civic life, including unions, clubs, organizations, educational institutions, and the arts. With its far-reaching empire of real estate, money, and business monopolies, and a web of laws, institutions, and mass media, the party silenced critics through ostracism, disempowerment, imprisonment, and sometimes death. With such a vast arsenal, the KMT protected and justified its corruption, assured its power, and ultimately established itself as the richest political party in the world. But by the year 2000, Taiwan had become a very different country. For the first time in decades, a new party, the Democratic Progressive Party (DPP) toppled the long-dictatorial KMT, and the long-accepted, corrupt governance and single-party rule were no longer considered legitimate.[13]

Taiwan's transformation from authoritarian dictatorship to a more pluralistic and transparent democracy was an arduous journey with multiple interactions and developments. Key in the development was a struggling, independent media that revealed corruption, offered new ideas and frameworks, and advocated for democracy and human rights.

Taiwan's transition was inclusive and relatively peaceful,[14] but what media helped usher in, new media threatens to destroy. Experts suggest that Taiwan's media landscape is now undermining what took years to establish.

MEDIA UNDER CHIANG, THE ELDER

"Communist!" That's what the KMT-controlled media said about hundreds of Taiwan's residents: "Communist infiltrator!" or "Communist agent!" They were fighting words that justified brutality and imprisonment. For some mainlanders living in Taiwan, fear of Communism was rooted in very real experiences. The Communist Party forces had waged a vicious war that sent them fleeing to Taiwan. Within the KMT, the fears were particularly pronounced. Party leaders held tightly to control of Taiwan through every means possible, with the hope that someday they would recapture mainland China from the Communists. But in the process, they overreached and violated countless human rights, justified as the means of "protecting" Taiwan from the community. Many in Taiwan accepted the oppression—some out of fear, some because of a lack of knowledge, and some because that was just "the way things were."[15]

President and KMT leader Chiang Kai-shek solidified the KMT's power into an unquestionable force in Taiwan. In less than two decades, he expanded party membership from one hundred thousand to nearly one million. But alongside reorganization and reform, Chiang ensured KMT's dominance through brutality, intolerance, and the silencing of criticism, particularly voices of native Taiwanese.[16]

Dissatisfied with the KMT and hungry for a more democratic system, a handful of advocates repeatedly sought to establish an alternative political party and a free media. Their efforts were consistently quashed and their leaders labeled "Communist" or "criminal" and imprisoned. That was the fate of Lei Chen and his *Free China Fortnightly* magazine.[17]

In addition to creating repressive laws, authorities sought to pacify their citizens through a vast media scheme that spewed anti-Communist ideology and elicited fear. A steady stream of media messages warned

Taiwan's residents of a "Communist menace" through broadcasts, newspapers, posters, and billboards.[18]

Under the elder Chiang, hardly a critical word could be uttered lest the critics face prison or death. The party controlled the vast majority of mass media either through direct ownership, business arrangements, or restrictive laws that controlled content and ownership of publications, arts, literature, and music. Through that control, officials justified brutish acts as legitimate punishment against "thieves, [gang members and], professional gamblers."[19]

The KMT controlled all three television stations and most of the thirty-three radio stations. Collectively, the party, government, and military owned most newspapers, newswires, and book publishing companies. Through professional arrangements, the KMT also wielded considerable control over privately held newspaper content: On news days, either the KMT or the Taiwan Garrison Command called publishers and editors to dictate the framing of events and stories. New media hardly had a chance. With strict licensing laws, the government prevented the establishment of additional newspapers by flatly refusing to license them to "unreliable" people.[20]

The government permitted a few non-KMT-affiliated weekly or monthly magazines but closely monitored their content. When they crossed an ideological line, the government suspended publication. During the early 1970s, in times of turbulence, economic growth, and an emerging, highly educated youth, one such magazine, the *Intellectual*, pushed the boundaries. In the *Intellectual*'s pages, fifteen writers argued that the goal of reunifying Taiwan and mainland China should not usurp human rights, rule of law, and economic prosperity. Officials sternly warned the press and arranged for the termination of fourteen of the fifteen writers from their academic jobs.[21]

With such harsh censorship, residents scarcely had a chance to hear substantive criticism of the KMT-controlled government or different ideas or perspectives. Even abroad, the KMT worked to silence dissent and criticism. Spies watched Taiwanese students studying overseas and censored information before it reached them. Occasionally, however, "subversive" material slipped into the students' hands, alerting, informing, and reframing politics and identity.[22]

The Students

They were young and studious and inspired by the West. Taiwanese students studying at American universities read texts about "decolonization of Asia and Africa . . . while the Vietnam War protests raged outside." US social movements of the 1960s successfully grabbed headlines and demanded civil rights and personal freedoms. As they absorbed new information and framing in US media, textbooks, and social movements, Taiwanese students understood Taiwan in a different light: "Taiwan had gone from being a Japanese colony to a Chinese colony." It was, as they saw it, "a classic imperial outpost" in which ethnicity determined one's lot in life.[23]

One student stumbled across *Taiwan Youth*, a Japanese-language political magazine that promoted "progressive ideas" and native "Taiwanese" consciousness, politics, and culture. After he subscribed, government spies intercepted the magazines and banished him from Taiwan. But with the experience and new framework internalized, he transformed into an organizer for Taiwan's coming democracy movement, teaching peaceful resistance with protests and sit-ins.[24]

CHIANG, THE YOUNGER

In 1975, during his fifth consecutive term as ROC president, Chiang Kai-shek passed away and was succeeded by his son, Chiang Ching-kuo. Facing increasing restlessness on the island and growing international pressure, including Taiwan's 1971 expulsion from the United Nations, the younger Chiang softened some of his father's hard-line policies. Vowing greater respect for human rights and a cleaner government, he reduced nonviolent criminals' sentences, prosecuted some internal government corruption, appointed more native Taiwanese to government posts, and cracked open the door for a limited, localized democracy. But "democracy" was hampered by several factors—continued oppression of dissidents, a well-oiled machine that traded political favors for political support, and a mass media that consistently gave KMT "extensive, favorable, year-round coverage." Heavy influence on editorial content and a ban on political advertising prevented non-KMT communications from reaching a mass audience.[25]

Before non-KMT publications were permitted to publish, government censors scrutinized them. But a group of intellectuals created a series of *dangwai* ("opposition") publications that grew and helped build a burgeoning democratic movement. In August 1975, the first exclusively Taiwanese dissent publication, the *Taiwan Political Review* (*TPR*) was born. *TPR* sought to "unite" and "focus" opposition forces, expose the KMT's flaws, and "attract more people" to its cause—it targeted particularly the new middle class, which had for years been inundated with messages suggesting that democracy advocates were "Communists." The publication advocated multiparty elections, freedom of speech and of the press, and the end of martial law, but it refrained from demanding Taiwanese independence lest the publishers face prison. To prevent confiscation, venders hid the magazine, and readers secretly passed their copies onto others.[26]

In December 1975, after a series of critical articles, the *TPR*'s fifth issue incurred the wrath of the KMT. Among its essays, the magazine published AN EVENING DISCUSSION WITH FOU CONG AND PROFESSOR LIOU. Another asked, MAY NOT THE CONSTITUTION AND NATIONAL POLICY BE CRITICIZED? Another called to LIFT MARTIAL LAW SOON. The government banned the publication and convicted its editor of sedition, for which he received a ten-year prison sentence.

Several successors emerged, including the bold *This Generation* and *Great Virtue*, but they were short lived. The groundbreaking *Taiwan Contention* again focused on KMT's weaknesses, rejected one-party dictatorship, and advocated for free speech and ending martial law.[27]

Taiwan had already been expelled from the UN after the US Nixon administration supported the mainland People's Republic of China (PRC) over Taiwan as the Republic of China. In 1978, US President Jimmy Carter withdrew formal recognition of Taiwan's ROC and instead recognized mainland People's Republic of China. The KMT reacted by postponing elections, but, under internal and international pressure, leaders considered increasing democratization in efforts to improve Taiwan's beleaguered image.[28]

The media publicly acknowledged the need to change. "We must Westernize," wrote the new *China Tribune*, a bimonthly publication serving mainlanders on Taiwan. "Whether from a historical perspective or the realistic requirements of the nation, it can affirmatively be said that we must learn from the Western powers and must accept Westernization. Everything in the world takes the West as the mainstream; in other words, the Western powers are the world's leaders." But while advocating for Westernizing, the publication opposed Taiwan's independence, calling it a "stupid course" that invited "suicide."[29]

"Does everyone still remember the heartfelt excitement and fervor created by the *Taiwan Political Review*?" asked the first issue of the *Eighties*, which emerged in the wake of *TPR*'s demise. The magazine was a self-proclaimed reincarnation of *TPR*, renamed to bypass censors and continue the work of its predecessor, although with a more moderate tone. But perhaps the greatest leap forward came with the work of another *TPR* executive and the launch of *Meilidao*.[30]

A BEAUTIFUL ISLAND

In 1979, *dangwai* leaders Huang sin-Chieh and Shih Ming-teh launched a bold magazine, *Meilidao* (Formosa, or "beautiful island"), suggesting Taiwan was separate and independent of mainland China. With its defiant name, *Meilidao* again advocated for democracy and Western-style rights. But it also argued for the right to overthrow illegitimate or tyrannical governments by force and broached ultrasensitive matters, including the taboo February 28 Incident and a distinct Taiwanese identity.

As writers pushed for democratic reform and hammered the government for prioritizing economic development over social justice, *Meilidao* became the second most popular publication on the island, second only to the Taiwanese *TV Guide*. With twelve offices around the island, the magazine staff established service centers and discussion groups to further the "island-wide network of anti-hegemonic opinion and activism."

After right-wing vigilantes attacked their centers, the *Meilidao* journalists planned a human rights demonstration. On December 10, the anniversary of the Universal Declaration of Human Rights, magazine staff organized a massive rally to acknowledge the day. But they had one problem: without the requisite permit, their demonstrations were illegal.[31]

Wearing riot gear, police arrived at the commemoration and physically blockaded the area. As thousands of people gathered, attempting to join the rally, officers sprayed tear gas at demonstrators, drove vehicles into the crowd, and blocked the exits. Angry participants railed at police, who retaliated. The altercation injured several officers and hundreds of rally participants.[32]

The KMT-controlled media denounced the demonstrators as lawless "mobsters" who attacked police with clubs and weapons. Their programs showed images of high officials and famous entertainers visiting the hospitalized police officers.

"[*Meilidao* leaders] attempted to carry out their goal of overthrowing the government by illegal means through simultaneous implementation of the long-range and short-range power-seizure plans," said President Chiang Ching-kuo in the KMT's mass circulation newspaper *United Daily News*. "[They] made radical statements to besmirch the government, undermine solidarity, make trouble, and engender conflict by shouting false slogans about human rights, democracy, and freedom." Even the more liberal *China Tribune* criticized the *dangwai* leaders for using "distorted" arguments to abet violence.[33]

Meilidao publishers, however, told a different story: "[The government] treated the general public as enemies," said legislator and *Meilidao* publisher Huang sin-Chieh at a press conference. Attendees, according to event spokespersons, had no clubs or weapons, only sticks and bamboo torches, which they extinguished at the behest of the police. Nonetheless, said the journalists, they regretted the resulting violence.[34]

The regrets failed to satisfy the government. Officials shut down *Meilidao*, revoked eighty-four other magazine licenses, suspended another thirteen, and took legal actions against twenty-two more. Police arrested *Meilidao*'s executives, except for two who fled—Shih and Hsu Hsin-liang—which created the "biggest manhunts in Taiwan's history." Officials finally captured Shih as he was undergoing reconstructive surgery "to alter his appearance." Hsu escaped into exile in the United States.[35]

The government charged *Meilidao* executives with sedition and antigovernment activities, held them in solitary confinement, forced them to stand for two days at a time, and subjected them to sleep deprivation and terrifying threats. Agents interrogated the executives, sometimes for sixty straight hours.[36]

"This is how you will end up," said police to Formosa vice president and one of the *Meilidao* eight, Lu Hsiu-lien, while showing her photos of a bullet-ridden corpse and a death notice sent to the deceased's widow. Officers bludgeoned Assemblyman Lin Yi-hsiung, a leader in the Dangwai movement and one of the *Meilidao* eight; the attack prompted his mother to call Amnesty International. The next day, she and Lin's twin seven-year-old daughters were stabbed to death. Lin's third daughter survived but was badly wounded.[37]

After one hundred days of a grueling existence, the *Meilidao* leaders signed "confessions" that carried prison sentences ranging from twelve years to life behind bars. It was a lighter sentence than the death penalty demanded by the ROC's vice president. Other demonstration participants, including high-level church officials from the Presbyterian Church, also faced trials, and thirty-three people were sentenced to prison.[38]

Although dissenting publications had been crushed, the government allowed remaining media to cover the trials. One newspaper, the *China Times* (*Zhonggua Shibao*), published the entire transcript, revealing sympathetic defendants and an abusive KMT government determined to prosecute the journalists without sufficient evidence. Throughout the trial, defendants apologized for the violence and injuries to police and reiterated their goals—to "end one party rule," not to overthrow the government. "Do you honestly think we would attempt to overthrow the government with sticks and bamboo torches?" asked one defendant. Other defendants disclosed their prison experiences: Yao Chia-wen said interrogators forced him to copy and sign a "confession" that officials wrote, and Lu cried while she recalled the threats and interrogations.[39]

While the *"Meilidao* Eight" languished in prison, many Taiwanese voters revolted, electing former political prisoners and the wives and attorneys of the jailed journalists. Campaigning on the *"Meilidao* incident," the wife of *Meilidao*'s Yao Chia-wen garnered the most votes for the national assembly.[40] The KMT was losing ground, but the *Meilidao* movement was also damaged.

"In the long-term interest of Taiwan, to carry out democracy on the island is far more urgent and important than unification with China," declared former *Meilidao* journalists from prison before they launched hunger strikes.[41] Other *dangwai* leaders formed new organizations, such as the Taiwan Association for Human Rights and the Dangwai Research Association for Public Policy, and more magazines. Government officials force-fed the hunger strikers, outlawed the organizations, and banned and confiscated the magazines.

When bombs exploded in two newspaper buildings and on a bus, officials blamed former *Meilidao* publisher Hsu Hsing-liang. The "traitor" and his "frenzied rebels are persistently doing evil to the extent of ruining means of public transport," they publicly said. "Their purpose is to disrupt social order, carry out bloody terrorist activities and threaten the government with the use of terrorism."[42]

Internationally, Taiwan became notorious for quashing free speech and free media. The Committee to Protect Journalists identified the KMT government as having imprisoned more journalists than any other noncommunist country. But when the efforts to silence the criticism reached US shores, Taiwan's KMT suffered a much larger blow.

Scandals

The KMT government's long arm reached to the shores of California and into the garage of Chinese-American journalist Henry Liu. Liu had persuaded his Taiwan editors to send him to the United States, where he continued writing while operating two businesses—a gift shop and the business of informing. But although he informed intelligence agencies in three different countries—the United States, China, and Taiwan—what ostensibly cost him his life was an unflattering biography he penned about Taiwan's president, Chiang Ching-kuo. KMT agents warned Liu to refrain from publishing the book and reportedly paid him to rewrite it.[43]

On October 15, 1984, Liu entered his garage, where two gunmen wearing wigs were waiting for him. The gunmen, members of a notorious international organized crime ring, the Bamboo Union, ambushed Liu, and with two bullets in the stomach and one to the head, Liu was dead. The gunmen had acted on their "duty," as defined by high-ranking Taiwanese intelligence officers, they said during their trials.[44]

"In Taiwan, it is your job, your duty to kill Communists," said Chang An-lo, a member of the Bamboo Union who implicated the president's son as part of the murder plot. "The government printed on [the killers'] minds that Henry Liu was a Communist. It wasn't until after that murder that they found out he was just a writer."[45]

The death was "politically motivated," said Liu's wife, Helena, to the Associated Press, accusing even higher ranking Taiwanese officials of organizing the slaying. Already the death had prompted a flurry of bad press for Taiwan. TAIWAN ROLE PROBED IN KILLING, wrote the *Washington Post*.[46] DEATH OF CRITIC OF TAIWAN LEADER STIRS FEAR AMONG CHINESE IN US, wrote the *New York Times*,[47] and later PAPER SAYS AUTHOR WROTE OF RIFT IN TAIWAN.[48] The negative media attention continued in the United States throughout the killers' trials.

After initially denying its involvement, the Taiwanese government admitted that its intelligence agents had played a role in Liu's death. It prosecuted several high-ranking Defense Ministry intelligence officers, including its intelligence chief.[49] "The government is deeply shocked by the involvement of our intelligence officials in Liu's murder," read the KMT government's official statement. "The intelligence agency under the National Defense Ministry will be thoroughly investigated. The government has condemned violence as an expression of political views and is determined to severely punish those who have broken the law."[50]

The slaying and subsequent publicity aggravated relations between Taiwan and the United States, which called for the extradition of the officials accused. Taiwan refused.[51] But the crime spawned convictions of several gang members and high-ranking intelligence officials. (In Taiwan, however, prison sentences were drastically shortened.)[52]

The Liu murder was one of several consecutive scandals publicly bruising the KMT's image. In another scandal, just before an election, two cabinet ministers were forced to resign for their involvement with two hundred million dollars in illegal loans. Another embarrassment was a decade-long scheme in which business officials reprocessed garbage and sold it as cooking oil to restaurants. A *New York Times* exposé asserted, DOMESTIC SCANDALS AND TRADE FEARS LEAVE TAIWAN UNCERTAIN. Then, the United States reprimanded Taiwan for arresting the publisher of a Los Angeles–based newspaper on sedition charges. She had reportedly attempted to negotiate a peace agreement between Taiwan and China.[53]

The Media's Cat and Mouse

In the wake of scandals, a battered image, and a slumping economy, the government softened its media oppression. Although police made fewer arrests, dissident publications still faced banning, confiscation, and suspensions when they broached "subversive" subjects. When the dissenting magazine the *Eighties* published details of the Liu murder, for example, it prompted the Taiwan Garrison Command to ban the issue and confiscate two-thirds of the magazines.

It certainly wasn't the first time that this publication faced government suppression. Over the years, officials suspended the *Eighties* five different times, once for publishing excerpts of the president's diary during his youthful exploration of Communism. But when confronted by suspension, editor Antonio Chiang simply changed the magazine's name and proceeded with another issue. The *Eighties* later became the *Asian* and then the *Current*, which was banned after it posed the question: DOES THE MINISTER OF THE INTERIOR UNDERSTAND DEMOCRACY?[54]

Progress Magazine's staff didn't get off quite so easily. In March 1985, after the government banned thirty of its issues, one hundred club-wielding police officers burst into *Progress*'s offices to confiscate critical articles. They injured three of the magazine's top executives and fined them for "obstruction."[55]

The KMT government justified its censorship because magazines printed "things that were completely made up," according to officials. The only prohibitions, according to censors, were advocating Communism, overthrowing the government, or agitating. But journalists also endured the government's wrath if they wrote "embarrassing" material about senior KMT members.[56]

Dangwai political candidates grew more vocal, distributing leaflets and staging rallies. But they could not compete with the KMT's "big" media control. So the KMT routinely won most elections with large margins.[57] Yet distrust was growing, and as the Taiwanese people grew more informed, they became increasingly agitated with their government.

Reform

Unrest was spreading in Taiwan, and President Chiang capitulated, offering negotiations and reforms. In mid-July 1986, he successfully pushed to replace the "emergency decree" with the National Security Law; he eliminated military trials for civilians, legalized political parties, ended military censorship of media, released several political prisoners, and expanded licensing for some media—those that opposed Communism and supported the island's reunification with China. For many, however, the advances were merely a "cover" to mask KMT's "authoritarian rule with an overcoat of democracy."[58]

"Ending martial law only removed one of many obstacles to democracy in Taiwan," argued DPP leader Hsieh Chang-ting as he stood before sixty demonstrators beating drums and gongs. They will not "celebrate" until "all these obstacles are removed."[59]

Thousands of Taiwanese expressed their dissatisfaction. They demonstrated in the streets, demanding new policies and better media: environmentalists fought nuclear and petrochemical pollution; farmers protested unlimited imports, unfair business practices, and lack of insurance; workers organized strikes, stopping work in vital operations, such as railroads; television viewers protested biased political coverage. The government conceded on some issues: it established a two-hundred-fifty million-dollar compensation fund, shut down polluting facilities, and enacted new, more open elections and election laws.[60]

With the eased restrictions, journalists released several new publications, including the defiant *Capital*, the name itself implying the once-forbidden issue of Taiwanese independence. Its debates ventured into the long-taboo question of Taiwan's independence.[61] But despite softened media laws, the government still relentlessly hounded certain journalists, like Cheng Nan-rong. Cheng published *Freedom Era Magazine*, in which he openly advocated for Taiwanese independence and a new constitution. Officials charged him with printing "seditious" articles, but Cheng refused to appear in court. On April 7, 1989, four hundred police officers surrounded his building to arrest him on charges that could bring the death penalty. Rather than acquiescing, Cheng protested the press infringement by setting himself and his building on fire.[62]

In the next election, Cheng's widow, Yeh Chu-lan, continued his advocacy, and in Taiwan's first multiparty elections she ran for a seat in the 256-seat Legislative Yuan.[63] While three government-run television stations heavily favored the KMT candidates, rarely covering opposition candidates, newly legalized, fledgling newspapers such as the *Independence Evening News* and the *Independence Morning News* revealed a faux democracy with "big bucks" vote-buying and other election irregularities. Voters openly admitted to selling their votes, some for as little as eight dollars each. The KMT party sued the *Independence Morning News* for its coverage. But through these alternative media, word was leaking out. Although the KMT still won most seats, Yeh was elected to the Legislative Yuan.[64]

THE AIR OF DEBATE

"This is 89.5, the Voice of Taiwan. You're on the air," said Charles Chiang early on election morning.

"The incumbent [KMT] candidate for Taipei mayor [is losing]," said one caller.

"KMT is spreading lies," claiming opposition candidates are planning to destroy temples, said another.

A third caller encouraged widespread poll watching to prevent election fraud.[65]

With the emergence of new radio stations, political debate was alive like never before in Taiwan. Although the government lifted the radio ownership ban in 1993 and relinquished forty-two FM channels, it established cumbersome licensing rules that locked out undercapitalized broadcasters.[66] Without the prerequisite capital, some broadcasters opted for illegal "pirate" stations. Among them was the Voice of Taiwan (VOT), broadcasting in the once-banned native Taiwanese language. Over the airwaves, VOT broadcasters reported government corruption, embarrassed officials, and encouraged callers to speak their minds and to resist what they believed was unfair, unjust, or improper.[67]

In native Taiwanese, Voice of Taiwan broadcaster Hsu Jung-chi (Hsu Rong-chi) railed against unfair auto insurance laws and the purported demolishing of a historic monument. Thousands gathered to demonstrate, including the station's more devout listeners—Taiwan's more than ten thousand taxi drivers. Police poured in to break up the protest, but angry demonstrators relentlessly pelted them with sticks and stones and burned their police cars. Parts of Taiwan descended into an angry bedlam.[68]

For inciting a riot and causing a public disturbance, police slapped handcuffs onto Hsu and two others, and the court sentenced them to eight months in prison.[69] But once out on bail, Hsu fled to the United States and broadcast from exile in California. In his absence, Hsu's wife, Lin Shiou-ching, managed the station, continuing the native Taiwanese broadcasts to ensure that "housewives and common people" could "hear about the government."[70]

In the face of stiff fines and lengthy prison sentences, the alternative Democratic Progressive Party (DPP) launched its own pirate broadcasting operation—a television station to "crack" the KMT's television monopoly.[71] By the end of 1994, Taiwan's media landscape featured more than three hundred newspapers, three hundred cable television stations, and forty illegal radio stations.[72]

In efforts to close down the pirate operations, some seven thousand police descended onto fourteen illegal stations, seized eleven of fourteen transmitters, and confiscated their equipment. But broadcasters simply rebuilt their stations, resumed broadcasting, and called upon listeners to "hit back."

With new sources of information and new framing, an emboldened citizenship altered the political landscape. In a landmark Tapei city election, the DPP mayoral candidate toppled the KMT incumbent. Increasingly, Taiwanese no longer believed in reunification with China—80 percent called it unrealistic.[73]

Although the KMT and the government maintained control of the three major television channels, in 1995, the government licensed a new company, People Broadcasting Corp, and lifted foreign media restrictions.[74] The growing legal freedoms prompted new journalism norms and public expectations. But despite less political censorship, mergers and consolidation created new constraints—the pressures of profit.[75]

The New Censorship

"The end of censorship is but a myth," said journalism professor Chen Shih-Meng in a communication journal. Taiwan was still "under the manipulation of political and business interests . . . real freedom has to come from within, through the awakening of press professionals who care about and want to defend their editorial independence and judgment."[76]

While government censors relented, journalists confronted pressure from media executives who controlled content to gain profits. It was a battle indicative in the system of "money politics," according to political science professor Hu Fu.[77]

"Before, the Government Information Office, [the] police, and the KMT's department of Cultural Affairs all had a say but now, no [government or KMT party] official would dare call up and tell us what to write and not to write," said Su Tzen-ping, editor in chief of the *Independence Morning Post*.[78] Under financial strain, the *Independence Morning Post* sold to Taipei businessman and KMT politician Chen Cheng-chung and, increasingly, its politics leaned toward the KMT, silencing "the one, true independent voice," according to journalism professor Lo Ven Hwei. Top editorial staff resigned, and some seven hundred journalists poured into the streets to fight profit-motivated editorial control, calling for "editorial covenants" to protect the "free flow of correct information and pluralistic opinion" necessary for democracy.[79]

The *Independence Morning Post* was only one medium that ostensibly traded journalistic integrity for profits, leading some journalists to resign in protest. "I no longer want to be a puppet," said award-winning television newscaster Lee Yen-chiu before she resigned from her job as a China Television Systems anchor. The Best Anchor Award she had received should be "renamed the Best Puppet Award," she said.

Still, by the late 1990s, Taiwan's media landscape featured a rich diversity: 361 newspapers, 242 news agencies, 5,480 magazines, 5,325 publishing houses, 1,615 record companies, and 194 television channels, including 8 news channels and 4 national television networks. Among the media was the new television station Formosa Television, launched in 1997.[80]

By the year 2000, for the first time since the KMT took power in Taiwan, the DPP presidential candidate won, ending the one-party rule on the island. Although the KMT returned to power in 2008, the politics and culture of Taiwan profoundly changed, no longer accepting authoritarianism or blatant corruption.[81]

But the new media, while more diverse, has also become more of a prisoner to the rule of profit and the direction of their wealthy investors in China. Media scholars lament the new profit-oriented content: increased sensationalism, inaccuracy, unjustified bias, and polarization, which, they fear, threaten to undermine the long work of early journalists.[82]

Taiwan's Changes

Taiwan's transformation emerged from a relentless struggle by a group of intellectual journalists. Under threat by the authoritarian, one-party government that harassed, fined, and imprisoned them, these journalists consistently pushed the boundaries. Through their publications, they built opposition movements, exposed the flaws in the system, and slowly persuaded their audiences to reject corruption and join in a stand for democracy.[83] When the government forced magazines into closure, the publishers and journalists simply continued in a different forum or under a different name.[84]

After years of oppressing journals and journalists, Taiwan's ruling KMT, under increasing internal and international pressures, finally relented and freed the media from military, party, and government control. The new publications were followed by broadcasts that offered alternative perspectives and challenged the corrupt norms that had previously been accepted. Through the new media framing, the opposition leaders built a culture that rejected one-party authoritarian rule and practices such as vote buying, and ultimately undermined the KMT's legitimacy. By the year 2000, the one-party system had collapsed. The DPP twice won the presidency—a feat that scarcely would have been possible in the old environment—and in 2000 the new People First Party formed and won legislative seats.[85] But Taiwan's power struggles continue: On the eve of the 2004 election, for example, one candidate was shot. The other parties said the shooting was staged to win sympathy.[86]

In more recent times, Taiwan's mass media have been criticized for behaving more like a "stumbling block" than a facilitator of democracy, according to media critics. Instead of control by a single party, the drive for advertising dollars and the concentration of media ownership have "tabloidized" Taiwan's media. As a result, much of Taiwan's media have abdicated their strong sense of ethics and social responsibility and diminished their important content in pursuit of profit, prompting media and democracy advocates to once again lead reform movements.[87]

PART 4

MEDIA AND SOCIAL CHANGE

Chapter 10

The Tipping Point:
Ending Five Thousand Years
of Violence on Girls

Soroya was thirteen when her mother decided that it was time to make her into a "woman." Luring her out of the home with a promise to buy her "some gifts," she instead transported Soroya to a doctor's house, where Soroya found herself tied down on an operating table. The local anesthetic reduced the pain, but she heard the *snip, snip, snip* as they cut off her clitoris and labia, then sewed up what remained of her genitalia, leaving a tiny opening to allow for urination and menstruation. Because Soroya was the daughter of a general, she was among the minority whose female genital cutting (FGC) procedure was performed by a surgeon with surgical tools and anesthesia.[1] Most of the other one hundred thirty million women who have undergone the procedure are more like Tiziana. At eleven years of age, a group of women pinned Tiziana to the ground while a midwife, providing no anesthetic, cut off Tiziana's external genitalia. Tiziana endured the agony, believing it was "her moral duty" and the only way for her to become a "real woman."[2]

For centuries throughout many parts of Africa and Asia, young women and girls have endured the removal of their external genitalia, often with unsterilized or crude cutting tools. In some countries, the girls are also infibulated with stitches, thread, or thorns, leaving only a small entrance for the passing of blood and urine.[3] Often considered a rite of passage, the practice has been customary and required of young women and girls in order to marry and to belong to a community.

Families generally feel compelled to submit their daughters to the cutting to ensure the girls' futures as wives and respected community members. But sometimes, if a family rejects the procedure, community members or relatives kidnap the girls in order to "purify" them.[4]

Before marriage, in some customs, the family of the groom-to-be

237

inspects the young woman to ensure that she has been "properly" cut and stitched lest the wedding be canceled. On her wedding night, the scarring over the infibulated woman's vagina is forced back open, usually by her husband.

In some African countries, such as Senegal, the practice came with a celebration of the girls' entering womanhood and the preparation for their upcoming marriages and childbearing. Communities gathered in traditional public ceremonies, beat drums, and danced. The girls were "feted and showered with presents." Their families were "honored" in this once-in-a-lifetime event.[5] But because the ceremonies and the customs were deeply secretive and women were forbidden to speak about them, the girls rarely knew what was going to happen to them. To the jubilant sounds of drums, dance, and song, women sequentially pinned down dozens of girls, then began the cutting and stitching. After the procedure, the girls were also sworn to secrecy, particularly about any suffering or complications resulting from the operation. Should they dare to break the silence, the spirit of Ngir-Ngiro would attack them, they were told.[6]

"Believe me, it's not something you can see twice," said one witness of the cutting process.[7] The pain from the cutting and stitching is only the beginning of some girls' agony. Later in their lives, some young girls and women, like Soroya and Tiziana, become severely ill, either from infections, hemorrhaging, ulceration, cysts, scarring, or childbirth complications. Many have died, either as a result of the cutting itself or subsequent complications.

More than one hundred thirty million women alive today have undergone the four-thousand-year-old practice often referred to as "circumcision," according to the World Health Organization (WHO). In countries such as Somalia, Guinea, and Mali, FGC is nearly universal; more than 92 percent of all women have undergone FGC as a routine procedure to reach womanhood, achieve societal acceptance, and have families. In Egypt, Sierra Leone, Sudan, Eritrea, Gambia, and Djibouti, more than 75 percent of women have been circumcised.

In some cultures, like those in Somalia and Sudan, by removing the "fleshy encumbrance" many of the women felt more beautiful and feminine. The process, they believed, made them more honorable and civilized, enhanced their fertility, better protected their wombs, and tightened the vaginal opening. They considered "uncircumcised" women to be like "barbarians."[8]

In other traditions, the practice was considered vital to either prevent "misfortune" or protect a family's honor. "Uncut" girls were considered dirty and thus marginalized, ostracized, and rejected by the community. They were the "laughing stock of the community."[9]

It is like "social death" for a girl or woman to forego the procedure, said Molly Melching, founder of Tostan, a nongovernmental development organization in Africa.[10]

"We would have nothing to do with any woman who was not cut," said one traditional cutter.

International journalists, writers, activists, and filmmakers exposed the practice as harmful to girls, and for decades feminist groups and health organizations attempted to end FGC with campaigns that focused on health risks, pain, and the moral "wrongness" of the procedure. It was "a system of torture that has crippled one hundred million people," according to an article in the *New York Times*. "Every year [FGC] takes at least two million more into an existence of suffering, deprivation and disease." But while the books and films lifted the practice from secrecy, most cultures that practiced FGC ignored the information, chose not to believe it, and rejected the crusade altogether. They felt personally disparaged, their custom turned into a "disease," and their practitioners made into pariahs.[11]

But deep inside rural Senegal, on July 31, 1997, something changed. A group of Senegalese villagers assembled for a different kind of celebration. The community gathered in drumming circles wearing their best traditional costumes. Their palms pounded steady tribal rhythms; their bodies danced with full spirit and joy, flinging baskets into the air; and their voices chanted and sang in unison. But instead of celebrating the rite of passage for the next wave of girls, village elders and public figures stood and spoke—about human rights, women's health, and children's education. The practice of cutting young girls' genitalia, they said, had ended for them.

In the following year, 1998, thirteen additional communities in an area called Mbour, where 94 percent of women had undergone FGC, celebrated their renunciation of the practice. As a movement to end FGC mushroomed, it entered neighboring countries where FGC was even more widely practiced. Across western Africa, for the first time, masses of people were questioning their long-standing "sacred" ritual.

Abandoing the cutting tradition was one among many changes spreading in Senegal. Communities were transforming in fundamental ways and tackling issues that had for too long seemed intractable. They established democratic community councils to discuss and decide important issues and developed plans to end malnutrition and child abuse. Across villages, literacy increased, while domestic and community violence and forced childhood marriages decreased. Ultimately, said observers, FGC's elimination was a "by-product" of a larger transformation, one that was based on new understandings about human rights, responsibilities, and democracy.

By 2008, four thousand communities had abandoned FGC, and Senegal's federal government created a plan for its total eradiction. Such a change—ending a four-thousand-year-old practice that was held to be commonsense and sacred—rarely occurs in the course of humanity. It begs the question: after so many campaigns to end FGC failed, why and how did such a profound change come about? It began as a personal awakening for a small group of women trying to better their village life and grew into a media phenomenon that spread first throughout Senegal, then to other parts of western Africa.

THREE STAGES OF SOCIAL CHANGE IN SENEGAL

Stage One: The Epiphany

It began in the small rural community of Malicounda-Bambara, just outside of Thies, home to a few thousand Senegalese people. There, as part of an "empowerment" program that they codesigned, thirty-five mothers sat in a circle and chose their ten-year goals: obtain running water, electricity, and better work.[12] The goal setting emerged from a nonprofit organization called Tostan that began as a program to help children learn to read in their own Wolof language. But Tostan evolved into a goal-setting and problem-solving adult education program that situated its workshops within classes that emphasized literacy, health, human rights, and democracy.[13] Taught in "modules," each layer of the classes led its participants deeper into understanding the connections between human health, disease, their bodies, their communities, human rights, and democracy.[14] It was in this setting that the question of FGC first arose. While for centuries, FGC had been too taboo to discuss—for fear of provoking bad spirits—an anatomical chart made the subject nearly impossible to avoid. These thirty-five women had never seen unaltered female bodies, nor learned about the functions of their reproductive organs. And the shocker: women in other parts of the world were not "cut." By the end of the health sessions, the women realized that FGC—not "bad spirits"—was causing their girls' illnesses.[15] Their tradition had a health cost.

The human rights and democracy sessions prompted more epiphanies: "We're now aware that we have the right to a normal and dignified sexual life. Our daughters also," remarked one participant. "I [can] no longer impose my will on my children and grandchildren," said another.[16] And through the program, women, many for the first time, felt empowered to speak and to facilitate change. "Tostan taught us that it is OK to speak our mind," said Oureye Sall to the *Christian Science Monitor.* "I could say that I think our traditions need to change."[17]

Within the contexts of human rights, democracy, and health for their families and communities, these women decided to spare their own girls from "the custom." Using traditional theater and storytelling, the women explained to their own community what they had learned. With democratic principles and a "no shame, no blame" approach, the village, together, chose to "never again" cut its girls.

But protecting their daughters from FGC's health risks carried with it potential social disasters. Because social norms required FGC, abandoning the practice would "ruin" their daughters' chances for starting a family and belonging to the larger community.[18] Their only choice, therefore, was to persuade other communities to follow the same path. That would require a public campaign to explain their decision about a very private matter. It was a daunting task to which these mothers were firmly commited.

Stage Two: Going Public

The village of Malicounda-Bambara prepared for a ceremony. They invited friends, relatives, and acquaintances from other communities, and a UNICEF (United Nations Children's Fund) representative invited twenty journalists.[19] Women dressed in bright, festive colors, and the community gathered into a celebratory circle, dancing and chanting to steady, rhythmic drumming. With festivities, traditional song, dance, theater, and exuberance, they feted the end of "the custom."[20]

The July 1997 ceremony became national and international news, spreading through television, radio, magazines, and newspapers. For two weeks, French- and national-language broadcasts featured the decisions, and television news aired parts of their play and interviews with the women and religious leaders.[21]

The wide coverage introduced ideas that many villagers had never considered, and most media portrayed the women as courageous, intelligent, and dedicated to health and human rights. They framed ending FGC as a commitment to human rights. One newspaper, *Le Soleil*, depicted them as "revolutionaries." In its cartoon, for example, the women were shown "burning down the circumcision hut." Behind the hut, a relieved young girl said "thank you" in Bambara.[22]

Senegal's President Abdou Diouf praised their decision and encouraged others to follow Malicounda-Bambara's path. "The time to change these ancient practices has arrived," declared President Diouf. "We must vigorously fight against female genital cutting. . . . I appeal for the Malicounda experience to be followed and to spread throughout Senegal." Diouf called for new laws criminalizing FGC and for countrywide cooperation to end FGC in their country.[23] Under Diouf's proposal, parents and traditional "cutters" could face up to five years in jail.[24]

While the women received high praise in some circles, more conservative Senegalese condemned them. How dare they openly discuss a taboo topic?[25] These matters "should not be discussed publicly," asserted some of the village men.[26] "This is a vulgarity that people do in the West. Have you no shame?" asked another.[27]

One newspaper mischaracterized their practice, causing rancor within some villages. How could they dispense with their long-standing tradition? They must have been bribed, some argued.[28] Others threatened the women, sneered at them, and accused the Tostan program of creating a ruse to turn their women into prostitutes. But despite a few negative articles, the bulk of media disseminated the idea that FGC might be unhealthy, sparking debates and discussions where there was previously an overwhelming silence.

The media campaign, on its own, had not been enough, the women realized. They needed to supplement it with personal discussions that would spark communities to act independently in their own best interest. In one discussion, a sixty-six-year-old imam, Demba Diawara, from a neighboring village, implored the women to reconsider their decision. But the women persuaded Diawara to query the women in his own community about their experiences with "the practice."[29]

"I had no idea, no idea," said Diawara about the tales he heard. "If we had known . . . we would have insisted that the women end FGC many years ago."

Diawara endorsed their decision and, realizing the potential grief, joined in their effort to abandon FGC more universally. "If [our relatives and neighboring communities] do not agree with our decision to end FGC, we will have insurmountable problems," he said. "Our children will not be able to marry their children."[30] Throughout the region, Diawara facilitated community discussions; while some stormed out of the meetings, others understood the larger concerns.[31]

On February 14, 1998, thirteen communities in the Diabougou region celebrated the end of FGC. On June 12, another community in Medina Cherif abandoned the custom. The public events stimulated another flurry of media attention, garnering enough news to spread to the United States and prompt a personal appearance by then First Lady Hillary Clinton. Appearing on national Senegalese television, Clinton embraced the Malicounda-Bambara women and personally thanked them for their courage.[32]

Yours is a "great movement," declared Clinton, as she acknowledged the struggle that change agents confront. "It is not easy for women and men to come together to stand against and speak out against a key ancient custom."[33]

Among some, however, Clinton's highly public moment elicited revolt. FGC is "normal," they said. This effort was simply a trick by "white people. . . . I saw Mrs. Clinton come and denigrate our culture!" shouted one woman who had watched the news program on television. But even among those who decried the changes, important questions had arisen.[34]

In 1999, the Senegalese parliament acted on the president's goal, outlawing FGC and imposing harsh criminal sanctions on practitioners.[35]

But the practice was still long from dead, and law enforcement officers could hardly arrest entire villages that continued the practice. "I will go to jail if need be," said Muntago Tall to the *Christian Science Monitor*. "I will happily die, rather than be forced to renounce what I believe."[36]

As word spread through local and national media, abandoning communities simultaneously "adopted" their neighbors, adding a one-on-one approach to the public campaign. The secret taboo had also become a regular matter of public debate, and many, for the first time, questioned the wisdom of their tradition. Critical mass was building, and revelations were occurring. But along with the realizations about FGC's dangers came painful self-reflection: from the village of Diagoune, Fatou, a Senegalese mother of four girls, turned her brown eyes down in sadness, realizing that her seven-year-old daughter, who died two days after she underwent FGC, had likely died from the procedure.[37] "Everywhere I looked, I saw her face," said Fatou. "Today, I still see her face as if she were here." The new knowledge, however, prompted Fatou's decision to spare her youngest daughter.[38]

Darietou Dieme also came to understand that FGC had compromised her ability to have more children. Like other victims of the tradition, her organs, altered from FGC, were damaged, and she bled intensely while giving birth.[39]

In late 1999, a historic moment arrived. People walked for miles to witness the event. Among traditional Faluni musicians, singers, dancers, and tribal rhythms, leaders declared: "We, 105 villages, forever renounce the practice. . . . The negative consequences of this practice . . . the opinion and advice of religious leaders and human right [leaders] encouraged us in making this decision. We thus announce our . . . commitment to disseminate this decision, not only in our own community but throughout the country and even throughout the world. We pay homage to the pioneer community [that] began this movement. We . . . thank the media for the important role they continued to play in informing the populations on the problems linked to the practice."[40]

Representing more than eighty thousand villagers, twenty-five hundred people joined in a circle to celebrate a future in which women and girls would be free from FGC-related pain and health complications. In observance were twenty-seven journalists who witnessed the event and listened to the heartrending stories of little girls dying from the operation.

Another wave of positive media attention built upon the earlier ones.

Radio programs sent the news into remote villages still practicing FGC. National television coverage and articles appearing on the front page of four daily newspapers instigated widespread discussions.[41]

Two years later, Tostan organizers launched a broadcast program specifically to share their concepts and facilitate dialogue over the air-waves. Through Tostan Radio Broadcasts, they penetrated deeper into six of Senegal's eleven regions. Every Saturday afternoon, Oumou Diop and Malick Niang sat before their radio microphones, hosting discussions and debates on a wide range of human-interest issues—environmental protection, human health, human rights, and democratic participation. "Under the Debate Tree" featured experts and open phone lines to explore contexts, connections, and best practices within the communities, using the model of critical thinking and nonjudgment that had been featured in the Tostan classrooms. They aired calls from listeners deeply opposed to changing their practices of childhood marriage and FGC, and calls from supporters who shared their stories, successes, and losses. The open forum allowed people to explore ideas while learning from others' experiences without blame or shame. Audiences listened in groups, then continued the discussions after the broadcasts ended.[42]

"Each week has a theme," explained Tostan's Cody Donahue. "It can be about malaria prevention, voting and elections, or human rights."[43]

Through these combined approaches—radio, newspapers, television, theater, song, and village-to-village "adoptions"—the concepts of human rights, democracy, health, and critical thinking that had propelled the movement toward FGC abandonment spread in Senegal. International media, including newspapers in Senegal, praised the changes, calling them "landmark" and "historic."

SEVENTY VILLAGES OF THE FOUTA SAY "NO" TO THE PRACTICE OF EXCISION, read one 2005 *Le Soleil* headline. "November 13, 2005 will be the date in history when Fouta . . . will end this ancient practice," read the article. "The authorities have given support and sympathy [for ending] feminine genital mutilation and forced childhood marriage."[44]

When professional "cutters" joined the effort to end the practice, the media was right there with them. *La Journal* covered the day that cutter Sall "put away her knife." Sall acknowledged, "It is always difficult to abandon your career, but when this practice puts human life in danger, it is better to do something else."[45]

Le Soleil announced "Marakissa's turn to bury forever the ancient practice of excision and ending childhood marriage" and acknowledged "the work of Tostan in partnership with UNICEF." From the NGO's advocacy, the people in Marakissa "realized the harmfulness of these practices and envision the bright future, promising to respect the rights of women's physical integrity and education."[46]

The paper quoted a traditional cutter who explained her new awareness about the "dangers of the practice." While they supported tradition, the cutters wanted to "promote health . . . and rights and dignity of each person."[47] The article's meaning was clear: the practice of FGC was in conflict with those goals.

As more communities chose these larger goals, they too publicly agreed to relinquish the tradition. It is "undemocratic" if our daughters have no part in the decision, they acknowledged.

For others, health concerns drove their decisions. "We came to the conclusion that many of the health problems of our girls came from FGC," said a local villager.

"We were determined to end the source of our problems and improve the overall health of the community . . . to give our girls a better future," asserted another.[48] "We abandoned a harmful practice that violated our human right to good health. Today we are even more in harmony with our traditions and culture. We are more Bambara than ever!"[49]

Some villagers continued the practice, "no matter how many declarations" against it, according to *L'Observateur*, which noted in its March 2006 newspaper, EXCISION PERSISTS AT TAMBACOUNDA. With the consent of the parents, "the [cutter] was preparing her blade, scissors, and other [tools] to cut five young girls, the youngest of whom was seven years of age." While warning of continued FGC, the article reminded readers of the young girls who had perished from the procedure.[50]

Stage Three: The "Tipping Point"

By 2007, through the two-tiered movement, two thousand communities and 40 percent of Senegalese had publicly abandoned FGC. On August 6, 2007, Dakar's Radio Television Sengalaise (RTS) marked the tenth anniversary of the first declaration abandoning the practice.[51] Although some women and girls were still subjected to genital cutting, even within communities that had renounced the practice,[52] leaders in the Senegalese movement believed they had achieved the "critical mass" or "tipping point" to completely end the practice in Senegal.[53]

As more people understood the risks and watched their neighboring communities abandon FGC, the custom lost its acceptability. By 2009, the social norm had largely been reversed in Senegal. It was "almost normal" to hear about a new declaration abandoning FGC and to hear, "Of course, we do not practice FGC. . . . We are promoting the health and well-being of girls and women and have nothing to do with promoting a practice that we now know can harm the girls who are the future of our country."[54]

At the end of that year, FGC had been abandoned in 4,121 of the five thousand FGC-practicing communities in Senegal. The fifty-first celebration fell on February 21, 2010, when another 256 villages together renounced FGC and forced childhood marriages. Media again embraced the moment, acknowledging that "the world is witnessing a great change."[55] Less than ten days later, the government of Senegal launched a national action plan to "seize on momentum created by local communities and the NGO Tostan to end the [FGC] practice" by 2015. SENEGAL: TOTAL END OF FEMALE GENITAL CUTTING NOW IN SIGHT, read one headline. "The crusade against female genital cutting and child/forced marriage will meet its end this Sunday," stated another.[56]

In a complete revolution about FGC, practicing FGC became stigmatized. Villagers had to "hide [the practice of FGC] in order to do it," explained Malick Diagne, deputy director of Tostan at the time. "We have changed the mentality . . . in such a way that it is not cool or politically correct to do excision [in Senegal]."[57]

BEYOND SENEGAL

The news and explanations for abandoning FGC spread into other parts of Africa. With the newspapers, Tostan's radio program, and international radio like Radio France, which broadcast some of the declarations live, people in neighboring countries heard about the growing movement.[58] In 2006, communities in Guinea and Burkina Faso began abandoning FGC. After widespread media coverage, Gambians began debating whether to preserve or eradicate the tradition. By the end of 2009, 364 communities in Guinea, 48 in Gambia, 34 in Somalia, and 23 in Burkina Faso had all declared an end to the ancient practice, largely as a result of the programs and positive publicity that came from Senegal.[59]

Media have also stimulated thought in other countries about FGC. Through radio dramas, films, media advertisements, and television programs, nonprofit organizations addressed issues of FGC in countries such as Kenya and Sudan. In Kenya, the Population Communication International worked with local Kenyan writers to create a highly popular radio drama, *If Assisted, Assist Yourself*, that reached millions of families. Roughly 40 percent of Kenyan households tuned in to the program, which spawned a book and a comic strip in the Kenyan daily newspaper *Taifa Leo*. In addition to FGC, Sudan's 144-episode radio drama *Ashreat Al Amal* engaged issues of gender equality, HIV/AIDS prevention, and FGC through the female characters facing decisions and the tribulations related to them. Through the stories and characters, the program's audiences have come to better understand the issues and the choices that they themselves face.[60]

ATTAINING CUSTOM CHANGE

Senegal's shift in the practice of FGC resulted from multiple efforts. Fundamentally, access to information and concepts related to health and human rights along with training in critical thinking led thirty-five community members to understand the connection between FGC and their health issues. That knowledge led the women to decide, on their own, that the practice was an obstacle to their larger goals and commitments: FGC risked their daughters' well-being, and, without their girls' consent, the decisions about imposing FGC on them were undemocratic.

Because of the stigma associated with being "uncut," the women knew that the culture itself had to change, lest their daughters become outcasts. So they, along with a local imam, became change agents. Their public renunciation of FGC began a ripple that was magnified by a two-pronged track—they "adopted" other communities and pursued publicity through mass media, the latter of which took a once-secretive custom and made it a publicly debatable subject. Vital to the campaign were positive aspirations and framing. To these women, FGC was not "mutilation." Rather, the practice directly contradicted their broader goals related to human rights and health.

Media coverage alone may not have attained the same results in such a short period of time, say organizers. But the media were essential for three critical reasons: they created awareness about the bigger concepts; they lifted the issue from secrecy; and they associated FGC's end with important goals that protected girls and advanced human rights. Through mass media, the advocates disseminated the idea that FGC was unnecessary, not part of their religion, and had serious health consequences. Journalists spread this basic information and used the positive, human-rights frames as the basis for FGC's abandonment. With this framework, the end of FGC was part of the communities' positive commitments, not an abandonment of tradition.

With this issue circulated in public, advocates used their social networks and the expansion of Tostan classes to better explain the concepts. And with public declarations, they engaged both—media and social networks—while demonstrating that tradition and culture would still be alive even if they abandoned FGC.[61]

Media also regularly publicized the NGOs' positive activities, particularly those of Tostan, which organized marches, immunization programs, human-rights workshops, seminars for women, and other events that dealt with poverty, forced childhood marriage, FGC, and assisting "street children."[62] The positive image generated from the coverage helped the organizations continue their work.

Broadcast media were the most important, according to independent surveys.[63] Some 72 percent of Senegalese women heard about the issues on the radio or television, and 58 percent agreed that it influenced their opinion about the practice. In urban Gambia, 69 percent heard about the issue on radio or television, of which 24 percent said it influenced their opinion. Rural Gambians reported slightly less exposure.[64]

While social networking and the NGOs' work were at the core of the transformation, media were vital to facilitate the "tipping point." By demonstrating the growing acceptance of FGC's renunciation, mass media coverage prevented the social shunning of a people accepting change. "Social change occurs through 'public moments,'" explained Gannon Gillespie of Tostan. "Everyone needs to see that everyone else is changing. . . . It has to be public. If it's not, it won't succeed."[65]

PART 5

MEDIA'S ROLE IN THE FATE
OF THE WORLD

Chapter 11

The Fate of the World: Media and Climate Change

I t was early 1986. James Hansen looked over the results of his study and was deeply disturbed by what he had found. Head of the National Aeronautics and Space Administration (NASA) Goddard Institute for Space Studies since 1981, Hansen—along with his fellow research scientists—had measured the earth's surface air temperatures dating back to 1880. Although there was some temperature variation, the 1980s clearly contained the four hottest years on record, and the heating trend was continuing.[1] Hansen knew that this pattern, should it continue, could have dire consequences for life on Earth.

Hansen's work built upon earlier science that had, for more than two decades, documented a heating planet, its connection to carbon dioxide (CO_2) emissions, and its potentially devastating consequences—rising sea levels that would flood low-lying coastal areas and damage agriculture and ecosystems. Those findings were checked and double-checked by other scientists.[2]

In 1988, Hansen sat before the dais at the Senate Natural Resources Committee to deliver the bad news, translate the scientific findings, and explain to the policymakers what the results meant for human existence. His assessment was unequivocal: "Global temperatures are the highest on record." With 99 percent confidence, we can state that global warming "is happening now" and that the "greenhouse" effect is changing our climate now.[3]

Because of his training as a scientist, Hansen chose his words carefully, but he didn't mince them. "We can ascribe with a high degree of confidence a cause-and-effect relationship between the greenhouse effect and observed warming," he said to the receptive audience. What that meant, he explained, was more droughts and forest fires on one end, wilder and more frequent flooding on the other, and hundreds of millions of climate refugees.[4]

253

Hansen's assertive testimony and subsequent interviews put him center stage in the energy debate. In a powerful headline, the *New York Times* declared, HIS BOLD STATEMENT TRANSFORMS THE DEBATE ON GREENHOUSE EFFECT. The article acknowledged that Hansen "was risking his reputation as a cautious and careful scientist" to proclaim his findings with such certainty.[5]

Although scientists were slowly arriving at similar conclusions, very few scientists followed Hansen's lead, leaving him largely alone to argue for thwarting potential devastation in the coming decades.[6] But that same year, the World Meteorological Organization and the United Nations Environmental Program established an international panel of top scientists from around the world to assess the reality of the situation. With hundreds of expert authors and scientific reviewers from dozens of countries, the new body's reports would undergo comprehensive scrutiny to present the most realistic picture of the problem. They called it the Intergovernmental Panel on Climate Change (IPCC).[7]

The 1990s broke another heat record, with 1998 as Earth's hottest year since 1880. Overwhelmingly, scientific studies confirmed that the planet was getting hotter because of human activities, as affirmed by the IPCC's 2001 report.[8] Despite the evidence, policymakers and the public did little to reduce greenhouse gas emissions. The next decade grew even hotter. In fact, it was the hottest decade on record, containing eight of the hottest years to date, according to the World Meteorological Organization.[9] Glaciers were melting. Species were disappearing.[10] The consensus that humans were causing global warming reached across the major scientific bodies, including the National Academy of Sciences, the American Meteorological Society, the American Geophysical Union, and the American Association for the Advancement of Science.[11]

Scientific studies increasingly demonstrated that life on Earth was in peril. In 2005, eleven of the world's major national scientific academies issued a joint statement, declaring that "the scientific understanding of climate change is now sufficiently clear to justify nations taking prompt action. It is vital that all nations identify cost-effective steps that they can take now to contribute to substantial and long-term reduction in net global greenhouse gas emissions."[12]

Polls reflected a public that wanted policymakers to take corrective action. In 2005, 73 percent of US residents said they wanted the United

States to sign the international Kyoto Protocol climate agreement, and 86 percent wanted their president and other leaders to limit greenhouse gas emissions.[13]

Attempting to close the gap between scientific knowledge and comprehension of policymakers and the public, Hansen escalated his warnings, sounding alarms that might be "shocking to the body politic." The planet had reached the brink of a "dangerous tipping point," he said, and the world needed to take rapid action to "defuse the global warming time bomb." His speeches, articles, and civic activities consistently urged rapid change to avert crisis.[14] The "elements of . . . a global cataclysm are assembled," he said.[15]

Was Hansen exaggerating? How bad were things, really? The prestigious panel of scientists, the IPCC, reviewed the entire catalog of scientifically conducted, peer-reviewed[16] climate science and concluded Earth's fever and its cause were "unequivocal." Evidence was piling up that the world was getting hotter and ecosystems were collapsing. Without serious reduction of greenhouse gases, disasters loomed—extreme weather patterns, acidic oceans, floods, intensified storms, melting glaciers, droughts, and food and water shortages around the world. Unless dramatic changes were made, said the IPCC, in roughly thirty years, 20 to 30 percent of plant and animal species would become extinct; more than seventy-five million people would face a water shortage; and tens of millions would experience devastating floods and food shortages, along with disease, malnutrition, thirst, and ultimately deaths.[17]

Most climate scientists abandoned their penchant for understatements. They now stood with Hansen, openly expressing concerns that policymakers and the public were not acting quickly enough. Even the IPCC panel, they said, had downplayed the climate threat, particularly those of rising sea levels. New studies confirmed that things were clearly worsening for life on the planet.[18]

In the United States, 77 percent of the public understood that there was "solid evidence of global warming," according to polls conducted in 2006 and 2007. In 2008, the number dropped slightly, to 71 percent.[19] Among policymakers, the knowledge gap was reflected down party lines, according to a poll conducted by the *National Journal*. It found that 95 percent of Democrats agreed with the statement, "It's been proven beyond a reasonable doubt that the earth is warming because of man-made problems." Only 13 percent of Republicans agreed.[20]

Then something baffling happened. Although the scientific consensus continued to solidify, public concern about global warming dramatically subsided. Despite overwhelming scientific evidence, by mid-2010, 40 percent of the US public expressed skepticism, believing that climate change and its consequences were exaggerated. Only 12 percent were particularly concerned about global warming, according to a Yale University poll.[21] Other parts of the world reported similar skepticism. Only 26 percent of Britons believed that "climate change is happening and is now established as largely man-made," according to a BBC public opinion survey.[22] Germans, too, diminished the climate's importance, with only 42 percent concerned, down from 62 percent a few years earlier.[23]

That low level of belief and interest seeped into public policies. While scientists called for revolutionary changes, in 2010 US Congress failed to pass even incremental reforms, and the Copenhagen climate conference yielded weak results and no real agreement. Why was skepticism growing among the public and policymakers at the very time that the science was most certain?

The answer lay partly in mass media's coverage of climate science and scientists. Most mass media, where people interface with science, reported a "debate" about climate science, when no substantive debate existed in the scientific community.[24] The climate "debate" emerged not from climate science but from fossil fuel–company back rooms to thwart climate policies. It was a page torn from the playbook of the tobacco industry, which manufactured doubt about science to keep people smoking.[25] It was a tried-and-untrue propaganda campaign that would convince people that climate science was still uncertain. Why did journalists fall for it?

THE TRIED-AND-UNTRUE
TOBACCO CAMPAIGN

To keep people smoking and prevent passage of new protective laws, the tobacco industry blazed a trail of deception, showing future industries the way to continue profiting at the expense of people's health. At each stage, before legislatures, media, schools, and other public forums, cigarette company spokespersons countered the health science, using a covert web of faux groups, hired scientists, and millions of dollars in publicity campaigns to dismiss the ever-growing body of evidence that demonstrated the destruction encased in their products. Their strategy was overwhelmingly comprehensive, blanketing audiences with one simple argument: the science was too uncertain to warrant protective laws.[26]

The consortium of front groups and hired scientists masked the true nature of the campaign, provided cover for the tobacco companies, and generated false credibility. Hidden behind innocuous names were active groups seeking to stifle and discredit the science and scientists and obstruct public-interest policies for commerce. Tobacco companies paraded their front groups—the Tobacco Industry Research Committee (later called the Tobacco Institute), the National Smokers Alliance, and the Advancement of Sound Science Coalition (TASSC)—as if they were upstanding organizations, authentically pursuing science. In reality, they were created by the industry specifically to thwart protective policies by attacking the research and the researchers that indicated protection was warranted.[27] TASSC ventured beyond cigarettes and railed against health protection efforts that attempted to reduce public exposure to harmful substances such as asbestos and radon. It was all part of a concerted plan to manufacture "doubt."[28]

"Doubt is our product, since it is the best means of competing with the 'body of fact,'" wrote the industry's public relations firm Brown and Williamson. The science about cigarettes' health dangers and addictive nature was as certain as any science can be. People were dying from long-term exposure to cigarette smoke. But with enormous profits at stake, tobacco companies sought to obfuscate the health findings with an arsenal of hollow rhetoric.[29] In addition to using front organizations, the tobacco industry paid select employees in organizations such as the World Health Organization (WHO) to spread misinformation and attack evidence. In case that failed to carry the doubt, they also attacked the institutions themselves.[30]

In this campaign, it was vital to have credentialed scientists willing to obscure and counterargue scientific findings and present alternative explanations. Among those scientists was Frederick Seitz, a once-prestigious scientist who left academia in 1978 to oversee tobacco giant R. J.

Reynolds's medical research program. For a handsome salary, he awarded forty-five million dollars in tobacco-supplied funding toward efforts to dispute the tobacco health link and to focus blame on other potential causes of lung cancer and heart disease.[31]

The story did not have a happy ending. Millions of people died prematurely while the tobacco industry reaped enormous profits.[32] The all-encompassing scheme became a prototype for other industries, which followed the same pattern: create front groups, rent scientists, pay them well, and generate an overwhelming, steady misinformation campaign to steer policymakers and the public toward the industry's favored political ends.

The Deception Machine

"Victory will be achieved when average citizens understand (recognize) uncertainties in climate science" and when the public "recognition of uncertainty becomes part of the 'conventional wisdom.'" This was the goal of the Global Climate Science Team (GCST) and the means to destroy policies that might stem the looming disasters of climate change.[33]

Starting months after Hansen's Senate committee testimony, several fossil-fuel companies gathered together to form a series of organizations, including the Global Climate Coalition, the Greening Earth Society, and the Information Council on the Environment (ICE), the latter in collaboration with the National Coal Association and the Edison Electric Institute. Through these groups, the industry sowed confusion about climate change and convinced many that global warming was a hoax. Millions of dollars that could have been used to develop clean technologies was instead used to fund efforts to derail scientifically established realities that could affect the fate of the world. Like the cigarette alliance, this small group of collaborators first denied that the planet was heating up, then characterized it as a natural or "good" phenomenon, arguing that increased heat and carbon dioxide had positive effects on Earth.[34]

ExxonMobil was the most aggressive. As evidence about the planet's heat problem mounted, three oil companies—BP, Shell, and Texaco—abandoned the Global Climate Coalition, while Exxon (now Exxon-Mobil) created another group, GCST, and resuscitated the cigarette industry's TASSC under a slightly different name—The Advancement of

Sound Science Center (also TASSC).[35] TASSC sought to persuade the "public to question—from the grassroots up—the validity of scientific studies," to "show that science does not support the Kyoto [Protocol]" and to "inform the media about uncertainties in climate science."[36]

Simultaneously, between 1998 and 2005, ExxonMobil endowed roughly sixteen million dollars to several additional organizations, such as the Competitive Enterprise Institute, the American Enterprise Institute, the Cato institute, the American Council for Capital Formation Center for Policy Research, the American Legislative Exchange Council, the Committee for a Constructive Tomorrow, the International Policy Network, Frontier of Freedom, the Center for Science and Public Policy, the George C. Marshall Institute, the Heartland Institute, and Tech Central Station.[37] Although many of these organizations shared directors, memberships, and funding sources, their message was funneled separately through their own channels, creating an illusion of independent criticism.[38] Between 2005 and 2008, the oil refinery company Koch Industries outspent ExxonMobil in funding many of these same climate-science denial organizations.[39]

Together, the compendium of groups—with multiple public forums, articles, books, videos, and press releases—barraged and inundated journalists, policymakers, and the public with misinformation, manipulated data, "diversionary reframing," half-truths, and flat-out untruths—but not sound science—in an effort to make it appear that there was no problem.[40]

While carbon dioxide was overheating the planet, the deniers' material made the reverse argument: Mass increases in carbon dioxide were good for us, they claimed, making a "better world. . . by the burning of fossil fuels." We are "greening" the earth by returning carbon dioxide to the atmosphere, claimed the George C. Marshall Institute's "Greening of Planet Earth" video. It is "a natural byproduct of man's industrial evolution."[41]

From 1990 to 1997, these groups produced or circulated more than two hundred books, press releases, policy papers, and essays, filling the public sphere with their messages. They compounded the effect by appearing on broadcast programs, buying advertisements, writing op-ed articles, and sponsoring policy forums, press conferences, and speeches.[42]

Science "Advisers"

To make convincing arguments, the fossil fuel industry needed a few people with academic credentials that would allow their claims to be taken seriously by media professionals, policymakers, and the public, though not necessarily by other scientists. Their recruitment list contained former research scientists who had abandoned the research endeavor but understood it well enough to consistently reject the climate science findings on behalf of the tobacco and oil industries.[43]

Scientific research is a rigorous process of confirmation or refutation in which findings are verified by independent experimentation. Scientists share data to be double-checked by other scientists, present their findings in the language of probability, and remain open to refutation by additional scientific testing. This rigorous approach played right into the hands of the industries determined to derail public-safety policies. Despite the realities of climate change, the naysayers' fierce denials overpowered the circumspect approach of research scientists trained to speak in a language of uncertainty and entertain counterarguments.[44]

Most global warming deniers are not bona fide climate research scientists. Although some had historically performed climate-related research, most had given up scientific research and instead had become affiliated with industry-funded organizations and think tanks. But they are well versed enough in the scientific method to use it against those discoveries and scientists that might threaten the fossil fuel industry's financial goals. Rather than engaging in legitimate scientific research, ExxonMobil's science advisers used slick presentations to argue about "gaps in the scientific basis" and to insist on "certainty" before enacting precautionary policies, while knowing "certainty" is a rarity in the scientific vernacular.[45]

Within the scientific community, the anti–global warming arguments had little credibility. No respected, peer-reviewed science journal published the efforts to rebut global warming findings—with one exception. The journal *Climate Research* published an article by astrophysicists Willie Soon and Sallie Baliunas that disputed the warming trend. But to make their argument, Soon and Baliunas ostensibly misrepresented previous scholars' work, which caused a revolt among the cited scholars, followed by "protest" resignations of *Climate Research* editors and an apology by its publisher, who said the journal "should have been more careful and insisted on solid evidence."[46] Both Soon and Baliunas became ExxonMobil darlings, affiliated with roughly nine organizations funded by the oil giant.[47]

Soon partnered with former University of Virginia professor Patrick Michaels to coedit the George C. Marshall Institute's *Shattered Consensus: The True State of Global Warming*, a book that challenged climate science data and findings. Michaels has been affiliated with ten ExxonMobil-funded organizations and received substantial funds from the fossil fuel industry to write denials.[48] In one testimony, Michaels attempted to discredit Hansen's research by altering the charts that Hansen had used to demonstrate possible future climate scenarios. On these charts, Hansen had drawn three curves to represent the three possible outcomes—a "low side," the "likely" scenario, and a "high side." Michaels erased the two lower curves, leaving only the "high side" curve and falsely presented that graphic as a representation of Hansen's complete work.[49]

Because their materials were scientifically substandard and thus inadequate for publication in respected science journals, the naysayers created their own publishing opportunities through their affiliated organizations, such as Michaels's own newsletter, *World Climate Review*, financed in part by the fossil fuel industry. Then they recycled their arguments in mainstream media, beginning with small-town newspapers, and gradually built the appearance of credibility.[50]

For people who don't read peer-reviewed journals, the arguments sounded plausible. Titles like ISSUES ON THE CURRENT STATE OF CLIMATE SCIENCE: A GUIDE FOR POLICY MAKERS AND OPINION LEADERS seemed legitimate. But the articles were a ruse: Because they could not refute the facts such as melting Arctic glaciers and species extinctions, they used a false logic that cited glaciers not yet inventoried, catalogued newly discovered species, and blamed the sun for any appreciable warming.[51]

The Government

Philip Cooney had long served as a lawyer-lobbyist with the American Petroleum Institute. But as chief of staff to the chairman at George W. Bush's White House Council on Environmental Quality, he had access to government science before Congress or the public did. In efforts to control the information, Cooney altered scientific reports before their release, buried them beneath discredited, oil industry–funded reports, or suppressed them altogether—despite vital materials that might have saved lives. One suppressed report, completed before Hurricane Katrina devastated the Gulf, warned of increased hurricane intensity in the region. In another, Cooney suppressed the EPA's conclusions about public health endangerment from greenhouse gas emissions. Rick Piltz, senior associate with the government's Climate Change Science Program, released the materials to the media before resigning in protest.[52]

Cooney was not the first government official to muzzle science and scientists. High-level political officials have repeatedly prevented the public from receiving important scientific information. But Republican politicians and administrations have been far more hostile to science and scientists, sometimes attacking and intimidating them in public settings.[53] During the climate-change hearings of 1997, for example, 53.8 percent of testimony came from industry while only 3.8 percent came from natural scientists and 15.4 percent from environmental organizations.[54] Congress members such as Senator James Inhofe (R-OK) and Representative Dana Rohrabacher (R-CA) elevated industry's output above peer-reviewed scientists and used the bully pulpit to argue against an "established consensus" on global warming.[55]

The second Bush administration increased censorship and established prohibitions to prevent certain scientific knowledge from reaching the public. Among scientists they most wanted silenced was James Hansen. Although past administrations had fiddled with Hansen's statements, he had "never seen anything approaching the degree to which information flow from scientists to the public has been screened and controlled as it is now," Hansen told the *New York Times*.[56] Political appointees scrutinized his calendar, edited his research statements, dismantled parts of his agency website, and forbade him from speaking with particular media outlets. When he was permitted to speak with journalists, administration officials accompanied him.[57]

How could climate science get a fair shake in the media with this level of censorship and manipulation? It would take a super vigilant corps of journalists to dig beneath the claims and thoroughly understand the science. But given the structures of journalism—the sources they use, the definition of "news" (drama and scandal, for example), the structure of "objective" news (false balance), and the pressure of deadlines—it was no contest.

NO CONTEST: THE JOURNALISTS

The mainstream media had been covering climate science as far back as 1932, and during the 1950s,[58] the *Saturday Evening Post*, the *New York Times* and the *Christian Science Monitor* all acknowledged humanity's contribution to global warming. "Today, more carbon dioxide is being generated by man's technological processes than by volcanoes, geysers, and hot springs," wrote Waldemar Kaempffert in the *New York Times* in 1956. "Every century, man is increasing the carbon dioxide content of the atmosphere by 30 percent—that is, at the rate of 1.1 degrees Celsius in a century. It may be a chance coincidence that the average temperature of the world since 1900 has risen by about this rate. But the possibility that man had a hand in the rise cannot be ignored."[59]

"Industrial activity is flooding the air with carbon dioxide gas," explained Robert C. Cowen in the *Christian Science Monitor* in 1957. "This gas acts like the glass in a greenhouse. It is changing the earth's heat balance. . . . Every time you start a car, light a fire or turn on a furnace, you're joining the greatest weather 'experiment' men have ever launched. You are adding your bit to the tons of carbon dioxide sent constantly into the air as coal, oil, and wood are burned at unprecedented rates."[60]

Although the media sporadically covered climate science in the 1960s and 1970s, it was Hansen's 1988 testimony before the US Senate committee that catapulted the issue into the national spotlight. The increased coverage and growing scientific consensus prompted even conservative politicians such as George H. W. Bush and Margaret Thatcher to campaign about solving the problem of global warming.[61] But as naysayers inundated journalists with materials, including slick publications, the coverage shifted—even though the materials not never peer-checked for accuracy and largely were funded by the fossil fuel industry.[62]

As the industry developed and effectuated its misinformation campaign, many media increasingly gave industry spokespersons time, space, and credibility—usually equal footing to the verified, peer-reviewed science.[63] Even as the science became more certain about the anthropomorphic causes of climate change, the media still equivocated. In 1995, for example, the climate scientists agreed that the causal relationship between global warming and human activity had been *demonstrated*, but the *New York Times* reported that "human activity is a *likely* cause of the warming."[64]

From 1988 through 2002, mainstream newspapers including the *New York Times*, the *Washington Post*, the *Los Angeles Times*, and the *Wall Street Journal* regularly "balanced" industry's aggressive contrarians with circumspect scientists as if industry's advocacy was equally credible to verified, established science.[65] In some of those years—1995, 1996, and 1997—mainstream news organizations cited the naysayers *more* than the published scientists,[66] creating the illusion of a "debate" about the planet's hotter temperature, even though there was no substantive debate within the scientific community. As climate scientists called for "revolutionary" changes, media and policymakers focused on incremental reform.[67]

Some publications, such as the *Wall Street Journal*, gave preferential treatment to the naysayers. The paper published an op-ed piece authored by Frederick Seitz that attacked IPCC lead author Ben Santer. With no evidence to support his claim, Seitz accused Santer of fraud. After Santer and forty IPCC lead authors replied with a full explanation of IPCC's process, the *Wall Street Journal* delayed their letter's publication, substantively edited it before printing it, and deleted the cosigners' names. The *Wall Street Journal* then published additional Seitz and Fred Singer diatribes, accusing Santer and the IPCC of "scientific cleansing" because they did not include material that had been disproved in the panel's final report.[68]

Until 2002, most US elite media gave this handful of aggressive deniers a public platform commensurate with serious, highly credentialed climate scientists.[69] And although bona fide climate scientists far outnumbered the contrarians, they hardly had a chance in the public eye until a handful of revelations emerged that reestablished their preeminence—at least temporarily.

A Partial News Shift

"There might be people who don't believe gravity exists, but that doesn't mean journalists should include their views for 'balance' every time they report on something falling," wrote Julie Hollar in the media watchdog publication *Extra!*[70] After a series of scientific revelations coupled with political developments, most elite newspapers accepted the scientific consensus and reflected that in their pages.[71] Some journalists checked the naysayers' claims for veracity before printing them. George Monbiot of the British newspaper the *Guardian* investigated two of Singer's claims—that glaciers were advancing rather than shrinking and that Singer allegedly had published a supportive peer-reviewed article in *Science*, a prestigious journal. After searching every issue of *Science* in the alleged publication year (1989), Monbiot could not turn up such an article; and the World Glacier Monitoring Service data showed that glaciers were, in fact, melting.[72] Singer's claims were simply untrue. Hansen's talks drew large audiences that were attended by, among others, BBC Radio, the *New York Times*, ABC News, the *International Herald Tribune*, and the *Washington Post*, and he was widely quoted as a preeminent climate scientist.[73] And the Bush administration's attempts to silence Hansen and other scientists became international news, reported across the United Kingdom, Australia, and the United States. In 2004, the *New York Times* detailed some of the administration's efforts to hide scientific information from the public. Many media followed suit, keeping the issue of censoring science alive for more than a month.[74]

In 2007, political changes fueled more robust media coverage. With the climate on their agenda, Democrats gained control of both houses of Congress; the US Supreme Court decided the EPA's role in regulating greenhouse gases; and California passed groundbreaking climate legislation, signed into law by actor-turned-governor Arnold Schwarzenegger. To disambiguate the science, former vice president Al Gore dispelled the myth of a scientific debate in his film, *An Inconvenient Truth*. The film penetrated every aspect of mass media, including news, business, entertainment, and style.[75]

In Great Britain, Prime Minister Tony Blair publicly acknowledged climate change, and Virgin Group mogul Richard Branson pledged three billion dollars toward renewable energy and biofuel initiatives. The Royal Society formally requested that ExxonMobil's UK division stop its disinformation campaigns, and the long-awaited report, *Stern Review on the Economics of Climate Change*, urged quick action to stem the economic catastrophes wrought by climate change.[76]

That same year, the IPCC unequivocally pinned the roots of climate change on humanity's fossil fuel energy consumption and showed a 70 percent growth in greenhouse gas emissions between 1970 and 2004. The panel warned of dire consequences if humanity failed to reduce its emissions. The *Guardian* revealed financial offers by ExxonMobil-funded think tank, the American Enterprise Institute, of more than ten thousand dollars for scientists and economists to dispute the IPCC's report.[77] For their work on climate change, the IPCC and former vice president Gore won the prestigious Nobel Peace Prize.[78]

With these developments, most journalists stopped countering science with naysayers, and some took an additional step. In December 2009, fifty-six newspapers in forty-five countries and twenty languages "united" to publish a joint editorial expressing the "profound emergency" of climate change facing the world. First drafted and published by the *Guardian* of London, the newspapers together warned their readers of the stark reality: "In scientific journals, the question is no longer whether humans are to blame but how little time we have got left to limit the damage." All fifty-six newspapers called upon policymakers to resist blame and to "seize opportunity from the greatest modern failure of politics. . . . If we [fifty-six newspapers from forty-five countries], with such different national and political perspectives can agree on what must be done, then surely our leaders can too."[79]

While most newspapers came to understand and accept the scientific consensus, unfortunately, broadcast and cable media, still the primary source of news, did not. The major networks and CNN continued presenting a "false balance."[80] In private settings, some cable hosts, including CNN's Larry King, dismissed the urgency. "Nobody cares about fifty years from now," he said to Hansen.[81] Some local broadcasters openly challenged the science and the scientists' integrity.[82] Fox News and AM talk-radio broadcasters relentlessly attacked science and scientists.[83] The mixed messages may have been confusing, but a new series of events reverted the frame back to one of false debate.

REVERSION

The climate "debate" reemerged not because of any new scientific discoveries but because hackers stole hundreds of private e-mails belonging to key climate scientists at East Anglia University and because media professionals fell for a "scandal" that wasn't. In their e-mails, scientists had strategized about combating industry's efforts to obfuscate climate realities. Feeling "under siege" by the skeptics, the scientists worried that "any stray comment or data glitch could be turned against them" and contemplated withholding specific data to prevent misuse, knowing that doing so is unacceptable in research science.[84] The denial machine scoured through the hundreds of stolen e-mails and seized upon a sentence as "evidence" that global warming was a "hoax." The sentence referred to a statistical "trick" used to calculate a "particular set of tree-ring data" in an effort to "remove the incorrect impression given by the tree rings" that temperatures didn't rise in the years between 1960 and 1999, when "instrumental data clearly showed that [those years] were [warmer]," explained scientist Phil Jones, the author of the e-mail.[85]

The naysayers quickly pounced upon single words and sentences without contexts and understandings in order to misconstrue their meanings and create the illusion of a scandal. "This is not a smoking gun; this is a mushroom cloud," declared Patrick Michaels in the *New York Times*.[86] Flooding media with the "trick" language, the climate-change deniers obtained wide coverage with their misinterpretations and accusations.[87]

The timing couldn't have been worse—it was just before the international conference on climate in Copenhagen, and the misleading climate "debate" was back. In December 2009, global warming coverage surged. But the increased coverage wasn't principally about either the science or the policies that might address the climate problem. Instead, it was another "debate" between scientists and the industries' deniers, the latter touting proof of a "hoax." Journalists across twelve countries underreported climate science during the Copenhagen summit, with only 10 percent of their column space dedicated to science.[88]

The pattern of coverage continued. During the six months after its release, the e-mail theft led to hundreds of stories. The blogosphere and Twitter were equally, if not more, alive. The focus across media was not on solving the climate problem but about "tainted" science and the "motivation" of scientists. Although many journalists and media professionals recognized the soundness of the science, others blindly followed the shill.[89] The *Wall Street Journal* published more than a dozen "Climategate"-related articles, most which criticized the scientists and questioned the integrity of their research. Its op-ed pieces suggested that the researchers had "blackballed" dissenting scientists and "manipulated" the peer-reviewing process for money—research funding.[90] That assertion spread into newspaper coverage worldwide. Few articles, meanwhile, addressed that the e-mails were obtained illegally, and meaningful dicussions about resolving the climate problem dwindled.[91]

The Sinister Ones

While withholding data is improper in the world of science, stealing private information is deeply unethical.[92] Many journalists hardly admonished the thieves while implicating "sinister" scientists, who, incidentally, have since been cleared of any wrongdoing.[93] Without researching the claim, a number of reporters, particularly broadcasters, simply repeated the industry's Climategate "scandal" framing. A *CBS Evening News* teaser asked, "Did some scientists fudge the numbers to make climate change look worse than it is?" Its correspondent claimed the hacked e-mails "cast doubts" on the science and attempted to explain temperature change. CNN's teaser asked, GLOBAL WARMING: TRICK OR TRUTH? and in the segment asked a reporter to "do a little reality check on climate change" to "try to separate fact from fiction." A roundtable debate featured mathematician Stephen McIntyre and lawyer Chris Horner in two of three spots.[94] The reporter, Tom Foreman, referred to scientists as "supporters" and pitted them against "skeptics" who said, "We've got a lot more time to study this and figure out if we're right or wrong." Another CNN broadcaster, Rick Sanchez, suggested that the e-mails "reveal that there may have been some shenanigans going on with some of the leading scientists."[95]

The Scientists Explain

On BBC News, Jones, author of the e-mail, reiterated that he was "100 percent confident that the climate has warmed" and that "most of the warming since the 1950s is due to human activity." He explained that pre-1880 temperatures were simply "more uncertain" than the latter periods. But media such as the *Wall Street Journal*, the *New York Post*, and Fox News ignored his explanation and the overall heating trend, fixated on one era in which heating was not statistically significant, and misrepresented Jones's words.[96] The *New York Post*'s February 22, 2010, editorial claimed that he "admitted that temperatures in the Middle Ages were warmer than they are today" and "confessed that there had been no statistically significant warming in the past fifteen years," a theme repeated by Fox News, which further claimed that Jones said there had been "no warming over the past fifteen years."[97] In the United Kingdom, the

British *Daily Mail* claimed that Jones had made a "U-turn."[98] These arguments were then repeated on AM talk shows, Fox News, and climate-change denial blogs, which "fixated" on Jones, referring to him as a "disgraced scientist" and arguing that he "admitted that not only is global warming not caused by man, but nothing significant is happening!"[99]

Former Republican vice presidential candidate Sarah Palin entered the fray, igniting international coverage with her statements: Because of the "appalling actions by so many climate-change experts," Palin argued that President Obama should boycott climate negotiations in Denmark in order to "not be a party to fraudulent scientific practices." The Academy of Motion Picture Arts and Sciences, she suggested, should rescind Al Gore's Oscar for *An Inconvenient Truth*.[100]

The e-mail hacking spawned official investigations into the scientists' work, including a thorough review of the IPCC report, which confirmed the integrity of both the science and the scientists. The investigations found that the IPCC's 2007 report contained two mistakes—one pertaining to an overestimation of Himalayan glacier recession and one pertaining to water shortages. (The IPCC calculated between 75 and 250 million people facing water shortage, but a Dutch investigation suggested the number is closer to 90 to 220 million people.) The science, however, according to the investigations, was uncompromised.[101]

Naysayers still pumped more scorn and ridicule through talk radio, Fox News, and the denial blogosphere, which lambasted climate science and scientists with emotionally laden pejoratives such as *hoax*, *con*, and *conspiracy*. It was the fodder with which program hosts could convince audiences that they were being fooled by evil scientists.

A SNOWBALL'S CHANCE IN HELL

A cold 2009–2010 winter and an East Coast February snowstorm became another opportunity to misinform the public and deride climate science on AM talk shows. Syndicated radio host Rush Limbaugh was among the most vocal. In February 2010, he called climate change a hoax, a big lie, a fraud, or a falsehood on at least nine of his shows. On February 17, he argued that climate change is "not about global warming or saving the planet." Rather, he claimed, it is a plot geared toward "advancing socialism [and] Marxism . . . expanding government and taking away people's freedom and liberty and raising their taxes."[102] Scientists and advocates calling for stemming global warming, said Limbaugh, have "done more damage than even Bill Ayers wanted to."[103] Among them was former vice president Al Gore. "Al Gore—ought to be subject to being sued."[104] In fact, Limbaugh linked the Democrats' climate-change rhetoric to al Qaeda leader Osama bin Laden.[105]

Limbaugh is among many talk-show hosts spreading conspiracy theories about scientifically established phenomena. Like Limbaugh, Fox News host Glenn Beck called climate change a "scam" and claimed that there had been "zero warming for over a decade."[106]

Among conspiracy-minded bloggers, science on climate change was being "driven by one-world-government seekers hoping to find a vehicle by which to command other nations . . . and their citizens," and that "genuine science was never involved."[107] Said another, "it is only the United Nations which will arbitrate what is correct environmentalism."[108]

Facing Realities

The year 2010 was marked by floods, fires, extinctions, record-breaking temperatures, and melting ice sheets.[109] In July, flooding destroyed and damaged seven hundred thousand homes in Pakistan, upending the lives of between fourteen and twenty million people, a disaster that humanitarian groups say is worse than the Haiti earthquake of 2010, Hurricane Katrina in 2005, and the Indian Ocean tsunami of 2004 combined.[110] Wildfires engulfed large areas of Russia while droughts shriveled millions of acres of its wheat. In the United States, unprecedented torrential rains deluged Tennessee, Oklahoma, and Arkansas. In August 2010, the Petermann Glacier, a one-square-mile chunk of ice, broke away from Greenland's ice sheet. According to a global inventory of species, 21 percent of known mammals and 30 percent of known amphibians face extinction, a faster rate of species decline than expected.[111] As oceans grow in acidity as a result of warmer temperatures, biodiversity and food security are increasingly threatened.[112] In the face of these daunting changes that threaten life on Earth, the US Senate failed to pass a climate bill, and the Copenhagen climate conference yielded little, due in part to tepid public pressure on policymakers. At the end of the hottest decade on record, the United Nations once more attempted to achieve consensus on an agreement to address global warming.

Media's Role in the Fate of the World

How could a handful of industry-sponsored science advisers convince masses of people that global warming, an established scientific phenomenon, was unreal or, worse, a hoax? It took three groups of political actors: industry's advocates, government officials, and mass media professionals.

Fossil fuel companies funded science advisers and created and sponsored front groups to obfuscate the science and sow confusion. This group of science advisers recycled their loud denial arguments through multiple channels.[113] Their rhetoric, which at times was wildly dishonest, created an illusion of scientific uncertainty, making it appear that the greenhouse effect was not occurring—or that if it were occurring, that it was natural and "good."

Government officials, particularly Republicans, aided and abetted these arguments. They hid the research from other public officials, the press, and the public while diminishing research scientists.

Without checking the veracity of the naysayers' statements, many journalists gave equal footing to denialists and real climate scientists, ultimately framing established climate science as "he-said-she-said" and creating an illusion that there were two sides to the climate science. Then, without adequate research and more credible sources, many followed the deniers' lead in pursuing the so-called Climategate scandal that turned out to be a ruse. Eager for controversy, some journalists seized upon a handful of words that turned errors in judgment into evidence of a conspiracy that unjustly tarnished climate scientists and misled the public on the seriousness of global warming. Other media professionals, particularly those affiliated with the more emotionally and ideologically driven cable programs, AM radio broadcasts, and Internet blogs blatantly joined the deniers, dishing out scorn and ridicule toward scientists. With the flood of confusion, much of the public never understood the realities of climate change. Policymakers failed to act, ultimately leaving a potentially cataclysmic problem unmitigated.

Before the industry's concerted attacks, most scientists had avoided engaging in politics to focus their time and efforts toward new scientific discoveries and research. Since the attacks, however, hundreds of scientists are now discussing ways to communicate the global warming realities directly to the public. The Geophysical Union has enlisted seven hundred climate scientists to readily speak with policymakers, journalists, and the public in efforts to correct misinformation.[114]

Chapter 12

The Sounds of Silence: Groups, Societies, and Media's Role

THE SOCIAL-PSYCHOLOGICAL BACKDROP: SOCIAL GRAVITY

The young men were stripped bare and chained; with bags placed over their heads, they were forced to simulate sodomy with other "prisoners." "That's the way dogs do it, isn't it?" the "guards" screamed. "Why don't you make like a dog?"[1]

It was just one of many humiliating acts that the "guards" forced the "prisoners" to do. They chained them to beds, forced them to withhold bodily functions, and deprived them of sleep. But these young men were not really prisoners, nor were their captors really prison guards. Rather, they were highly intelligent, psychologically healthy Stanford University students, many of whom were peace activists. But within three days, at the flip of a coin that determined their roles, some morphed into abusive guards, taunting, humiliating, and torturing their colleagues, while the others became "zombielike" prisoners. If the coin had landed the other way, reversing their roles, the same result would likely occur because they all shared psychological, social, and intellectual profiles. The 1971 Stanford Prison Experiment, as it became known, gave us a dose of reality about human behavior: Normal, peace-loving people can quickly become cruel abusers through a simple alteration of the situation's norms and assigned roles.[2]

This and many psychological experiments have raised questions about the degree to which thoughts, emotions, attitudes, identity, ideology, and behavior are individually determined and to what degree they are determined by larger groups and societies. Wild behavioral and atti-

273

tudinal differences appear from culture to culture, sometimes even from city to city. In one city, an abandoned car with its hood open is stripped of all its valuable parts while in another city, the car's hood is gently closed to protect it from rain.[3] In one part of the world, people believe they are "special," while in another they shun "specialness."[4] The same person, taken from one situation to the next, behaves and thinks differently in the new setting. What one knows to be true becomes questionable if the rest of the group disagrees—even when it comes to something as fundamental as the length of a line.[5]

Groups and roles weaken personal autonomy and often blind individuals to aspects of reality. Belonging to groups elicits allegiances, intergroup emotions, and "us versus them" thinking. It triggers "groupthink," a potentially dangerous phenomenon in which members of the groups develop beliefs of invulnerability, inherent morality, stereotypes of outsiders, and self-censorship to avoid falling out of the group's graces.[6] Group members cheer for their cohorts and boo at the "others." They tend to express pride and loyalty for their "own" and apathy, indifference, or disdain for outsiders, particularly in the face of competition. And what is particularly remarkable is that these phenomena occur even when the groups are *completely arbitrary* creations and membership is randomly assigned.[7] This was demonstrated in an experiment in which psychologists randomly assigned normal, young, middle-class, white, Protestant boys into two fabricated groups that the experimenters called "Rattlers" and "Eagles" and created a competitive game. Despite group members having no ethnic, religious, physical, or gender differences, they favored their "own" members, believing that they were "brave" and "friendly," while they stereotyped the "others" as "no-good cheats" and "rotten cussers."[8]

Groups are generally mental constructs, created to simplify a very complex world into organized, more easily understood categories, which on their own are not particularly harmful. Although many groups form organically as a result of birthplace, interest, or some shared aspect of life, others are actually artifacts, initiated in someone's mind, then through communication made into "reality," which can carry material consequences.[9] In Rwanda, the physical features that came to distinguish the Hutus from the Tutsis, for example, were largely established by European settlers who then lavished benefits onto one group based on those characteristics. In reality, the two groups had more commonalities than differences.[10] In Nazi Germany, Nazi leaders determined who was "a Jew" based on how many grandparents were Jewish, not one's religion, culture, or practice, then codified that group definition into the Nuremberg laws. Historic categorization of identity groups (such as the Canaanites and Philistines) have all but disappeared, while modern categories (such as Bangladeshis and East Timorians) have emerged or become more pronounced.[11]

Similarly, large groups such as nations and states have often been created, defined, and demarcated based on prevailing ideas about what "should" be. The idea of nationhood based on language or ethnicity such as a Slavic state (Yugoslavia), for example, emerged largely from thinkers connected to the French Revolution and German Romanticism. Intellectuals also developed and propagated the concept of separate nationhood based on ideas of "great" historical nations—the Great Serbia, Croatia, and Bosnia.[12] These are "imagined communities" in which members will never meet most of their group's fellow constituents.[13] Still, within imagined communities, members develop intergroup characteristics, emotions, and behaviors and adapt intergroup values, morals, speech patterns, codes, and symbols. They form bonds with one another, set up boundaries between themselves and the "outsiders," and shift the world into the lens of "us" and "them." On the state level, these groups physically separate themselves from the "others" with enforceable boundaries, standing armies, and a willingness to "die" for one's group. Citizenships are created, borders are enforced, and powerful social laws emerge.[14]

Social laws, such as public opinion, personal reputation, or cultural fashions, establish what is considered acceptable within the group and are often as powerful as laws promulgated by the state. Group members tend to obey social laws, lest they be outcast, isolated, or shunned. Often social laws are harmless: The laws of fashion, for example, may prevent a man from wearing a pink suit. But what happens when these social laws are unjust or harmful? "Even when people see plainly that something is wrong, they will [go silent] if public opinion and the consensus . . . [speak] against them." This is the "spiral of silence" that renders some members of a group or society mute.[15] And while it is not universal— there is always room for dissent—social pressures make dissenting from the norm very difficult. What is the media's role in the construction of groups, societies, social laws, and silencing?

THE ROLES OF MEDIA AND GROUP

In order for ideas—groups, their boundaries, membership criteria, and social laws—to become "real," they need to be communicated and accepted by other people. Those with the broadest reach—those with access to media—have the means to propagate their ideas, whether their ideas are meritorius or destructive. So, through media, some social constructs, such as group boundaries, stereotypes, frames, and social laws, get more exposure, promotion, and favorable presentation. Over time, these ideas harden, increasingly seeming concrete and true.[16] The categories, divisions, and characteristics of Hutus, Tutsis, Jews, Catholics, Africans, Communists, Socialists, and other groups, for example, became "true" in people's minds as a result of their repetition in mass media. These "realities" then influenced and guided behavior and caused a further demarcation of "us" from "them."

Media also profoundly affects existing social laws. In Senegal, for example, social laws had long required that young girls undergo female genital cutting (FGC) in order to be accepted as part of their communities. "Uncut" women were considered dirty and thus outcast. It took a thoughtful, concerted campaign to introduce and promote new concepts and frames that showed the incompatibility of FGC with health and human rights. Without mass media to propagate these concepts, FGC would likely still be the criterion determining fitness for marriage and community.

In some cases, media frames fueled the birth of nations. Through media, journalists such as Thomas Paine in his popular pamphlet-style publication, *Common Sense*, planted the seeds of independent statehood for what became the United States. In *Common Sense*, Paine regularly attacked the old country's feudal system and insisted that leaders— whether monarchs, tyrants, or legislators—had power only through citizens' consent and their granting of that power. This framework allowed the revolutionaries to envision themselves not as "traitors" but as "pioneers and forefathers struggling to create a better world for future generations." Through the media, such as *Common Sense*, readers began to imagine "life without a monarch," inspiring the Declaration of Independence and the Revolutionary War. Paine then used his medium to continue spreading revolutionary ideas, such as ending slavery and limited suffrage, by framing them as unacceptable and disgraceful.[17]

In the reverse, media also encouraged the dissolution of nations or states, such as the case of Yugoslavia's breakup, in part, by emphasizing factional groups. The nationalist media, beginning in Serbia, then in Croatia, emphasized divisions between ethnic groups and stereotyped the "others" as evil outsiders who should be ousted from "our" land. Those media, similar to the nationalist media of Rwanda and Nazi Germany, made associations with a socially constructed ethnic group a primary determinant for matters of life and death, affecting many for whom ethnicity had been essentially meaningless for decades. This kind of framework also makes ethnic differences seem primordial or biological, when in reality they are largely social artifacts and, in some cases, products of the last centuries.[18]

Once groups are formed, media tend to reinforce them, their characteristics, and their boundaries, whether they are "ethnicities," "nations," or other types of divisions, making them seem solid, permanent *things* rather than dynamic, fluid, socially constructed ideas.[19] This reinforcement makes change difficult, largely because it becomes hard to imagine or accept counterinformation that challenges the concepts and stereotypes about the "others" and the world that *seem* factual and real.[20]

Of course, in and of themselves, groups, political parties, societies, and states are not problematic and, in fact, have advanced many of humanity's loftiest aspirations. But danger arises when, through media, people convey interpretations that provoke negative emotions, stereotypes, blame, scapegoating, and their associated behaviors, often in favor of more benefits for those in one's own group. This occurs in the framing process. By taking massive amounts of data and distilling them into simpler frames, media professionals suggest meanings and interpretations for events, situations, and people. These meanings can either exacerbate conflicts and other problems or help resolve them.[21] Although some simplification is necessary to convey a complicated world in a short amount of time and space, some of the chosen frameworks can be profoundly detrimental. They propel absolutism, blind us to the subtle yet meaningful aspects of people and situations, and silence alternative points of view—which can, in turn, enable destruction agendas to flourish.

When media fixate on stereotypes and group differences, for example, audiences can lose sight of the many qualities, characteristics, and values they have in common, thereby creating the illusion of great chasms of separateness.[22] Oversimplification, stereotypes, and the illusion of unchanging societies make intergroup cooperation and conflict resolution far more difficult. The myths that groups or their members "are just this way" or "have always been this way" are gross simplifications that can have enormous consequences.

In the worst cases, media perpetuate stereotypes that diminish the "others" as categorically evil or subhuman, which opens the door for human rights violations.[23] But if media emphasize commonalities among people and broader shared goals and frames for which group members can strive together, then the illusions of great separation can fade, and groups can reconcile, collaborate, and cooperate or resolve issues together.[24]

Even subtle stereotypes and illusions can affect outcomes. While missing the deeper social and political dynamics, for example, many in the Western media portrayed the Bosnian war as an ancient, cyclical, never-ending, tribal war. This portrayal reportedly dissuaded the United States and others from intervening to protect human rights until after thousands had already perished.[25]

Changing frames can change outcomes. The same events and issues presented in different frames evoke markedly different responses. For example, in an experimental setting, people were more tolerant of a Ku Klux Klan rally when it was presented in a "free speech" frame than when it was framed as an issue of public safety.[26]

Under trying conditions, such as hardship or scarcity, certain frames can inflame public opinion and make cruelty acceptable. Perhaps the worst damage is done when static group simplifications and stereotypes combine with blame. "Blame frames" fault persons or groups for complex sociopolitical problems that they alone did not create, while exempting others, be they societies or institutions, from their respective roles and responsibilities. In essence, these frames ignore the multiple factors that collectively created the state of affairs and instead distill the complex situations into simplistic narratives with "bad guys" who cause the problems and "good guys" who are victims or heroes.[27] When these frameworks are consistent and repetitive across media outlets, they can seem like real explanations, particularly to people without access to all the contexts and additional facts. Worse yet, regular use of blame framing can act to reduce critical thinking on multiple issues, leading some people to rely on simplistic, black-and-white explanations.

Blame also stirs emotions such as anger or hate toward "the perpetrators," and the expectations of imminent harm elicit fear, a combination that historically has been used to justify civil or human rights abuses against constructed enemies and has contributed to self-fulfilling prophecies.[28] If conflicts become real and violent, the media tend to favor and portray one position, usually that of the establishment, as righteous and superior, while painting their constructed opponents as nefarious.[29] In apartheid South Africa, for example, without critically examining the government's role in creating a hostile racial environment, many Afrikaans mass media blamed black "terrorists" who, after decades of discrimination and abuse, violently railed against the government. In pre-democracy Taiwan, pro-KMT media blamed "Communists" for social problems without considering the government's oppressive practices that gave rise to the reformers' efforts.[30] In the genteel culture of Chile, where it could "never happen," widespread blame frames, disinformation, and stereotypes made the case for brutality and loss of life. Fueled by this framing, the most solid democracy in South America crumbled, and the gracious culture in which Chileans addressed each other as "madam" and "gentleman" deteriorated into violent chaos.[31]

In their extreme form, blame frames spawn an atmosphere of hate. At its worst, blame is a powerful component of the genocidal frame.

THE GENOCIDAL FRAME: STIRRING EMOTIONS THROUGH BLAME, HATE, AND FEAR

In worst-case scenarios, negative group stereotypes combine with four other components to form a "genocidal frame": the static, dehumanizing, or evil depictions; blame for serious sociopolitical problems; a "grand" cause that requires the elimination of the "bad guys"; and a "kill-or-be-killed" dichotomy. Under conditions of hardship and with a single, dominant message, the genocidal frame, when widely believed, can convince populations to support or, at least, turn a blind eye to the elimination of "the others" for the sake of rescuing their "own" community.

During the Holocaust and the Rwandan genocide, journalists stereotyped all members of particular identity groups as evil and subhuman, blamed them for a catalog of sociopolitical problems, and offered the "only solution"—preemptively eliminating all members of that group to prevent the "bad guys" from annihilating the "good guys." The Hutus blamed and targeted Tutsi "cockroaches." The Nazis blamed the international Jewish conspiracy and their collaborators. In both cases, the groups were portrayed as evil at their core and thus unchangeable.

Similarly, during the Bosnian war, many journalists blamed "the other" groups, depicted as evil, for the problems in the former Yugoslavia. Several Serbian journalists blamed "Albanian terrorists," the Muslim mujahideen, and Ustashas, which triggered similar retaliatory characterizations in the other groups' media. In all three of these cases mass media couched the destruction in language that made it seem vital for larger goals, such as majoritarian democracy, rescuing their people or humanity itself, or creating a utopia.

ROLE-PLAY AND DISTORTIONS

Heroes and villains, superstars and outcasts, leaders and followers, terrorists and freedom fighters—these social constructs rely upon and fit within narratives and frames that cast people into unrealistic (if not contrived) roles that delimit and caricature people and make them appear one-dimensional. When media disseminate these characteristics, they distort reality in ways that materially impact people's lives. In Serbian media, Slobodan Milošević was cast as the hero who was rescuing Serbs from the throes of a genocide being perpetrated upon them by their neighbors. Yet to the rest of the former Yugoslavia, Milošević was a villain who was responsible for the ruthless oppression and killing of countless Bosniaks, Croats, and Kosovars. Nazi media cast Adolf Hitler as their fearless Führer who restored Germany's dignity and reclaimed its rightful place among the nations of Europe. To most of the rest of the world, he was a vicious killer.

Media built these "heroes" by disseminating selective information and simplistic narratives and frames. Believing fully in these constructed ideas made many citizens blind to the enormity of their leaders' objectives and actions. In fiction those portrayed as heroes rarely do wrong, but reality is often entirely different.

Just as heroes are constructed, so are villains. They emerge through similarly selective information, crafted frames, and manufactured narratives. Audiences saturated in these media portrayals often cannot recognize any value in the perspectives of those people who have been cast into the role of villains. The simplified roles can promote cyclical hostility and finger-pointing, perpetuate conflict, and prevent efforts to resolve differences. During the early sabotage campaign in apartheid-era South Africa, for example, many of the Afrikaans media regularly portrayed Nelson Mandela and other antiapartheid leaders as "terrorists" without offering any contexts from which to understand the African National Congress's motivations toward violence. When Mandela was cast in the one-dimensional role of a terrorist, his argument for a multiracial democracy was difficult for many in the Afrikaans community to accept. International media, however, came to portray Mandela as a freedom fighter working toward apartheid's end. Similarly, in the Unionist media of the six counties/Northern Ireland, Republican leaders such as Gerry Adams and Martin McGuinness were cast as terrorists, while in pro-Republican media they were depicted as freedom fighters and protectors of the Irish Catholic community. As the caricatures subsided, efforts to obtain a peace agreement advanced.

On a much less dramatic level, many media distort individuals and groups through oversimplified character roles.[32] In the United States many media treat change agents, advocates challenging systemic injustice, and those holding minority opinions as outcasts and radicals.[33] While this treatment is most pronounced in programs that ridicule those with alternative viewpoints—or call people "Nazis," "traitors," or "a virus"—other media belittle or glorify in subtler ways. In the face of ridicule, many people eschew becoming agents of change, even when change is warranted.

SILENCING AND STATUS QUO

In this book's three worst-case scenarios—the Rwandan genocide, the Holocaust, and the Bosnian war—the leaders of the genocides and ethnic cleansing efforts took control of the media to ensure the greatest penetration of their message and to silence alternative perspectives. As part of this silencing, authorities seized the channels of communication and eliminated dissenters, change agents, and journalists who didn't toe the authority's party line. This was accomplished in multiple ways, including by job termination, defamation, or death—in all cases casting their adversaries as enemies. In Rwanda, Nazi Germany, and the former Yugoslavia, authorities silenced the vast majority of public dissent. Similar efforts to silence journalists and alternative information were made in apartheid-era South Africa, Chile, Taiwan, and the warring Burundi.

Authoritarian regimes are not the only setting in which silencing or gatekeeping occurs, however. In the United States, for example, numerous journalists and broadcasters have been fired for airing unpopular viewpoints. In one case, CNN fired a young journalist after she publicly admitting feeling pressured to use a specific frame, and another was terminated when she rejected the use of a "bad guy" caricature. CNN also forced the resignation of its chief news executive after he criticized the US military's attack on war reporters. Networks have also censored material or fired journalists when they sought to report dangerous corporate activities. In one incident, Fox TV in Tampa, Florida, terminated the jobs of two reporters after they refused to acquiesce to an exposé about the connection between cancer and growth hormones in milk.[34] In the 1990s, around the time of the ABC–Disney merger, the president of ABC News suppressed a report that was to be aired about child molesters working at Disney's theme parks. And while doing business with China, NBC rebuked a sports reporter who, during his report, mentioned China's human rights abuses.[35]

Eliminating nonconforming journalists is one of many ways that important information, ideas, and perspectives are omitted from the public sphere. Journalists and media professionals also self-censor, either to conform to their institutional expectations, to protect their careers, or to protect the media entity from bad publicity.

Silencing takes on more blatant forms as well. After the WikiLeaks November 2010 release of a trove of sensitive documents, including classified US cables, the nonprofit organization came under tremendous attack from government officials, media personalities, and some traditional journalists. Several public figures denounced WikiLeaks founder Julian Assange as a terrorist; some called for his assassination. Simultaneously, governments and corporations sought to destroy the organization. Companies such as MasterCard, Visa, and PayPal cut off the funding channels for WikiLeaks; Amazon.com threw the organization off its cloud-computing platform; and the United States led efforts to destroy the WikiLeaks website. The United States launched an investigation into prosecuting Assange. Before releasing the diplomatic cables that ran him afoul of the US government, Assange had won several journalism awards, including Amnesty International's New Media Award and the Index of Censorship's Freedom of Expression Award, for WikiLeaks's work in exposing unethical government and business conduct.[36]

Through the frames, norms, routines, and gatekeeping methods, media organizations also exclude important information, people, and ideas as if they don't exist or are unworthy of consideration.[37] But these omissions and gatekeeping hide, camouflage, and distort realities. They generate illusions and misunderstandings about sociopolitical developments and ultimately do injustice to societies by taking away the citizenry's choice and power. In Chile, for example, when the mainstream media essentially hid the government's torture program, most Chileans did not know about the torture and therefore could not take action. Similarly, in early apartheid South Africa, many Afrikaans-language audiences did not fully understand the human rights concerns behind the ANC's sabotage campaigns. In Mexico and Taiwan, before aggressive journalists exposed it as improper, the electorate either knew little of the system's corruption or merely accepted it as "just the way it is." And in the United States, many sectors of the public hear little if anything about corporate wrongdoing or many international developments, again robbing them of the first critical element necessary to take action: accurate information.[38]

Gatekeeping has another detrimental effect: It serves to narrow public opinion and the associated norms and cultures. Public opinion "depends on who talks and who keeps quiet," explained Elisabeth Noelle-Neumann in her 1984 book, *The Spiral of Silence*.[39] When gatekeepers allow only certain ideas, "hopes, and dreams" to go "through the gate into public consciousness,"[40] they limit what is possible, in part, by generating two illusions: that there is nothing more to be considered and that there is consensus, which can trigger a detrimental "spiral of silence."[41] In the spiral of silence, many "keep quiet even when people see plainly that something is wrong,"[42] or they "join the majority point of view even when they have no doubt that it is false."[43] Together, the silence and "bandwagon" types of conformity feed each other and shove important knowledge and thought underground. If a frame becomes accepted as a truth, the sense of consensus becomes more pronounced, bolstering the illusions further. From this state of affairs, new norms and cultures develop as if they are the natural order of things. "It's just the way things are."[44]

THE COSTS OF SILENCING

Silencing always has a cost, usually perpetuating a status quo and limiting a society's knowledge and development, which naturally affects the individuals within the society. In the words of the political communication scholar W. Lance Bennett, media often limit "who we think we are and what we think we are doing."[45] By robbing audiences of important knowledge and ideas that might otherwise prompt action, silencing ties the public's hands; it often prevents progress and ensures that the status quo continues. Although this can be benign, it can also perpetuate dangerous customs and ways of understanding the world. In extreme cases, as media portrated their systems and myths as perfectly normal in Nazi Germany, Rwanda, the former Yugoslavia, apartheid-era South Africa, Taiwan, Mexico, and Chile, human rights abuses persisted because they were either masked, hidden, or purported to be "common sense." In some of these situations, with no alternative frames, masses of people either accepted the logic and abuses or ignored them.[46]

Silencing also stifles democracies. Because media tend to set the public's agenda, when they omit issues and policies, those issues and policies are often forgotten by the masses. When absent from the agenda, important matters can be left unaddressed, which again makes problem solving difficult.[47]

Framing Distortions

"Blame" and "heroes-versus-villains" are two of many frames used in media to distill complex situations into simple, understandable stories. All frames suggest their meanings by the information the framers choose to include, exclude, and highlight, as well as through use of contexts, reference points, and emphases. They often suggest that some ideas, principles, perspectives, and people should be favored and considered legitimate while others should be devalued and delegitimized. They can suggest roles and responsibilities and set up expectations about the future. But by their very nature, frames are incomplete and biased, promoting certain understandings over others, which then shape their audience's emotions, thoughts, and judgments related to a spetrum political developments, people, and institutions.[48]

Over time, the frequent repetition of a few exclusive frames creates a generally accepted, sometimes distorted notion of "common sense." But that common sense blocks more comprehensive understandings, which makes that "reality" *seem* real and fixed. Because these frames are mostly hidden, embedded in their own cultures, their effects are subconscious.[49] And the "special genius" of this process is that its effect is completely invisible—seeming "normal and natural," so much so that its effect is completely invisible.[50] Though hidden beneath the surface, frames have very real effects. They motivate actions and inactions that can collectively influence the shape of societies and matters of life or death. In the case of climate change, for example, media used a seemingly harmless "debate" frame, characterized by "he-said-she-said" opposing views. In an ostensible effort to report on all sides of an issue, the media made it appear that global warming was still being debated among research scientists when, in fact, no meaningful debate exists in the scientific community. The frame ultimately misinformed members of the public and left an immense problem unmitigated.[51]

Certain frames and narratives can also trigger emotions, which again motivate decision making and action. Particular tones, narratives, and frames can imply guilt, innocence, fairness, or injustice. They can establish expectations or spark ridicule. Through these implications, frames can diminish or exalt people and their ideas and provoke actions and public policy change.[52] Powerful emotions such as hate and rage can lead to intolerance, violence, and support for abusive policies. When people hear only negative framing that focuses on the troublesome aspects of society without also supplying levelheaded, well-considered solutions, societies can descend into hopelessness, apathy, and cynicism.[53] Collectively, the constructed meanings, understandings, and misunderstandings shape cultures and unleash an array of psychological reactions—intergroup emotions, beliefs, and behaviors that together shape political outcomes.

When frames remain unchallenged, over time they can become "hardwired" into the brain, like computer operating systems that function without thought. With repetition, certain words trigger neurological connections that operate subconsciously and viscerally. By some estimates, our subconscious and reflexive responses account for roughly 98 percent of our attitudes and behaviors.[54] Without counterbalancing points of view to consider, these frames become the only reality that some people ever know.

CHANGE FRAMES, CHANGE THE WORLD?

Given the potentially negative impact of overly simplistic caricatures, frames, and narratives, it is vital to explore whether different and more accurate media frames foster rational problem solving and better societies. There is evidence that they can. When Burundi's media blamed "the others" and depicted them as "monsters," the carnage continued. But in perhaps one of the least likely places for reconciliation, journalists helped their audiences understand the underlying dynamics of the conflict and humanized the "others," allowing violence to subside. As journalists sorted fact from rumor and demonstrated the groups' mutual humanity, constructive social dialogue and a sense of community developed.[55]

During the Northern Ireland civil conflict, journalists reported the horrors of intercommunal violence, but they also recognized when paramilitary leaders authentically changed their approach and called for dialogue. As the previously hostile parties called for peaceful solutions, political leaders and media professionals reframed the political situation—from a war against "terrorists" and "criminals" to a complex political situation with conflicting interests between legitimate parties that had legitimate grievances needing to be redressed and reconciled. Most media openly endorsed the resulting peace agreement.[56] While the situations in both Burundi and Northern Ireland remain imperfect, the internecine violence has largely been replaced with dialogue.

In South Africa, antiapartheid activists, political leaders, and journalists used new frames about multiracial democracy to essentially construct a new country. Once the new South Africa was established, by broadcasting and covering the Truth and Reconciliation Commission hearings, media helped establish a shared history and a common ground among former adversaries while setting a new national foundation rooted in human rights. The process allowed former enemies to better understand one another within the larger contexts of the conflict.[57]

The "no-blame frame" has been important in facilitating positive social change. The mass abandonment of female genital cutting (FGC), for example, may not have been possible had change agents blamed FGC practitioners or stigmatized the custom. Instead, advocates situated FGC within the aspirational frames of health, human rights, and democracy. With the "human rights for all" frame and with fundamental information about FGC's health risks, thousands of communities realized that the practice conflicted with their larger goals.[58]

THE POWER OF MEDIA

Media are inextricably intertwined with events, political leaders, and societies, which collectively construct outcomes. As media influence people, cultures, and societies, those people and cultures, in turn, influence the media. And while media are not all-powerful, their might increases if their frames go unnoticed, uncountered, and unchallenged. Through repetition, pervasiveness, and domination of the public stage, one-sided views can become so widespread that they seem ordinary, commonplace, true, and natural.[59] And although some people "know better" and successfully repel divisive messages—even under the worst of circumstances (such as resistance groups during the Holocaust, the Rwandan genocide, and the Bosnian war)—without mass media to communicate their perspectives, their ability to affect public opinion is diminished, making substantive change improbable.[60]

People don't blindly accept media's frames. Their acceptance depends on numerous factors, including the types of frames used, their prior knowledge of the issues, and available countermessages. But most people don't have direct access to or extensive knowledge about many complex subject matters, such as science and international politics. So although political leaders and scientists play an important role in conveying information, their messages are typically filtered through media frames, from which the public derive their understandings. These understandings then collectively shape cultures, emotions, and beliefs, which in turn shape decisions, actions, and, of course, the concrete outcomes.[61]

With new technologies, such as the Internet, social networking, and the increasing numbers of television channels, the construction of a coherent and collective social reality has become more muddled, with a greater number of people contributing to political meanings and spreading responsibility for framing.[62] While this has enhanced the communication and framing power for many more people, it also has the potential to make matters much worse.

Chapter 13

Kill the Messenger

"Television [has] shrunk the world and [has] in the process become a great weapon for eradicating ignorance and promoting democracy," wrote Nelson Mandela after meeting the Inuit people in Alaska. They had watched his release on television and the transformation of South Africa from a deeply unjust country into an evolving democracy, and there he was, live and in person. "*Viva, ANC!*" (African National Congress), they shouted. Mandela's plight had reached communities that couldn't be farther from South Africa.[1]

It was through mass media that much of the world was in solidarity with Mandela's quest for a multiracial, democratic South Africa. That solidarity helped facilitate the first step in his vision, one that could only take shape in an environment that rejected and shunned the system's iniquities. Through the live broadcasts of the Truth and Reconciliation Commission hearings, the old South Africa was laid to rest, making way for the birth of a new one. But just as television and other mass media can be a great "weapon for eradicating ignorance and promoting democracy," they can also be a weapon that eradicates democracy and promotes ignorance, along with other less desirable ends.

Because the world of politics is fluid, dynamic, and ever changing, Mandela's dream continues to ebb and flow, relying on the next generation of policymakers' and media leaders' communications and activities to construct, along with the public, the next set of outcomes. Such is true of every political situation, whether great achievements, great disasters, or somewhere in between. Every moment gives people an opportunity to nurture and affect the next great achievement or to avert imminent disaster. Political outcomes are constant works in progress and "worlds of our making," shaped by our collective communications, meanings, understandings, and behaviors.[2]

Media are like DNA for social systems, offering us the codes and information by which we organize ourselves. They offer glue for modern societies—common reference points, events, meanings, frames, and social laws that guide our thinking and behaviors. When the information is flawed—like a mutant gene in our DNA—the system can malfunction. As eloquently stated by European scholar Dusan Reljic, without uninhibited and accurate information, "democratic institutions will corrupt . . . markets will collapse . . . information about new artists, trends, [and] culture will degenerate." Media are not "just another appliance . . . a toaster with pictures," he wrote, referring to comments by Mark Fowler, former chair of the Federal Communications Commission.[3]

CHANGING MEDIA, CHANGING WORLD

What was shaped yesterday by the press, television, and radio, today is shaped by many additional media—the Internet, social networking, cell phone cameras, and new channels, formats, and developing communication technologies. With changing technologies, mass communications have become more dynamic and interactive, which is also altering the world's political dynamics—some for better, some for worse.[4] The Internet has opened channels that might have otherwise been closed, boosting the ability of citizen journalists to investigate and disseminate realities that might be missed by both media conglomerates and state media, and, in some ways, democratizing access to "speech." In Burma, trampled citizens uploaded video footage of brutal government crackdowns. In Iran, protesters uploaded their fight for democracy before an international audience.[5] In Mexico, citizen journalists exposed the brutal drug wars via Twitter and blogs.[6] In Tunisia, citizens communicated and organized through an array of media, including Twitter and Facebook, to circumvent state restrictions on media and stand for a more fair and just society. Using cell phone cameras and computers, Tunisians uploaded photos and videos of government crackdowns throughout the country to share with fellow citizens. The Zine El Abidine Ben Ali regime caught on, sending hackers in to steal the entirety of Tunisians' passcodes, delete their Facebook profiles, and block access. But Facebook security teams used reconfiguring, rerouting, and blocking technologies to protect users. By January 8, 2011, several hundred thousand additional Tunisians had joined Facebook, sharing information, videos, and thoughts about Tunisia's political situation, concluding that it was time for a new government in their country. With the support of the Tunisian military, the Tunisian people ended the twenty-three-year dictatorship. Tunisians then turned back to Facebook as a tool for deliberation in their quest to create a new government.[7]

Through both traditional and new media, Tunisia's success spread throughout the world, inspiring a wave of activity throughout the Middle East. A second revolution followed, toppling the long-standing repressive Hosni Mubarak regime in Egypt, which had also attempted to control information and communication. In fact, for five days in late January 2011, Egypt's government cut off most of the country's Internet and cell phone service in efforts to disrupt the developing protests. Egyptians turned to other media, including voice technology, enabled by Google, with which they could connect to Twitter via telephone.[8]

The Internet has enhanced connections and collaborations across borders and allowed people to take some matters and some aspects of framing their experiences into their own hands. These connections enable people to bypass traditional media in exposing critical situations and to work together to improve lives.[9] But there is a darker side. The Internet has also become a mill for rumormongering, hate baiting, disseminating lies, and organizing malevolent ends. Doctored videos, photographs, and other material circulated over the Web become mainstream news before they are fact-checked, wreaking havoc on innocent people's lives.[10] The blogosphere has been used as a hotbed for destructive rumors, blame frames, and negative emotions, enclosing people in a hateful echo chamber whose effects can lead to injurious behavior or indifference to the fate of fellow human beings.[11]

As the foundational building blocks for frames, meanings, emotions, and beliefs, words and their arrangement matter, perhaps more now—in an age of instant communication—than ever before.[12] When they justify, legitimize, or teach deadly beliefs and behaviors, or harden people to accept such an environment, they can mean life or death. Advanced communication technologies can make matters worse, particularly when they combine with more sophisticated and increasingly accessible lethal technologies. Today, one person or small group can destroy an entire city of one hundred thousand with easy, small-scale modern technologies, according to defense specialists.[13] "Fifty years ago it took an invading army or massive aerial bombardment to cause such carnage, but today the same effect can be caused by a single nuclear, chemical, or biological weapon. . . . Any organization that wants the tools of mass destruction will have them," wrote Stephen Younger, former director of the US Department of Defense's Defense Threat Reduction Agency.[14] A vial containing a deadly new virus intentionally leaked at a major world airport, a "do-it-yourself" briefcase-sized nuclear weapon kit sold to the highest bidder—the capacities already exist and are expanding.[15] In the face of the dizzying array of potential threats to life and limb, it seems increasingly unrealistic and useless to continue focusing valuable talent and resources on building bigger and better weapons, rather than building a better humanity. For the latter, we may need to "kill the messenger." Not journalism itself and certainly not journalists, but perhaps some of the premises, structures, systems, and approaches to mass media that serve to stifle and oppress people and threaten life itself.

BETTER MEDIA, BETTER HUMANITY?

At first, it may sound like a ridiculous concept—media's role in elevating humanity. Obviously, media do not provide such fundamentals as food and shelter that psychologists suggest people need before they can reach for higher pursuits.[16] Most professional journalists reject such a role, believing that their job is simply to report facts accurately and objectively. But journalists' roles are not neutral: the subjects they choose, the questions they ask, the sources on which they rely, and the focus of their lens favor particular interpretations and help construct a particular kind of reality and humanity.[17] Although professional journalists generally do not blatantly propagandize, because mass media are embedded in particular ideologies and cultures, through their frames, narratives, and choice of stories, they naturally—and usually subconsciously—support, legitimize, or delegitimize those ideologies, cultures, and ways of thinking. All media systems have a subtle element of advocacy, often through the hidden reproduction of cultural symbols and their choices about what should be included or excluded. Journalists rely upon their own emotions, culture, values, and ideologies to decide what is newsworthy and draw conclusions about the framing of the events they choose to cover and the story lines they develop from them.[18] Because "facts do not frame themselves," the arrangements of the facts impact the meanings that are delivered.[19]

The collecting and reporting of "news" biases the information conveyed due to its very nature—its definition, brevity, and sources. Some define news as "novelty without change"; others identify it as the "violation of values," both of which spring from a particular interpretation of the world. News gathering tends to focus on activities of authorities and on dramatic events, crises, scandals, disagreements, and cynicism, all of which shape a particular outlook.[20] Relying upon authorities as primary sources, for example, usually results in authority-favored framing, and focusing on conflict creates a sense of controversy, even when there is none.[21]

For better or for worse, media play at least four roles in humanity's future. First, they either feature or ignore information that allows individuals and societies to know about and respond to important matters that might improve their lives and their communities. Second, through framing, media help shape meanings and understandings about issues, each other, and the world around them. Third, they help construct systems and cultures, elevating some norms, roles, and values and deprecating others. Systems and cultures, in turn, impact whom we become—as a society and as individuals—in a dynamic process. Fourth, media set up expectations and provoke emotions that encourage certain behaviors, which together contribute to the construction of another set of events.[22]

The Information and Contexts

A familiar maxim holds that "you can't teach philosophy to a hungry man," meaning that people cannot pursue higher ground before their basic survival needs are met.[23] Although feeding the hungry and ensuring people's safety are not in media's direct purview, media convey the information and contexts that allow individuals and societies to address and resolve these fundamental matters. If, for example, mass media fail to report and connect important issues such as poverty, government abuse, and citizen violence, societies generally can't know about and appropriately respond to them. But when media do convey the information, as they did in Senegal, life-altering changes can occur. When villagers in Senegal learned new concepts related to human health, human rights, and democracy, they changed several practices: They abandoned female genital cutting (FGC), ended forced childhood marriages, and established democratic councils for their villages. Through mass media, the concepts spread throughout Senegal and into additional countries, ultimately facilitating mass abandonment of FGC, which had long been held as commonsense and socially obligatory. Thousands of girls were spared the pain and illness associated with the practice.[24]

Because mass media call attention to certain issues while ignoring others—thereby setting the public's agenda and priming their considerations—they leave some matters and information unknown and neglected.[25] Neglect can leave major problems to fester and develop into epidemics, which can spiral sectors of society downward, stunt their development, and, in turn, affect other sectors of society.

Through framing, mass media also convey meanings, understandings, and misunderstandings about the issues, people, and groups while often implicitly suggesting whether the issues are intractable or resolvable. And although some simplicity is necessary to untangle a complicated world, oversimplification of sociopolitical matters can exacerbate problems and generate bigger ones. But if media make it possible for societies to comprehend the deeper mechanisms of sociopolitical or economic problems, people can be better positioned to solve them.[26]

Culture and Systems

Among the many ways that media affect humanity is their shaping of culture and social systems within a dynamic process of social construction. Human beings are inherently social creatures who tend to conform to their culture and social system—the roles, customs, values, and social laws in which they are immersed—and are inclined to gravitate toward pursuits and behaviors that are accepted and rewarded in those systems.[27] Some cultures and social systems encourage the emergence of extraordinary humanitarians, such as Mahatma Gandhi or Martin Luther King Jr., who model magnanimity, generosity, and dedication to the benefit of all humanity. Other systems, through social shunning and restrictive rules, destroy exemplars and their causes, either literally or figuratively. Similarly, while some cultures honor "war heroes" or powermongers, peaceful societies censure violence and the violent as underdeveloped behavior and character.[28]

Social systems and cultures are ever changing, discarding old norms, roles, and values and adopting new ones—sometimes for better, sometimes for worse. Because of their reach and amplification, mass media are an integral part of these social transformations. They suggest models of attitude and behavior, legitimize and promote some ideas, values, and frames, and diminish, obscure, or silence others.[29]

Expectations, Meanings, and Emotions

Through frames and narratives, media often set up expectations about the future, which trigger emotions—such as fear and anger—and their associated behaviors.[30] For example, a mass-disseminated narrative creating the expectation of an attack by an "enemy" on "us," whomever the "us" may be, can elicit fear, anger, or hatred,[31] prompting support for defensive action or even a preemptive strike. In Nazi Germany, the former Yugoslavia, and Rwanda, the media's narratives promoted expectations that their enemies were plotting a genocide, prompting support for "preemptive" attacks. It also occurred in Burundi, costing about five thousand lives in one preemptive slaying. Conveying these expectations set the dominoes in place to create wars and genocides that might not have happened without media's dissemination. This kind of content can fuel self-fulfilling prophecies in a wide range of sociopolitical phenomena.

Given media's ability to disseminate and influence for better or for worse, how should we use these powerful tools to our best collective advantage? How can we build a better media?

BUILDING A BETTER MEDIA

We have yet to explore mass media's highest and best use. Better media can equip individuals and societies to sensibly resolve sociopolitical problems and conflicts and to support the realization of their potential.[32] Among the important shifts, better media would include vastly more beneficial information, problem solving, deep analysis, and more accurate frames—filling the missing pieces of today's media.

Sins of Omission 1: The Holes in Most Mass Media

In November 2009, two top scientists calculated with meticulous detail how to power the entire world with renewable energy. In the cover story of the prestigious scientific journal *Scientific American*, Stanford University's Mark Jacobson and University of California–Davis's Marc Delucchi explained the obstacles and opportunities to achieving a world powered by sun, wind, and geothermal energy. They demonstrated the superiority of renewable energy, drew the road map for achieving this goal, and explained the hurdles that must be overcome—the greatest of which was a dearth of political will.[33]

As the world faces a most profound threat from climate change, one might expect the work of Delucchi and Jacobson to have commanded wide coverage in media. But the duo received requests for only a few interviews, while loud climate-change deniers and "Climategate" pushers ruled the headlines, captured worldwide attention, and thwarted even incremental policy changes. The omission of Jacobson and Delucchi juxtaposed against the headline-stealing denialists highlights one element of media's missing content: levelheaded assessments and solution providers, such as scientists, peacemakers, and others ready and able to make a difference, if they are just given the chance.

What if media had broadly covered the work of Delucchi and Jacobson or similar thinkers? Perhaps policymakers and the public would be closer to solving the climate problem. At minimum, their calculations and careful explanations would have allowed societies to make better-informed decisions about clean, renewable energies, rather than engage in irrelevant debates and character attacks.

When disseminated to enough people, this kind of information, which exists across numerous issue areas, can change the considerations, approaches, and relationships to seemingly intractable problems. And although critical thinkers and problem solvers could contribute ideas about answers to these important questions, they don't always fit well within the normal media frames and are therefore sparsely featured in much of today's mass media. Instead, most media tend to repeatedly recycle the same sources and present problems with no solutions.

Sins of Omission 2: Deep Analysis

Edward Scott Jr. made his fortune by cofounding BEA Systems, which he sold to Oracle for $8.5 billion. After a distinguished career in government, Scott focused on entrepreneurism and had not delved deeply into the world's intricate political issues. But in the year 2000, Link TV, a small, progressive channel, aired the documentary *Deadly Embrace: Nicaragua, the World Bank, and the International Monetary Fund* (IMF), which detailed the crippling effects of the IMF's "structural adjustment" policies on the developing Latin American country. Through the documentary, Scott gained new insights about the roots of Nicaragua's economic troubles, which prompted him to seek more knowledge and spend a chunk of his fortune—initially ten million dollars—toward the improvement of globalization policies. Scott's life soon became enriched with efforts toward big political changes that would assist in eradicating poverty and life-threatening illnesses.[34]

By helping one very capable person understand the roots of widespread poverty in some developing countries, a single documentary aired on one small channel may affect the well-being of millions of people. If media regularly conveyed more deep analysis in such a way that greater numbers of people grasped the nature of sociopolitical developments, the polarization in our world might subside; people could engage in more meaningful ways, and an enlightened society could emerge and resolve many additional problems.

How might more people be able to access greater breadth, depth, critical thought, diverse and pluralistic ideas, and rational solutions? In part, it would require addressing the invisible forces that drive the production of mass media's content. Some of those forces are structural—embedded in the media institutions' goals, legal environment, the definition of "news," and the recruiting, training, and rewarding of journalists and media professionals. Other forces are cultural, ideological, and psychological. Together these invisible forces impact the internal operations of mass media—its leadership and ethics—and ultimately who and what is heard, read, and seen in media content.

INVISIBLE FORCES 1

Systems and Structures

News Corporation's chairman and chief executive officer (CEO) Rupert Murdoch said on his company's Global Energy Initiative's website that he is "committed to addressing [the corporation's] impact on climate change and lowering the energy use of its businesses." News Corporation, which owns Fox News and several other media companies, took aggressive steps to combat climate change and reduce its own greenhouse gas emissions to zero in 2010 through carbon offsets, and it bragged that it was the first global media company to achieve such a goal. News Corporation subsidiary Dow Jones has committed to building a 4.1 megawatt solar power installation on its property in New Jersey, making it among the largest commercial solar power systems on a single site, according to its website.[35] If the CEO of News Corporation acknowledges the need to mitigate climate change, why, then, does his subsidiary, Fox News, loudly disseminate denial messages about established facts of climate change? The answer lies partly in the structure and goals of the publicly traded, for-profit mass media: Their content is designed to attract the biggest audience in order to sell advertising to other large corporations, even if that means conveying disinformation masked as journalism. As content grows wilder and more circuslike, it attracts larger audiences and translates into greater financial success for the company. But these benefits come with societal costs and consequences.

Free Media and Profit

Scholars have long asserted that free media help inform and protect citizens by their independent reporting and analysis. But when media's goals are exclusively focused on generating profits, journalists are not "free" to pursue substantive analysis.[36] Rather, they are constrained by the need to continuously increase profit and consequently must bypass considerable important content in favor of mass-appeal material, even when the omissions and inclusions might damage people or societies. Simplicity, drama, cynicism, episodic coverage, and superficial content replace complexity, depth, and substance. But while eye-catching content attracts large audiences, all that is popular is not necessarily good, as such content crowds out important societal information and cost-cutting measures thwart excellence and breadth of coverage.[37]

Because journalists are constrained by corporate goals, this model, in reality, is not free media. Free media liberate their journalists from such limitations so that they can offer deep analysis in what they believe to be of public interest.

Commercial media operators argue that they are simply giving people what they want. But perhaps "what people want is not necessarily what people need."[38] Part of the news media's job is "to tell the public . . . what it needs to know."[39] When they fail to do so, the costs may be larger than they appear. Under the profit-only goal, mass media professionals are sometimes forced to reach for the lowest common denominator—reaching to the depths of conflict, destruction, and ultra-simplification without meaningful explanations or solutions. The regular degrading of humanity, the ongoing reduction in complexity, critical thinking, and reduced knowledge can plunge societies into spirals of cynicism and worse.[40] Lowering standards of thinking, principles, and ethics may have the unintended consequence of reducing societies in tandem—drawing out the worst in people.

When companies incorporate goals related to the "public good," the "public interest," or a related mission, they can balance their motives with the offer of critical information and analysis. Several models attempt this, and each has strengths and weaknesses. In addition to the profit-only model, scholars most often lament the state-owned media model, which, when controlled by authoritarians or other government actors, is also not free.

Public and Government-Run Media

Government-sponsored media take many shapes. Under authoritarian governments, they can dangerously shore up the government's ideology and legitimacy, even when the government is abusive. In Nazi Germany and wartime Yugoslavia, the government-owned and government-sponsored mass media supported their respective regimes, even while those governments committed atrocities. The South African Broadcasting Corporation (SABC) in apartheid-era South Africa also acquiesced to government-driven ideologies. In Mexico and Taiwan, government-sponsored private media respectively turned a blind eye or justified government abuses.

In democratic settings, however, if there is an impenetrable wall between mass media content and other state functions, public media can be relatively free to serve the public interest and make important intellectual and cultural contributions.[41] If the walls are breached, however, these state media lose their freedoms. During Northern Ireland's "Troubles," for example, both British and Irish governments mandated a broadcasting ban, forbidding journalists from airing the voices of "terrorists," which often included elected officials. The ban tied journalists' hands and limited their ability to offer what they believed was important public information. BBC journalists attempted to circumvent the ban by showing the forbidden person speaking while using actors to lip-sync their statements. But while some BBC journalists made a mockery of the censorship, they could only go so far. By some accounts, the attempted silencing of the Irish Republican movement merely prompted the Republicans to use other means of being heard—including intensified sabotage.

The nature of institutions also limits dissemination of nongovernmental perspectives and frames. Even the most independent journalists face the invisible social forces that arise from being immersed in an institution.[42] When part of any system, people tend to conform to the dominant customs and ways of doing and seeing things. Sometimes conformity is necessary to succeed or avoid collision (such as driving on one side of the road to avoid an accident, using particular words to be understood, or following professional customs to keep one's job).[43] But sometimes people conform subconsciously simply by being steeped in the social system and thus being unaware of alternative ways of thinking or doing.

Alternative Models

Mission-driven, independent mass media are important alternatives to for-profit and government media. With alternative structures such as trusts, nonprofit organizations, and hybrids, mission-driven media journalists can better resist pressures from both the government and the media executives' drive for profit. With a trust, for example, resources are channeled toward a particular purpose rather than toward benefiting shareholders or proprieters. The trust-owned *Guardian* of London's purpose, to protect journalistic independence, freedom, and "liberal values," has been a key force behind the newspaper's pursuit of bold and independent journalism. With the climate change issue, for example, the *Guardian* led its media competitors in two ways: its reporter was one of the few who investigated and debunked the global warming naysayers' assertions; and the paper drafted and led a consortium of international newspapers in jointly publishing an editorial calling upon leaders to rectify the climate problem. The *Guardian* has also been a leader in exposing human rights abuses: For example, a *Guardian* reporter led investigations into British companies' substandard treatment of African laborers in South Africa. His reports prompted other British media to follow suit.

Nonprofit and Community Media

In Burundi, while most mass media content reflected their respective factions' violent perspectives, nonprofit media such as Studio Ijambo, Radio Publique Africaine, and Radio Isanganiro helped audiences sort rumor from fact and offered vital information and perspectives on the violence to help communities better understand the nature of the conflict, rebuild their lives, and reestablish social bonds. Their work helped facilitate intercommunity reconciliation during the vicious war, even while political leaders continued fighting. These media are among numerous nonprofit and community mass media that are making important contributions all over the world. Freed from the profit motives and usually exempt from state influence, these media are much better situated to offer independent analysis and programming.

Ijambo and similar media projects derive support from international, nonprofit, media-support organizations such as Search for Common Ground, Fondation Hirondelle, International Media Support, and Interviews Network. These organizations provide various levels of training, equipment, and other support to establish solid, community-based journalism in crisis areas that might help to facilitate peace and enhance human dignity. With a strong emphasis on empowering local communities to establish high levels of journalism, their projects have grown throughout the world's most troubled regions.

While the advantages of nonprofit organizations include greater independence, funding can be a struggle. Because they often rely on philanthropists and the generosity of patrons, their independence can be compromised, especially in times of economic hardship, often when perhaps independent media are needed most. They can also be compromised if the goals and ideologies of their funders or other powerful interests conflict with their own. The case of WikiLeaks, noted earlier, may be an extreme example. The website's release of diplomatic cables prompted a massive effort by corporations and the US government to compromise its ability to raise funds.[44]

The Cooperative Model

In Mexico, while most mass media acted as PRI-government cronies, the journalist-run cooperatives *Excelsior* and *Uno Mas Uno* offered vital underreported information, nongovernment perspectives, and a much-needed challenge to corruption. In cooperative media, workers—often both the journalists and the support staff—jointly own and manage the organization. Cooperatives are often nonprofit and democratically run, giving each worker-owner one vote in decision making; but they can take other forms as well. Like most nonprofit organizations, they can also face funding constraints.

Open Source

In open-source media, like Wikipedia, Wikinews, Indy-media, open blogs, and media exchange programs, individuals within a broad, decentralized network collaborate and openly contribute to the ever-changing media, collectively shaping the content. With people regularly adding their own expertise and correcting others' errors via the Internet or related technologies, open-source media evolves, improves, and can bridge countries and cultures. Because of their open, communal nature, they are generally free and independent of government or corporate influence and offer information unattainable through larger, established media. But their openness, which usually allows anyone to contribute, can also compromise accuracy, particularly if they do not have professional staff to fact-check, without which inaccurate information can be disseminated as fact.

WikiLeaks uses an aspect of open-source technology and allows whistle-blowers to deliver material through a relatively secure electronic medium. The website exposed wide-ranging activities of questionable morality by governments and organizations that had not been published by traditional media outlets. For example, it posted a confidential video showing US troops opening fire on approximately a dozen civilians in Iraq, including two Reuters journalists. One gunman remarked, "Ha ha, I hit 'em."[45] As mentioned, after winning the 2009 Amnesty International New Media Award, WikiLeaks founder Julian Assange shocked the world by releasing a trove of classified US diplomatic cables. The cables included information about Tunisia that helped confirm the Tunisians' widespread suspicions about their government's corrupt activities.[46] Assange maintains that WikiLeaks has filled a void generated by the failures of traditional journalism.

The impact of WikiLeaks on journalism, government, and the law is still unclear, but, at minimum, it has raised vital questions about transparency, journalistic responsibility, whistle-blower protection, and media freedoms.[47]

Institutional Media

Since the early 1920s, Wisconsin Public Radio has experimented with a cross-pollination of educational and public affairs information through its institutional sponsor, the University of Wisconsin. The station was an early broadcaster of news, book readings, classroom materials, and a wide range of public-interest material, offering a glimpse of what is possible through institutional mass media. This model, particularly when connected to educational institutions, has great promise for developing and disseminating excellent and expansive content. With a built-in apprentice program, the sponsoring colleges and universities can simultaneously train new media professionals and connect the wider community to the knowledge and critical thinking usually imparted in university classrooms. With the wealth of knowledge available from university scholars, institutional media can share important scientific discoveries, vital information, and deeper analyses. Through their journalism programs, many schools and universities already have facilities to publish and broadcast and the capacity to experiment with new management and reporting structures. In addition to institutional mass media, interuniversity media can share resources, disseminate the best information across institutions, and highlight the vital contribution of scholars alongside important news and analysis.

Entertainment and Politics

"Have you ever put lipstick on a pig?" asked late-night talk-show host David Letterman of then presidential candidate Barack Obama. After a brief pause, the candidate retorted, "The answer would be 'no' but it might be fun." He then added, "This is sort of silly season in politics," referring to the attacks on his remarks about Senator McCain's economic plans. Obama's appearance on the late-night talk show was part of a bigger trend that mixes serious political matters with comedy and other entertainment programs. The next day, then Republican presidential candidate John McCain appeared on ABC's *The View*, a talk show hosted by Barbara Walters and four other female panelists. They challenged McCain's veracity and logic on a range of political and constitutional issues. One panelist challenged the truth of a McCain advertisement, while another reminded McCain that the "originalist" constitutional philosophy he had espoused also supported slavery. Before the New Hampshire Primary elections of 2008, five million people had watched a viral Internet music video, "Crush on Obama," starring a woman who became known as "Obama Girl."

The blend of entertainment and politics can connect less politically attentive people with important public information through drama, comedy, and other related programs. In the United States, Comedy Central's *The Daily Show with Jon Stewart* has become a leading source of news for young people. Comedian-commentators Jon Stewart, Stephen Colbert, Bill Maher, and numerous other personalities are among a growing crop of media professionals who enlighten while they entertain. Some call Stewart a modern-day Edward R. Murrow, who is considered one of America's greatest broadcast journalists.[48]

Across cultures, entertainment programs are helping to heal divisions in war-torn communities. Programs such as *Our Neighbors, Ourselves* in Burundi helped to dispel erroneous beliefs about the "other" ethnic group. Other programs such as *The Team*, a drama about a fictional soccer team, entertain while demonstrating the necessity of cooperation for goal attainment. Versions of *The Team* air in fifteen countries, such as in Kenya, where there are forty-two distinct tribes. In Macedonia, a children's series significantly changed the kids' willingness to play with someone of another ethnic group. Before the program, only 30 percent of kids said they would invite children from other ethnic groups home to play; after eight episodes, that number increased to 60 percent.[49]

These programs offer plots with conflict resolution, bringing adversaries together to accomplish a common goal.[50] But other, more divisive programs can be dangerous: by falsifying information, misleading audiences, deriding and ridiculing others, and further polarizing people, they entertain at the expense of truth and social harmony.[51]

INVISIBLE FORCES 2: LEGAL STRUCTURES AND INSTITUTIONAL SUPPORT

While media can and should have multiple uses—for example, entertainment, communication, education—they should also enhance the welfare of humanity as a whole and contribute to wiser and more self-aware societies. Societies that foster excellence and civic and democratic participation need independent, free media to both reflect their evolution and offer a wide range of diverse perspectives, voices, and information from which to learn about and understand the world. Such a media environment requires legal and institutional structures—statutes, law enforcement, and resources—to protect and sustain information diversity, openness, accuracy, and accessibility, while preventing the development of a malicious, dishonest, or homogenized public space. This fine line requires careful implementation to protect journalists and independent mass media institutions while refining the distinction between free speech and more dangerous "fighting words" in the public sphere.

Protecting the Right to Information

In article 19(2) of the International Covenant on Civil and Political Rights, a multilateral United Nations treaty, international law recognizes a right to information and freedom of expression. But ensuring that right is complicated. It requires protecting journalists; bridging the "digital divide" between those who do and do not have access to information technology; ensuring that free and independent media organizations can do their work without interference by states, corporations, or others trying to thwart knowledge; and protecting diverse information, its sources, and the media institutions that report it, even when the material is uncomfortable.

Protecting the Right to Information by Protecting the Journalists

It is impossible to get vital information if the safety of journalists and other mass media professionals is compromised. International institutional structures must be established to ensure that journalists can safely obtain and deliver vital information without intimidation, punishment, and harm designed to silence the dissemination of information and alternative points of view. Between 1992 and 2011, some 852 journalists were killed on the job. Of these cases, 544 have not been prosecuted, according to the Committee to Protect Journalists (CPJ). In 2010 alone, 44 journalists were killed—fewer than the 77 slain in 2009, according to the CPJ. Many lost their lives while attempting to expose corruption, not while reporting in combat zones. Another 145 journalists are imprisoned, most of them in China (34), Iran (34), and Cuba (22);[52] more than 450 journalists live in exile for fear of being persecuted or killed.[53] Preventing future deaths of journalists calls for creation of international legal and structural protections on which journalists can rely in times of danger.

Access to Information

As our human right to information and knowledge is increasingly recognized as a means to better our own lives and communities, more resources need to be dedicated to bridging the information technology gap. This requires developing supportive infrastructures, expanding the reach of technology, and establishing enforceable international agreements to open and broaden Internet access and use.[54] Both the developing world and developed nations need these tools to ensure that access to accurate and unbiased sources of knowledge is available to all, rich or poor. Only with the free flow of accurate information can the dark shadows of hate, exploitation, and prejudice be overcome by the light of reason and thoughtful deliberation.

Media consolidation and concentration of ownership are the enemies of information diversity and pluralism, serving only media owners, not the public. To prevent narrow-minded discourse from dominating the public sphere, legal structures including antitrust laws, protections for net neutrality (unrestricted and unbiased Internet access and flow), treaties, and other thoughtful regulation are needed to help limit concentrated ownership and related forces that strangle the flow of independent information.

In addition to national and international laws, institutions, and resources should be dedicated to support bottom-up, independent, community-based media *and* intercommunity media. Locally based media can empower and engage people while they develop new publications, broadcast operations, and Internet channels. These media can also honor local cultures, share wisdom from diverse sources, channel talents into productive, cooperative efforts, and expand their creativity, skills, and knowledge.

With new technologies, intercommunity media can bridge across communities in virtual collaboration to exchange ideas and dialogue about common concerns irrespective of religion, ethnicity, age, sex, nationality, or other characteristics. While social networking has already enhanced these capabilities, more can be done through community centers, nongovernmental organizations (NGOs), schools, and universities, expanding potential solutions across borders and adding to the international marketplace of ideas. Each can share its unique knowledge, and together they can collaborate on mutually important projects, fostering cross-cultural trust and idea interchanges that can enlighten and elevate human potential.

With mission-oriented pilot projects, international institutions can aid cooperation, collaboration, democratic deliberation, conflict resolution, and multiculturalism through public affairs, comedy, and drama. Democratically structured media can also serve as microcosms, developing skills to practice democracy and conflict resolution. Internal and independent checks can correct their course if their missions become mired in selfish motives.

INVISIBLE FORCES 3:
BUILDING BETTER JOURNALISM

While news-oriented journalism has made enormous contributions, news and the internal media structures that produce it only partly serve the needs of an informed global society. The forces that shape news— including the recruiting, training, and rewarding of journalists, the beat system, the sources on whom they rely, the definition of news, and social forces such as ideology, culture, and institutional power—all shape what the world receives through news-based journalism.[55]

Recruiting

Journalists and other media professionals, whether on-air broadcasters, print and electronic reporters, or behind-the-scenes producers, are political leaders who wield considerable power. Thus, selecting the best and the brightest as media leaders is crucial to assure great content. But media professionals are most often placed in leadership positions without being democratically elected and are chosen for a wide array of reasons, including political alliances, ideologies, attractiveness, and popularity— none of which guarantees great insight or wisdom. While authoritarian regimes select journalists to fit their own ideologies or political goals (often power and resources), corporate media executives have also chosen journalists, in part, for their ideologies and for their mass appeal to aid them in attaining higher ratings, which ultimately brings in more advertising dollars.[56]

Professional Training and Rewarding

All professions need introspection, honest assessments, and development to keep improving and adjusting to the needs of changing times and circumstances. Journalism is no different. And in some ways, because of journalism's reach and potential influence, such introspective assessments and improvements are even more critical. Over the past several decades, Western journalists were trained to get the "scoop" and "break the news," through "beats" and official sources. That generally meant forgoing important civic phenomena in favor of dramatic events, crises, and scandals, without adequate explanations to better understand the underlying nature of the stories covered. It also meant magnifying differences and conflicts while losing sight of areas of agreement, shared values and commitments, as well as available avenues for reconciliation. While covering the words and actions of officials is important, relying upon them and their frames to accurately explain events fails to give the breadth and depth needed by the public to fully comprehend the real issues and situations.[57]

While news is important, the current approach to news may not be enough to convey the richness of the reality and resolve today's complicated issues. Humanity would benefit if the journalism profession reexamined and adjusted its old routines, training methods, and reward structures to better address societies' changing needs. To accomplish this, the profession could establish its own oversight institute or work with existing ones to reflect on areas of weakness, suggest improvement, and help the public sort out the veracity of the media's reports.

Ethics and Careerism

In most professions that have the ability to significantly injure others by their words or behaviors, oversight bodies have been established. Doctors have medical boards; lawyers have bar associations; scholars have institutional review boards; democratic politicians have elections and checks by the other governmental arms, such as independent courts and investigative committees. Similarly, most of these professions—such as doctors and lawyers—have ethics training requirements to ensure that minimum ethical standards are understood and maintained and have put punitive measures in place for those who violate the standards. In essence, these institutions work to ensure that professionals minimize their potential harm. But there is little in the way of offering oversight or ethics training to mass media professionals who, because of their reach and influence on the climate of social ethics, can do as much damage, and in some cases, more damage, than other professionals. Mass media touch all the other professions and communities and weigh heavily in the construction of society's principles and values.

How does a society embrace ethical media without impinging on media's freedoms? One proposal by the International Federation of Journalists (IFJ) argues for independent press councils to monitor media and guard the principles that guide their professionals. Those principles are outlined in the organization's "Declaration of Principles on the Conduct of Journalists":

(1) Respect for truth and for the right of the public to truth is the first duty of the journalist.

(2) In pursuance of this duty, the journalist shall at all times defend the principles of freedom in the honest collection and publication of news, and of the right of fair comment and criticism.

(3) The journalist shall report only in accordance with facts of which he/she knows the origin. The journalist shall not suppress essential information or falsify documents.

(4) The journalist shall use only fair methods to obtain news, photographs and documents.

(5) The journalist shall do the utmost to rectify any published information which is found to be harmfully inaccurate.

(6) The journalist shall observe professional secrecy regarding the source of information obtained in confidence.

(7) The journalist shall be aware of the danger of discrimination being furthered by the media, and shall do the utmost to avoid facilitating such discrimination based on, among other things, race, sex, sexual orientation, language, religion, political or other opinions, and national or social origins.

(8) The journalist shall regard as grave professional offenses the following:
   (a) plagiarism;
   (b) malicious misrepresentation;
   (c) calumny, slander, libel, unfounded accusations;
   (d) acceptance of a bribe in any form in consideration of either publication or suppression.

(9) Journalists worthy of the name shall deem it their duty to observe faithfully the principles stated above. Within the general law of each country the journalist shall recognize in professional matters the jurisdiction of colleagues only, to the exclusion of every kind of interference by governments or others.[58]

"It is hardly possible for one journalist to be 'ethical' on [his or her] own without engaging with colleagues," argued IFJ president Jim Poumelha. "Journalists who do not want to be mouthpieces for owners or political dogma, or other vested interests need the support of their colleagues," he said, advocating for a strong journalism union, milieu, and structure to enable and elevate strong ethical standards.[59] Together, media institutions can empower independent oversight organizations to collectively guard against journalistic activities that conflict with fundamental principles while encouraging those that elevate journalism and generate trust from their audiences.

Balancing Principles

Some principles are not quite as clear as the issues of truth telling and will require some debate among media professionals and scholars. Among them is the issue of free speech. How does a society protect free speech and political thought while also protecting people from the harms that arise from particular kinds of speech that, for example, incite violence? This issue needs discussion in order to find the distinction that protects free speech while preventing injury to others. In many cases presented in this book, media played a large role in creating the environments conducive to human rights abuses and genocide. The answers are not yet clear. Some scholars argue for solid institutions and regulations to ensure that unfettered speech does not become fratricidal or genocidal.[60] Others suggest that "real freedom has to come from within, through the awakening of press professionals who care about and want to defend their editorial independence and judgment."[61] And some argue that the answer to destructive speech is more speech. But many of the potential harms can also be abated—or at least addressed—if media professionals create or engage oversight structures in a meaningful way.

While avoiding a "slippery slope" that might hamper free speech, laws and institutions must protect against the dissemination of harm-provoking speech, such as incitement to violence, "fighting words," and blatant disinformation, while protecting authentic free expression. Fine-tuning those demarcations will require engagement of media professionals and legal and communication scholars.

HOLDING CANDLES TO THE DARKNESS

As the pillars of journalism are increasingly challenged—by new technologies, new media, and the collapse of press industries—I advocate reexamining the approach to mass media, particularly journalism. While media may or may not have "direct effects," through these snapshots in time I hope to have shown how, under many circumstances, media messages do collectively have real consequences in constructing outcomes. They can imperil or help rescue. They can stoke the flames of war or help facilitate peace; they can enrich or impoverish human existence, dialogue, diplomacy, and democracy; and they can help protect human rights or provoke their violation. Media can be tools of enlightenment or weapons of ignorance and darkness. Through shaping meanings, identities, and other commonsense realities, media help create a kind of reality that can be life altering, expanding and elevating what is possible for individuals, communities, and the fate of Earth itself.

Knowing that so much more is possible, both for humanity as a whole and for individuals, media can contribute to the building of a better humanity, as a starting point, through four primary shifts: (1) by disseminating a fuller range of important information and perspectives, (2) by offering deeper understandings about sociopolitical issues, (3) by featuring well-considered, rational, or emotionally intelligent solutions, and (4) by airing the exemplars, offering models and legitimacy for "higher" values and pursuits and those who exhibit them. These four shifts might allow people and societies to see their own shortcomings, attain greater comprehension of vital issues, address neglected societal problems from well-founded critical thought, and encourage people to expand their own potential. But more is possible and necessary, given the crossroads that we face. The potential is there to bring out the best in humanity; to end wars and other devastation; to contribute to transparent, democratic governance that serves the public good; and to enrich humanity with the promise of discovering a higher purpose. These goals require considerable structural support—for example, laws and institutions for protecting and promoting an independent, sophisticated, and introspective media corps that is ready to learn, evolve, and share its wisdom with its audiences. In essence, we must strive for a media corps that will do more than report; we need one that will disentangle truth from lies and push the boundaries of what is possible for humanity, while bringing lasting understanding to the widest audience and helping societies resolve public-interest matters and heal old wounds.

NOTES

Foreword

1. C. Wright Mills, *White Collar* (New York: Oxford University Press, 1951), p. 333.
2. C. Wright Mills, *The Power Elite* (New York: Oxford University Press, 1956), pp. 302–303.
3. See, for example, Robert W. McChesney, *The Problem of the Media: U.S. Communication Politics in the Twenty-First Century* (New York: Monthly Review Press, 2004).

Preface

1. There has been considerable work around this idea, including Steven Livingston, "Clarifying the CNN Effect: An Examination of Media Effects According to the Type of Military Intervention" (Research Paper R-18, Joan Shorenstein Center on the Press, Politics, and Public Policy, Kennedy School of Government, Harvard University, Cambridge, MA, 1997); Piers Robinson, "The CNN Effect: Can the News Media Drive Foreign Policy?" *Review of International Studies* 25, no. 2 (1999): 301–309; Philip Seib, *Headline Diplomacy: How News Coverage Affects Foreign Policy* (Westport, CT: Greenwood Publishing Group, 1996); Eytan Gilboa, "Effects of Global Television News on U.S. Policy in International Conflict," in *Media and Conflict in the Twenty-First Century*, ed. Philip Sieb (New York: Palgrave MacMillan, 2005), pp. 1–32.

Introduction

1. Jim David Adkisson, handwritten manifesto, *Knoxville News Sentinel*, February 10, 2009, http://web.knoxnews.com/pdf/021009church-manifesto.pdf (accessed February 27, 2011), linked at Jamie Satterfield, "Church Shooter Pleads Guilty; Letter Released," *Knoxville News Sentinel*, February 10, 2009, http://webcache.googleusercontent.com/search?q=cache:ZQhB0B-K2sMJ:www.knoxnews.com/news/2009/feb/10/church-shooter-pleads-guilty-letter-released/+Jamie+Satterfield,+%E2%80%9CChurch+Shooter+Pleads+Guilty,+Knoxville+News+Sentinel&cd=1&hl=en&ct=clnk&gl=us&source=www.google.com (accessed February 27, 2011); Hayes Hickman and Don Jacobs, "Suspect's Note Cites 'Liberal Movement' for Church Attack," Knoxville News Sentinel, July 28, 2008, http://webcache.googleusercontent.com/search?q=cache:tCHbD79gAL4J:www.knoxnews.com/news/2008/jul/29/suspects-note-cites-liberal-movement-church-attack/+Hayes+Hickman+and+Don+Jacobs.+Knoxville+News+Sentinel+Co.+%28July+28,+2008%29&cd=1&hl=en&ct=clnk&gl=us&source=www.google.com (accessed February 27, 2011).
2. Adkisson, manifesto.

3. Hickman and Jacobs, "Suspect's Note Cites 'Liberal Movement' for Church Attack."

4. Ibid.

5. Ibid.

6. Satterfield, "Church Shooter Pleads Guilty."

7. Michael Savage, as quoted in Rory O'Connor, *Shock Jocks: Hate Speech and Talk Radio* (San Francisco: Alternet Books, 2008); Bill Moyers, "Rage on the Radio," *The Journal*, September 12, 2008, http://webcache.googleusercontent.com/search?q=cache:oDx7JjHKIsUJ:www.pbs.org/moyers/journal/09122008/profile.html+Bill+Moyers,+The+Journal+%28September+12,+2008&cd=1&hl=en&ct=clnk&gl=us&source=www.google.com (accessed February 27, 2011).

8. Michael Savage, November 13, 2009, archived on http://www.mediamatters.org.

9. These are the numbers reported in newspapers and Web magazines, including *Talkers Magazine*, although the numbers fluctuate some, http://talkers.com/online/?p=71, http://www.michaelsavage.wnd.com/index.php?fa=PAGE.view&pageId=10421, http://www.trn1.com/talkers-top-heavy-hundred; Michael Massing, "Un-American: Have You Listened to the Right-Wing Media Lately?" Columbia Journalism Review, January/February 2009, http://www.cjr.org/essay/unamerican_1.php (accessed March 3, 2011).

10. Rush Limbaugh, May 11, 2010, archived on http://www.mediamatters.org.

11. Ann Coulter on *The O'Reilly Factor*, May 7, 2010.

12. Ann Coulter, *Treason: Liberal Treachery from the Cold War to the War on Terrorism* (New York: Crown Forum, 2010), p. 1.

13. Media Matters for America, "Conservative Media Frequently Accuse Progressives of 'Raping' Americans," November 19, 2009, http://mediamatters.org/research/200911190048.

14. Rush Limbaugh, May 2, 2010, archived on http://www.mediamatters.org.

15. Media Matters for America, "Conservative Media Frequently Accuse."

16. Ibid.

17. Massing, "Un-American."

18. Media Matters for America, "Conservative Media Frequently Accuse"; Noah Lederman, "Playing the Nazi Card: Comparing Obama to Hitler Becomes a Standard Right-Wing Trope," *Extra!* March 2010, pp. 10–11.

19. Lederman, "Playing the Nazi Card," pp. 10–11.

20. Sarah Sobieraj and Jeffrey M Berry, "From Incivility to Outrage: Political Discourse in Blogs, Talk Radio, and Cable News," *Political Communication* 28, no. 1:19–41.

21. Harris Poll, March 24, 2010, posted at http://www.mediamatters.org; Marty Kaplan, "How Dumb Do They Think (Know) We Are," *Jewish Journal*, March 26, 2010, http://www.jewishjournal.com/marty_kaplan/article/how_dumb_do_they_think_know_we_are_20100326/ (accessed March 3, 2011).

22. Ibid.

23. Ibid.

24. Harris Poll, March 24, 2010; Marty Kaplan, "How Dumb Do They Think

(Know) We Are"; Media Matters for America, "No Surprise That Harris Poll Finds Republicans Believe GOP Smears of Obama," October 25, 2010, http://media mat-ters.org/research/201003250048. One study finds that AM talk-radio listeners are more misinformed than listeners of moderate radio such as National Public Radio (NPR): Richard C. Hofstetter, David Barker, James T. Smith, Gina M. Zari, and Thomas A. Ingrassia, "Information, Misinformation on Political Talk Radio," *Political Research Quarterly* 52 (1999): 353–69.

25. Mark Potok, "The Year in Hate & Extremism, 2011," *Southern Poverty Law Center Intelligence Report* 141 (Spring 2011), http://www.splcenter.org/get-informed /intelligence-report/browse-all-issues/2011/spring/the-year-in-hate-extremism-2010; Southern Poverty Law Center; Department of Homeland Security, Office of Intelligence and Analysis, "Rightwing Extremism: Current Economic and Political Climate Fueling Resurgence in Radicalization and Recruitment," April 7, 2009, http://www.fas.org/ irp/eprint/rightwing.pdf (accessed March 3, 2011).

26. Ibid.

27. Mark Potok, "Rage on the Right: The Year in Hate and Extremism," Southern Poverty Law Center, *Intelligence Report* 137 (Spring 2010), http://www.splcenter.org/get-informed/intelligence-report/browse-all-issues/2010/spring/rage-on-the-right (accessed March 3, 2011); Potok, "Year in Hate & Extremism."

28. Larry Keller, "Fear of FEMA," Southern Poverty Law Center, *Intelligence Report* 137 (Spring 2010), http://www.splcenter.org/get-informed/intelligence-report/browse-all-issues/2010/spring/fear-of-fema (accessed March 3, 2011).

29. Paul Krugman, "Climate of Hate," Newy York Times, January 9, 2011, http://www.nytimes.com/2011/01/10/opinion/10krugman.html (accessed March 3, 2011).

30. Jordy Yager, "Lawmakers Facing More Threats," Hill, April 27, 2011, http://thehill .com/homenews/house/157897-lawmakers-under-threat (accessed May 2, 2011).

31. Boone, "Swastika Painted."

32. Krugman, "Climate of Hate."

33. "Tucson Firefighter Refused to Respond," *New York Times*, February 17, 2011, http://www.nytimes.com/2011/02/18/us/18tucson.html (accessed March 3, 2011).

34. Jean Seaton, "The New 'Ethnic' Wars and the Media," in *The Media of Conflict: War Reporting and Representations of Ethnic Violence*, ed. Tim Allen and Jean Seaton (New York: St. Martin's Press, 1999), pp. 43–63.

35. Monroe Price and Mark Thompson, *Forging Peace: Intervention, Human Rights, and the Management of Media Space* (Indianapolis: Indiana University Press, 2002), p. 42.

36. David Altheide, *Creating Fear: News and the Construction of Crisis* (New York: Walter de Gruyter, 2002).

37. Massing, "Un-American."

38. Price and Thompson, *Forging Peace*, p. 1.

39. Examples for this are contained with the chapters in this book.

40. For citations, please see chapter 1 on Rwanda.

41. For citations, see chapter 1.

42. See citations in chapter 2 on the Holocaust.

43. For citations, please see chapter 3 on Bosnia and chapter 2 on the Holocaust.

44. Vahakn N. Dadrian, *The History of the Armenian Genocide: Ethnic Conflict from the Balkans to Anatolia to the Caucuses* (Providence: Berghahn Books, 1995).

45. Price and Thompson, *Forging Peace*, p. 1.

46. For citations, please see chapter 4 on Burundi.

47. Gordon Adam and Lina Holguin, "The Media's Role in Peace-Building: Asset or Liability?" (presentation at Our Media 3 Conference, Barranquilla, Colombia, May 19–21, 2003), http://ics.leeds.ac.uk/papers/pmt/exhibits/1769/mediainpeace.pdf (accessed March 3, 2011).

48. For citations, please see chapter 5 on Northern Ireland.

49. For citations, please see chapter 7 on Chile.

50. For citations, please see chapter 6 on South Africa.

51. For citations, please see chapter 6.

52. For citations, please see chapter 9 on Taiwan and chapter 8 on Mexico.

53. For citations, please see chapter 10 on Senegal.

54. This is further discussed in chapters 12 and 13. There is a large body on constructionism, including Nick Onuf, *World of Our Making: Rules and Rule in Social Theory and International Relations* (Columbia: University of South Carolina Press, 1989); William A. Gamson, David Croteau, William Hoynes, and Theodore Sasson, "Media Images and the Social Construction of Reality," *Annual Review of Sociology* 18: 373–93; Murray Edelman, *Politics as Symbolic Action: Mass Arousal and Quiescence* (Chicago: Markham Publishing, 2001); Ann M. Crigler, "Making Sense of Politics: Constructing Political Messages and Meanings," in *The Psychology of Political Communication*, ed. Ann N. Crigler (Ann Arbor: University of Michigan Press, 1998); Russell W. Neuman, Marion R. Just, and Ann N. Crigler, *Common Knowledge: News and the Construction of Political Meaning* (Chicago: University of Chicago Press, 1992), pp. 1–10. For a discussion on how constructionism relates to conflict, see Seaton, "New 'Ethnic' Wars and the Media."

55. For citations, please see chapter 11 on climate change.

56. Alexis Madrigal, "The Inside Story of How Facebook Responded to Tunisian Hacks," *Atlantic*, January 24, 2011, http://www.theatlantic.com/technology/archive/2011/01/the-inside-story-of-how-facebook-responded-to-tunisian-hacks/70044/ (accessed March 3, 2011); "Egypt Internet Comes Back Online," BBC News: Technology, February 2, 2011, http://www.bbc.co.uk/news/technology-12346929 (accessed March 3, 2011); Matt Richtel, "Egypt Cuts off Most Internet and Cell Service," *New York Times*, January 28, 2011, http://www.nytimes.com/2011/01/29/technology/internet/29cutoff.html (accessed March 3, 2011); Mike Giglio, "The Cyberactivists Who Helped Topple a Dictator," *Newsweek*, January 15, 2011, http://www.newsweek.com/2011/01/15/tunisia-protests-the-facebook-revolution.html (accessed March 3, 2011); on changing power, see Joseph Nye, *The Future of Power* (New York: Public Affairs Books, 2011); for the role of Al Jazeera aggregating social networking posts, see Philip Seib, "Thank You, Al Jazeera," *Huffington Post*, January 24, 2011, http://www.huffingtonpost.com/philip-seib/thank-you-al-jazeera_b_812724.html (accessed March 3, 2011).

Chapter 1: Hate as a Contagion

1. Names are fictional, but the accounts are real.

2. Scott Straus and Richard Lyons, *Intimate Enemy: Images and Voices of the Rwandan Genocide* (New York: Zone Books, 2006), p. 40.

3. Straus and Lyons, *Intimate Enemy*.

4. Peter Landesman, "A Woman's Work," *New York Times Magazine*, September 15, 2002, http://www.nytimes.com/2002/09/15/magazine/a-woman-s-work.html (accessed March 3, 2011).

5. Straus and Lyons, *Intimate Enemy*.

6. Alison Des Forges, *Leave None to Tell the Story* (New York: Human Rights Watch, 1999), p. 212.

7. Straus and Lyons, *Intimate Enemy*.

8. Jean Hatzfeld, *Machete Season: The Killers in Rwanda Speak: A Report* (New York: Farrar, Straus, and Giroux, 2005), p. 68.

9. Ibid., p. 100.

10. Ibid., pp. 100–101.

11. Ibid., pp. 103–104.

12. Ibid., pp. 131–33.

13. Jean Hatzfeld, *Life Laid Bare: The Survivors in Rwanda Speak* (New York: Other Press, 2006).

14. Mahmood Mamdani, *When Victims Become Killers: Colonialism, Nativism, and the Genocide in Rwanda* (Princeton, NJ: Princeton University Press, 2001).

15. Roméo Dallaire, *Shake Hands with the Devil: The Failure of Humanity in Rwanda* (New York: Random House, 2003).

16. Nick Hughes, "Exhibit 467: Genocide through a Camera Lens," in *The Media and the Rwandan Genocide*, ed. Allan Thompson (Ann Arbor: Pluto Press, 2007), pp. 231–34.

17. Dallaire, *Shake Hands with the Devil*.

18. Ibid., p. 277.

19. Des Forges, *Leave None to Tell the Story*, p. 15.

20. Ibid.; note that there were enclaves where Tutsis and Hutus together resisted the genocide.

21. Straus and Lyons, *Intimate Enemy*; Gerald Caplan, "Rwanda: Walking the Road to Genocide," in *The Media and the Rwandan Genocide*, ed. Allan Thompson (Ann Arbor: Pluto Press, 2007), pp. 20–40.

22. Mamdani, *When Victims Become Killers*; Alain Destexhe, *Rwanda and Genocide in the Twentieth Century* (New York: New York University Press, 1995).

23. Caplan, "Rwanda"; note that there is some dispute: Shaharyar M. Khan, *The Shallow Graves of Rwanda* (New York: I. B. Tauris, 2000), suggests there had been massacres, but for the most part the tribes lived harmoniously.

24. Richard H. Dekmejian, *Spectrum of Terror* (Washington, DC: CQ Press, 2007).

25. Linda Melvern, *Conspiracy to Murder: The Rwandan Genocide* (New York: Verso, 2004).

26. Des Forges, *Leave None to Tell the Story*.

27. Ibid.; Mike Dottridge, "Notes on Circumstances That Facilitate Genocide: The Attention Given to Rwanda by the Media and Others Outside Rwanda Before 1990," in *The Media and the Rwandan Genocide*, ed. Allan Thompson (Ann Arbor: Pluto Press, 2007), pp. 242–47; note that the numbers of refugees range from 450,000 to nearly 800,000.

28. Des Forges, *Leave None to Tell the Story*.

29. Melvern, *Conspiracy to Murder*.

30. Des Forges, *Leave None to Tell the Story*, p. 49.

31. Des Forges, *Leave None to Tell the Story*.

32. Ibid.

33. Ibid.

34. Hatzfeld, *Machete Season*, p. 71.

35. Dallaire, *Shake Hands with the Devil*.

36. Alison Des Forges, "Call to Genocide: Radio in Rwanda, 1994," in *The Media and the Rwandan Genocide*, ed. Allan Thompson (Ann Arbor: Pluto Press, 2007), pp. 41–54.

37. Caplan, "Rwanda."

38. Des Forges, "Call to Genocide"; Radio Télévision Libre des Milles Collines (RTLM) transcripts.

39. Des Forges, "Call to Genocide," p. 2; Darryl Li, "Echoes of Violence: Considerations on Radio and Genocide in Rwanda," in *The Media and the Rwandan Genocide*, ed. Allan Thompson (Ann Arbor: Pluto Press, 2007), pp. 90–109.

40. RTLM transcripts; Li, "Echoes of Violence."

41. Jean-Pierre Chrétian, "RTLM Propaganda: The Democratic Alibi," in *The Media and the Rwandan Genocide*, ed. Allan Thompson (Ann Arbor: Pluto Press, 2007), p. 56.

42. Kantano Habimana, RTLM transcripts, tape 0004.

43. Ibid.

44. Valerie Bemeriki, RTLM transcripts, tape 0008.

45. Dele Olojede, "When Words Could Kill," *Newsday*, April 4, 2004, http://www.pulitzer.org/archives/6922.

46. Habimana, RTLM transcripts, tape 0035.

47. Bemeriki, RTLM transcripts, tape 0016.

48. Ibid., tape 0035.

49. Jean-Marie Vianney Higiro, "Rwandan Private Print Media on the Eve of the Genocide," in *The Media and the Rwandan Genocide*, ed. Allan Thompson (Ann Arbor: Pluto Press, 2007), p. 73.

50. Fred Grunfeld and Anke Huijboom, *The Failure to Prevent Genocide in Rwanda: The Role of Bystanders* (Boston: Martinus Nijhoff Publishers, 2007), p. 25.

51. Ibid., p. 22.

52. Marcel Kabanda, "*Kangura*: The Triumph of Propaganda Refined," in *The Media and the Rwandan Genocide*, ed. Allan Thompson (Ann Arbor: Pluto Press, 2007), pp. 62–73.

53. RTLM transcripts; Des Forges, "Call to Genocide," p. 48.

54. Des Forges, *Leave None to Tell the Story*, p. 73.

55. Ibid.

56. Habimana, RTLM transcripts, tape 0011.

57. RTLM transcripts.

58. Des Forges, *Leave None to Tell the Story*, p. 72.

59. Hatzfeld, *Machete Season*, p. 15.

60. Ibid., p. 49.

61. Ibid., p. 47.

62. Ibid.

63. Ibid., p. 231.

64. Frodouald Karamira, RTLM transcripts, tape 0008.

65. Ananie Nkurunziza, RTLM transcripts, tape 0022.

66. Habimana, RTLM transcripts, tape 0016.

67. Li, "Echoes of Violence."

68. Nkurunziza, RTLM transcripts, tape 0016; Habimana, RTLM transcripts, tape 0014, May 29, 1994.

69. Gaspard Gahigi, RTLM transcripts, tape 0011.

70. Habimana, RTLM transcripts, tape 0011.

71. Ibid., tape 0109.

72. Gahigi, RTLM transcripts, tape 0011; Des Forges, "Call to Genocide," p. 49.

73. Habimana, RTLM transcripts, tape 0011.

74. BBC News: World: Africa, "Rwanda Arrests 'Hate Radio' Journalist," June 21, 1999, http://news.bbc.co.uk/2/hi/africa/374375.stm (accessed March 3, 2011).

75. Habimana, RTLM transcripts, tape 0004.

76. Hatzfeld, *Machete Season*.

77. Habimana, RTLM transcripts, tape 0035; Des Forges, "Call to Genocide," p. 48, citing Jean-Pierre Chrétien and Reporters Sans Frontières, *Rwanda: Les Médias du Génocide* (Paris: Karthala, 1995), p. 205.

78. Li, "Echoes of Violence."

79. Hatzfeld, *Machete Season*, p. 15.

80. Bemeriki, RTLM transcripts, tape 0008.

81. Karamira, RTLM transcripts, tape 0008.

82. Hatzfeld, *Machete Season*, p. 15.

83. Ibid., p. 219.

84. Georges Ruggiu, RTLM transcripts, tape 0004.

85. Habimana, RTLM transcripts, tape 0004; Des Forges, *Leave None to Tell the Story*.

86. Ruggiu, RTLM transcripts, tape 0004.

87. Habimana, RTLM transcripts, tape 0109.

88. Ibid., tape 0004.

89. Des Forges, "Call to Genocide," p. 48, citing Chrétien and Reporters Sans Frontières, *Rwanda*, p. 300 (see note 77).

90. Bemeriki, RTLM transcripts, tape 0008.

91. Habimana, RTLM transcripts, tape 0004.

92. Des Forges, *Leave None to Tell the Story*.

93. Karamira, RTLM transcripts, tape 0004.

94. Des Forges, *Leave None to Tell the Story*; Stanilas Simbizi, RTLM transcripts, tape 0004.

95. Emmanuel Mbilizi, RTLM transcripts, tape 0008.

96. Ruggiu, RTLM transcripts, tape 0004.

97. Karamira, RTLM transcripts.

98. Chrétien, "RTLM Propaganda"; although historically Tutsis had considerable power for their population size, they composed only roughly 10 percent of the Rwandan population. Thus, with an overwhelming majority, the Hutus would benefit from a majoritarian democracy.

99. RTLM transcripts, tape 0004.

100. Des Forges, *Leave None to Tell the Story*, citing from Association des Femmes Parlementaires pour la Défense des Droits de la Mere et de l'Enfant, "Toute la Vérité sur la Guerre d'octobre 1990 au Rwanda," Kigali, Rwanda, February 1991 (an English version of the pamphlet differs slightly from the original French (International Commission); Bemeriki, RTLM transcripts, tape 0008.

101. RTLM transcripts, tape 0008.

102. Gahigi, RTLM transcripts, tape 0004.

103. Ibid.

104. Habimana, RTLM transcripts, tape 0016.

105. RTLM transcripts, tape 0109.

106. Habimana, RTLM transcripts, tape 0109.

107. Simbizi, RTLM transcripts, tape 0008.

108. Karamira, RTLM transcripts, tape 0008.

109. Hitimana, RTLM transcripts, tape 0122.

110. Habimana, RTLM transcripts, tape 0004.

111. Habimana, RTLM transcripts, tape 0035.

112. Ibid.

113. Karamira, RTLM transcripts, tape 0008.

114. Habimana, RTLM transcripts, tape 0004; Karamira, RTLM transcripts, tape 0008.

115. Chrétien, "RTLM Propaganda," p. 57.

116. Gahigi, RTLM transcripts, tape 0016.

117. Straus and Lyons, *Intimate Enemy*, p. 39.

118. Ibid., p. 88.

119. Ibid., p. 87.

120. Scott Straus, "What Is the Relationship between Hate Radio and Violence? Rethinking Rwanda's 'Radio Machete,'" *Politics & Society* 35 (2007): 609.

121. Straus and Lyons, *Intimate Enemy*, p. 85.

122. Hatzfeld, *Machete Season*, p. 175.

123. Straus and Lyons, *Intimate Enemy*, p. 39.

124. Des Forges, "Call to Genocide," p. 49, citing T. Sindikubwabo, Discours du Président Théodore Sindikubwabo prononcé le 19 avril à la Préfecture de Butare, Government of Rwanda, Kigali, Rwanda, 1994.

125. Des Forges, "Call to Genocide," p. 48; RTLM transcripts.

126. Mbilizi, RTLM transcripts, tape 0008.

127. Roméo Dallaire, "The Media Dichotomy," in *The Media and the Rwandan Genocide*, ed. Allan Thompson (Ann Arbor: Pluto Press, 2007), pp. 12–19.

128. Charles Mironko, "The Effect of RTLM's Rhetoric of Ethnic Hatred in Rural Rwanda," in *The Media and the Rwandan Genocide*, ed. Allan Thompson (Ann Arbor: Pluto Press, 2007), pp. 125–35.

129. Des Forges, "Call to Genocide."

130. Straus, "What Is the Relationship between Hate Radio and Violence?"

131. Some experts argue that it is more than 800,000 people; others say more than 500,000.

Chapter 2: Conspiracy and Murder

1. Eve Nussbaum Soumerai and Carol D. Schulz, *Daily Life during the Holocaust* (Westport, CT: Greenwood Press, 1998).

2. Ibid., p. 16.

3. Manus Midlarsky, *The Killing Trap: Genocide in the Twentieth Century* (New York: Cambridge University Press, 2005), pp. 136–37; Richard H. Dekmejian, *Spectrum of Terror* (Washington, DC: CQ Press, 2007), p. 245, citing Eric Erikson, Young Man Luther (New York: W. W. Norton, 1958), pp. 14–15.

4. Hilmar Hoffmann, *The Triumph of Propaganda: Film and Socialism, 1933–1945* (Providence: Berghahn, 1996), p. 86, citing Georg Simmel.

5. Soumerai and Schulz, *Daily Life during the Holocaust*, p. 58.

6. Ibid., pp. 28–29.

7. William Shirer, *The Rise and Fall of the Third Reich* (New York: Simon and Schuster, 1960); Soumerai and Schulz, *Daily Life during the Holocaust*, pp. 35, 57–58; Dekmejian, *Spectrum of Terror*, p. 249.

8. Soumerei and Schulz, *Daily Life during the Holocaust*, p. 37.

9. Norman Naimark, *Fires of Hatred: Ethnic Cleansing in Twentieth-Century Europe* (Cambridge, MA: Harvard University Press, 2007), pp. 66–67.

10. Ian Kershaw, *Hitler: A Biography* (New York: W. W. Norton), p. 457.

11. Naimark, *Fires of Hatred*, p. 67, citing the diary of Joseph Goebbels, as noted in Saul Friedlander, *Nazi Germany and the Jews: The Years of Persecution, 1933–1939*, vol. 1 (New York: HarperCollins, 1977); Jeffrey Herf, *The Jewish Enemy: Nazi Propaganda during World War II and the Holocaust* (Cambridge, MA: Belknap Press of Harvard University Press, 2006); Alexander G. Hardy, *Hitler's Secret Weapon: The 'Managed' Press and Propaganda Machine of Nazi Germany* (New York: Vantage Press, 1967), p. 171.

12. Dekmejian, *Spectrum of Terror*; Herf, *Jewish Enemy*; Soumerai and Schulz, *Daily Life during the Holocaust*.

13. Hardy, *Hitler's Secret Weapon*, p. 171.

14. Dekmejian, *Spectrum of Terror*, citing Robert Melson, *Revolution and Genocide: On the Origins of the Armenian Genocide and the Holocaust* (Chicago: University of Chicago

Press, 1996), p. 248; Primo Levi, *Survival in Auschwitz: The Nazi Assault on Humanity* (New York: Collier-Macmillan, 1971); Soumerai and Schulz, *Daily Life during the Holocaust*, pp. 105, 187; Isaiah Trunk, *Jedenrat: The Jewish Councils in Eastern Europe under Nazi Occupation* (New York: Macmillan, 1972), p. 151; Raul Hilberg, *The Destruction of the European Jews* (Chicago: Quadrangle Books, 1967).

15. Hilberg, *Destruction of the European Jews*; Soumerai and Schulz, *Daily Life during the Holocaust*.

16. Yaffa Eliach, *Hasidic Tales of the Holocaust* (New York: Oxford University Press, 1982), p. 54.

17. Ibid., p. 53.

18. Ibid., p. 54.

19. Naimark, *Fires of Hatred*, p. 61; David Welch, "Propaganda and Indoctrination in the Third Reich: Success or Failure?" *European History Quarterly* 17 (1987): 403; Soumerai and Schulz, *Daily Life during the Holocaust*.

20. Dekmejian, *Spectrum of Terror*.

21. Naimark, *Fires of Hatred*, p. 60.

22. Hardy, *Hitler's Secret Weapon*, pp. 174–75 and 177–78.

23. Donald L. Niewyk, *The Columbia Guide to the Holocaust* (New York: Columbia University Press, 2000).

24. Hoffmann, *Truimph of Propaganda*, p. 90; Robert Edwin Herzstein, *The War That Hitler Won: The Most Infamous Propaganda Campaign in History* (New York: G. P. Putnam's Sons, 1978); Randall Bytwerk, e-mail exchange with the author; Daniel Jonah Goldhagen, *Hitler's Willing Executioners: Ordinary Germans and the Holocaust* (New York: Vintage, 1997); Dekmejian, *Spectrum of Terror*.

25. Aristotle Kallis, *Nazi Propaganda and the Second World War* (New York: Palgrave McMillan, 2005), p. 67; Herzstein, *War That Hitler Won*; Dekmejian, *Spectrum of Terror*, p. 247; Hoffmann, *Triumph of Propaganda*.

26. Herf, *Jewish Enemy*; David Welch, "Nazi Propaganda and the Volksgemeinschaft: Constructing a People's Community," *Journal of Contemporary History* 39 (2004), pp. 213–38; David Welch, "Propaganda and Indoctrination in the Third Reich: Success or Failure?" Hoffmann, *Triumph of Propaganda*, pp. 92–93; Herzstein, *War That Hitler Won*, pp. 22–23; Naimark, *Fires of Hatred*, citing Adolf Hitler, *Mein Kampf*, trans. Malph Mannheim (Boston: Houghton Mifflin, 1999).

27. Naimark, *Fires of Hatred*, pp. 58, 63, citing Adolf Hitler's speeches on June 24, 1920, and *Mein Kampf*, p. 327 (see note 26); Herf, *Jewish Enemy*; Jay Baird, *The Mythical World of Nazi War Propaganda 1939-1945* (Minneapolis: University of Minnesota Press, 1974).

28. Herzstein, *War That Hitler Won*, p. 22; Herf, *Jewish Enemy*; Welch, "Propaganda and Indoctrination"; Welch, "Nazi Propaganda"; Dekmejian, *Spectrum of Terror*.

29. Herf, *Jewish Enemy*; Dekmejian, *Spectrum of Terror*.

30. Naimark, *Fires of Hatred*, pp. 58, 59, 61, citing *I Shall Bear Witness: The Diaries of Victor Klemperer* (London: Wedenfeld and Nicolson, 1998), p. 122; Baird, *Mythical World*.

31. Norman Naimark, *Fires of Hatred*, p. 59, citing Kershaw, *Hitler* (see note 10), and

Kershaw, *Hitler, 1889–1936: Hubris* (New York: W. W. Norton, 1999), p. 152; Naimark, *Fires of Hatred*, citing Elke Fröhlich, ed., *Die Tagebücher von Joseph Goebbels* (Munich: K. G. Sauer, 1996), p. 141; Herf, *Jewish Enemy*; Hoffmann, *Triumph of Propaganda*; Welch, "Nazi Propaganda"; Dekmejian, *Spectrum of Terror*, p. 247.

32. Welch, "Propaganda and Indoctrination"; Welch, "Nazi Propaganda," p. 218.

33. Welch, "Propaganda and Indoctrination," pp. 409, 415; Randall Bytwerk, e-mail exchange with the author, 2010.

34. David Welch, *The Third Reich: Politics and Propaganda* (New York: Routledge, 1993); Hardy, *Hitler's Secret Weapon*.

35. Horst Bergmeier and Rainer E. Lotz, *Hitler's Airwaves: The Inside Story of Nazi Radio Broadcasting and Propaganda Swing* (New Haven: Yale University Press, 1997); Eric Rentschler, *The Ministry of Illusion: Nazi Cinema and Its Afterlife* (Cambridge, MA: Harvard University Press, 1996); Herzstein, *War That Hitler Won*.

36. Randall L. Bytwerk, "The Argument for Genocide in Nazi Propaganda," *Quarterly Journal of Speech* 91, no. 1 (February 2005): 39.

37. Randall L. Bytwerk, *Bending Spines: The Propagandas of Nazi Germany and the German Democratic Republic* (East Lansing: Michigan University Press, 2004), p. 15; Bytwerk, "Argument for Genocide."

38. Herf, *Jewish Enemy*, pp. 222–23.

39. Jeffrey Herf, "The 'Jewish War': Goebbels and the Antisemitic Campaigns of the Nazi Propaganda Ministry," *Holocaust and Genocide Studies* 19, no. 1 (Spring 2005): 51–80.

40. Baird, *Mythical World*; Herf, "'Jewish War.'"

41. Ibid.

42. Herf, *Jewish Enemy*, p. 282, citing *Der Volkische Beobachter*, February 5 and July 24, 1941.

43. Joseph Goebbels, "Jews Are Guilty," *Das Reich*, November 16, 1941, courtesy of German Propaganda Archive at http://www.calvin.edu/academic/cas/gpa/goebl.htm.

44. Ibid.

45. Ibid.

46. Ibid.

47. Bytwerk, "Argument for Genocide," p. 42.

48. Randall L. Bytwerk, *Julius Streicher: Nazi Editor of the Notorious Anti-Semitic Newspaper* Der Stürmer (New York: Cooper Square Press, 2001); Hardy, *Hitler's Secret Weapon*, pp. 82–83; Julius Streicher, "The Way to Slavery," *Der Stürmer*, August 1939, from the German Propaganda Archive at http://www.calvin.edu/academic/cas/gpa/ds5.htm.

49. Bytwerk, *Julius Streicher*, p. 52.

50. Ibid., pp. 56, 104; "Die Geheimplane Gegan Deutschland Enthult," *Der Stürmer*, July 1933, from the German Propaganda Archive, http://www.calvin.edu.

51. "Briefkasten," *Der Stürmer*, no. 19, 1935, from the German Propaganda Archive at http://www.calvin.edu/academic/cas/gpa/ds6.htm; Ernst Hiemer, "When Will the Jewish Danger Be Over?" Der Stürmer, 1942, from the German Propaganda Archive, http://www.calvin.edu/academic/cas/gpa/ds11.htm; Bytwerk, Bending Spines, pp. 89, 121.

52. Bytwerk, *Julius Streicher*; Bytwerk, *Bending Spines*, pp. 89, 121.

53. Bytwerk, "Argument for Genocide," pp. 43–44.

54. Rentschler, *Ministry of Illusion*; Hoffmann, *Triumph of Propaganda*, p. viii; Herzstein, *War That Hitler Won*.

55. Hoffman, *Triumph of Propaganda*, pp. vi, vii, x, xi, 143.

56. Herf, *Jewish Enemy*, p. 41; Baird, *Mythical World*, p. 6; Bytwerk, *Bending Spines*, pp. 16, 113.

57. Bytwerk, "The Argument for Genocide"; Herf, "The 'Jewish War.'"

58. Welch, *Third Reich*, p. 148 (see note 34), citing Goebbels, March 25, 1933; Philipp Gassert, "This Is Hans Fritzsche: A Nazi Broadcaster and His Audience," *Journal of Radio and Audio Media* (April 2010): 81–103; Herf, Jewish Enemy; Herf, "Jewish War.'"

59. Herf, *Jewish Enemy*, p. 39; Herf, "'Jewish War,'" p. 56.

60. Radio transcripts from the German Propaganda Archive, http://www.calvin.edu.

61. Bergmeier and Lotz, *Hitler's Airwaves*, p. 16.

62. Herzstein, *War That Hitler Won*; Gassert, "This Is Hans Fritzsche," citing M. Groth, "Ein Publizist im Dritten Reich: Vorstudien zu einer Biographie von Hans Fritzsche" (unpublished master's thesis, Munster, 1979).

63. Gassert, "This Is Hans Fritzsche," p. 11.

64. Herzstein, *War That Hitler Won*, p. 180; Bergmeier and Lotz, *Hitler's Airwaves*.

65. Welch, "Propaganda and Indoctrination," p. 413.

66. Hardy, *Hitler's Secret Weapon*, pp. 54, 118, 124–25; Herzstein, *War That Hitler Won*.

67. Hardy, *Hitler's Secret Weapon*, pp. 153–54.

68. Bergmeier and Lotz, *Hitler's Airwaves*, pp. 5–6.

69. Hoffmann, *Triumph of Propaganda*, p. 110; Bergmeier and Lotz, *Hitler's Airwaves*, p. 156; Welch, "Propaganda and Indoctrination"; Soumerai and Schulz, *Daily Life during the Holocaust*, p. 42; German Propaganda Archive at http://www.calvin.edu.

70. Baird, *Mythical World*, p. 4; Bergmeier and Lotz, *Hitler's Airwaves*, p. 3.

71. Bergmeier and Lotz, *Hitler's Airwaves*; Hoffmann, *Triumph of Propaganda*.

72. Herf, *Jewish Enemy*; Hardy, *Hitler's Secret Weapon*, p. 188.

73. Hardy, *Hitler's Secret Weapon*, pp. 189–90, 192.

74. Naimark, *Fires of Hatred*, p. 61.

75. Baird, *Mythical World*, pp. 25–26; Herzstein, *War That Hitler Won*, p. 17; Herf, *Jewish Enemy*; Julius Yourman, "Propaganda Techniques within Nazi Germany," *Journal of Educational Sociology* 13, no. 3 (November 1939): 148–63.

76. Randall Bytwerk, "Argument for Genocide"; Goldhagen, *Hitler's Willing Executioners*; Kallis, *Nazi Propaganda and the Second World War*.

77. Hoffmann, *Triumph of Propaganda: Welch*, "Propaganda and Indoctrination."

78. Herf, *Jewish Enemy*, p. 38.

79. Bytwerk, "Argument for Genocide," p. 42.

80. Gassert, "This Is Hans Fritzsche," citing Ian Kershaw, "How Effective Was Nazi Propaganda?," in *Nazi Propaganda: The Power and Limitations*, ed. David Welch (London: Croom Helm, 1983), pp. 180–205; Welch, "Propaganda and Indoctrination"; Tim Mason, *Nazism, Fascism, and the Working Class* (Cambridge: Cambridge University Press, 1995); Welch, *Nazi Propaganda*, citing Tim Mason, *Social Policy in the Third Reich: The*

Working Class and the National Community (New York: Oxford University Press, 1993); Elisabeth Noelle-Neumann, *The Spiral of Silence: Our Social Skin* (Chicago: University of Chicago Press, 1984); Bytwerk, "Argument for Genocide," p. 19.

81. Bytwerk, "Argument for Genocide."

82. Gassert, "This Is Hans Fritzsche," citing Kershaw, "How Effective Was Nazi Propaganda?"(see note 80); Welch, "Propaganda and Indoctrination"; Mason, *Nazism, Fascism, and the Working Class*; Welch, *Nazi Propaganda*, citing Mason, *Social Policy in the Third Reich* (see note 80); Noelle-Neumann, *Spiral of Silence*; Bytwerk, "Argument for Genocide," p. 19.

Chapter 3: Killing in the Name Of . . .

1. For the sake of simplicity, the phrase "Serb forces" pertains to all of the military or paramilitary forces that were fighting on behalf of Serbia or the "greater Serbia." While this trades precision for generalization, it avoids the confusion arising from multiple parties and acronyms, which are better handled in a book that can help to distinguish them. Because the military in Serbia was known to be supporting many of the paramilitaries, while it is an oversimplification, it is not inaccurate to refer to all of them as Serb forces.

2. Djemo is a fictional name used by Rezak Hukanovi in his memoir describing his experience in Omarska: *The Tenth Circle of Hell: A Memoir of Life in the Death Camps of Bosnia* (New York: Basic Books, 1996), p. 7.

3. Ibid.

4. Helsinki Watch (a division of Human Rights Watch), *War Crimes in Bosnia-Herzegovina*, vol. 2 (Los Angeles and New York: Human Rights Watch, 1993), p. 43.

5. Hukanović, *Tenth Circle of Hell.*

6. Ibid., p. 10.

7. Ibid.

8. Ibid.

9. Ibid.

10. Ibid.

11. Hukanović, *Tenth Circle of Hell.*

12. Ibid.

13. Ibid.

14. Ibid., p. 44.

15. Ed Vulliamy, *Seasons in Hell: Understanding Bosnia's War* (New York: St. Martin's Press, 1994).

16. Hukanović, *Tenth Circle of Hell.*

17. Ibid., p. 62.

18. Ibid., p. 74.

19. Ibid., p. 105.

20. This refers to the cruelty, not to the numbers of people. Louis Begley, foreword to *Stripping Bare the Body: Politics, Violence, War*, by Mark Danner, (New York: Nation Books, 2009), p. xii.

21. Roy Gutman, *A Witness to Genocide: The Pulitzer Prize-Winning Dispatches on the "Ethnic Cleansing in Bosnia"* (New York: Macmillan, 1993), p. 47.

22. Center for Investigation and Documentation of the Association of Former Prison Camp Inmates of Bosnia-Herzegovina (CID), *I Begged Them to Kill Me: Crime against the Women of Bosnia-Herzegovina* (Sarajevo: CID, 2000).

23. Gutman, *Witness to Genocide*, p. 41.

24. Vulliamy, *Seasons in Hell*, pp. 323–24; International Criminal Tribunal for the Former Yugoslavia, Indictment against Jadranko Prli , Bruno Stojic, Slobodan Praljak, Milivov Petkovic, Valentin Coric, and Berislav Pusic, Case No. IT-04-74-T, June 11, 2008.

25. CID, *I Begged Them to Kill Me*, p. 107; Helsinki Watch, *War Crimes*, p. 33.

26. CID, *I Begged Them to Kill Me*, p. 301.

27. Ibid., p. 105.

28. Ibid.

29. Ibid., pp. 151, 246.

30. CID, *I Begged Them to Kill Me*; Slavenka Drakulic, *They Would Never Hurt a Fly: War Criminals in the Hague* (New York: Viking Penguin, 2004), pp. 52, 58; Helsinki Watch, *War Crimes*, p. 24.

31. CID, *I Begged Them to Kill Me*, p. 97. *Balinkura* is a derogatory term used to disparage or denigrate Muslim Bosniak women in the former Yugoslavia.

32. Ibid., p. 197.

33. Associated Press (AP), "Serb Mortar Barrage Kills Playing Children," *Courier-Mail*, October 12, 1992, 49; Yigal Chazan and Ian Traynor, "Carnage in Sarajevo Bread Queue," *Guardian*, May 28, 1992, 1; Vulliamy, *Seasons in Hell*, pp. 81–82; Natasha Byron Narayan, "Mortars Cut Down Youth of Sarajevo," *Guardian*, June 28, 1993, 10.

34. Vulliamy, *Seasons in Hell*.

35. Human Rights Watch, War Crimes in Bosnia-Herzegovina: Abuses by Bosnian Croat and Muslim Forces in Central and Southwestern Bosnia-Herzegovina (September 1, 1993), http://www.hrw.org/en/reports/1993/09/01/abuses-bosnian-croat-and-muslim-forces-central-and-southwestern-bosnia-hercegovin.

36. Tim Judah, *The Serbs: History, the Myth, and the Destruction of Yugoslavia* (New Haven: Yale University Press, 2009); Norman Naimark, *Fires of Hatred: Ethnic Cleansing in Twentieth-Century Europe* (Cambridge, MA: Harvard University Press, 2001).

37. Vulliamy, *Seasons in Hell*; Judah, *Serbs*; Naimark, *Fires of Hatred*. Human rights groups, such as Helsinki Watch, and other experts, including Naimark and Midlarsky, wrote that the Serbs were the primary aggressors and violators of human rights. Assaults by Bosniaks (Muslims) were mostly attributed to acts of individual retaliation. Midlarsky says that while all engaged in ethnic cleansing, the Serbs committed the worst acts: Manus Midlarsky, *The Killing Trap: Genocide in the Twentieth Century* (New York: Cambridge University Press, 2005).

38. Gutman, *Witness to Genocide*, p. 95; Emir Suljagic, *Postcards from the Grave* (London: Saqi Books, 2005), p. 91.

39. Eric Stover, *The Witness: War Crimes and the Promise of Justice in the Hague* (Philadelphia: University of Pennsylvania Press).

40. Samantha Power, *A Problem from Hell: America in the Age of Genocide* (New York: Basic Books, 2002); David Hirsh, *Law against Genocide: Cosmopolitan Trials* (Portland: Glasshouse Press, 2003); Drakulic, *They Would Never Hurt a Fly*, p. 97. Serbs argue that the Srebrenica slaughter was in retaliation for an offensive by Bosniak Muslim forces that killed Serb civilians in the village of Kravice. The International Criminal Tribunal for the former Yugoslavia (ICTY) acknowledges that between June 1992 and March 1993 "a number of Serbs" were captured by Bosniak Muslim forces that beat many Serbs to death.

41. Helsinki Watch, *War Crimes*, p. 8; Pal Kolsto, *Media Discourse and the Yugoslav Conflicts: Representations of Self and Other* (Burlington, VT: Ashgate Publishing, 2009); Gregory Kent, *Framing War and Genocide: British Policy and News Media Reaction to the War in Bosnia* (Cresskill, NJ: Hampton Press, 2006).

42. Drakulic, *They Would Never Hurt a Fly*, p. 74; CID, *I Begged Them to Kill Me*, pp. 103, 180, 191, 233, 265; Bette Denich, "Unmaking Multiethnicity in Yugoslavia: Media and Metamorphoses," in *Neighbors at War: Anthropological Perspectives on Yugoslav Ethnicity, Culture, and History*, ed. Joel M. Halpern and David Kideckel (University Park: Pennsylvania State University, 2000); Misha Glenny, *The Fall of Yugoslavia: The Third Balkan War* (New York: Penguin Books, 1992); Judah, *Serbs*.

43. Drakulic, *They Would Never Hurt a Fly*, p. 89.

44. Zlatiborka Popov-Momčinović, interview with the author, Pale, Bosnia, September 2010.

45. Sabrina Ramet, *The Three Yugoslavias: State-Building and Legitimation, 1918–2005* (Washington, DC: Woodrow Wilson Center Press, 2006).

46. Naimark, *Fires of Hatred*, pp. 148–49; Laura Silber and Allan Little, *Yugoslavia: Death of a Nation* (New York: Penguin Books, 1996); Bogdan Denitch, *Ethnic Nationalism: The Tragic Death of Yugoslavia* (Minneapolis: University of Minnesota Press, 1994), p. 62.

47. Naimark, *Fires of Hatred*; Ramet, *Three Yugoslavias*, p. 7; Mirjana Prosic-Dvornic, "Serbia: The Inside Story," in *Neighbors at War: Anthropological Perspectives on Yugoslav Ethnicity, Culture, and History*, ed. Joel M. Halpern and David Kideckel (University Park: Pennsylvania State University, 2000), pp. 316–39.

48. Ramet, *Three Yugoslavias*; Helsinki Watch, *War Crimes*.

49. Ramet, *Three Yugoslavias*; Joel M. Halpern and David A. Kideckel, eds., *Neighbors at War: Anthropological Perspectives on Yugoslavia Ethnicity, Culture, and History* (University Park: Pennsylvania State University, 2000); Naimark, *Fires of Hatred*.

50. Naimark, *Fires of Hatred*, pp. 144–45.

51. First called the Kingdom of Serbs, Croats, and Slovenes and included Bosnia; Ramet, *Three Yugoslavias*; Naimark, *Fires of Hatred*. Kosovo and Vojvodina were given autonomy later under a new constitution.

52. Denitch, *Ethnic Nationalism*.

53. Denich, "Unmaking Multiethnicity in Yugoslavia."

54. Ibid., p. 40; Naimark, *Fires of Hatred*; Judah, *Serbs*.

55. Naimark, *Fires of Hatred*; Kent, *Framing War and Genocide*; Kolsto, *Media Discourse*; Vulliamy, *Seasons in Hell*; Mark Thompson, *Forging War: The Media in Serbia, Croatia, Bosnia and Herzegovina* (Luton and Bedfordshire: University of Luton Press, 1999).

56. Noel Malcolm, *Bosnia: A Short History* (London: Papermac, 1994), p. 222; Kent, *Framing War and Genocide*, p. 72.

57. Zlatko Dizdarevic, *Sarajevo: A War Journal* (New York: Fromm International, 1993), p. 6.

58. In the rural areas, intermarriage was less common, but the ethnic groups were still amicable, according to Vulliamy, *Seasons in Hell*.

59. Kemal Kurspahic, *Prime Time Crime: Balkan Media in War and Peace* (Washington, DC: United States Institute of Peace Press, 2003), p. 114; Stuart Kaufman, *Modern Hatreds: The Symbolic Politics of Ethnic War* (Ithaca, NY: Cornell University Press, 2001); Kent, *Framing War and Genocide*, p. 72, citing Chuck Sudetic, *Blood and Vengeance: One Family's Story of the War in Bosnia* (New York: W. W. Norton, 1998); Drakulic, *They Would Never Hurt a Fly*.

60. Hukanović, *Tenth Circle of Hell* ; Kolsto, *Media Discourse*; Kent, *Framing War and Genocide*.

61. Ramet, *Three Yugoslavias*; Julie Mertus, *Kosovo: How Myths and Truths Started a War* (Los Angeles: University of California Press, 1999).

62. Emil Pinkas, interview with the author, Sarajevo, Bosnia, September 2010.

63. Ramet, *Three Yugoslavias*; Thompson, *Forging War*; Robert English, interview with the author, 2009.

64. Thompson, *Forging War*; Denich, "Unmaking Multiethnicity in Yugoslavia"; Rajko Mursic, "The Yugoslav Dark Side of Humanity: A View from a Slovene Blind Spot," in *Neighbors at War: Anthropological Perspectives on Yugoslavia Ethnicity, Culture, and History*, ed. Joel Halpern and David A. Kideckel (University Park: Pennsylvania State University, 2000), pp. 56–81.

65. Thompson, *Forging War*; Silber and Little, *Yugoslavia*, p. 244.

66. Kurspahic, *Prime Time Crime*, p. 29.

67. Thompson, *Forging War*, p. 53.

68. Malcolm, *Bosnia*.

69. Ramet, *Three Yugoslavias*.

70. Ibid., p. 320.

71. Thompson, *Forging War*; Naimark, *Fires of Hatred*, p. 150; Silber and Little, *Yugoslavia*, p. 31; Vladimir Andri and Nedim Hogic, interviews with the author, Sarajevo, 2010; Robert English, e-mail memorandum to the author, 2010.

72. Ramet, *Three Yugoslavias*; Mertus, *Kosovo*; Glenny, *Fall of Yugoslavia*. Some argue that Miloševi also paid unemployed young men to travel around and participate in these rallies: Silber and Little, *Yugoslavia*; Denich, "Unmaking Multiethnicity in Yugoslavia," p. 47.

73. Kurspahic, *Prime Time Crime*, p. 30; Mertus, *Kosovo*.

74. Renaud de La Brosse, "Political Propaganda and the Plan to Create a 'State for all Serbs': Consequences of Using the Media for Ultra-Nationalist Ends," report compiled at the request of the Office of the International Criminal Tribunal for the Former Yugoslavia, 2003.

75. Kurspahic, *Prime Time Crime*, pp. 34–35; Silber and Little, *Yugoslavia*, p. 37.

76. Ramet, *Three Yugoslavias*; Kurspahic, *Prime Time Crime*, p. 35; Silber and Little, *Yugoslavia*.

77. Ibid.

78. Quotes slightly varied in these accounts: Naimark, *Fires of Hatred*, pp. 150–51; Kurspahic, *Prime Time Crime*, p. 35; Kent, *Framing War and Genocide*, pp. 20–21; Ramet, *Three Yugoslavias*, p. 343.

79. Silber and Little, *Yugoslavia*; Kurspahic, *Prime Time Crime*; Thompson, *Forging War*; Kent, *Framing War and Genocide*; Naimark, *Fires of Hatred*.

80. Kurspahic, *Prime Time Crime*, p. 36; Silber and Little, *Yugoslavia*.

81. Kurspahic, *Prime Time Crime*, p. 37; Kent, *Framing War and Genocide*, p. 20; Ramet, *Three Yugoslavias*, p. 344; Judah, *Serbs*, p. 163.

82. Kurspahic, *Prime Time Crime*, p. 37; Ramet, *Three Yugoslavias*, p. 344. Judah states that approximately 10,000 appeared at the memorial (*Serbs*).

83. Kurspahic, *Prime Time Crime*, p. 47, citing Rajko Djurdjevic, *Duga*, September 17–30, 1988.

84. La Brosse, "Political Propaganda," p. 41, citing Gavro Marjanović, *Politika*, December 6, 1988.

85. *Politika*, July 1, 1989, in La Brosse, "Political Propaganda"; Thompson, *Forging War*; Kurspahic, *Prime Time Crime*; Kent, *Framing War and Genocide*.

86. La Brosse, "Political Propaganda," citing *Politika*, November 5, 1988, and October 1989. *Politika* had three daily papers and ten magazines.

87. La Brosse, "Political Propaganda," citing letter signed by Vojislav K. Stajanovic, president of the Association of University Teachers and Scholars of Serbia, *Politika*, February 9, 1990.

88. Jack Snyder and Karen Ballentine, "Nationalism and the Marketplace of Ideas," *international Security* 21, no. 2 (Fall 1996): 5–40; Thompson, *Forging War*.

89. Kurspahic, *Prime Time Crime*, p. 36; Thompson, *Forging War*, p. 56; "Hate's Hold on Yugoslavia's News," *New York Times*, Editorial, November 7, 1992.

90. Helsinki Watch (a division of Human Rights Watch), *Open Wounds: Human Rights Abuses in Kosovo* (New York: Human Rights Watch, 1993), pp. 101–103.

91. Blaine Harden, "Serbian Leader Derides U.N. Sanctions," *Washington Post*, Foreign Service, May 31, 1992, A1; Chuck Sudetic, "Tens of Thousands Call for Removal of Serbia's Leader," *New York Times*, June 1, 1992, 1; Mark Thompson, *Forging War*, p. 57; La Brosse, "Political Propaganda," citing Vojislav Stojanovi , *Politika*, February 9, 1990.

92. Kurspahic, *Prime Time Crime*, p. 29, citing Branka agaš, *The Destruction of Yugoslavia* (London: Verso, 1993).

93. Thompson, *Forging War*, pp. 54, 55; Silber and Little, *Yugoslavia*.

94. Kent, *Framing War and Genocide*, pp. 23, 24; Martin Shaw, "The Kosovan War, 1998–1999: Transformations of State, War and Genocide in the Global Revolution," *Sociological Research Online* 4 (1999), http://ideas.repec.org/a/sro/srosro/1999-52-1.html.

95. Kurspahic, *Prime Time Crime*, pp. 43–44.

96. Ibid., p. 44.

97. Ibid., pp. 42–43; Robert Marquand, "Serbia's State-Run Media Are a Weapon of War," *Christian Science Monitor*, January 26, 1993, 2; Silber and Little, *Yugoslavia*.

98. La Brosse, "Political Propaganda," p. 43; Thompson, *Forging War*; "Hate's Hold on Yugoslavia's News," p. 20.

99. Kurspahic, *Prime Time Crime*, p. xxii; Silber and Little, *Yugoslavia*.

100. La Brosse, "Political Propaganda," citing accounts from journalist Goran Mikic. This ostensibly appeared in local and international headline news, including Reuters (November 20, 1991) and ITV, and throughout Serb media.

101. La Brosse, "Political Propaganda," citing Risto Djogo on TV Pale.

102. Kurspahic, *Prime Time Crime*; Thompson, *Forging War*, p. 67.

103. Kurspahic, *Prime Time Crime*, p. 41.

104. Thompson, *Forging War*, pp. 72, 74, 88; Kurspahic, *Prime Time Crime*; Kent, *Framing War and Genocide*, p. 21.

105. Thompson, *Forging War*.

106. Kurspahic, *Prime Time Crime*, p. xviii; Sylvia Poggioli and Bob Edwards, "Bosnia Media Struggle against Government Control," *Morning Edition*, National Public Radio, April 6, 1992.

107. Silber and Little, *Yugoslavia*, p. 142, citing *Vjesnik* on May 7, 1991.

108. Kurspahic, *Prime Time Crime*, p. xxii.

109. Gutman, *Witness to Genocide*, p. xxvi.

110. Ibid., p. xxviii; Naimark, *Fires of Hatred*.

111. Kurspahic, *Prime Time Crime*, p. 97, citing Branka Magaš, "The Destruction of Bosnia and Herzegovina," in *Why Bosnia? Writings on the Balkan War*, ed. Rabia Ali and Lawrence Lifschultz (Stony Creek, CT: Pamphleteer's Press, 1993), p. 253.

112. Kurspahic, *Prime Time Crime*, pp. 119–20.

113. Silber and Little, *Yugoslavia*; Kent, *Framing War and Genocide*, p. 76. Although he declared this publicly, Izetbegovi also said in parliament that he "would sacrifice peace for a sovereign Bosnia-Herzegovina," according to Silber and Little, Yugoslavia, p. 211.

114. Kurspahic, *Prime Time Crime*, p. 99; Kent, *Framing War and Genocide*, p. 76, on neutrality.

115. Poggioli and Edwards, "Bosnia Media Struggle"; Blaine Harden, "Bosnia-Herzegovina on the Brink: Yugoslav Republic Seeks to Steer Clear of Ethnic Carnage by Showing Political Flexibility," *Washington Post*, Foreign Service, January 15, 1992, A17.

116. Thompson, *Forging War*, p. 212, citing Noel Malcolm, *Bosnia: A Short History* (New York: New York University Press, 1994). Many Bosnian Serbs, led by two members of the shared presidency, did not vote; 99 percent of those who voted cast a vote for independence.

117. Kurspahic, *Prime Time Crime*, p. 99; Vulliamy, *Seasons in Hell*, p.73.

118. Kurspahic, *Prime Time Crime*, p. xii.

119. Ibid., p. 98; Thompson, *Forging War*, p. 214.

120. Thompson, *Forging War*, pp. 214, 215; Hukanović, *Tenth Circle of Hell*, p. 4; Kent, *Framing War and Genocide*, p. 81, citing S. Letica, "The West Side Story of the Collapse of Yugoslavia and the Wars in Slovenia, Croatia, and Bosnia-Hercegovina," in *This Time We Knew: Western Responses to Genocide in Bosnia* (New York: New York University Press, 1996), pp. 163–87.

121. Hukanović, *Tenth Circle of Hell*.

122. Thompson, *Forging War*, p. 82; Marcus Tanner, "Belgrade Sacks Anti-Miloševi Journalists," *Independent*, January 14, 1993.

123. Mirsad Abazovi , interview with the author, Sarajevo, September 2010.

124. Hukanović, *Tenth Circle of Hell*, pp. 5, 7, 9.

125. Abazović, interview.

126. La Brosse, "Political Propaganda," August 4, 1991.

127. La Brosse, "Political Propaganda," citing Jovan Raskovic on Serbian television; Kent, *Framing War and Genocide*; Judah, *The Serbs*.

128. Kent, *Framing War and Genocide*, p. 81, citing D. Rieff, *Slaughterhouse: Bosnia and the Failure of the West* (London: Vintage, 1995).

129. La Brosse, "Political Propaganda," p. 3, citing Biljana Plavsic, *Svet*, September 6, 1993.

130. La Brosse, "Political Propaganda," Biljana Plavsic, *Oslobodjenje*, May 1994.

131. Hukanović, *Tenth Circle of Hell*, pp. 6, 7.

132. Poggioli and Edwards, "Bosnia Media Struggle."

133. Ibid.; Helsinki Watch, *War Crimes*; Thompson, *Forging War*, pp. 218–21; Vulliamy, *Seasons in Hell*; Yigal Chazan and Ian Traynor, "Serbs Bombard Bosnian Capital," *Guardian*, April 22, 1992, 20; Kurspahic, *Prime Time Crime*, pp. xviii–xix.

134. Chazan and Traynor, "Serbs Bombard Bosnian Capital."

135. John F. Burns, "Tape Order Loud and Clear: 'Burn It All,'" *New York Times*, June 9, 1992.

136. Dizdarevic, *Sarajevo*, p. 9; Kurspahic, *Prime Time Crime*, p. 106.

137. Gordana Knezevic, "Karadžić: Looking for a Monster, and Finding Only a Man," Radio Free Europe, November 3, 2009.

138. Kurspahic, *Prime Time Crime*, pp. 106–107.

139. Ibid., p. 105.

140. Marcus Gee, *Globe and Mail*, March 17, 1993.

141. Helsinki Watch, *War Crimes*.

142. John F. Burns, "Bosnian Shelling Lifts Civilian Toll," *New York Times*, July 24, 1992, 3.

143. Six remained missing at the time of Helsinki Watch's publication. Marcus Gee, *Globe and Mail*, March 17, 1993; Helsinki Watch, *War Crimes*, p. 121.

144. Andrew Culf, "BBC Man Hurt in Bosnia Is TV Reporter of Year," *Guardian*, February 24, 1993, 6; Miami Herald, "ABC-TV Producer Killed in Sarajevo," August 14, 1992, 12; David Rohde, *Endgame: The Betrayal and Fall of Srebrenica, Europe's Worst Massacre Since World War II* (New York: Farrar, Straus, and Giroux, 1997).

145. Thompson, *Forging War*, pp. 82, 220, citing M. Camo, *Balkan War Report* (February–March 1993), p. 18.

146. Gutman, *Witness to Genocide*, pp. xxxi, xxxii; Kent, *Framing War and Genocide*; Power, *Problem from Hell*; Kemal Kurspahic, "Objectivity without Neutrality: A Bosnian Journalist Reflects on the Value of Testifying about the Crimes of Genocide," *Neiman Reports* (Spring 2003), http://www.nieman.harvard.edu/reportsitem.aspx?id=101240; Vulliamy, *Seasons in Hell*; Silber and Little, *Yugoslavia*, p. 249.

147. Kent, *Framing War and Genocide*, p. 2.

148. Vulliamy, *Seasons in Hell*, p. 81.

149. Mark Danner, *Stripping Bare the Body: Politics, Violence, War* (New York: Nation Books, 2009), pp. 205–206.

150. Kent, *Framing War and Genocide*, pp. 3, 6, citing Rieff, *Slaughterhouse: Bosnia and the Failure of the West* (New York: Simon and Schuster, 1995).

151. Graham Spencer, *Media and Peace*, citing F. Hartmann, "Bosnia," in *Crimes of War* (New York: W. W. Norton, 1999).

152. Danner, *Stripping Bare the Body*, pp. 205–206.

153. Ibid., p. 213.

154. Ibid.

155. Thompson, *Forging War*, p. 121.

156. Kurspahic, *Prime Time Crime*, p. 103.

157. Vulliamy, *Seasons in Hell*, p. 42.

158. Kent, *Framing War and Genocide*, citing Sudetic, *Blood and Vengeance*, pp. 98–101 (see note 59).

159. Rohde, *Endgame*, p. 390.

160. La Brosse, "Political Propaganda," pp. 25–26, citing what was shown on Belgrade Television on September 26, 1993.

161. Mirsad Abazović, interview.

162. Drakulich, *They Would Never Hurt a Fly*.

163. Kent, *Framing War and Genocide*; Thompson, *Forging War*; Rohde, *Endgame*.

164. Zala Volcic, "Blaming the Media: Serbian Narratives of National(ist) Identity," *Journal of Media and Cultural Studies* 20, no. 3 (September 2006): 313–30.

165. Denitch, *Ethnic Nationalism*, p. 20.

166. See discussion on the spiral of silence in chapter 13.

167. Jean Seaton, "The New 'Ethnic' Wars and the Media," in *The Media of Conflict: War Reporting and Representations of Ethnic Violence*, ed. Time Allen and Jean Seaton (New York: St. Martin's Press, 1999), pp. 43–64; Kaufman, Modern Hatreds; Kent, *Framing War and Genocide*; Denitch, *Ethnic Nationalism*.

Chapter 4: Averting Genocide

1. Alexis Sinduhije, "Ijambo: 'Speaking Truth' amidst Genocide" (Discussion Paper D-30, Joan Shorenstein Center for Press, Politics, Public Policy, Harvard University, Cambridge, MA, July 1998).

2. Ibid.; Marie-Soleil Frere, *The Media and Conflicts in Central Africa* (Boulder, CO: Lynne Rienner Publishers, 2007); Alexis Sinduhije, e-mail exchange with the author, 2010; BBC, "Timeline: Burundi: A Chronology of Key Events," December 11, 2010, http://news.bbc.co.uk/2/hi/africa/1068991.stm (accessed May 11, 2011).

3. Sinduhije, e-mail.

4. Frere, *Media and Conflicts in Central Africa*, p. 12; Bryan Rich, "One David, Two Goliaths: The Struggle for Independent Media in Burundi," *Nieman Reports* (Winter 1997); Asgede Hagos, *Greater Horn of Africa Peace Building Project, Case Study Six: Media*

Intervention in Peace Building in Burundi—The Studio Ijambo Experience and Impact (Washington, DC: Management Systems International, March, 2011), p. 3.

5. Hagos, "Media Intervention in Peace Building in Burundi," p. 21.

6. Sinduhije, "Ijambo," p. 5.

7. John Marks, interview, aired on the *Insighters*, KPFK and WPRR, 2010.

8. Sinduhije, "Ijambo."

9. Frere, *Media and Conflicts in Central Africa*.

10. Ibid., p. 12.

11. Sinduhije, "Ijambo," p. 3.

12. Sinduhige, "Ijambo."

13. Ibid.

14. Ibid., p. 4.

15. Ibid.

16. Ibid.

17. Ibid., p. 5.

18. Ibid., p. 6.

19. Ibid., p. 5.

20. Ibid.

21. Sinduhije, "Ijambo"; Michael Skoler, "Burundi Radio Project Races to Ease Hutu-Tutsi Tensions," National Public Radio, June 29, 1996.

22. Skoler, "Burundi Radio Project Races to Ease Hutu-Tutsi Tensions."

23. Sinduhije, "Ijambo," p. 8.

24. Frere, *Media and Conflicts in Central Africa*, pp. 16–17.

25. Sinduhije, "Ijambo"; Frere, *Media and Conflicts in Central Africa*.

26. Excerpt of Radio Democracy, broadcast in French, then rebroadcast on National Public Radio, June 29, 1996.

27. Frere, *Media and Conflicts in Central Africa*, pp. 16–17.

28. Ibid.

29. Sinduhije, "Ijambo," p. 7.

30. Marvin Kalb, "'Free, Fact-Based News': A Weapon for Education in Africa," *Harvard International Journal of Press/Politics* 4 (1999).

31. Sandra Melone, Georgios Terzis, and Ozsel Beleli, "Using the Media for Conflict Transformation: The Common Ground Experience," *Berghof Handbook for Conflict Transformation* (Berlin, Germany: Berghof Research Center for Constructive Conflict Management, April 2002).

32. Frere, *Media and Conflicts in Central Africa*.

33. The numbers in Rwanda of those who died range from 500,000 to 800,000. Search for Common Ground memorandum entitled "George E. Moose Letter," provided via an e-mail message to the author.

34. Marks, interview.

35. Ray Robinson and Lena Slachmuijlder, "Peace Radio Finds a Home in Burundi," *USAID in Africa: News, Updates and Resources from USAID's Bureau for Africa* (Fall 2003).

36. Frere, *Media and Conflicts in Central Africa*.

37. Hagos, "Media Intervention in Peace Building in Burundi," p. 16.

38. Sinduhije, "Ijambo."

39. Rich, "One David, Two Goliaths."

40. Richard Parker, introduction to "Ijambo: 'Speaking Truth' amidst Genocide," by Alexis Sinduhije (Discussion Paper D-30, Joan Shorenstein Center for Press, Politics, Public Policy, Harvard University, Cambridge, MA, July 1998); Frere, *Media and Conflicts in Central Africa*; Marks, interview; Hagos, "Media Intervention in Peace Building in Burundi."

41. Rich, "One David, Two Goliaths"; Marks, interview.

42. Bryan Rich, interview with the author, October 7, 2010.

43. Hagos, "Media Intervention in Peace Building in Burundi," p. 24; Sinduhije, "Ijambo."

44. Sinduhije, "Ijambo."

45. Ibid., p. 16.

46. Ibid., p. 13.

47. Skoler, "Burundi Radio Project Races to Ease Hutu-Tutsi Tensions"; Sinduhije, "Ijambo."

48. Diana Cahn, "Studio Ijambo Trying to Bridge Hutu–Tutsi Divide in Burundi," Associated Press, March 9, 1998.

49. Sinduhije, "Ijambo," p. 13.

50. Ibid., p. 11.

51. Ibid., p. 14.

52. Ibid.

53. Rich, "One David, Two Goliaths."

54. Frere, *Media and Conflicts in Central Africa*, p. 21.

55. Alexis Sinduhije, "A War Reporter Tries to Understand What Courage Is: 'Thinking about Courage Becomes a Reflection on Humanity,'" *Nieman Reports* (Summer 2006): 18.

56. Hagos, "Media Intervention in Peace Building in Burundi," p. 21.

57. Frere, *Media and Conflicts in Central Africa*, p. 22.

58. This is a translation from Radio Isanganiro from Kirundi into English.

59. Ibid.

60. Ibid.

61. Ibid.

62. Ibid.

63. Marks, interview.

64. Ibid.

65. Hagos, "Media Intervention in Peace Building in Burundi."

66. James Astill, "Burundi Heals Wounds with Touch of Soap," *Guardian Unlimited* (*Observer*), May 4, 2003.

67. Transcript published in *Harper's Magazine*, "Banana Split," January 2001.

68. Ibid.

69. Ibid.

70. Ibid.

71. Ibid.

72. Astill, "Burundi Heals Wounds."

73. Ibid.; Gordon Adam and Lina Holguin, "The Media's Role in Peace-Building: Asset or Liability?" (presentation at Our Media 3 Conference, Barranquilla, Colombia, May 19–21, 2003), http://ics.leeds.ac.uk/papers/pmt/exhibits/1769/mediainpeace.pdf (accessed March 3, 2011).

74. Rich, interview.

75. Karl Vick, "In Burundi, Confessions of Genocide: On Film, Killers Purge Souls to Heal Nation," *Washington Post*, August 30, 1999, A01.

76. Ibid.

77. Ibid.

78. Peter Uvin, *Life after Violence: A People's Story of Burundi* (London: Zed Books, 2009).

79. Marks, interview.

80. Rich, interview.

81. Marks, interview.

82. Robinson and Slachmuijlder, "Peace Radio Finds a Home."

83. Rich, interview.

84. Uvin, *Life after Violence*.

85. BBC News, "Burundi Opposition Leader Jailed."

86. Radio France Internationale (Paris), "Six Opposition Party Members Arrested," *Africa News*, August 9, 2010.

Chapter 5: Peace at the Edge

1. Patrick is a fictional name, but the accounts are based on the October 30, 1971, Amnesty International Report on Northern Ireland: *A Report on Allegations of Ill-Treatment Made by Persons Arrested under the Special Powers Act After 8 August* (Nottingham: Amnesty International, Russell Press, 1971), http://cain.ulst.ac.uk/events/intern/docs/amnesty71.htm.

2. Conflict Archive on the Internet (CAIN), an archive of information related to the Troubles and Northern Ireland from 1968 until the present day, based at the University of Ulster and affiliated with Northern Ireland Social and Political Archive (ARK) and International Conflict Research Institute (INCORE), http://cain.ulst.ac.uk/events/intern/chron.htm.

3. Amnesty International Report on Northern Ireland, October 30, 1971.

4. Ibid.

5. Ibid.

6. Mari Fitzduff, *Beyond Violence: Conflict Resolution Process in Northern Ireland* (New York: United Nations University Press, 2002); Martin McGinley, e-mail exchange with the author, 2010.

7. Fitzduff, *Beyond Violence*, citing L. De Paor, *Divided Ulster* (Harmondsworth: Penguin, 1970), p. 154; *Unionists* is a term that came later and referred to those wishing to maintain union with Great Britain.

8. Fitzduff, *Beyond Violence*, citing Cameron Report, *Disturbances in Northern Ireland: Report of a Commission Appointed by the Governor of Northern Ireland* (Belfast: HMSO, 1971).

9. Fitzduff, *Beyond Violence*, p. 4.

10. Tim Pat Coogan, *The Troubles: Ireland's Ordeal and the Search for Peace* (New York: Palgrave, 2002), p. 34.

11. CAIN; Coogan, *The Troubles*; David McKittrick, interview with the author, August 2009; Eamonn McCann, interview with the author, 2009; Don Mullen and John Scally, *Bloody Sunday: Massacre in Northern Ireland* (Niwot, CO: Roberts Rinehart Publishers, 1997). Unionists called the city Londonderry.

12. Fitzduff, *Beyond Violence*.

13. Coogan, *The Troubles*, p. 33; David McKittrick and David McVea, *Making Sense of the Troubles: The Story of the Conflict in Northern Ireland* (Chicago: New Amsterdam Books, 2002), pp. 70–71.

14. Coogan, *The Troubles*; CAIN; McGinley, e-mail.

15. McKittrick and McVea, *Making Sense of the Troubles*.

16. Mullen and Scally, *Bloody Sunday*.

17. A total of 1,874 detainees were Catholic. See CAIN. Note that these are overall internment numbers through 1975.

18. Free Derry was declared autonomous from British rule by the Irish Catholic community.

19. Mullen and Scally, *Bloody Sunday*, p. 203; Fulvio Grimaldi, *Blood on the Street* (Derry: Guildhall Press, 1998); CAIN. Some said the dye was red, not purple.

20. Mullen and Scally, *Bloody Sunday*.

21. Ibid., p. 96.

22. Ibid., p. 95; Eamonn McCann, from CAIN; Grimaldi, *Blood on the Street*.

23. Mullen and Scally, *Bloody Sunday*, p. 205; David McKittrick, Seamus Kelters, Brian Feeney, and Chris Thornton, *Lost Lives: The Stories of the Men, Women, and Children Who Died as a Result of the Northern Ireland Troubles* (Edinburgh and London: Mainstream Publishing, 1999).

24. Mullen and Scally, *Bloody Sunday*.

25. Ibid.

26. Ibid.; McKittrick et al., *Lost Lives*.

27. McKittrick and McVea, *Making Sense of the Troubles*, p. 77.

28. CAIN; Mullen and Scally, *Bloody Sunday*; McKittrick et al., *Lost Lives*. There are slight variations in the accounts.

29. Ibid.

30. Amnesty International Report on Northern Ireland, October 30, 1971.

31. *Republicans* was the term usually designated for those attempting to unite the "six counties" of Northern Ireland with the Republic of Ireland, even if it meant using violence.

32. McKittrick and McVea, *Making Sense of the Troubles*, p. 78.

33. Other estimates suggest that there were 100,000 people in this march.

34. CAIN; David McKittrick et al., *Lost Lives*; Mark O'Brien, "Disavowing Democracy: The Silencing Project in the South," in *Political Censorship and the Democratic State: The Irish Broadcasting Ban* (Portland: Four Courts Press), pp. 48–61.

35. Alasdair McDonnell, interview with the author, August 2009.

36. McKittrick et al., *Lost Lives*.

37. The Provisional IRA (PIRA) denied planting this bomb and warnings were not given prior to its detonation (as is usually the PIRA practice). McKittrick et al., *Lost Lives*, p. 16.

38. *Loyalists* was the term for those who were "loyal" to Great Britain and were willing to use violence to prevent being forced into a "united Ireland."

39. McKittrick et al, *Lost Lives*; McKittrick and McVea, *Making Sense of the Troubles*.

40. Paul Bew and Gordon Gillespie, *Northern Ireland: A Chronology of the Troubles, 1968–1999* (Lanham, MD: Scarecrow Press, 1999), pp. 47–48.

41. Ibid.

42. Bew and Gillespie, *Northern Ireland*; Peter Taylor, *Behind the Mask: The IRA and Sinn Fein* (New York: TV Books, 1999); Billy Hutchinson, interview with the author, August 2009; author interviews with Loyalists and Unionists who have not agreed to being identified, 2009 and 2010.

43. Taylor, *Behind the Mask*, p. 165.

44. Hutchinson, interview; author interview with former Loyalist paramilitary members, 2009, 2010. Some indicated that they were acting as vigilantes.

45. Taylor, *Behind the Mask*, pp. 171–72.

46. One account says the rounds fired by the army were rubber bullets (according to Taylor, *Behind the Mask*), but the number of dead suggest that at some point the army fired live ammunition. The PIRA emerged at the end of 1969 and was distinct from the official IRA, but, for the sake of simplicity, this chapter uses the acronym *IRA* to include the PIRA.

47. Taylor, *Behind the Mask*. The degree to which the IRA shot is disputed by witnesses.

48. McKittrick and McVea, *Making Sense of the Troubles*; Bardon, *A History of Ulster* (Belfast: Blackstaff Press, 1992).

49. W. D. Flackes and Sydney Elliot, *Northern Ireland: A Political Directory, 1968–1993* (Belfast: Blackstaff Press Limited, 1994).

50. McKittrick et al., *Lost Lives*.

51. Taylor, *Behind the Mask*.

52. McKittrick and McVea, *Making Sense of the Troubles*.

53. Taylor, *Behind the Mask*; McKittrick et al., *Lost Lives*.

54. Ibid.

55. Bew and Gillespie, *Northern Ireland*; McGinley, e-mail.

56. Political status had been won as a condition for talks in 1972, then taken away. Coogan, *The Troubles*, p. 162; Peter Taylor, *Behind the Mask*, p. 237.

57. Martin Dillon, *The Shankill Butchers: The Real Story of Cold-Blooded Mass Murder* (New York: Routledge, 1989).

58. Coogan, *The Troubles*; McKittrick and McVea, *Making Sense of the Troubles*; Taylor, *Behind the Mask*; Gerry Adams, in his book *Before the Dawn* (New York: William Morrow, 1996), argued that the "no-wash" was forced onto the prisoners because their toilet facilities were withdrawn, p. 279.

59. Taylor, *Behind the Mask*, p. 281.

60. The five demands included the right to wear their own clothes rather than prison uniforms, the right to refuse prison work, the right of free association with other prisoners, the right to one visit, one letter, and one parcel per week, and regaining their remission rights. CAIN; Brendan O'Brien, *The Long War: The IRA & Sinn Fein* (Dublin: O'Brien Press, 1999); David McKittrick, "Remembering Bobby Sands," *Independent*, May 5, 2006, http://www.independent.co.uk/news/uk/this-britain/remembering-bobby-sands-476884.html.

61. CAIN.

62. Richard Davis, *Mirror Hate: The Convergent Ideology of Northern Ireland Paramilitaries, 1966–1992* (Brookfield, VT: Dartmouth Publishing, 1994).

63. Brian Rowan and Eamonn Mallie, interviews with the author, August 2009 and September 2010; David Miller, *Don't Mention the War: Northern Ireland, Propaganda, and the Media* (Boulder, CO: Pluto Press, 1994).

64. Hume and Clinton were the most public leaders about standing with Adams in a way that helped him build credibility among those who mistrusted him. While most journalists with whom I spoke emphasized Hume, this particular quote belongs to Mallie (interview); Brendan McCourt emphasized the importance of Clinton in securing the peace agreement (interview with the author, August 2009).k/events/bsunday/chron.htm (accessed May 11, 2011).

65. Multiple leaders deserve credit, particularly Britain's former prime minister Tony Blair, but they are not named due to the length considerations in this chapter.

66. Hutchinson, interview. Hutchinson was one of the initiators of peace talks through clergy while he was still in prison.

67. CAIN, February 2, 1972, http://cain.ulst.ac.uk/events/bsunday/chron.htm. (accessed May 11, 2011).

68. Liz Curtis, *Ireland the Propaganda Wars: The British Media and the Battle for Hearts and Mind* (Concord, MA: Pluto Press, 1984).

69. McKittrick and McVea, *Making Sense of the Troubles*, p. 78. The words belong to Sir John Peck. David Butler, *The Trouble with Reporting Northern Ireland* (Brookfield, VT: Ashgate Publishing, 1995).

70. *Derry Journal*, "It Was Willful Murder, Say Priests," January 31, 1972. The date on this newspaper is unclear due to the quality of the electronic copy. It is featured at the Museum of Free Derry.

71. *New York Times*, January 31, 1972.

72. Maureen Mulvihill, "Camera Does Not Lie: Revisiting Bloody Sunday," *New Hibernia Review* 6, no. 4 (2002): 151–54.

73. Curtis, *Ireland*, p. 45.

74. Emphasis mine. Simon Winchester, "13 Killed as Paratroops Break Riot," *Guardian*, January 13, 1972, http://www.guardian.co.uk/uk/1972/jan/31/bloodysunday.northernireland.

75. Curtis, *Ireland*, p. 25.

76. CAIN, February 2, 1972.

77. Taylor, *Behind the Mask*; author interview with a Republican leader who has not consented to be identified, 2009.

78. Tim Pat Coogan, *On the Blanket: The Inside Story of the IRA Prisoners' 'Dirty' Protest* (New York: Palgrave MacMillan, 1997), pp. 156–57.

79. Miller, *Don't Mention the War*, p. 28; Curtis, *Ireland*, p. 10.

80. Miller, *Don't Mention the War*.

81. Ed Maloney, "Censorship and 'The Troubles,'" in *Political Censorship and the Democratic State: The Irish Broadcasting Ban*, ed. Mary P. Corcoran and Mark O'Brien (Dublin: Four Courts Press, 2005), pp. 99–113.

82. Bill Rolston, "Political Censorship," in *War and Words: The Northern Ireland Media Reader*, ed. Bill Rolston and David Miller (Belfast: Beyond the Pale Publications, 1996), pp. 235–44.

83. Niall Meehan, "How RTE Censored Its Censorship," *Sunday Business Post*, April 20, 2003, http://gcd.academia.edu/NiallMeehan/Papers/75310/How_RTE_censored_its _censorship; Rolston, "Political Censorship."

84. Graham Ellison and Jim Smyth, *The Crowned Harp: Policing Northern Ireland* (London: Pluto Press, 2000), http://cain.ulst.ac.uk/issues/police/docs/ellison/ellison00b.htm.

85. The British Parliament passed a series of bills: the Emergency Provisions Act of 1978 prohibited journalists from collecting information that could be used by terrorists or to solicit or invite support for illegal organizations; the Prevention of Terrorism Act made the IRA illegal in Britain and required information about anyone involved in terrorism to be handed to police; the Police and Criminal Evidence Act gave police power to seize any material from persons, including journalists. Author interview with a Sinn Fein leader who did not consent to be identified, August 2009; McKittrick and McVea, *Making Sense of the Troubles*.

86. Ibid.

87. Staff writer, "Remembering," *Sunday Journal*, August 10, 2008, http://www.sunday journal.ie/mary-nelis/Remembering.4374961.jp?articlepage=3.

88. Ibid.

89. Coogan, *On the Blanket*. For the importance of the murals, see Bill Rolston's books, including *Politics and Painting: Murals and Conflict in Northern Ireland* (Madison, NJ: Fairleigh Dickinson University Press, 1991).

90. Danny Morrison, interview with the author, August 2009; also, author interview with another Sinn Fein leader who has not consented to being identified, August 2009; for the murals, see Rolston, *Politics and Painting*.

91. "Mosquito" press was said to be biting away at the mainstream press.

92. Tom Hartley, interview with the author, August 2009; Máirtín Ó Muilleoir, interview with the author, August 2009; Morrison, interview; author interview with a Sinn Fein leader who has not consented to being identified, 2009.

93. This estimate was given by the publication's former editor and Sinn Fein communications director Danny Morrison, who was also the editor of the paper. Other Sinn Fein members and some researchers estimated it at 60,000 at its peak.

94. Danny Morrison noted that the Telex machine was rented and they simply replaced it with another one (interview). Davis, *Mirror Hate*; Liz Curtis, "Republican Publicity," in *War and Words: The Northern Ireland Media Reader*, ed. Bill Rolston and David Miller (Belfast: Beyond the Pale Publications, 1996), pp. 265–305. Personnel were held in jail for various periods. Morrison was jailed for five years at one time.

95. Coogan, *On the Blanket*, pp. 169–82.

96. Staff writer, "Remembering."

97. Coogan, *On the Blanket*, p. 174.

98. Davis, *Mirror Hate*, p. 60.

99. Ibid.

100. McKittrick, interview.

101. Davis, *Mirror Hate*.

102. Editorial Report, "Ulster By-Election Victory by Hunger Striker Robert Sands," BBC Summary of World Broadcasts, April 14, 1981.

103. Ray Wilkinson with Tony Clifton, "An IRA Man Wins a Seat in Commons," *Newsweek*, April 20, 1981, 59.

104. Gwen Smith, "Irish Hunger Striker 'Very Noble Person, Belfast Priest Found," *Globe and Mail*, April 25, 1981.

105. Newspapers throughout the world followed the events; *Irish bloodbath* was part of the headline for the article by Jeffrey Simpson, "Vigilantes Active: Both Sides Prepare for Irish Bloodbath," *Globe and Mail*, May 1, 1981.

106. *Economist*, "Hope Starved in Ulster" and "West Germany; A Death without Much Resonance," April 25, 1981, 69 (US ed., 65).

107. BBC, "'Counter-Terror' from Ulster Catholics Predicted," April 25, 1981.

108. Yuny Ustenko, "London's 'Terror' in Ulster, 'The Whirlwind Gathers Momentum,'" BBC Summary of World Broadcasts, April 27, 1981.

109. Reuters, "Bobby Sands Dies Day 66 of Fast," *Globe and Mail*, May 5, 1981.

110. Gerry Adams, *A Farther Shore: Ireland's Long Road to Peace* (New York: Random House, 2003).

111. Ibid.

112. BBC Summary of World Broadcasts, "Other Reports: Apartheid in South Africa—and Northern Ireland," *Radio Peace and Progress*, May 8, 1981.

113. Adams, *Farther Shore*, p. 295, citing a quote from the *New York Daily News*.

114. Adams, *Farther Shore*, p. 296, citing a quote from the *Irish Press*.

115. Ed Maloney, "Closing Down the Airwaves: The Story of the Broadcasting Ban," in *The Media and Northern Ireland*, ed. Bill Rolston (Hampshire: Macmillan Academic and Professional Limited, 1991); Tim Cooke, "Prepared for War, Ready for Peace? Paramilitaries, Politics and the Press in Northern Ireland" (Discussion Paper D-31, Joan Shorenstein Center for Press, Politics, Public Policy, Harvard University, 1998), p. 10.

116. Quote from *Irish News*, January 1989; Maloney, "Closing Down the Airwaves."

117. Morrison, interview. A cursory review of newspapers supports his assertion.

118. Author interview with political leaders and reporters revealed this.

119. McKittrick, interview; McKittrick, "Sinn Fein Leaders Raise Hopes with Talk

of Peace: About 2,000 People Marched in Belfast Yesterday to Mark the 21st Anniversary of the Start of Internment in Northern Ireland," in*dependent*, August 10, 1992, http://www.independent.co.uk/news/uk/sinn-fein-leaders-raise-hopes-with-talk-of-peace-about-2000-people-marched-in-belfast-yesterday-to-mark-the-21st-anniversary-of-the-start-of-internment-in-northern-ireland-david-mckittrick-reports-1539427.html (accessed May 11, 2011).

120. McKittrick, interview.

121. From PBS, "Behind the Mask: The IRA & Sinn Fein," http://www.pbs.org/wgbh/pages/frontline/shows/ira/conflict/hunger.html.

122. This revelation was broken by journalist Eamonn Mallie; Mallie, interview; McKittrick, interview.

123. Sinn Fein was excluded from the forum.

124. McKittrick, interview.

125. Ibid. McKittrick mentioned that eleven columns denounced Hume for speaking with Adams; Brian Rowan, interview with the author, August 2009.

126. Mallie, interview.

127. Ibid.

128. "John Hume—Ireland's Peacemaker," Social Democratic and Labor Party (SDLP), http://www.sdlp.ie/index.php/about_sdlp/john_hume/ (accessed May 11, 2011).

129. Gerry Adams (presidential address, Ard Fheis, 1989).

130. McKittrick, interview.

131. CAIN.

132. McKittrick, interview.

133. *Irish News*, "A New Era," October 1, 1994, 1.

134. The increase in coverage was evident from skimming the newspapers from 1988 to 1998.

135. Among the political leaders with whom I spoke, Sir "Reg" Empey said that Mitchell really enabled the peace process through his fair approach (interview with the author, September 2010).

136. *Irish News*, "Blessed Are the Peacemakers," and "A Tale of Two Leaders: Bill Clinton and Gerry Adams Shake Hands on the Falls," November 1995.

137. These headlines were on November 29, 2005.

138. Mallie, interview; Rowan, interview.

139. Martin McGinley, interview with the author, August 2009.

140. Mallie, interview.

141. Author interview with a reporter covering the Troubles who asked not to be identified, 2010.

142. Terry McLaughlin, interview with the author, August 2009; McGinley, interview.

143. Martina Purdy, conference paper delivered to the author via e-mail, 2010.

144. Rowan, interview; Brian Rowan, e-mail exchange with the author, 2010.

145. Author interview with a leading journalist covering the Troubles and peace process, 2010. Other journalists did not agree with this, however.

146. McCann, interview. Of the dozen journalists I interviewed in Northern Ireland,

two, McCann and McLaughlin, were critical of the peace process and the final 1998 agreement.

147. Gadi Wolfsfeld, *Media and the Path to Peace* (Cambridge: Cambridge University Press, 2004).

148. Mallie, interview.

149. Fitzduff, interview, August 2009.

150. Harold Goode, interview with the author, August 2009; he mentioned the "chuckle brothers," which referred to Sinn Fein's Martin McGuinness and the Democratic Unionist Party's Ian Paisley, the latter of whom had opposed the peace process and refused to sign it because of Sinn Fein's engagement. The two now work together in government under the power-sharing agreement; Cooke, "Prepared for War."

Chapter 6: In Black and White

1. Albie Sachs, *The Jail Diary of Albie Sachs* (New York: McGraw-Hill, 1966).

2. Albie Sachs, interview with the author, February 2010.

3. Afrikaners were white settlers who migrated to South Africa from Holland.

4. *Truth and Reconciliation Commission Summary Report and Transcripts* (March 21, 2003): 63 (for transcripts, see http://www.justice.gov.za/trc/special/index.htm#mh; for reports, see http://www.justice.gov.za/trc/report/index.htm and http://www.info.gov.za/otherdocs/2003/trc/); Robert Horwitz, *Communication and Democratic Reform in South Africa* (New York: Cambridge University Press, 2001); Don Pinnock, "Writing Left: The Journalism of Ruth First and *The Guardian* in the 1950s," in *South Africa's Alternative Press: Voices of Protest and Resistance, 1880-1960*, ed. Les Switzer (New York: Cambridge University Press, 1997), pp. 308–30.

5. William A. Hachten and C. Anthony Giffard, *The Press and Apartheid: Repression and Propaganda in South Africa* (Madison: University of Wisconsin Press, 1984), p. viii; *Truth and Reconciliation Commission Summary Report and Transcripts*, pp. 63, 64.

6. Sachs, *Jail Diary of Albie Sachs*, pp. 147, 152, 284.

7. ANC Freedom Charter; Chenhamo C. Chimutengwende, *South Africa: The Press and the Politics of Liberation* (Half Moon Bay, BC: Barbican Books, 1978), p. 76. Other attendees of the conference were the South African Indian Congress, the South African Colored People's Organization, the White South African Congress of Democrats, the South African Congress of Trade Unions, and the Federation of South African Women.

8. Sachs, *Jail Diary of Albie Sachs*; *Truth and Reconciliation Commission Summary Report and Transcripts* (October 29, 1998), citing the hearing in Johannesburg from September 15 to 17, 1997 (for the entire report, see http://www.info.gov.za/otherdocs/2003/trc/, dated March 21, 2003); Les Switzer, "South Africa's Resistance Press under Apartheid," in *South Africa's Resistance Press: Alternative Voices in the Last Generation of Apartheid*, ed. Les Switzer and Mohammad Adhikari (Athens: Ohio University Press, 2000), pp. 1–78.

9. *Time*, "South Africa: The Sharpeville Massacre," April 4, 1960, http://www.time.com/time/magazine/article//0,9171,869441,00.html; Ambrose Reeves, "The Sharpeville Massacre—A Watershed in South Africa," http://www.sahistory.org.za/pages/library

resources/articles_papers/1960-sharpeville-massacre-rev-ambrose.html; James Zug, *The* Guardian: *The History of South Africa's Extraordinary Anti-Apartheid Newspaper* (East Lansing: Michigan State University, 2007). The official number of people shot dead is sixty-nine; however, this number is contested.

10. *Time*, "South Africa"; Reeves, "Sharpeville Massacre."

11. *Time*, "South Africa"; Zug, *Guardian*.

12. James Zug, "Far from Dead: The Final Years of *The Guardian*, 1960–1963," in *South Africa's Resistance Press: Alternative Voices in the Last Generation under Apartheid*, ed. Les Switzer and Mohammad Adhikari (Athens: Ohio University Press, Center for International Studies, 2000), pp. 128–75.

13. *New York Times*, Abstract, April 9, 1970, 13, col. 5.

14. Zug, "Far from Dead."

15. Les Switzer and Mohammad Adhikari, eds., *South Africa's Resistance Press: Alternative Voices in the Last Generation under Apartheid* (Athens: Ohio University Press, Center for International Studies, 2000); Sachs, interview with the author.

16. Albie Sachs, interview, *Insighters*, KPFK 90.7 FM Los Angeles and WPRR, http://www.alternet.org/story/145976/lessons_from_a_revolutionary%27s_lifetime_crusade _for_justice/.

17. Sachs, *Jail Diary of Albie Sachs*, p. 105.

18. Ibid., p. 26.

19. Ibid.

20. Ibid., p. 114.

21. Ibid., p. 109.

22. Judith Mason, "The Man Who Sang and the Woman Who Kept Silent," in *The Strange Alchemy of Life and Law*, by Albie Sachs (New York: Oxford University Press, 2009), pp. vii–viii.

23. Sachs, *Jail Diary of Albie Sachs*, p. 147.

24. Indres Naidoo, *Robben Island: Ten Years as a Political Prisoner in South Africa's Most Notorious Penitentiary* (New York: Vintage Books, 1983).

25. Ibid., pp. 22–23.

26. Sachs, *Jail Diary of Albie Sachs*, pp. 122–24.

27. Sachs, *Jail Diary of Albie Sachs*; Zug, *The* Guardian, p. 225.

28. Allister Sparks, *Tomorrow Is Another Country: The Inside Story of South Africa's Road to Change* (New York: Hill and Wang, a division of Farrar, Straus, and Giroux, 1995), pp. 24–25.

29. "Coloreds" were lighter-skinned, usually a mix of African and white.

30. Albie Sachs, *Soft Vengeance of a Freedom Fighter* (Los Angeles: University of California Press, 1990); Sachs, interview with the author.

31. Ibid.

32. Sparks, *Tomorrow Is Another Country*.

33. Ibid.

34. Sachs, interview with the author; Ron Krabill, "Symbiosis: Mass Media and the Truth and Reconciliation Commission of South Africa," *Media Culture Society* 23 (2001): 567.

344 NOTES

35. Sachs, interview with the author.

36. Switzer, "South Africa's Resistance Press under Apartheid."

37. James Sanders, *South Africa and the International Media, 1972–1979: A Struggle for Representation* (London: Frank Cass Publishers, 2000), citing Mervyn Rees and Chris Day, *Muldergate: The Story of the Info Scandal* (New York: Macmillan, 1980), p. 172.

38. Sachs, interview with the author; Gordon S. Jackson, *Breaking Story: The South African Press* (San Francisco: Westview Press, 1993); Horwitz, *Communication and Democratic Reform*; Desmond Tutu, *Truth and Reconciliation Commission Summary Report and Transcripts* (October 29, 1998), citing the hearing in Johannesburg from September 15 to 17, 1997 (for transcripts, see http://www.justice.gov.za/trc/special/index.htm#mh; for reports, see http://www.justice.gov.za/trc/report/index.htm and http://www.info.gov.za/otherdocs/2003/trc/); Lyn S. Graybill, *Truth and Reconciliation in South Africa: Miracle or Model?* (Boulder, CO: Lynne Rienner, 2002).

39. Tutu, *Truth and Reconciliation Commission Summary Report and Transcripts*, opening remarks; Horwitz, *Communication and Democratic Reform*; Graybill, *Truth and Reconciliation in South Africa*; Pinnock, "Writing Left"; Sachs, interview with the author.

40. Horwitz, *Communication and Democratic Reform*; Tutu, *Truth and Reconciliation Commission Summary Report and Transcripts*; Graybill, *Truth and Reconciliation in South Africa*.

41. Allister Sparks, e-mail exchange with the author, October 2010; Gordon S. Jackson, *Breaking Story*. Another Afrikaans-language paper that opposed apartheid was *Pro Veritate*. It existed from the early 1960s to the late 1970s, according to the library and archives at Stanford University.

42. Tim Du Plessis, "Newspaper Management Keeps Quiet about Its Role in Apartheid: In the Afrikaans Press, Some Reporters Decide to Testify," *Neiman Reports* (Winter 1998).

43. Horwitz, *Communication and Democratic Reform*.

44. Radio Freedom transcript, South African History Online, http://www.sahistory.org.za/ (accessed May 13, 2011).

45. Switzer, "South Africa's Resistance Press under Apartheid"; Sachs, interview with the author.

46. Switzer, "South Africa's Resistance Press under Apartheid," pp. 275, 276, 295–97; Pinnock, "Writing Left," pp. 308, 315; Zug, "Far from Dead."

47. Pinnock, "Writing Left," pp. 312–13, 315.

48. Ibid., p. 316.

49. Switzer, "South Africa's Resistance Press under Apartheid," p. 291.

50. Zug, "Far from Dead"; Switzer, "South Africa's Resistance Press under Apartheid," p. 299; Pinnock, "Writing Left," p. 316–17.

51. Pinnock, "Writing Left," pp. 316–18.

52. Ibid.

53. Pinnock, "Writing Left"; Switzer, "South Africa's Resistance Press under Apartheid."

54. Zug, "Far from Dead"; Zug, *Guardian*.

55. Zug, "Far from Dead," p. 141; Zug, *Guardian*, p. 192.

56. Zug, "Far from Dead," p. 148.

57. Ibid., pp. 145–46.

58. Zug, "Far from Dead," p. 153; Zug, *Guardian*, p. 212.

59. Zug, "Far from Dead," pp. 153–54; Zug, *Guardian*, p. 213.

60. Zug, *Guardian*, p. 215.

61. Ibid., p. 216.

62. Zug, "Far from Dead"; Zug, *Guardian*, p. 220.

63. Zug, "Far from Dead," p. 163; Pinnock, "Writing Left," p. 328.

64. Some of the publications included *Workers' Unity, Sechaba, Mayibuye*, and *Dawn*. Peter Limb, "African Workers in the Afrikan National Press, 1900–1960," in Switzer and Adhikar, *South Africa's Resistance Press* (see note 15).

65. Neville R. Choonoo, "The Sophiatown Generation: Black Literary Journalism," in Switzer and Adhikar, *South Africa's Resistance Press* (see note 15), pp. 257, 259–60; South Africa History Online, http://www.sahistory.org.za/ (accessed May 13, 2011).

66. Chimutengwende, *South Africa*, p. 69; Choonoo, "Sophiatown Generation," p. 260; Horwitz, *Communication and Democratic Reform*.

67. Radio Freedom, as reported by BBC World Broadcasts, December 8 and 10, January 14, 1982; July 9, 1982; and January 19, 1993, LexisNexis.

68. Horwitz, *Communication and Democratic Reform*; Graybill, *Truth and Reconciliation in South Africa*; Mohamed Adhikari, "You Have the Right to Know: South, 1987–1994," in Switzer and Adhikar, *South Africa's Resistance Press* (see note 15).

69. Paul J. Vorster, "The *Rand Daily Mail*: The Rise, Decline, and Demise of a Once Great Daily," *World Communication* 15, no. 2 (Fall 1986); *New York Times*, June 29, 1969, LexisNexis; Benjamin Pogrund, "Obituary: Laurence Gandar," *Independent*, November 17, 1998.

70. Pogrund, "Obituary."

71. Ibid.; Donald G. McNeil, "Laurence Gandar, Apartheid Critic, Dies at 82," *New York Times*, November 16, 1998; *New York Times*, Abstract, June 29 and July 11, 1969; Vorster, "The *Rand Daily Mail*."

72. *Time*, "South Africa"; *New York Times*, abstract, July 13, 1969.

73. Charles Mohr, *New York Times*, October 1, 1974, LexisNexis; FRELIMO was a movement in Mozambique fighting for independence.

74. Chimutengwende, *South Africa*, pp. 68, 69.

75. Mbulelo Vizikhungo Mzamane and David R. Howarth, "Representing Blackness: Steve Biko and the Black Consciousness Movement," in Switzer and Adhikar, *South Africa's Resistance Press* (see note 15); Chimutengwende, *South Africa*, p. 85.

76. Mzamane and Howarth, "Representing Blackness," p. 181.

77. Mzamane and Howarth, "Representing Blackness"; Chimutengwende, *South Africa*, p. 85.

78. Mzamane and Howarth, "Representing Blackness."

79. Ibid. The Bantu Homelands Citizenship Act of 1970, in essence, denied black South Africans of South African citizenship and instead declared that they were citizens of their ethnic group. The Bantu Self-Government Act of 1959 created ten territories separate from white South Africa that would be recognized as the homelands or Bantustans for black South Africans.

80. Hachten and Giffard, *Press and Apartheid*; Hachten and Giffard, *Press and Apartheid*, p. 4, citing a July 18, 1978, interview with Benjamin Pogrund; Switzer, "South Africa's Resistance Press under Apartheid," in Switzer and Adhikar, *South Africa's Resistance Press* (see note 15), pp. 1–78. Altogether, more than six hundred died during the riots, but not in this first confrontation.

81. Switzer, "South Africa's Resistance Press under Apartheid"; Jackson, *Breaking Story*.

82. Mzamane and Howarth, "Representing Blackness."

83. Jay Ross, "Key South African Black Dies in Custody: US Officials Criticize Death of Moderate Black Leader," *Washington Post*, September 14, 1977.

84. Associated Press, September 15, 1977, LexisNexis.

85. Maureen Johnson, Associated Press, September 15, 1977, LexisNexis; Raymond Caroll with Peter Younghusband, "Steve Biko Is Dead," *Newsweek*, September 26, 1977; Associated Press, September 15, 1977, LexisNexis.

86. Johnson, Associated Press, September 15, 1977, LexisNexis; Judy Yablonky, Associated Press, September 18, 1977, LexisNexis.

87. Maureen Johnson, Associated Press, September 15 and 16, 1977, LexisNexis.

88. Maureen Johnson, Associated Press, October 7 and 25, 1977, LexisNexis; Judy Yablonky, Associated Press, October 8, 1977, LexisNexis; *Economist*, "How Did Steve Biko Die?" October 15, 1977; David B. Ottaway, "Biko Autopsy Said to Show He Died of Head Blow," *Washington Post*, October 26, 1977, A1.

89. Maureen Johnson, Associated Press, October 7 and October 25, 1977, LexisNexis; Judy Yablonky, Associated Press, October 8, 1977, LexisNexis; *Economist*, "How Did Steve Biko Die?"; Ottaway, "Biko Autopsy."

90. James Sanders, *South Africa and the International Media, 1972–1979: A Struggle for Representation* (London: Frank Cass Publishers, 2000).

91. Reuters, "S. African Editor Urges Ostracism," *Globe and Mail*, January 9, 1978; Hachten and Giffard, *Press and Apartheid*, p. 6; Associated Press, October 12, 1977, LexisNexis; Maureen Johnson, Associated Press, October 19, 1977, LexisNexis.

92. Maureen Johnson, Associated Press, October 19, 1977, LexisNexis.

93. Judy Yablonky, Associated Press, November 24, 1977, LexisNexis; Reuters, "Acid Coated T-Shirt Hurts Editor's Child," *Globe and Mail*, November 25, 1977; BBC News, "SA Activist Donald Woods Dies," World Edition, August 19, 2001, http://news.bbc.co.uk/2/hi/africa/1499587.stm; "On This Day 1978: Newspaper Editor Flees South Africa," January1, http://news.bbc.co.uk/onthisday/hi/dates/stories/january/1/newsid_2459000/2459845.stm.

94. Hachten and Giffard, *Press and Apartheid*, pp. 6–7; Caryle Murphy, "S. Africa Imperils Court, Press Freedom," *Washington Post*, Foreign Service, November 30, 1979.

95. Murphy, "S. Africa Imperils Court."

96. Sanders, *South Africa and the International Media*.

97. Ibid.

98. *Time*, "South Africa"; Alfred C. Ames, "Evil in South Africa: A Convincing Account," *Chicago Daily Tribune*, September 4, 1960. The *New York Times* covered the Sharpeville massacre a minimum of eight times.

99. Parliamentary Staff, "MPs to Join Protest Vigil," *Guardian*, March 3, 1961; Sanders, *South Africa and the International Media*.

100. John Hughes, "World Attention Turns on Apartheid," *Christian Science Monitor*, January 12, 1961, 1.

101. Sanders, *South Africa and the International Media*, p. 110. A big part of this series related to British companies that were working in South Africa.

102. News Dispatches, "Post's Jim Hoagland Wins Pulitzer Prize, *Washington Post*, *Times-Herald*, May 4, 1971.

103. David B. Ottoway, "Backlash against U.S. Engulfs South African Moderates," *Washington Post*, June 29, 1977.

104. Sanders, *South Africa and the International Media*; Trevor Brown, "Did Anybody Know His Name? US Press Coverage of Biko," *Journalism Quarterly* 57, no.1 (1980): 31–44; *Washington Post* website.

105. Carrol with Younghusband, "Steve Biko Is Dead."

106. Associated Press, September 15, 1977, LexisNexis; Carrol with Younghusband, "Steve Biko Is Dead."

107. Associated Press, September 13, 1977, LexisNexis.

108. *Washington Post*, Editorial, September 15, 1977.

109. Jay Ross, "Key South African Black Dies in Custody: US Officials Criticize Death of Moderate Black Leader," *Washington Post*, September 14, 1977.

110. Associated Press, September 15, 1977, LexisNexis; *Washington Post*, "Demands Mount for Resignation of S. African in Biko Death Case," September 17, 1977; Judy Yablonky, Associated Press, September 18, 1977, LexisNexis; Reuters, "Police Blocked MDs, Inquest Told," *Globe and Mail*, November 22, 1977; *Washington Post*, "Move to Hospitalize Biko Halted," November 22, 1977.

111. Associated Press, September 17 and 27, 1977, LexisNexis.

112. David B. Ottoway, "Death of Jailed Black Puts South African Justice on Trial," *Washington Post*, October 18, 1977.

113. Jay Ross, "US Will Send Top Delegation to S. African's Rites," *Washington Post*, September 24, 1977; Matt Franjola, Associated Press, September 25, 1977, LexisNexis.

114. *Economist*, "After Biko's Death," October 15, 1977, p. 9; South Africa Correspondent, "You're Banned, You're Jailed; You're Underground," *Economist*, October 22, 1977.

115. *Washington Post*, May 4, 1978, editorial.

116. Hsinhua correspondent, "No Brutal Suppression Can Stave Off Vorster Regime's Doom," Xinhua General News Service, October 22, 1977.

117. Jim Hoagland, "*Battle of South Africa*: CBS Reports: South Africa: A Stark and Chilling Documentary from CBS," *Washington Post*, September 1, 1978; BBC Summary of World Broadcasts, "The Iniquities of the South African Bantustans," February 6, 1982; James F. Smith, AP News Special, Associated Press, August 5, 1982, LexisNexis; Xinhua General News Service, "People's Daily Demands Release of Nelson Mandela," August 5, 1982; *Globe and Mail*, "Around the World: Third Decade in Prison," August 6, 1982.

118. Xinhua General News Service, "South African Regime's Repression of Black People Condemned at UN?" October 22, 1977; Samuel Koo, Associated Press, November 4, 1977, LexisNexis. (Only Israel continued to supply arms.)

119. Susanna McBee, "House Censures 'Repressive' South African Tactics," *Washington Post*, November 1, 1977; *Chemical Week*, "Yale Warns of Divestiture," July 12, 1978.

120. Reuters, "S. African Editor Urges Ostracism"; black South African journalists, however, criticized Woods for "exploiting" his friendship with Biko for a book, according to Caryle Murphy, "S. African Blacks Assail White Editor," *Washington Post*, Foreign Service, July 6, 1978.

121. Xinhua General News Service, "South African Blacks Call for Release of Nationalist Leader," March 22, 1980; Manuel Escott, "Daughter Launches Bid to Free Black Nationalist in S. Africa," *Globe and Mail*, April 9, 1980; Arthur Gavshon, "Jailed African Leader Calls for Overthrow of South African Government," Associated Press, June 10, 1980.

122. James F. Smith, AP News Special, Associated Press, August 5, 1982, LexisNexis.

123. Gavshon, "Jailed African Leader Calls for Overthrow of South African Government"; *Globe and Mail*, "Letter from Mandela Smuggled to India," August 27, 1981.

124. Associated Press, "Europeans Criticize South Africa," June 20, 1980, LexisNexis; BBC, "China Calls for Release of Nelson Mandela," August 11, 1982.

125. Associated Press, "Anne Wins Chancellor Ballot," February 17, 1981, LexisNexis; United Press International, "Royal Footsteps," February 17, 1981, LexisNexis; Associated Press, "S. Africa Denies U.S. Congressional Request to Visit Black Leader," July 24, 1981, LexisNexis; BBC Summary of World Broadcasts, "People's Daily Calls for Release of S. Africa's Political Prisoners," October 13, 1982, LexisNexis.

126. Associated Press, "Nelson Mandela Named Honorary Citizen of Rome," February 16, 1983, LexisNexis; BBC Summary of World Broadcasts, "Points from Speeches by Other Leaders," March 16, 1983; Laurie Johnston and Susan Heller Anderson, "City College to Honor Jailed Apartheid Opponent," *New York Times*, March 22, 1983; Associated Press, "King Carlos, Nelson Mandela Awarded Simon Bolivar Prize," June 16, 1983, LexisNexis; D. Buckley, "Mandela Honor," *Telegraph*, May 5, 1986.

127. D. Buckley, "Union Takes a Hard Line," *Telegraph*, February 17, 1986; BBC Summary of World Broadcasts, "NUM Rally in Soweto: Election of Nelson Mandela as Life President," February 18, 1986.

128. Robert Weller, Associated Press, March 17, 1983, LexisNexis.

129. Holger Jensen, *Newsweek*, February 14, 1983, LexisNexis.

130. James F. Smith, AP News Special, Associated Press, August 5, 1982, LexisNexis; Howard Simons, "Conscience of South Africa," *Washington Post*, February 23, 1986.

131. Simons, "Conscience of South Africa."

132. James F. Smith, AP News Special, Associated Press, August 5, 1982, LexisNexis.

133. United Press International, April 7, 1983, LexisNexis; Xinhua General News Service, "Foreign Journalists Searched, Arrested in South Africa," March 17, 1983; *Economist*, "South Africa: Bang on the Door," March 19, 1983.

134. Ross, "US Will Send Top Delegation"; Associated Press, March 18, 1983, LexisNexis.

135. All in the 1980s, circa 1982. Except Sachs diary; Dan van der Vat, "Books: Ruler in Exile," *Guardian*, January 30, 1986.

136. Sparks, *Tomorrow Is Another Country*; Christopher Merrett and Christopher Saunders, "The *Weekly Mail*, 1985–1994," in Switzer and Adhikar, *South Africa's Resistance Press* (see note 15); *Christian Science Monitor*, "Jailed ANC Leader Rejects Offer of Freedom," March 12, 1984.

137. Radio Freedom transcripts from BBC Summary of World Broadcasts (October 12, 1979; January 14, 1981; November 9, 1982; February 23, 1985; and January 19, 1993, respectively), LexisNexis.

138. Radio Freedom transcripts from BBC Summary of World Broadcasts (June 1, 4, and 7, 1982; March 8, 1984; May 21 and 23, 1985; November 5, 1982; and January 13 and September 5, 1984), LexisNexis; Reuters, "South African Non-Whites Urged to Resist," *Globe and Mail*, September 5, 1985.

139. Reuters, "Riots Greet Commonwealth Group, Botha Pressed to Arrange Peace Talks," *Globe and Mail*, May 14, 1986; Reuters, "Western Style Democracy Ruled out for South Africa," *Globe and Mail*, April 18, 1986.

140. Sparks, *Tomorrow Is Another Country*; Merrett and Saunders, "The *Weekly Mail*."

141. Jeremy Seekings, "The Media of the United Democratic Front, 1983–1991," in Switzer and Adhikar, *South Africa's Resistance Press* (see note 15); Switzer, "South Africa's Resistance Press under Apartheid"; Joseph Lelyveld, "Foes of Apartheid Hold Large Rally," *New York Times*, August 22, 1983.

142. Seekings, "Media of the United Democratic Front"; Switzer, "South Africa's Resistance Press under Apartheid," pp. 244–45; Lelyveld, "Foes of Apartheid Hold Large Rally."

143. Seekings, "Media of the United Democratic Front," p. 236.

144. Ibid., pp. 241–43; Keyan G. Tomaselli, "Ambiguities in Alternative Discourse," in Switzer and Adhikar, *South Africa's Resistance Press* (see note 15); Ineke Van Kessel, "*Grassroots*: From Washing Lines to Utopia," in Switzer and Adhikar, *South Africa's Resistance Press* (see note 15); Mohamed Adhikari, "You Have a Right to Know: *South*, 1987–1994," in Switzer and Adhikar, *South Africa's Resistance Press* (see note 15), pp. 334–35; Jackson, *Breaking Story*.

145. Sparks, *Tomorrow Is Another Country*; Merrett and Saunders, "The *Weekly Mail*."

146. Hachten and Giffard, *Press and Apartheid*, pp. 12–18.

147. Paul J. Vorster, "The *Rand Daily Mail*," pp. 129–44; Hachten and Giffard, *Press and Apartheid*, pp. 12–18.

148. Necklacing involves putting a tire around a person and lighting it on fire. Merrett and Saunders, "The *Weekly Mail*," pp. 462, 466.

149. Merrett and Saunders, "The *Weekly Mail*," p. 466.

150. Ibid.

151. Switzer, "South Africa's Resistance Press under Apartheid"; Sparks, *Tomorrow Is Another Country*. Some suggest the government funded the violence.

152. Seekings, "Media of the United Democratic Front," p. 247.

153. Chris Dafoe, "Simon's Graceland Show a Seductive Mix," *Globe and Mail*, June

24, 1987; P. Wicks, "0 Pays Tribute to Nelson Mandela," *Telegraph*, September 16, 1987; R. Gibson, "Mandela, the Struggle for Justice," *Sunday Mail*, September 20, 1987.

154. Howard Simons, "Conscience of South Africa," *Washington Post*, February 23, 1986.

155. Seumas Milne, "Beating Out the Theme for Mandela's Freedom," *Guardian*, June 1, 1988; Robin Hill, "Live Aid Revisited, Almost," *Sydney Morning Herald*, June 6, 1988; Karen Pakula, "Today's People," *Sydney Morning Herald*, June 13, 1988.

156. Milne, "Beating Out the Theme for Mandela's Freedom"; Hill, "Live Aid Revisited"; Pakula, "Today's People."

157. Merrett and Saunders, "The *Weekly Mail*," p. 476; Sparks, *Tomorrow Is Another Country*.

158. Sparks, *Tomorrow Is Another Country*.

159. Ibid.

160. F. W. de Klerk, "Opening of Second Session of 9th Parliament of Republic of South Africa" (speech, February 2, 1990), http://www.info.gov.za/speeches/1996/101348690.htm (accessed May 13, 2011).

161. Ibid.

162. BBC Summary of World Broadcasts, Radio Freedom transcript, April 11, 1990, LexisNexis.

163. Sachs, *Strange Alchemy of Life and Law* (see note 22), pp. 24–25.

164. Sachs, interview with the author.

165. Ibid.

166. Du Plessis, "Newspaper Management Keeps Quiet about Its Role in Apartheid."

167. Krabill, "Symbiosis," p. 568.

168. Du Plessis, "Newspaper Management Keeps Quiet about Its Role in Apartheid."

169. Krabill, "Symbiosis"; Daniel Dayan and Elihu Katz, *Media Events: The Live Broadcasting of History* (Cambridge, MA: Harvard University Press, 1992), p. 9.

170. Sachs, interview with the author.

171. Tutu, *Truth and Reconciliation Commission Summary Report and Transcripts*, chap. 6, para. 1; Du Plessis, "Newspaper Management Keeps Quiet about Its Role in Apartheid."

172. Hachten and Giffard, *Press and Apartheid*, p. 3.

173. Guy Berger, "Alternative Voices in the Last Generation," in Switzer and Adhikar, *South Africa's Resistance Press* (see note 15), p. xi.

Chapter 7: One Nation, Ripped Apart

1. Mark Ensalaco, *Chile under Pinochet: Recovering the Truth* (Philadelphia: University of Pennsylvania Press, 2000), p. 24; Heraldo Munoz, *The Dictator's Shadow: A Political Memoir* (New York: Basic Books, 2008), p. 14.

2. Munoz, *Dictator's Shadow*.

3. Ibid., pp. 13–14.

4. Ibid., p. 14.

5. Munoz, *Dictator's Shadow*, p. 13; Steve J. Stern, *Battling for Hearts and Minds:*

Memory Struggles in Pinochet's Chile (Durham, NC: Duke University Press, 2006); Pamela Constable and Arturo Valenzuela, *A Nation of Enemies: Chile under Pinochet* (New York: W. W. Norton, 1991); Rosalind Bresnahan, "Radio and the Democratic Movement in Chile 1973–1990: Independent and Grass Roots Voices during the Pinochet Dictatorship," *Journal of Radio Studies* 9, no. 1 (2002): 161–81; Ken Leon-Dermota, . . . *And Well Tied Down: Chile's Press under Democracy* (Westport, CT: Praeger, 2003).

6. Munoz, *Dictator's Shadow*, p. 11.

7. Constable and Valenzuela, *Nation of Enemies*, p. 24.

8. Constable and Valenzuela, *Nation of Enemies*; Marc Cooper, *Pinochet and Me: A Chilean Anti-Memoir* (New York: Verso, 2001).

9. Salvador Allende, speech quoted in Bresnahan, "Radio and the Democratic Movement"; Stern, *Battling for Hearts and Minds*, p. 12; Cooper, *Pinochet and Me*, p. 39.

10. Constable and Valenzuela, *Nation of Enemies*; Stern, *Battling for Hearts and Minds*, p. 175; *Time*, "Chile: Scenario for Chaos," September 10, 1973, http://www.time.com/time/magazine/article/0,9171,907835,00.html.

11. Munoz, *Dictator's Shadow*, p. 17; Bresmahan, "Radio and the Democratic Movement"; Constable and Valenzuela, *Nation of Enemies*.

12. Munoz, *Dictator's Shadow*; Bresnahan, "Radio and the Democratic Movement in Chile."

13. Constable and Valenzuela, *Nation of Enemies*; Peter Winn, "*Weavers of Revolution: The Yarur Workers and Chile's Road to Socialism* (New York: Oxford University Press, 1986).

14. Constable and Valenzuela, *Nation of Enemies*, p. 19.

15. John Dinges, e-mail exchange with the author, 2010; Constable and Valenzuela, *Nation of Enemies*, p. 20; Munoz, *Dictator's Shadow: New York Times*, September 12, 1973, LexisNexis.

16. Munoz, *Dictator's Shadow*, p. 47; Stern, *Battling for Hearts and Minds*; Constable and Valenzuela, *Nation of Enemies*.

17. Constable and Valenzuela, *Nation of Enemies*.

18. Ibid., p. 23; quote belongs to Carlos Alberto Cruz; Stern, *Battling for Hearts and Minds*.

19. These are conservative estimates, according to Stern, *Battling for Hearts and Minds*, p. xxi.

20. Carlos Catalan, "Mass Media and the Collapse of a Democratic Tradition in Chile," in *Media and Politics in Latin America*, ed. Elizabeth Fox (Beverly Hills: Sage Publications, 1988), pp. 45–55; Bresnahan, "Radio and the Democratic Movement"; Marc Cooper, interview with the author, May 19, 2010.

21. Elizabeth Fox, ed., "Media Policies in Latin America: An Overview," in *Media and Politics in Latin America* (Beverly Hills: Sage Publications, 1988), pp. 6–35; Bresnahan, "Radio and the Democratic Movement"; Catalan, "Mass Media and the Collapse."

22. Catalan, "Mass Media and the Collapse"; Leon-Dermota, . . . *And Well Tied Down*; Bresnahan, "Radio and the Democratic Movement," citing M. C. Lasagni, P. Edwards, and J. Bonnefoy, *La Radio en Chile: Historia, Modelos, Perspectivas* (Santiago:

CENECA, 1985) and H. Uribe, "Prensa y periodismo Politico en los Anos 60/70," in *Mori res la Noticia*, ed. E. Carmona (Santiago: J & C Productores Graficos Ltda, 1998).

23. Elizabeth Fox, ed., *Media Policies in Latin America* (Beverly Hills: Sage Publications, 1988); Bresnahan, "Radio and the Democratic Movement."

24. Winn, *Weavers of Revolution*; Constable and Valenzuela, *A Nation of Enemies*.

25. Some spell this "Dunney." "Doonie" is Peter Kornbluh's spelling.

26. Leon-Dermota, . . . *And Well Tied Down*.

27. Peter Kornbluh, "The *El Mercurio* File," *Columbia Journalism Review* 43, no. 3 (2003): 14–19. Experts such as John Dinges argue that Nixon would likely have done this anyway.

28. Quote from Kornbluh, "*El Mercurio* File," p. 14; CMPC (Compania Manufacturera de Papeles e Cartones S.A.) produced all Chilean newsprint, according to Leon-Dermota, . . . *And Well Tied Down*, p. 17.

29. Kornbluh, "*El Mercurio* File," citing Rockefeller memoir.

30. Kornbluh, "*El Mercurio* File," citing Seymour Hersh, *The Price of Power: Kissinger in the Nixon Whitehouse* (New York: Summit Books, 1983); Peter Kornbluh, *The Pinochet File: A Declassified Dossier on Atrocity and Accountability* (New York: New Press, 2003), p. 4.

31. Leon-Dermota, . . . *And Well Tied Down*; Kornbluh, "*El Mercurio* File."

32. Kornbluh, "*El Mercurio* File"; Peter Kornbluh, "The Chile Coup—The US Hand," *iF Magazine*, October 25, 1998, http://www.globalresearch.ca/articles/KOR309 A.html; Stern, *Battling for Hearts and Minds*, pp. 13–14; Winn, *Weavers of Revolution*; Edward Korry, testimony as reported in *Washington Post*, "Korry, Ex-Envoy to Chile, Wants to Testify at Sorensen Hearings," January 10, 1977, A2. To Korry, that is a "monstrous simplification" that paints Chilean history solely in terms of CIA "bully boys kicking around small and innocent social democrats." Korry does not question that Nixon plotted against Allende, but he says that the Kennedy and Johnson administrations—in league with US corporations—first established the precedent of massive US interference in Chilean politics. *Newsweek*, "Diplomacy: Man without a Country," January 10, 1977, 25. In an interview with David Frost, Nixon said that it was an Italian businessman who warned him about Allende, according to the Associated Press article by George Gedda, May 25, 1977.

33. Constable and Valenzuela, *Nation of Enemies*, p. 23.

34. Kornbluh, "*El Mercurio* File"; Winn, *Weavers of Revolution*.

35. Kornbluh, "Chile Coup"; Carlos Huneeus, *The Pinochet Regime* (Boulder, CO: Lynne Rienner, 2007); John Dinges, *The Condor Years: How Pinochet and His Allies Brought Terrorism to Three Continents* (New York: New Press, 2004).

36. Kornbluh, "Chile Coup"; Kornbluh, "*El Mercurio* File," p. 22; Stern, *Battling for Hearts and Minds*, pp. 13–14; Huneeus, *Pinochet Regime*; Dinges, *Condor Years*; Munoz, *Dictator's Shadow*, p. 85.

37. Winn, *Weavers of Revolution*, p. 71.

38. Roger Burbach, *The Pinochet Affair: State Terrorism and Global Justice* (New York: Zed Books, 2003), p. 14; Stern, *Battling for Hearts and Minds*; Huneeus, *Pinochet Regime: Time*, "Chile: Scenario for Chaos."

39. Winn, *Weavers of Revolution*, p. 75; Stern, *Battling for Hearts and Minds*, p. 14.

40. Leon-Dermota, . . . *And Well Tied Down*; Cooper, *Pinochet and Me*.

41. Fox, "Media Policies in Latin America"; Bresnahan, "Radio and the Democratic Movement."

42. Kornbluh, "*El Mercurio* File"; Constable and Valenzuela, *Nation of Enemies*, p. 26; Stern, *Battling for Hearts and Minds*, p. 16; Cooper, *Pinochet and Me*, p. 26; Ensalaco, *Chile under Pinochet*.

43. Stern, *Battling for Hearts and Minds*, p. 16; *Time*, "Chile: Scenario for Chaos"; Constable and Valenzuela, *Nation of Enemies*; Leon-Dermota, . . . *And Well Tied Down*.

44. Kornbluh, "*El Mercurio* File"; Stern, *Battling for Hearts and Minds*, pp. 13–14; Huneeus, *Pinochet Regime*; Dinges, *Condor Years*.

45. Constable and Valenzuela, *Nation of Enemies*.

46. Fred Simon Landis, "Psychological Warfare and Media Operations in Chile, 1970–1973" (PhD diss., University of Illinois at Urbana–Champaign, 1975), p. 59.

47. Close to $8.4 million in today's dollars, according to Kornbluh, "*El Mercurio* File."

48. Kornbluh, "Chile Coup." Nixon argued this point in a televised interview with David Frost, according to the Associated Press article written by George Gedda on May 25, 1977.

49. Catalan, "Mass Media and the Collapse."

50. Landis, "Psychological Warfare," p. 115.

51. Landis, "Psychological Warfare"; Stern, *Battling for Hearts and Minds*, p. 21.

52. Stern, *Battling for Hearts and Minds*, pp. 21–22; Landis, "Psychological Warfare," pp. 57, 183.

53. Leon-Dermota, . . . *And Well Tied Down*, p. 4.

54. Constable and Valenzuela, *Nation of Enemies*, p. 154.

55. Landis, "Psychological Warfare and Media Operations in Chile," p. 191.

56. Ibid., p. 193.

57. Leon-Dermota, . . . *And Well Tied Down*, p. 4.

58. Stern, *Battling for Hearts and Minds*, p. 23; Constable and Valenzuela, p. 26.

59. Stern, *Battling for Hearts and Minds*, pp. 22–23; Constable and Valenzuela, *Nation of Enemies*, p. 28.

60. Stern, *Battling for Hearts and Minds*, pp. 22–23; Landis, "Psychological Warfare."

61. Constable and Valenzuela, *Nation of Enemies*, pp. 27–29, 144.

62. Constable and Valenzuela, *Nation of Enemies*, p. 27; Stern, *Battling for Hearts and Minds*, p. 15.

63. Cooper, *Pinochet and Me*, p. 2; Constable and Valenzuela, *Nation of Enemies*.

64. Burbach, *Pinochet Affair*, p. 15; Stern, *Battling for Hearts and Minds*, p. 63. Prats was eventually assassinated by Pinochet agents.

65. *Time*, "Chile: Scenario for Chaos."

66. Constable and Valenzuela, *Nation of Enemies*, p. 154.

67. Leon-Dermota, . . . *And Well Tied Down*, p. 19.

68. Cooper, *Pinochet and Me*, p. 26.

69. Ibid., pp. 29–30.

70. *Time*, "Chile: Scenario for Chaos."

71. Leon-Dermota, . . . *And Well Tied Down*; Stern, *Battling for Hearts and Minds*; Bresnahan, "Radio and the Democratic Movement."

72. Bresnehan, "Radio and the Democratic Movement"; Munoz, *Dictator's Shadow*; Leon-Dermota, . . . *And Well Tied Down*, p. 5. One slightly different account says that Radio Magallanes was also bombed but continued its broadcast temporarily on an emergency transmitter.

73. Munoz, *Dictator's Shadow*, p. 53; Bresnahan, "Radio and the Democratic Movement"; Huneeus, *Pinochet Regime*; Fox, "Media Policies in Latin America."

74. Kornbluh, "*El Mercurio* File."

75. Tim Frasca, "Fighting Back in Chile," *Columbia Journalism Review* 23, no. 4 (November/December 1984): 9–11.

76. Stern, *Battling for Hearts and Minds*; Constable and Valenzuela, *Nation of Enemies*; Kornbluh, "Chile Coup"; Kornbluh, "*El Mercurio* File."

77. Constable and Venezuela, *Nation of Enemies*, p. 156.

78. *New York Times*, September 14, 1973, LexisNexis.

79. Leon-Dermota, . . . *And Well Tied Down*, p. 13; Stern, *Battling for Hearts and Minds*.

80. Stern, *Battling for Hearts and Minds*, pp. 39–41.

81. Ibid., pp. 41–42; Constable and Valenzuela, *Nation of Enemies*, p. 154.

82. Stern, *Battling for Hearts and Minds*, pp. 42, 47; Constable and Valenzuela, *Nation of Enemies*, pp. 37, 152.

83. Stern, *Battling for Hearts and Minds*, pp. 42–45, 49.

84. Ibid., p. 39.

85. Ibid., pp. 51–53.

86. Ibid., pp. 46, 51–53.

87. Constable and Valenzuela, *Nation of Enemies*, p. 153.

88. Stern, *Battling for Hearts and Minds*, pp. 52–53, 98.

89. Dinges, *Condor Years*.

90. Ramon Marsano, "Chile: Anatomy of a Cover-up," *National Catholic Reporter* 11, no. 43 (October 10, 1975): 16.

91. Dinges, *Condor Years*, p. 236; John Dinges, interview with author; Brooke Gladstone, "Operation Colombo," interview with Peter Kornbluh in *On the Media*, National Public Radio, December 15, 2006; Munoz, *Dictator's Shadow*, pp. 94–95.

92. Constable and Valenzuela, *Nation of Enemies*, pp. 155–56.

93. Stern, *Battling for Hearts and Minds*, p. 64.

94. The report of the Chilean National Commission on Truth and Reconciliation (also known as the Rettig Report [Washington, DC: US Institute of Peace, 1991]) says ten journalists were killed; Bresnahan, "Radio and the Democratic Movement," cites H. Uribe as counting forty, "Prensa y periodismo politico en los anos 60/70" [Press and political journalism in the 1960s and 1970s], *Mori res la noticia* [Death is the news], ed. E. Carmona (Santiago: J & C Productores Graficos Ltda, 1998).

95. Munoz, *Dictator's Shadow*; Bresnahan, "Radio and the Democratic Movement"; Constable and Valenzuela, *Nation of Enemies*, p. 155.

96. Munoz, *Dictator's Shadow*, p. 53.

97. Constable and Valenzuela, *Nation of Enemies*, p. 144.

98. Stern, *Battling for Hearts and Minds*, pp. 73–74. Some may have lied to pollsters or may have been too afraid to express their true thoughts.

99. *New York Times*, September 13, 1973, LexisNexis.

100. *Time Magazine*, "Chile: The Bloody End of a Marxist Dream," September 23, 1973, http://www.time.com/time/magazine/article/0,9171,907929,00.html.

101. Ensalaco, *Chile under Pinochet*; Stern, *Battling for Hearts and Minds*, pp. 94, 95.

102. Stern, *Battling for Hearts and Minds*, pp. 95, 96–99, 101, cites Mexican paper *Excelsior*; a LexisNexus search also revealed several articles and wire service reports; Burbach, *Pinochet Affair*; Ensalaco, *Chile under Pinochet*.

103. Robert Schakne, "Chile: Why We Missed the Story," *Columbia Journalism Review* 14, no. 6 (March/April 1976): 60–62; David Binder, "U.S. Not Surprised," *New York Times*, September 12, 1973, 1, 19.

104. *Wall Street Journal*, September 12, 1973, col. 1.

105. *New York Times*, "Tragedy in Chile," September 12, 1973, editorial, col. 4, 16.

106. *New York Times*, "Angela Davis Leads Allende Rally Here," September 12, 1973, 1, 19.

107. *Time*, "Chile: The Bloody End of a Marxist Dream," September 24, 1973, http://www.time.com/time/magazine/article/0,9171,907929,00.html.

108. Schakne, "Chile: Why We Missed the Story."

109. Victoria Goff, "The Chile Solidarity Movement and Its Media: An Alternative Take on the Allende and Pinochet Years," *American Journalism* 24, no. 4 (2007): 95–125. Newsletters include the *Chile Newsletter, Chile Action Bulletin on Political Prisoners and Human Rights*, the *NACLA* newsletter, and *Chile Vencera*.

110. James Pringle, "The Exorcists," *Newsweek*, April 28, 1975, 42.

111. Jonathan Kandell, *New York Times*, May 5 and 25, 1975, abstracts from LexisNexis.

112. *New York Times*, "Chile: New Torture Causes," June 1, 1975, E3.

113. Dinges, *Condor Years*; *New York Times*, 1976, LexisNexis; Raymond Carroll with Henry McGee and Tessa Namuth, "The Long Arm of the DINA?" *Newsweek*, October 5, 1976, 59; Ensalaco, *Chile under Pinochet*.

114. Burbach, *Pinochet Affair*, p. 63; William R. Long, "An AP News Analysis," Associated Press, March 12 and March 16, 1977.

115. Ensalaco, *Chile under Pinochet*, p. 120.

116. Stern, *Battling for Hearts and Minds*.

117. Hanns Neuerbourg, Associated Press, March 9, 1977; Timothy S. Robinson, "Letelier Slaying Called Work of Cuban Exile Unit: Cuban Exiles, Chile DINA Linked to Letelier Slaying," *Washington Post*, September 8, 1977, A1; Stern, *Battling for Hearts and Minds*.

118. Stern, *Battling for Hearts and Minds*, pp. 144–46.

119. Karen DeYoung and John Dinges, "Chile Takes Steps to Liberalize Rule: Chilean Junta Edges toward More Liberal Government: US Probe in Letelier Death a Catalyst," *Washington Post*, April 17, 1978, A1.

120. Stern, *Battling for Hearts and Minds*, p. 96.

121. *New York Times*, "A Grim Anniversary in Chile," September 11, 1977, editorial, 16; Stern, *Battling for Hearts and Minds*; Ron Moreau, "Chile: After DINA," *Newsweek*, September 12, 1977, 50; Constable and Valenzuela, *Nation of Enemies*, p. 128.

122. Karen De Young, "Chile Trying to Polish Tarnished Image Abroad; Chile Finds It Hard to Polish Its Image," *Washington Post*, September 15, 1977, A1; Shirley Christian, Associated Press, January 5, 1978; De Young and Dinges, "Chilean Junta Edges toward More Liberal Government"; Constable and Valenzuela, *Nation of Enemies*; John Dinges, "Chile Silences 2 Main Voices of Once Independent Media," *Washington Post*, February 3, 1977, A14.

123. Burbach, *Pinochet Affair*; Stern, *Battling for Hearts and Minds*, pp. 35, 39; Constable and Valenzuela, *Nation of Enemies: Time*, "Chile: Scenario for Chaos."

124. Shirley Christian, Associated Press, December 21, 1977, LexisNexis.

125. Fox, "Media Policies in Latin America"; Munoz, *Dictator's Shadow*, pp. 57–58; Bresnehan, "Radio and the Democratic Movement"; Stern, *Battling for Hearts and Minds*, pp. 87, 308.

126. Bresnahan, "Radio and the Democratic Movement"; Munoz, *Dictator's Shadow*, p. 57.

127. Constable and Valenzuela, *Nation of Enemies*, p. 149.

128. Bresnahan, "Radio and the Democratic Movement"; Fox, "Media Policies in Latin America"; Dinges, *Condor Years*.

129. Stern, *Battling for Hearts and Minds*, p. 133; Bresnahan, "Radio and the Democratic Movement."

130. Dinges, interview.

131. Ibid.

132. Stern, *Battling for Hearts and Minds*, p. 135.

133. Associated Press, June 23, 1977, LexisNexis; Stern, *Battling for Hearts and Minds*, pp. 125, 149.

134. Stern, *Battling for Hearts and Minds*; Charles A. Krause, "Chileans End Hunger Strike after Pledge on Prisoners," *Washington Post*, June 8, 1978; Shirley Christian, Associated Press, June 8, 1978, LexisNexis; Associated Press, June 1, 1978, LexisNexis.

135. Stern, *Battling for Hearts and Minds*; Reuters, "Chile Arrests General after US Indictment," *Globe and Mail*, August 2, 1978; Charles A. Krause, "Chile Arrests Three Named in Letelier Indictment," *Washington Post*, August 2, 1978; Shirley Christian, Associated Press, August 13, 1978, abstract from Lexis Nexis; Charles A. Krause, "Public Reaction to Letelier Evidence Termed Crucial to Chile's Government," *Washington Post*, September 22, 1978.

136. Constable and Valenzuela, *Nation of Enemies*; Charles A. Krause, "Chileans Relax amid Improving Outlook for Rights," *Washington Post*, March 19, 1979.

137. Stern, *Battling for Hearts and Minds*, p. 124; Leon-Dermota, . . . *And Well Tied Down*.

138. Charles A. Krause, "Key Court Test Looms for Chile's Press Policy," *Washington Post*, June 27, 1979; Stern, *Battling for Hearts and Minds*; Charles A. Krause, "Letelier Verdict, Amply Covered in Chile, Has Little Impact," *Washington Post*, February 16, 1979.

139. Munoz, *Dictator's Shadow*, p. 140; Bresnahan, "Radio and the Democratic Movement"; Stern, *Battling for Hearts and Minds*, pp. 124, 127.

140. Bresnahan, "Radio and the Democratic Movement"; Charles A. Krause, "Key Court Test Looms for Chile's Press Policy."

141. Constable and Valenzuela, *Nation of Enemies*, p. 157.

142. Charles A. Krause, "Chile Again Puts Clamps on Dissent," *Washington Post*, October 16, 1979.

143. Ibid.

144. Leon-Dermota, . . . *And Well Tied Down*, p. 23.

145. Krause, "Chile Again Puts Clamps on Dissent."

146. Burbach, *Pinochet Affair*, p. 64.

147. Bresnahan, "Radio and the Democratic Movement."

148. Shirley Christian, an AP News Analysis, Associated Press, August 29, 1977, LexisNexis; Burbach, *Pinochet Affair*, p. 64.

149. Bresnahan, "Radio and the Democratic Movement," cites M. C. Lasagni, P. Edwards, and J. Bonnefoy, *La Radio en Chile: Historia, Modelos, Perspectivas* [Radio in Chile: History, Models, Prospects] (Santiago: CENECA, 1985).

150. Ibid.

151. William R. Long and Associated Press, March 26, 1977, LexisNexis; Bresnahan, "Radio and the Democratic Movement."

152. Stern, *Battling for Hearts and Minds*, p. 154.

153. *Newsweek*, "Chile: Church vs. State," November 15, 1976; William R. Long, Associated Press, March 26, 1977, LexisNexis.

154. Shirley Christian, Associated Press, December 7, 1978, LexisNexis; Stern, *Battling for Hearts and Minds*; Ensalaco, *Chile under Pinochet*.

155. Krause, "Chileans Relax amid Improving Outlook for Rights"; Stern, *Battling for Hearts and Minds: Washington Post*, "Probe Links Chile's Police to 11 Bodies," June 29, 1979; *Globe and Mail*, "Chilean Police Ruled Killers," July 2, 1979; Charles A. Krause, "8 Chilean Police Charged in Post-Coup Deaths of 15," *Washington Post*, July 4, 1979.

156. Stern, *Battling for Hearts and Minds*, pp. 160–61.

157. Shirley Christian, Associated Press, December 26, 1977, and January 4, 1978, abstracts from LexisNexis.

158. Karen DeYoung, "Favorable Image in Chile Shown by Polls for Junta," *Washington Post*, September 21, 1977. People sometimes lie to pollsters, and sometimes they are afraid to answer under conditions of intimidation.

159. Stern, *Battling for Hearts and Minds*, p. 171.

160. Tom Fenton, "Opposition Growing to Military's Proposed Constitution in Chile," Associated Press, August 31, 1980; Tom Fenton, "Demonstrate against Constitution," Associated Press, September 9, 1980; Tom Fenton, "Chileans Vote on New Charter," Associated Press, September 10, 1980.

161. Stern, *Battling for Hearts and Minds*, pp. 171–72.

162. Tom Fenton, "Pinochet Becomes Constitutional President," Associated Press, March 10, 1981.

163. Ensalaco, *Chile under Pinochet: Globe and Mail*, "International Report: Inflation in Chile," January 4, 1979.

164. Charles A. Krause, "Chilean Law Students Demonstrate against Government," *Washington Post*, September 6, 1979; Shirley Christian, Associated Press, September 11, 1978, LexisNexis; Xinhua General News Service, "Chilean Students in Solidarity with Detained Fellow Students," May 13, 1979.

165. Ensalaco, *Chile under Pinochet*, p. 135; Stern, *Battling for Hearts and Minds*, p. 251; Jackson Diehl, "Clashes Mark Massive Protest against Pinochet," *Washington Post*, June 15, 1983.

166. Stern, *Battling for Hearts and Minds*, p. 252; Diehl, "Clashes Mark Massive Protest against Pinochet."

167. Geri Smith, United Press International, June 21, 1983, LexisNexis.

168. Stern, *Battling for Hearts and Minds*, p. 252.

169. Ibid.

170. Anthony Boadle, "Chile Censors Strike Coverage," United Press International, June 19, 1983; Edward Schumacher, "Chile Coalition Calls a Nationwide Strike Beginning Thursday," *New York Times*, June 21, 1983; Jackson Diehl, "Chilean Unions Call National Protest Strike," *Washington Post*, June 21, 1983.

171. Boadle, "Chile Censors Strike Coverage."

172. Stern, *Battling for Hearts and Minds*, pp. 252, 258.

173. Ibid.

174. Ibid., pp. 259–60.

175. Ibid., pp. 260–61, 270–77, 279–80; Frasca, "Fighting Back in Chile."

176. Stern, *Battling for Hearts and Minds*, p. 301; Ensalaco, *Chile under Pinochet*, pp. 136–38.

177. Bresnahan, "Radio and the Democratic Movement."

178. Ibid.

179. Stern, *Battling for Hearts and Minds*, pp. 302–303.

180. Leon-Dermota, . . . *And Well Tied Down*, pp. 27–28; Stern, *Battling for Hearts and Minds*, p. 304.

181. Leon-Dermota, . . . *And Well Tied Down*, pp. 27–28; Stern, *Battling for Hearts and Minds*.

182. Ensalaco, *Chile under Pinochet*, p. 144.

183. Stephen Kinzer, "The Press in Chile, and One Bold Editor's Struggle," *New York Times*, October 20, 1983.

184. Richard Boudreaux, "Editor Jailed for Criticizing Military," Associated Press, September 27, 1983.

185. Lake Sagaris, "Published Critical Opinion Poll, Magazine Editor Jailed in Chile," *Globe and Mail*, April 12, 1984; Richard Boudreaux, "Chilean Press Comes Alive, but Government Resists," Associated Press, April 13, 1984.

186. Tina Rosenberg, "Letters from Chile," *Columbia Journalism Review* (September/October, 1987).

187. Stern, *Battling for Hearts and Minds*, pp. 322, 326.

188. United Press International, "Foreign News Briefs," November 25, 1983.

189. *Christian Science Monitor*, "On Election Eve, Chile Imposes Press Censorship," March 28, 1984; *Globe and Mail*, "Chilean Government Acknowledges Effect of National Protests," March 29, 1984; Boudreaux, "Chilean Press Comes Alive."

190. Reuters, "Protest by Chilean Press," *New York Times*, April 26, 1984.

191. Mark Ensalaco, *Chile under Pinochet*, p. 142.

192. Boudreaux, "Chilean Press Comes Alive."

193. Lake Sagaris, "Court Backs Pinochet Probe," *Globe and Mail*, May 12, 1984.

194. Leon-Dermota, . . . *And Well Tied Down*, p. 28; BBC Summary of World Broadcasts, "New Daily Newspaper in Chile," March 8, 1984, from Cooperativa; Tina Rosenberg, "Letters from Chile"; Frasca, "Fighting Back in Chile."

195. Boudreaux, "Chilean Press Comes Alive"; Rosenberg, "Letters from Chile."

196. Leon-Dermota, . . . *and Well Tied Down*, p. 28.

197. Ibid., pp. 28–29, 31; Stern, *Battling for Hearts and Minds*, p. 355.

198. Stern, *Battling for Hearts and Minds*, pp. 354–55.

199. Ibid., p. 354.

200. Boudreaux, "Chilean Press Comes Alive."

201. Bresnahan, "Radio and the Democratic Movement."

202. Stern, *Battling for Hearts and Minds*, pp. 357–58.

203. Rosenberg, "Letters from Chile."

204. Stern, *Battling for Hearts and Minds*, pp. 338, 341–42; Eugenio Tironi and Guillermo Sunkel, "The Modernization of Communications: The Media in the Transition to Democracy in Chile," in *Democracy and the Media: A Comparative Perspective*, ed. Richard Gunther and Anthony Mughan (New York: Cambridge University Press, 2000); Stern, *Battling for Hearts and Minds*.

205. Stern, *Battling for Hearts and Minds*, p. 342; Tironi and Sunkel, "Modernization of Communications."

206. Stern, *Battling for Hearts and Minds*, pp. 347–48.

207. Ibid., pp. 355, 380.

208. Tironi and Sunkel, "Modernization of Communications."

209. Munoz, *Dictator's Shadow*, p. 196.

210. Ibid.

211. Stern, *Battling for Hearts and Minds*, p. 355.

212. Munoz, *Dictator's Shadow*, p. 192.

213. Ibid. Munoz paraphrased the first part of Lagos's statement. He wrote, "He [Lagos] accused [Pinochet] of reneging on his 1980 promise not to run in 1989."

214. Ibid., p. 192.

215. Ibid.

216. Stern, *Battling for Hearts and Minds*, p. 372; Burbach, *Pinochet Affair*, p. 77.

217. Leon-Dermota, . . . *And Well Tied Down*.

218. Landis, "Psychological Warfare and Media Operations in Chile."

219. Constable and Valenzuela, *Nation of Enemies*, p. 144.

220. Leon-Dermota, . . . *And Well Tied Down*, pp. x–xi.

Chapter 8: Death of the Perfect Dictatorship

1. Richard J. Meislin, "For Mexicans, Concern Rises on Civil Rights," *New York Times*, September 23, 1984; Cynthia Tompkins and David William Foster, *Notable Twentieth-Century Latin American Women: A Biographical Dictionary* (Westport, CT: Greenwood Publishing Group, 2001).

2. Chappell Lawson, *Building the Fourth Estate: Democratization and the Rise of a Free Press in Mexico* (Los Angeles: University of California Press, 2002), p. 13; Larry Rohter, "Stiff Setback Seen for Ruling Party in Mexican Voting," *New York Times*, July 8, 1988; Isaac A. Levi, "Ruling Party Claims Election Victory," Associated Press, July 8, 1988.

3. Nadine Epstein, "Mexico's First Woman for Pres," *Ms.*, March 1988; Tompkins and Foster, *Notable Twentieth-Century Latin American Women*; Anthony DePalma, "Mexico City Journal: Among the Ruins of the Left, a Pillar Stands," *New York Times*, October 5, 1994, 4.

4. Tompkins and Foster, *Notable Twentieth-Century Latin American Women*; DePalma, "Mexico City Journal."

5. This is a rough translation of her quote.

6. Alan Robinson, "Mexico Shaken by Murder and Scandal before Presidential Election," *Times* (of London), July 5, 1988; Tompkins and Foster, *Notable Twentieth-Century Latin American Women*; DePalma, "Mexico City Journal."

7. James Anderson, "Majority of Mexicans Supporting Governing Party Candidate, Polls Say," Associated Press, June 21, 1988; Alan Robinson, "Mexican Opposition Demands Inquiry into Ballot 'Fraud,'" *Times* (of London), July 8, 1988; Soll Sussman, "Cárdenas Closes Campaign with Giant Downtown Rally," Associated Press, June 25, 1988.

8. Robinson, "Mexican Opposition Demands Inquiry"; Reuters, "Mexican Opposition Leaders Unite to Challenge Results," *New York Times*, August 5, 1988.

9. Levi, "Ruling Party Claims Election Victory"; Isaac A. Levi, "Ruling Party Candidate Winning, but Lowest Margin in 70 Years," Associated Press, July 9, 1988.

10. James Smith and Mary Beth Sheridan, "An End to the PRI Era—and Way of Life," *Los Angeles Times*, July 3, 2000, 1; Daniel Hallin, "Media, Political Power, and Democratization in Mexico," in *De-Westernizing Media Studies*, ed. Myung-Jin Park and James Curran (New York: Routledge, 2000).

11. Mary Jordan, "Mexico to Allow 'Dirty War' Trials: Court Strikes Down Statute of Limitations," *Washington Post*, Foreign Service, November 6, 2003, A21.

12. Alejandro Moreno, "The Coalition for Change: Voters and Parties in the 2000 Mexican Election," in *The Elections of 2000: Politics, Culture, and Economics in North America*, ed. Mary K. Kirtz, Mark J. Kasoff, Rick Farmer, and John C. Green (Akron, OH: University of Akron Press, 2006), pp. 21–49.

13. Lawson, *Building the Fourth Estate*, p. 25; Hallin, "Media, Political Power, and Democratization in Mexico." The phrase "perfect dictatorship" came from Peruvian novelist and politician Mario Vargas Llosa: Sallie Hughes, *Newsrooms in Conflict: Journalism and the Democratization of Mexico* (Pittsburgh: University of Pittsburgh Press, 2006).

14. Kate Doyle, "The Dead of Tlatelolco," *Proceso*, October 1, 2006, http://www .gwu.edu/~nsarchiv/NSAEBB/NSAEBB201/index.htm#article (accessed March 4, 2011); Ruben Sergio Caletti Kaplan, "Communication Policies in Mexico: An Historical Paradox of Words and Actions," in Media and Politics in Latin America, ed. Elizabeth Fox (Beverly Hills: Sage Publications, 1988), pp. 67–81; Lawson, Building the Fourth Estate.

15. Lawson, *Building the Fourth Estate*, p. 25; Hallin, "Media, Political Power, and Democratization in Mexico," p. 100.

16. Lawson, *Building the Fourth Estate*, pp. 48, 173; Hallin, "Media, Political Power, and Democratization in Mexico," p. 100; Alan Riding, "Mexico Reinstating Editor Ousted by Former Regime," *New York Times*, May 14, 1977; Alan Riding, "Ousted Journalists Start a Liberal Paper," *New York Times*, November 24, 1977, 7; Kaplan, "Communication Policies in Mexico."

17. Lawson, *Building the Fourth Estate*, pp. 1, 49; Ilya Adler, "The Mexico Case: The Media in the 1988 Presidential Election," in *Television, Politics, and the Transition to Democracy in Latin America*, ed. Thomas Skidmore (Baltimore, MD/Washington, DC: Johns Hopkins University Press/Woodrow Wilson Center Press, 1993); Kaplan, "Communication Policies in Mexico," p. 67.

18. Hallin, "Media, Political Power, and Democratization in Mexico," p. 99.

19. Joe Richman and Anayansi Diaz-Cortes, "The History Project: Radio Diaries: Mexico's 1968 Massacre: What Really Happened?" and "Transcript of Mexico '68: A Movement, a Massacre and the 40-Year Search for the Truth," National Public Radio, December 1, 2008.

20. Enrique Krauze, *Mexico: Biography of Power* (New York: HarperCollins, 1997); Richman and Diaz-Cortes, "History Project"; Larry Rohter, "20 Years after a Massacre, Mexico Still Seeks Healing for Its Wounds," *New York Times*, October 2, 1988.

21. Krauze, *Mexico*, p. 701; Richman and Diaz-Cortes, "History Project"; Rohter, "20 Years after a Massacre."

22. Richman and Diaz-Cortes, "History Project."

23. Quote belongs to Miguel Breseda, in Richman and Diaz-Cortez, "History Project."

24. Krauze, *Mexico*, p. 708.

25. Ibid., p. 720.

26. Barry Bishop, "Won't Cancel Olympics," *Chicago Tribune*, October 4, 1968. To this day, it is unclear how many perished in the attack: BBC News, "The Most Terrifying Night of My Life," October 2, 2008, http://news.bbc.co.uk/2/hi/americas/7646473.stm (accessed March 4, 2011); Krauze, *Mexico*, p. 720; Tlatelolco means "place of the gods," in Aztec.

27. Sam Dillon, "Anniversary of '68 Massacre Brings Facts to Light," *New York Times*, September 14, 1998.

28. Kaplan, "Communication Policies in Mexico"; Lawson, *Building the Fourth Estate*, p. 66.

29. Kaplan, "Communication Policies in Mexico," p. 69; Lawson, *Building the Fourth Estate*, p. 66; *New York Times*, "Mexican Newspaper Director Ousted," August 21, 1976; *New York Times*, "Three Win Cabot Awards at Columbia," November 1, 1971, p. 28.

30. Riding, "Ousted Journalists Start a Liberal Paper"; Riding, "Mexican Newspaper Director Ousted."

31. *New York Times*, "Liberal Editor in Mexico Begins New Magazine and Criticizes President," special issue, November 7, 1976.

32. *New York Times*, "Liberal Editor in Mexico Begins New Magazine."

33. Hallin, "Media, Political Power, and Democratization in Mexico"; Kaplan, "Communication Policies in Mexico"; Lawson, *Building the Fourth Estate*, pp. 67–68; Alan Riding, *New York Times*, July 10, 1976, 8, LexisNexis; Krauze, *Mexico*, p. 751.

34. *New York Times*, "Liberal Editor in Mexico Begins New Magazine."

35. Lawson, *Building the Fourth Estate*, pp. 67–68; Hallin, "Media, Political Power, and Democratization in Mexico"; Riding, "Ousted Journalists Start a Liberal Paper"; Riding, "Mexican Newspaper Director Ousted"; Hughes, *Newsrooms in Conflict*.

36. Lawson, *Building the Fourth Estate*, pp. 67–68; Hallin, "Media, Political Power, and Democratization in Mexico"; Riding, "Ousted Journalists Start a Liberal Paper"; Riding, "Mexican Newspaper Director Ousted."

37. Kaplan, "Communication Policies in Mexico," p. 69.

38. Ibid.

39. Alan Riding, "Canceled Subsidy Stirs Clash on Press Freedom," New York Times, June 22, 1982; Lawson, Building the Fourth Estate, p. 69.

40. Lawson, Building the Fourth Estate; Kaplan, "Communication Policies in Mexico," p. 69; Nick Anderson, Associated Press, November 3, 1996, LexisNexis.

41. Jonathan Alter, Joseph Contreras, and Jessica Kreimerman, "Reporters under the Gun," Newsweek, November 17, 1986.

42. Ibid.

43. Associated Press, September 19, 1985, LexisNexis; Lawson, *Building the Fourth Estate*, p. 100.

44. Lawson, *Building the Fourth Estate*, pp. 94, 99, 100, 102; Hallin, "Media, Political Power, and Democratization in Mexico," p. 105; Krauze, *Mexico*, p. 766.

45. Gerson Yalowitz, "A Horse Race in Mexico, Perhaps," *U.S. News & World Report*, February 1, 1988; Jonathan Steele, "Glacier Cracking under the Sun," *Manchester Guardian Weekly*, January 10, 1988.

46. Sergio Carrasco, "President Warns Inflation Will Continue," Associated Press, February 12, 1988.

47. Alan Robinson, "Opposition Claims Cheating as Poll Battle Warms Up," *Times* (of London), June 3, 1988.

48. Hallin, "Media, Political Power, and Democratization in Mexico," p. 99, citing Adler, "Mexican Case"; Hughes, *Newsrooms in Conflict*, p. 117.

49. Robinson, "Mexico Shaken by Murder and Scandal."

50. Ibid.; Larry Rohter, "As Mexicans Vote, Fraud Is Alleged," *New York Times*, July 7, 1988; Krauze, *Mexico*, p. 770.

51. William Branigin, "Mexico Votes Calmly amid Fraud Claims," *Washington Post*, July 7, 1988.

52. Krauze, *Mexico*, pp. 766, 770; Lawson, *Building the Fourth Estate*, pp. 94, 99, 100, 102; Hallin, "Media, Political Power, and Democratization in Mexico," p. 105.

53. Hallin, "Media, Political Power, and Democratization in Mexico," p. 102.

54. Tony Burton, "170 Killed as Explosions Flatten City," *Daily Mail* (London), April 23, 1992; *Evening Standard* (London), "200 Killed in Mexico 'Atom Bomb' Explosion," April 23, 1992.

55. Hughes, *Newsrooms in Conflict*; Martin Langfield, "Mexicans Seek the Guilty Ones as Blast Deaths Soar to 227," *Herald* (Glasgow), April 24, 1992.

56. Hughes, *Newsrooms in Conflict*; Alfredo Corchado, "Mexico's New Journalism," *Dallas Morning News*, May 4, 1977; Langfield, "Mexicans Seek the Guilty Ones." *Siglo* was launched in November 1991 by a former PRI politician, Alfonso Dau. Its vision came from political scientist and editor in chief Jorge Zepeda, who called on the paper to be in "service of the community"; Lawson, *Building the Fourth Estate*, p. 73.

57. Langfield, "Mexicans Seek the Guilty Ones."

58. Hughes, *Newsrooms in Conflict*, p. 117; Lawson, *Building the Fourth Estate*, p. 74.

59. Hughes, *Newsrooms in Conflict*, p. 3.

60. Ibid., p. 122.

61. Harry M. Cleaver, "The Zapatista Effect: The Internet and the Rise of an Alternative Political Fabric," *Journal of International Affairs* 51, no. 2 (Spring 1998): 621–40.

62. United Press International, "Clashes in Mexico between Peasants and Police Kill 11," January 1, 1994, LexisNexis; United Press International, "Mexican Army Repels 'Zapatista' Attack on Military Base," January 2, 1994, LexisNexis.

63. Paco Ignacio Taibo II, "Zapatistas! The Phoenix Rises," in *Zapatista Reader*, ed. Tom Hayden (New York: Avalon, 2002), p. 22 (originally in the *Nation*, March 28, 1994).

64. David Clark Scott, "Mexican Indians Seize Towns and Demand Land in Challenge to Salinas," *Christian Science Monitor*, January 1, 1994; Taibo, "Zapatistas!"

65. Deedee Halleck, "Zapatistas On-line," *NACLA Report on the Americas* 28 (1994): 30–32; Taibo, "Zapatistas!"

66. Joseph B. Frazier, "State Where Indians Attacked Plagued by Isolation, Backwardness," Associated Press, *Worldstream*, January 1, 1994, LexisNexis.

67. Scott, "Mexican Indians Seize Towns"; Krauze, *Mexico*.

68. Scott, "Mexican Indians Seize Towns."

69. Halleck, "Zapatistas On-line."

70. Samuel Prieto, "Rebels up Close en Route to Ocosingo," Television Azteca, January 4, 1994.

71. Betzy Villarreal and Juan de Dio Garcia, "Chiapas Governor Acknowledges Climate of Tension, *Uno Mas Uno*, March 11, 1994, 1, 9.

72. Juan Carlos Santoya, "Spokesman, Human Rights Ombudsman Discusses Events, Mexico City Radio," ACIR Network, January 1994; Television Azteca, "Clashes Continue," January 4, 1994.

73. Halleck, "Zapatistas On-line"; Hughes, *Newsrooms in Conflict: La Jornada*, "EZLN Issues Communiqué Commemorating Labor Day," May 2, 1994, 16.

74. Hughes, *Newsrooms in Conflict*; Gregory Gross, "A Distant Rebellion Has Tijuana Residents on Edge," *San Diego Union-Tribune*, January 13, 1994; Prieto, "Rebels up Close en Route to Ocosingo."

75. Hughes, *Newsrooms in Conflict*, p. 3.

76. BBC Summary of World Broadcasts, "Contradictory Reports on Demonstrations in Mexico City about Events in Chiapas," January 14, 1994, LexisNexis.

77. Halleck, "Zapatistas On-line," p. 31.

78. Lawson, *Building the Fourth Estate*, pp. 95, 104.

79. Lawson, *Building the Fourth Estate*, p. 50; Hallin, "Media, Political Power, and Democratization in Mexico."

80. John Rice, "Mexican Ruling Party Leader Assassinated, Country Rocked Anew," Associated Press, September 28, 1994.

81. Juan Walte and Michael Katz Lee, "Election Front-Runner in Mexico Shot, Killed," *USA Today*, March 24, 1991.

82. Lawson, *Building the Fourth Estate*, p. 1. *Malosos* means malignant.

83. Hallin, "Media, Political Power, and Democratization in Mexico."

84. Ibid.; Lawson, *Building the Fourth Estate*, p. 138.

85. Lawson, *Building the Fourth Estate*, pp. 139–40, 145.

86. Ibid., p. 93; *Washington Post*, "Deaths," April 20, 1997; Andrew Paxman, "'El Tigre' Turns Televisa over to His Young Cub," *Daily Variety*, March 10, 1997.

87. Lawson, *Building the Fourth Estate*, p. 109.

88. Ibid., pp. 110, 157, 160; Hallin, "Media, Political Power, and Democratization in Mexico"; Hughes, *Newsrooms in Conflict*.

89. Chappell Lawson and James A. McCann, "Television News, Mexico's 2000 Election and Media Effects in Emerging Democracies," *British Journal of Political Science* 35 (January 2004): 28.

90. Lawson, *Building the Fourth Estate*, p. 5.

91. Lawson, *Building the Fourth Estate*; Hallin, "Media, Political Power, and Democratization in Mexico."

92. Stephen Engelberg, "Mexico's Regional Newspapers Limit Reporting of Cartels' Role in Drug Violence," *ProPublica*, November 17, 2010, http://www.propublica.org/article/mexicos-regional-newspapers-limit-reporting-of-cartels-role-in-drug-violenc (accessed March 4, 2011); Albor Ruiz, "Concert to Benefit Mexican Journalists," *New York Daily News*, December 2, 2010; Jo Tuckman, "Twitter Feeds and Blogs Tell Hidden Story of Mexico's Drug Wars," *Guardian*, September 26, 2010; Andrew O'Reilly, "Journalists Are Major Targets in Mexico's Drug War; Bloggers Use Twitter to Report," *Latin America News Dispatch*, September 27, 2010, http://latindispatch.com/2010/09/27/journalists-are-major-targets-in-mexicos-drug-war-bloggers-use-twitter-to-report/ (accessed March 4, 2011). Some argue that the numbers of journalists who have been killed in the drug wars is underreported. For example, South Notes counted ten journalists killed in 2010 alone, http://www.southnotes.org/2011/01/04/2010-deadliest-year-for-mexican-journalists/ (accessed March 4, 2011). Newswatch states that more than eighty journalists have been either killed or disappeared since 2000, Newswatch Desk, "More Than 80 Journalists Have Disappeared or Been Killed in Mexico Since 2000," May 5, 2011, http://www.newswatch.in/newsblog/9509 (accessed May 19, 2011). According to the *Christian Science Monitor*, more than sixty have been killed in the past decade—ten of them in the past year, *Christian Science Monitor*, "Mexican Press Tagged 'Not Free' amid

Drug War Violence, Self-Censorship," http://www.csmonitor.com/World/Americas/2011/0502/Mexican-press-tagged-not-free-amid-drug-war-violence-self-censorship/(page)/2 (accessed May 19, 2011). And according to PRNewswire and the Associated Press, seven more were killed in 2010, making Mexico the second deadliest country for journalists, Associated Press, "Newseum Adds Names of 77 Slain Newspeople to Journalists Memorial, Including 59 from Last Year," *Washington Post*, May 16, 2011, http://www.washingtonpost.com/national/newseum-adds-names-of-77-slain-newspeople-to-journalists-memorial-including-59-from-last-year/ 2011/ 05/16/AFLXkp4G _story.html (accessed May 19, 2011); PRNewswire, "Newseum Will Host 2011 Journalists Memorial Rededication Ceremony on May 16: 59 Journalists Killed in 2010 Will Be Added—18 from Past Years," May 9, 2011, http://www.prnewswire.com/news-releases/newseum-will -host-2011-journalists-memorial-rededication-ceremony-on-may-16-121506034.html (accessed May 19, 2011).

Chapter 9: Regime Change II

1. Ko Shu-ling, "Taiwan: Lei Mei-lin Says She Still Bears a Grudge," *Tapei Times*, July 18, 2007, Asia Media Archives, http://www.asiamedia.ucla.edu/article-eastasia.asp?parentid=74164, accessed March 20, 2011.

2. Denny Roy, *Taiwan: A Political History* (Ithaca, NY: Cornell University Press, 2003), p. 78; Chin-Chuan Lee, "State, Capital, and Media: The Case of Taiwan," in *De-Westernizing Media Studies*, ed. Myung-Jin Park and James Curran (New York: Routledge, 2000), pp. 124–38.

3. Roy, *Taiwan*, pp. 80, 87; Daniel K. Berman, *Words Like Colored Glass: The Role of the Press in Taiwan's Democratization Process* (Boulder and San Francisco: Westview Press, 1992), p. 128.

4. Berman, *Words Like Colored Glass*, p. 175.

5. Ibid.

6. Ko Shu-ling, "Taiwan."

7. Ibid.; Chin-Chuan Lee, "State, Capital, and Media"; Roy, *Taiwan*, p. 88.

8. Berman, *Words Like Colored Glass*, p. 123; Roy, *Taiwan*, p. 87; George H. Kerr, *Formosa Betrayed* (New York: Da Capo Press, 1976).

9. Roy, *Taiwan*, pp. 89, 90.

10. *New York Times*, "Taiwan Jails Oppositionist," September 22, 1961; Roy, *Taiwan*, p. 88; *New York Times*, "Taiwan Aide Indicted: Su Will Be Tried for Treason by Chinese Nationalists," January 21, 1962.

11. *New York Times*, "Taipei, in Drive on Dissidents, Jails Writer and Other Intellectuals," July 3, 1969; Daniel Southerland, "Acid-Penned Chinese Writer Gains in Popularity," *Washington Post*, January 5, 1988, LexisNexis; Peter Chen Mail Wang, "A Bastion Created, a Regime Reformed, an Economy Reengineered, 1949–1970," in *Taiwan: A New History*, ed. Murray Rubenstein (Armonk, NY: M. E. Sharpe, 1999), p. 335; Berman, *Words Like Colored Glass*.

12. *New York Times*, "Taipei, in Drive on Dissidents, Jails Writer and Other Intellectuals"; Roy, *Taiwan*, pp. 92–93; Berman, *Words Like Colored Glass*, says prison term was nine years.

13. Dafydd Fell, "Political and Media Liberalization and Political Corruption in Taiwan," *China Quarterly* 184 (December 2005): 875–93; Gary D. Rawnsley and Ming-Yeh Rawnsley, "Regime Transition and the Media in Taiwan," in *Democratization and the Media*, ed. Vicky Randall (Portland, OR: Frank Cass, 1998); Roy, *Taiwan*, p. 152; Murray A. Rubinstein, ed., *Taiwan: A New History* (New York: M. E. Sharpe, 1999).

14. Fell, "Political and Media Liberalization"; Rawnsley and Rawnsley, "Regime Transition and the Media in Taiwan."

15. Roy, *Taiwan*; Rubinstein, *Taiwan*; Wang, "Bastion Created, a Regime Reformed."

16. Roy, *Taiwan*.

17. Ibid., pp. 80–84, 87–88; Steven J. Hood, *The Kuomintang and the Democratization of Taiwan* (Boulder, CO: Westview Press, 1997); Wang, "Bastion Created, a Regime Reformed," p. 335.

18. Roy, *Taiwan*, p. 79; Wang, "Bastion Created, a Regime Reformed."

19. Roy, *Taiwan*, p. 89.

20. Bruce Jacobs, "'Taiwanization' in Taiwan's Politics," *China Quarterly*, no. 68 (December 1976): 778–88; Rawnsley and Rawnsley, "Regime Transition and the Media in Taiwan"; Roy, *Taiwan*.

21. Roy, *Taiwan*, pp. 164–65; Lucien Pye, "Taiwan's Development and Its Implications for Beijing and Washington," *Asian Survey* 26, no. 6 (June 1986): 611–29; Linda Gail Arrigo, "From Democratic Movement to Bourgeois Democracy: The Taiwan Democratic Progressive Party in 1991," in *The Other Taiwan: Taiwan in the Modern World*, ed. Murray Rubinstein (New York: M. E. Sharpe, 1994), pp. 145–80.

22. Daniel C. Lynch, *Rising China and Asian Democratization: Socialization to "Global Culture," in Political Transformations of Thailand, China, and Taiwan* (Stanford: Stanford University Press, 2006).

23. Daniel C. Lynch, "Taiwan's Democratization and the Rise of Taiwanese Nationalism as Socialization to Global Culture," *Pacific Affairs* 75 no. 4 (Winter 2002): 565, 557–74; Jacobs, "'Taiwanization' in Taiwan's Politics."

24. Lynch, *Rising China and Asian Democratization*, p. 171; Rubinstein, *Taiwan*.

25. Roy, *Taiwan*, pp. 157, 161; Fell, "Political and Media Liberalization"; Rawnsley and Rawnsley, "Regime Transition and the Media in Taiwan."

26. Lynch, *Rising China and Asian Democratization*, pp. 173–74.

27. Berman, *Words Like Colored Glass*, pp. 185, 186; Roy, *Taiwan*, p. 165; Lynch, *Rising China and Asian Democratization*, p. 174; Lynch, "Taiwan's Democratization," p. 572.

28. Lynch, "Taiwan's Democratization," p. 573; Willie Ma, Associated Press, March 16, 1980, LexisNexis; Tun-Jen Chen, "Democratizing the Quasi-Leninist Regime in Taiwan," *World Politics* 41, no. 4 (1989): 479–99; Berman, *Words Like Colored Glass*.

29. Lynch, *Rising China and Asian Democratization*, pp. 176–77.

30. Berman, *Words Like Colored Glass*, p. 187.

31. Lynch, "Taiwan's Democratization," p. 573; Lynch, *Rising China and Asian Democratization*, p. 175; Roy, *Taiwan*, p. 167.

32. BBC Summary of World Broadcasts, "Anti-Government Riot in Kaohsiung," December 14, 1979, from AFP; Roy, *Taiwan*, p. 168; Ma, Associated Press; Bruce Jacobs, "'Taiwanization' in Taiwan's Politics," in *Culture, Ethnic, and Political Nationalism in Contemporary Taiwan*, ed. John Makeham and A-chin Hsiau (New York: Palgrave Macmillan, 2005), pp. 17–54.

33. Roy, *Taiwan*, p. 168; Ma, Associated Press; Lynch, *Rising China and Asian Democratization*, p. 178.

34. BBC Summary of World Broadcasts "Anti-Government Riot in Kaohsiung"; John Makeham and A-chin Hsaiu, eds., *Cultural, Ethnic, and Political Nationalism in Contemporary Taiwan*; A-chin Hsiau, "Epilogue: *Bentuhua*," in *Culture, Ethnic, and Political Nationalism in Contemporary Taiwan*, ed. John Makeham and A-chin Hsiau (New York: Palgrave Macmillan, 2005), pp. 261–76.

35. BBC Summary of World Broadcasts, "Taiwan: Chinese Attack on Press Restrictions in Taiwan, April 25, 1979, LexisNexis; Ma, Associated Press; Edith M. Lederer, "Taiwan Dissident Denies Favored Violent Overthrow," Associated Press, March 20, 1980; Lena H. Sun, "Taiwanese Abroad See New Hope for Democracy at Home," *Washington Post*, May 30, 1986.

36. Willie Ma, "Feminist Testifies about Coercion," Associated Press, March 16 and 19, 1980, LexisNexis; Lederer, "Dissident Denies Advocating Force."

37. Roy, *Taiwan*, pp. 168–69; Associated Press, "Eight to Be Tried for Sedition," February 20, 1980; Ma, Associated Press; Lynch, *Rising China and Asian Democratization*, p. 172.

38. Lederer, "Dissident Denies Advocating Force"; Roy, *Taiwan*, pp. 168–69.

39. Jacobs, "'Taiwanization' in Taiwan's Politics," in *Culture, Ethnic, and Political Nationalism in Contemporary Taiwan*; Roy, *Taiwan*; Associated Press, "Investigators Wrote His Confession," March 21, 1980; *Economist*, "Taiwan: Does Dissent Equal Sedition?" April 12, 1980.

40. Makeham and Hsaiu, *Cultural, Ethnic, and Political Nationalism in Contemporary Taiwan*; Roy, *Taiwan*, pp. 169, 175; Arrigo, "From Democratic Movement to Bourgeois Democracy."

41. Roy, *Taiwan*, p. 170; Annie Huang, "Dissidents Wary of Nationalist Claims for Democracy," Associated Press, July 15, 1987.

42. Roy, *Taiwan*, p. 171; BBC Summary of World Broadcasts, "Commentary following Bus Explosion Views Terrorist Activities," excerpts from commentary on June 14 regarding the explosion on a bus from Tainan to Kaoshiung, Taipei home service, June 21, 1983, LexisNexis.

43. David E. Kaplan, *Fires of the Dragon: Politics, Murder, and the Kuomintang* (New York: Atheneum, 1992); Ross Terrill, "Death of a Triple Agent," *Washington Post*, January 10, 1993; James O. Clifford, United Press International, October 17, 1984, LexisNexis; Jay Mathews, "Taiwan Role Probed in Killing," *Washington Post*, October 18, 1984.

44. Clifford, United Press International; Mathews, "Taiwan Role Probed in Killing"; Berman, *Words Like Colored Glass*.

45. Associated Press, "Gangster Alleges President's Son Had Ties to Liu Killing," May 10, 1985, citing the *Los Angeles Times*.

46. Mathews, "Taiwan Role Probed in Killing."

47. Fox Butterfield, "Death of Critic of Taiwan Leader Stirs Fears among Chinese in U.S.," *New York Times*, November 2, 1984.

48. Associated Press, "Around the World: Paper Says Slain Author Wrote of Rift in Taiwan," *New York Times*, November 4, 1984.

49. Wendel Chang, "Taiwan Defense Official Arrested in Journalist's Slaying," Associated Press, January 15, 1985; United Press International, "Taiwan Fires Military Intelligence Chief," January 15, 1985; Xinhua General Overseas News Service, "Taiwan Authorities Admit Intelligence's Involvement in Murder of Henry Liu," January 15, 1985; BBC Summary of World Broadcasts, "Taiwan Spokesman Confirms Involvement in Murder of Chinese American," January 16, 1985, LexisNexis; Reuters, "Taiwan Says Suspect Worked at Spy Agency," February 26, 1985.

50. Jay Mathews, "Taiwan Admits Role in Murder of U.S. Author," *Washington Post*, January 16, 1985.

51. Associated Press, "Taiwan Would Like to Sign Extradition Treaty with US," April 17, 1985; *Christian Science Monitor*, "Taiwan Rejects US House Call for Extradition of Liu Suspects," April 18, 1985; Associated Press, "China Denounces Verdict in Liu Killing," April 22, 1985.

52. Wendel Chang, Associated Press, April 18, 1985, LexisNexis; Steve Lohr, "Murder Trial Illuminates Taiwan's Dark Thoughts," *New York Times*, April 21, 1985.

53. Marvine Howe, "Domestic Scandals and Trade Fears Leave Taiwan Uncertain," *New York Times*, October 27, 1985; Julian Baum, "Taiwan Election Brings Heated Debate," *Christian Science Monitor*, November 15, 1985.

54. Steve Lohr, "Taiwan Magazines Play 'Mice' to the Censor's 'Cat,'" *New York Times*, February 4, 1985; Roy, *Taiwan*; Phil Brown, "Authorities Appear to Be Tolerating More Criticism," Associated Press, February 28, 1985; Howe, "Domestic Scandals and Trade Fears"; Berman, *Words Like Colored Glass*, p. 191.

55. Roy, *Taiwan*, p. 164.

56. Lohr, "Taiwan Magazines Play 'Mice' to the Censor's 'Cat.'"

57. Pye, "Taiwan's Development and Its Implications," p. 615; Roy, *Taiwan*, pp. 85, 87; Fell, "Political and Media Liberalization."

58. Huang, "Dissidents Wary of Nationalist Claims for Democracy"; Roy, *Taiwan*, p. 175.

59. Huang, "Dissidents Wary of Nationalist Claims for Democracy."

60. Arrigo, "From Democratic Movement to Bourgeois Democracy"; Roy, *Taiwan*, p. 175.

61. Chan Wai-Fong, "Taipei Media Faces Threat from Within," *South China Morning Post* (Hong Kong), 1994; Kao Chen, "Post-Martial Law Taiwan Media Still Lacks Freedom from Official Sanctions," *Straits Times* (Singapore), November 22, 1996.

62. Associated Press, "Dissident Publisher Burned to Death in Clash with Police," April 7, 1987; Roy, *Taiwan*, pp. 175–76; Annie Huang, "Vote-Buying Reported in Taiwan's First Democratic Election," Associated Press, December 2, 1989; Berman, *Words Like Colored Glass*.

63. John Pomfret, "Ballot-Rigging Charged in First Taiwan's First Multiparty Election," Associated Press, December 2, 1989 (title error in the original).

64. Huang, "Vote-Buying Reported in Taiwan's First Democratic Election."

65. Sheila Tefft, "With Their Own Limbaugh, Taiwanese Tune in to Politics," *Christian Science Monitor*, December 13, 1994.

66. Tefft, "With Their Own Limbaugh"; Rajiv Chandra, "Taiwan: Renegade Radio Roils Taipei Airwaves," Inter Press Service, December 15, 1994; Associated Press, "Taiwan to License Private TV Channel," *Worldstream*, January 28, 1994.

67. United Press International, "Radio Stations Challenge Crackdown," April 21, 1994; Chandra, "Taiwan."

68. Inter Press Service, "Taiwan: Radio Turns Taxi Drivers into Rebels on Wheels," August 11, 1994. Some reports say there were 40,000 taxi drivers.

69. United Press International, "Renegade Taiwanese Broadcaster Sentenced," October 1, 1994, LexisNexis.

70. Tefft, "With Their Own Limbaugh."

71. United Press International, "Pirate Television to Hit Airwaves," November 15, 1993; United Press International, "UPI Spotlight: Pirate Television to Hit Airwaves," November 14, 1993.

72. Tefft, "With Their Own Limbaugh."

73. Inter Press Service, "Taiwan"; Tefft, "With Their Own Limbaugh"; Satoshi Saeki, "Taiwan's President Pushing for Statehood," *Daily Yomiuri*, July 14, 1994.

74. Associated Press, "Taiwan's Government Approves First Private Television Network," June 16, 1995; United Press International, "Taiwan Lifts Foreign Media Restrictions," September 7, 1995; Kao Chen, "Post-Martial Law Taiwan Media Still Lacks Freedom from Official Sanctions."

75. Inter Press Service, "Taiwan."

76. Kao Chen, "Post-Martial Law Taiwan Media Still Lacks Freedom from Official Sanctions," *Straits Times* (Singapore), November 22, 1996.

77. Kao Chen, "Post-Martial Law Taiwan Media Still Lacks Freedom from Official Sanctions"; Chen Wai-Fong, "Taipei Media Faces Threat from Within."

78. Chen Wai-Fong, "Taipei Media Faces Threat from Within."

79. Ibid.

80. BBC Summary of World Broadcasts, "Cable TV Operators Urged to Improve Programming, April 18, 1997, LexisNexis; Rawnsley and Rawnsley, "Regime Transition and the Media in Taiwan"; Central News Agency (Taiwan), "Mass Media Growing Fast in Taiwan," October 16, 1997.

81. Fell, "Political and Media Liberalization."

82. BBC Summary of World Broadcasts, "Cable TV Operators Urged to Improve Programming"; Leanne Kao, "Media Wars," *Taiwan Review*, February 2, 2005; Daniel C. Lynch, e-mail exchange with the author, September 2010.

83. Berman, *Words Like Colored Glass*; Lynch, *Rising China and Asian Democratization*; Fell, "Political and Media Liberalization."

84. Berman, *Words Like Colored Glass*.

85. Lynch, "Taiwan's Democratization," p. 572; Fell, "Political and Media Liberalization."

86. Kathrin Hille, "Taiwan Stalemate as Parties Fight over Posts," *Financial Times*, December 16, 2004.

87. Ping-hung Chen et al., "A 21st Century Anthology of Media Criticism," Campaign for Media Reform (Taiwan), 1st ed., compiled and edited by Yu-Peng Lin, translated by Taipei Times Translation Section, January 21, 2008, http://twmedia.org; Chen-li Liu, "News Media Performance and Social Responsibility in Transitional Societies: A Case Study of Tabloidisation in Taiwan" (PhD diss., Loughborough University).

Chapter 10: The Tipping Point

1. Renee Tawa, "The Sunday Profile," *Los Angeles Times*, March 12, 1995.

2. United Nations Children's Fund (UNICEF); UN Women, "International Day against Female Genital Mutilation," February 6, 2007, http://www.unifemuk.org/news-international-day-against-female-genital-mutilation.php (accessed May 24, 2011).

3. Wairagala Wakabi, "Africa Battles to Make Female Genital Mutilation History," *World Report*, March 29, 2007; Maimouna Abdoulaye Barro, *Lancet* 369, no. 9567 (March 31, 2007); Vivienne Walt, "Village by Village, Circumcising a Ritual," *Washington Post*, June 7, 1998.

4. Pamela Constable, "Area Immigrants with Wounds That Won't Heal," *Washington Post*, November 3, 2008.

5. Population Council, "Breakthrough in Senegal: Ending Female Genital Cutting, the Process That Ended Female Genital Cutting in 31 Villages," Africa Operation Research and Technical Assistance Project II, 1999, p. 5.

6. Ibid.

7. Tostan, "Empowering Communities to Abandon Female Genital Cutting," http://www.tostan.org.

8. R. Shweder, "What about Female Genital Mutilation? And Why Understanding Culture Matters in the First Place," in *Engaging Cultural Differences: The Multicultural Challenge in Liberal Democracies*, ed. R. Shweder, M. Minow, and H. Markus (New York: Russell Sage Foundation Press, 2002).

9. Population Council, "Breakthrough in Senegal," p. 40.

10. Tostan, "Empowering Communities to Abandon Female Genital Cutting."

11. Karen Greiner, Arvind Singhal, and Sarah Hurlburt, "With an Antenna We Can Stop the Practice of Female Genital Cutting," *Investigacion y Desarrollo* 15, no. 2 (2007): 226–59; Shweder, "What about Female Genital Mutilation?" p. 220.

12. Diane Gillespie, "Villagers Ending Female Genital Cutting," *Seattle Post Intelligencer*, August 17, 2007; David Hecht, Linda Wertheimer, and Noah Adams, National Public Radio, July 22, 1998.

13. Ibid.

14. Molly Melching, "A Breakthrough," in *Eye to Eye: Women Practicing Development across Cultures*, ed. Susan Perry and Celeste Schenck (New York: Zed Books, 2001).

15. Ibid.

16. Population Council, "Breakthrough in Senegal," p. 40.

17. David Hecht, "Standing up to Ancient Custom," *Christian Science Monitor*, June 3, 1998.

18. Melching, "Breakthrough," citing Gerry Mackie, "Female Genital Cutting: The Beginning of the End," in *Female "Circumcision," in Africa: Culture, Controversy, and Change*, ed. Bettina Shell Duncan and Ylva Hernland (London: Lynne Rienner, 2000), pp. 253–81.

19. Population Council, "Breakthrough in Senegal," p. 41.

20. Peter Easton, Karen Monkman, and Rebecca Miles, "Social Policy from the Bottom Up," *Development in Practice* 13, no. 5 (November 2003): 445–58.

21. Population Council, "Breakthrough in Senegal"; Melching, "Breakthrough"; Easton, Monkman, and Miles, "Social Policy from the Bottom Up," pp. 445–58.

22. Population Council, "Breakthrough in Senegal," p. 41.

23. Ibid., p. 46.

24. David Hecht, "When a Law Sweeps in, Tradition Lashes Back," *Christian Science Monitor*, February 4, 1999.

25. Easton, Monkman, and Miles, "Social Policy from the Bottom Up."

26. Population Council, "Breakthrough in Senegal."

27. Hecht, "When a Law Sweeps In."

28. David Hecht and Linda Wertheimer, "Female Circumcision Educators" *All Things Considered*, NPR, July 22, 1998.

29. Easton, Monkman, and Miles, "Social Policy from the Bottom Up"; Population Council, "Breakthrough in Senegal."

30. Melching, "Breakthrough," p. 163.

31. Walt, "Village by Village."

32. Ibid.

33. Hecht, "When a Law Sweeps In."

34. Walt, "Village by Village."

35. Barbara Crossette, "Senegal Bans Cutting of Genitals of Girls," *New York Times*, January 18, 1999.

36. Hecht, "When a Law Sweeps In."

37. Tostan, "Empowering Communities to Abandon Female Genital Cutting."

38. Ibid.

39. Ibid.

40. Melching, "Breakthrough," pp. 168–69.

41. Ibid., p. 167.

42. Gannon Gillespie, interview with the author, 2010; Jamie Beth Lennahan, "Escaping Illiberal Liberalism: A Holistic Approach to Engaging with Culture" (PhD diss., University of Colorado, 2008); Tostan, 2006 Annual Report.

43. Cody Donahue, interview with the author, 2010.

44. *Le Soleil*, "70 Villages du Fouta Disent Non à la Pratique de l'excision," November 18, 2005.

45. *La Journal*, "Confidence of an Ancient Cutter," May 18, 2005.

46. Malick Ciss, "La Declaration de Marakissa Casse la Lame à 44 Villages," *Le Soleil*, May 20, 2005.

47. Ibid.

48. Tostan, "Empowering Communities to Abandon Female Genital Cutting."

49. Gillespie, "Villagers Ending Female Genital Cutting."

50. Pape Ouseynou Diallo, "L'Excision Persiste à Tambacounda," *L'Observateur*, March 23, 2006.

51. Radio Television Senegalaise, "RTS Midday News," August 6, 2006, obtained from Open Source Center; Molly Melching, "NGO Founder Says Education Is Key to End Female Genital Cutting," CO.NX Webchat Transcript, March 29, 2009, State Department Documents and Publications: News From America.co and the Washington File, http://www.uspolicy.be/headline/ngo-founder-says-education-key-end-female-genital-cutting (accessed May 31, 2011).

52. Gillespie, interview.

53. Helene Benga, Fatou Cisse, Babacar Mane, Inge Baumgarten, and Molly Melching, "The TOSTAN Program: Evaluation of a Community Based Education Program in Senegal," Population Council, GTZ, Tostan, August 2004 (funded by USAID, the United States Agency for International Development); Molly Melching, interview with the author, 2007.

54. Melching, "NGO Founder Says Education Is Key."

55. Kedougou, "Public Declaration for the Abandonment of Female Genital Cutting and Child/Forced Marriages," Tostan, Feburary 21, 2010.

56. "Senegal: Total End of Female Genital Cutting Now in Sight," *A Changing Life*, February 19, 2010, http://travellingspouse.blogspot.com/2010/02/senegal-total-end-of-female-genital.html (accessed May 27, 2011).

57. *Africa News*, "Human Rights: Growing Number of African Communities Focus on Women's Rights," August 11, 2004.

58. Donahue, interview.

59. Diane Gillespie and Molly Melching, "The Transformative Power of Democracy and Human Rights in Nonformal Education: The Case of Tostan," *Adult Education Quarterly*, March 26, 2010.

60. Greiner, Singhal, and Hurlburt, "With an Antenna We Can Stop the Practice of Female Genital Cutting."

61. Gillespie, interview.

62. Various press clippings and transcripts from Radio Television Senegalaise, June 30, 2007. Obtained from Open Source Center and Tostan.

63. Nafisatou J. Diop and Ian Askew, "The Effectiveness of a Community Education Program on Abandoning Genital Mutilation/Cutting in Senegal," *Studies in Family Planning* 40, no. 4 (2009): 307–18; Nafissatou J. Dip et al., "The Tostan Program: Evaluation of a Community Based Education Program in Senegal," August 2004, http://www.popcouncil.org/pdfs/frontiers/FR_FinalReports/Senegal_Tostan%20FGC.pdf (accessed May 27, 2011).

64. Bettina Shell-Duncan and Ylva Hernlund, "Summary Report: Contingency and Change in the Practice of FGC: Dynamics of Decision-Making in Senegambia" (unpublished paper, 2009).

65. Gillespie, interview.

Chapter 11: The Fate of the World

1. James Hansen and S. Lebedeff, "Global Trends of Measured Surface Air Temperature," *Journal of Geophysical Research* 92 (1987): 13345–72.

2. Naomi Oreskes and Erik M. Conway, *Merchants of Doubt: How a Handful of Scientists Obscured the Truth on Issues from Tobacco Smoke to Global Warming* (New York: Bloomsbury Press, 2010).

3. Philip Shabecoff, "Global Warming Has Begun, Expert Tells Senate," *New York Times*, June 24, 1988; Michael Weisskopf, "Scientist Says Greenhouse Effect Is Setting In," *Washington Post*, June 24, 1988; D. Costello, "Scientists Put More Heat on Congress," *Courier-Mail*, June 25, 1988.

4. James Hansen, "Global Warming Twenty Years Later: Tipping Points Near," June 23, 2008, http://www.columbia.edu/~jeh1/2008/TwentyYearsLater_20080623.pdf (accessed May 31, 2011).

5. John Noble Wilford, "His Bold Statement Transforms the Debate on Greenhouse Effect," *New York Times*, August 23, 1988.

6. Richard Kerr, "Newsfocus: Pushing the Scary Side of Global Warming," *Science* 316 (June 8, 2007).

7. Shardul Agrawala, "Structural and Process History of the Intergovernmental Panel on Climate Change," *Climatic Change* 39, no. 4 (1998): 621–42.

8. IPCC, 2001 report.

9. World Meteorological Organization, "2000–2009, the Warmest Decade," press release no. 869, December 8, 2009.

10. Ibid.; Michael McCarthy, "End of Alaotra Grebe Is Further Evidence of Sixth Great Extinction: Species Are Vanishing Quicker Than at Any Point in the Last 65 Million Years," *Independent*, May 26, 2010.

11. Naomi Oreskes, "Beyond the Ivory Tower: The Scientific Consensus on Climate Change," *Science* 306, no. 5702 (2004): 2686.

12. "Joint Science Academies' Statement, Global Response to Climate Change," June 7, 2005, published in the *Times* (of London) and other publications. The joint statement, noted here, included eleven academies.

13. WorldPublicOpinion.org, July 5, 2005, citing a poll conducted by Program on International Policy Attitudes/Knowledge Networks, "Americans on Climate Change 2005," http://www.worldpublicopinion.org/pipa/articles/btenvironmentra/79.php?nid=&id=&pnt=79&lb=bte (accessed May 19, 2011).

14. James Hansen, "Can We Defuse the Global Warming Time Bomb?" *Natural Science*, August 1, 2003; Kerr, "Newsfocus."

15. Hansen, "Global Warming Twenty Years Later."

16. Peer review is a process of evaluating, assessing, and verifying academic research. It is a "blind" process whereby submitters and reviewers do not know each other's identities.

17. IPCC Fourth Assessment Report Report (AR4), 2007.

18. Kerr, "Newsfocus."

19. Pew Research Center, "Fewer Americans See Solid Evidence of Global Warming: Modest Support for 'Cap and Trade' Policy," October 22, 2009, http://peoplepress.org/

2009/10/22/fewer-americans-see-solid-evidence-of-global-warming/ (accessed May 31, 2011). A 2008 Harris Poll found similar results.

20. *National Journal*, "Congressional Insiders Poll," February 3, 2007, 6–7; Maxwell T. Boykoff, "Flogging a Dead Norm? Newspaper Coverage of Anthropogenic Climate Change in the United States and United Kingdom from 2003 to 2007," *Area* 39, no. 4 (December 2007): 470–81.

21. *New York Times*, "Green Blog," April 27, 2010.

22. Elisabeth Rosenthal, "Climate Fears Turn to Doubts among Britons," *New York Times*, May 24, 2010.

23. Ibid.

24. Oreskes, "Beyond the Ivory Tower."

25. Oreskes and Conway, *Merchants of Doubt*; James Hoggan with Richard Littlemore, *Climate Cover-Up: The Crusade to Deny Global Warming* (Berkeley: Greystone Books, 2009); Chris Mooney, *The Republican War on Science* (New York: Basic Books, 2005); Seth Shulman, Kate Abend, and Alden Meyer, "Smoke, Mirrors, and Hot Air: How Exxon-Mobil Uses Big Tobacco's Tactics to Manufacture Uncertainty on Climate Science," Union of Concerned Scientists, January 2007, http://www.ucsusa.org/assets/documents/global_warming/exxon_report.pdf (accessed May 20, 2011).

26. Shulman, Abend, and Meyer, "Smoke, Mirrors, and Hot Air"; Oreskes and Conway, *Merchants of Doubt*; Hoggan and Littlemore, *Climate Cover-Up*; Mooney, *Republican War on Science*.

27. Shulman, Abend, and Meyer, "Smoke, Mirrors, and Hot Air," citing APCO Associates, Washington, DC, October 15, 1993, http://www.tobaccodocuments.org; Hoggan and Littlemore, *Climate Cover-Up*, pp. 17, 18, 20–22, 36.

28. Shulman, Abend, and Meyer, "Smoke, Mirrors, and Hot Air," pp.18–22, citing Philip Morris, "ETS Media Strategy," 1993, http://www.tobaccodocuments.org; Oreskes and Conway, *Merchants of Doubt*.

29. Shulman, Abend, and Meyer, "Smoke, Mirrors, and Hot Air," p. 7, citing Brown and Williamson, 1969, http://tobaccodocuments.org; Mooney, *Republican War on Science*, p. 47; Oreskes and Conway, *Merchants of Doubt*; Hoggan and Littlemore, *Climate Cover-Up*.

30. Shulman, Abend, and Meyer, "Smoke, Mirrors, and Hot Air," p. 7, citing Committee of Experts on Tobacco Industry Documents, World Health Organization, "Tobacco Company Strategies to Undermine Tobacco Control Activities," 2000, http://escholarship.org/uc/item/83m9c2wt#page-1; Hoggan and Littlemore, *Climate Cover-Up*.

31. Shulman, Abend, and Meyer, "Smoke, Mirrors, and Hot Air," pp. 16–19, citing M. Hertsgaard, "While Washington Slept," *Vanity Fair*, May 2006; Hoggan and Littlemore, *Climate Cover-Up*, p. 41.

32. World Health Organization, "Tobacco Free Initiative (TFI): Why Tobacco Is a Public Health Priority," http://www.who.int/tobacco/health_priority/en/ (accessed May 19, 2011).

33. Shulman, Abend, and Meyer, "Smoke, Mirrors, and Hot Air," p. 10, citing J. Walker, "Draft Global Climate Science Communication Plan," American Petroleum Institute, April 1998, Memorandum to GCST; Mooney, *Republican War on Science*, p. 82.

34. Hoggan and Littlemore, *Climate Cover-Up*, pp. 32–33; Ross Gelbspan, *The Heat Is On: The High Stakes Battle over Earth's Threatened Climate* (New York: Addison-Wesley Publishing, 1997); Shulman, Abend, and Meyer, "Smoke, Mirrors, and Hot Air"; Source-Watch, http://www.sourcewatch.org (accessed May 19, 2011).

35. Shulman, Abend, and Meyer, "Smoke, Mirrors, and Hot Air," pp. 9–13; Source-Watch; Andrew C. Revkin, "Industry Ignored Its Scientists on Climate," *New York Times*, April 23, 2009.

36. Shulman, Abend, and Meyer, "Smoke, Mirrors, and Hot Air," p. 10, citing APCO Associates, 1993; Hoggan and Littlemore, *Climate Cover-Up*, p. 37; Gelbspan, *Heat Is On*.

37. Shulman, Abend, and Meyer, "Smoke, Mirrors, and Hot Air," p. 14, citing ExxonMobil's corporate reports.

38. Shulman, Abend, and Meyer, "Smoke, Mirrors, and Hot Air."

39. Jane Mayer, "Covert Operations," *New Yorker*, August 30, 2010; Center for Public Integrity, http://www.publicintegrity.org/ (accessed May 31, 2011).

40. Aaron M. McCright and Riley E. Dunlap, "Defeating Kyoto: The Conservative Movement's Impact on US Climate Change," *Social Problems* 50, no. 3 (2003): 348–73, citing Matthew A. Crenson, *The Un-Politics of Air Pollution: A Study of Non-Decision Making in the Cities* (Baltimore, MD: Johns Hopkins University Press, 1971); Harvey Molotch, "Oil in Santa Barbara and Power in America," *Sociological Inquiry* 40 (1970): 131–44; William R. Freudenburg and Robert Gramling, *Oil in Troubled Waters* (Albany: State University of New York Press, 1994); Naomi T. Krogman, "Frame Disputes in Environmental Controversies," *Sociological Spectrum* 16 (1996): 373–400.

41. Hoggan and Littlemore, *Climate Cover-Up*; Ross Gelbspan, *Heat Is On*; "The Greening of Planet Earth (Part 1 of 2)," YouTube video, 15:00, posted by "Sea-horse1776," October 19, 2010, http://www.youtube.com/ watch?v=de6AHklxX1s; "The Greening of Planet Earth (Part 2 of 2)," YouTube video, 13:01, posted by "Sea-horse1176," October 20, 2010,http://www.youtube.com/ watch?v=jXLE6mdmGYI& feature=related.

42. Hoggan and Littlemore, *Climate Cover-Up*; McCright and Dunlap, "Defeating Kyoto"; Gelbspan, *Heat Is On*.

43. Shulman, Abend, and Meyer, "Smoke, Mirrors, and Hot Air"; Hoggan and Littlemore, *Climate Cover-Up*; McCright and Dunlap, "Defeating Kyoto."

44. Oreskes and Conway, *Merchants of Doubt*.

45. Ibid.; Hoggan and Littlemore, *Climate Cover-Up*; Shulman, Abend, and Meyer, "Smoke, Mirrors, and Hot Air."

46. Hoggan and Littlemore, *Climate Cover-Up*, p. 104; Shulman, Abend, and Meyer, "Smoke, Mirrors, and Hot Air."

47. Shulman, Abend, and Meyer, "Smoke, Mirrors, and Hot Air," citing Exxon-Mobil's corporate reports, 1998–2005.

48. SourceWatch.org lists much of Michaels' funding; Shulman, Abend, and Meyer, "Smoke, Mirrors, and Hot Air."

49. James Hansen et al., "Global Climate Changes as Forecast by Goddard Institute

for Space Studies: A Three-Dimensional Model," *Journal of Geophysical Research* 93, D8 (1998): 9341–64; Spencer Weart, *The Discovery of Global Warming: A Hypertext History of How Scientists Came to (Partly) Understand What People Are Doing to Cause Climate Change* (Cabridge, MA: Harvard University Press, 2008); Paul Krugman, "Swiftboating the Planet," *New York Times*, May 29, 2006; SourceWatch; Patrick Michaels, "Kyoto Protocol: A Useless Appendage to an Irrelevant Treaty, Testimony before the Committee on Small Business," 1998, also posted on the Cato Institute website, http://www.cato.org, and on the Daily Kos website, http://www.dailykos.com, by "Meteor Blades."

50. McCright and Dunlap, "Defeating Kyoto"; Oreskes and Conway, *Merchants of Doubt*, p. 203; Gelbspan, *Heat Is On*; Shulman, Abend, and Meyer, "Smoke, Mirrors, and Hot Air"; Hoggan and Littlemore, *Climate Cover-Up*.

51. Shulman, Abend, and Meyer, "Smoke, Mirrors and Hot Air"; Oreskes and Conway, *Merchants of Doubt*.

52. Rick Piltz, "The Denial Machine," *Index on Censorship* (2007): 72–81; Andrew Revkin, "Bush Aide Softened Greenhouse Gas Links to Global Warming," *New York Times*, June 8, 2005.

53. McCright and Dunlap, "Defeating Kyoto"; Mooney, *Republican War on Science*.

54. McCright and Dunlap, "Defeating Kyoto."

55. Ibid.; Mooney, *Republican War on Science*.

56. James Hansen, *Storms of My Grandchildren: The Truth about the Coming Climate Catastrophe and Our Last Chance to Save Humanity* (New York: Bloomsbury, 2009), p. 130; Piltz, "Denial Machine."

57. Piltz, "Denial Machine"; Hansen, *Storms of My Grandchildren*, pp. 125, 128–29.

58. Maxwell T. Boykoff and J. Timmons Roberts, "Media Coverage of Climate Change: Current Trends, Strengths, Weaknesses," *Human Development Report*, United Nations Development Project, 2007/2008 Report, p. 5, citing Albert Abarbanel and Thomas McClusky, "Is the World Getting Warmer?" *Saturday Evening Post*, July 1, 1950, 22–23, 57–63.

59. Boykoff and Roberts, "Media Coverage of Climate Change," citing Waldemer Kaempffert, "Science in Review," *New York Times*, October 28, 1956, N12; Boykoff and Roberts, "Media Coverage of Climate Change."

60. Boykoff and Roberts, "Media Coverage of Climate Change," citing Robert C. Cowen, "Are Men Changing the Earth's Weather?" *Christian Science Monitor*, 1957.

61. Boykoff and Roberts, "Media Coverage of Climate Change," citing S. Ungar, "The Rise and (Relative) Decline of Global Warming as a Social Problem," *Sociological Quarterly* 33, no.4 (1992): 483–501; Phillip Shabecoff, "Common Ground Seen on Warming of Globe," *New York Times*, 1988.

62. Oreskes and Conway, *Merchants of Doubt*, pp. 203, 207; on inundation of journalists, Eugene Linden, *Winds of Change: Climate, Weather, and the Destruction of Civilization* (New York: Simon and Schuster, 2006).

63. Boykoff, "Flogging a Dead Norm?"; S. C. Zehr, "Public Representations of Scientific Uncertainty about Global Climate Change," *Public Understanding of Science* 9 (2000); Boykoff and Roberts, "Media Coverage of Climate Change."

64. Oreskes and Conway, *Merchants of Doubt*, p. 202, emphasis added.

65. Maxwell T. Boykoff and Jules M. Boykoff, "Balance as Bias: Global Warming and the US Prestige Press," *Global Climate Change* 14 (2006):125–36; Boykoff and Roberts, "Media Coverage of Climate Change," p. 35.

66. McCright and Dunlap, "Defeating Kyoto," pp. 348–73.

67. Boykoff and Roberts, "Media Coverage of Climate Change," p. 34.

68. Oreskes and Conway, *Merchants of Doubt*, pp. 208, 210.

69. Boykoff and Boykoff, "Balance as Bias."

70. Julie Hollar, "'Climategate' Overshadows Copenhagen: Media Regress to the Bad Old Days of False Balance," *Extra!* February 2010.

71. Boykoff, "Flogging a Dead Norm?"

72. George Monbiot, "Junk Science," *Guardian*, May 10, 2005; Jay Ingram, "Climate Change Debate Off-Key," *Toronto Star*, May 14, 2005.

73. A LexisNexis search turns up hundreds of articles featuring Hansen; Hansen, *Storms of My Grandchildren*, p. 132.

74. *New York Times*, "Subverting Science," editorial, October 31, 2004; a LexisNexis search turns up articles in several English-language publications in the United Kingdom, Australia, and elsewhere. Rick Piltz's whistleblowing was the front page of the *New York Times* in the prior year. Revkin, "Bush Aide Softened Greenhouse Gas Links to Global Warming."

75. Boykoff, "Flogging a Dead Norm?"

76. Ibid.; Boykoff and Roberts, "Media Coverage of Climate Change," p. 35.

77. Ian Sample, "Scientists Offered Cash to Dispute Climate Study," *Guardian*, February 2, 2007.

78. Jennifer Good, "Climate Status Quo? The Newspaper Framing of Climate Change in Canada, the United States, and around the World, National Communication Association" (paper presented at the National Communication Association's 94th Annual Meeting, 2008), http://www.allacademic.com/meta/p_mla_apa_research_citation/2/50908040p259840_index.html (accessed May 31, 2011).

79. *Editor and Publisher*, "56 Papers in 45 Countries Publish Joint Editorial," December 6, 2009.

80. Maxwell T. Boykoff, "Tracking Global Warming's Media Profile: US Climate Coverage in the '00s," *Extra!* February 2010.

81. Hansen, *Storms of My Grandchildren*, p. 131.

82. Boykoff, "Tracking Global Warming's Media Profile."

83. Fox News, Sunday, December 13, 2009.

84. Andrew Revkin, "Hacked Email Is New Fodder for Climate Dispute," *New York Times*, November 21, 2009.

85. BBC, "Q&A: Professor Phil Jones," February 13, 2010, http://news.bbc.co.uk/2/hi/8511670.stm; Revkin, "Hacked Email Is New Fodder for Climate Dispute."

86. Revkin, "Hacked Email Is New Fodder for Climate Dispute."

87. A LexisNexis search turns up hundreds of articles on this.

88. James Painter, "Summoned by Science, Reporting Climate Change at Copen-

hagen and Beyond" (Oxford: Reuters Institute for the Study of Journalism, November 15, 2010).

89. Paul Hitlin, Tricia Sartor, and Tom Rosenstiel, "Media Debate Climate Change," December 15, 2009, LexisNexis; Pew Research Center's Project for Excellence in Journalism, New Media Index, "Global Warming Debate Rages on in Social Media," December 7–11, 2009, http://www.journalism.org/index_report/global_warming_debate _rages_social_media (accessed May 31, 2011); A LexisNexis search on the phrases "East Anglia" and "climate" turned up some six hundred articles for the period stated.

90. Bret Stephens, "Climategate: Follow the Money," *Wall Street Journal*, November 27, 2009; Curtis Brainard, "Hacked E-mails and Journalistic Tribalism: Climate Coverage Is Imperfect, but Is It Ideologically Biased?" *Observatory*, December 3, 2009, http://www.cjr.org/the_observatory/hacked_emails_and_journalistic.php (accessed May 31, 2011).

91. Several newspapers made reference to this in a LexisNexis search.

92. James Hansen, interview, the *Insighters*, KPFK and WPRR, 2010.

93. Hollar, "'Climategate' Overshadows Copenhagen"; Raphael G. Satter, "'Climategate' Investigation Vindicates Scientists, Finds Research Reliable," *Huffington Post*, July 7, 2011, http://www.huffingtonpost.com/2010/07/07/climategate-investigation_0_n _637622.html (accessed May 27, 2011); Travis Walter Donovan "'Climategate' Investigation Clears U.S. Scientists," *Huffington Post*, February 24, 2011; Stephen Dinan, "Investigation Clears 'Climategate' Participants," *Washington Times*, July 7, 2010, http://www .washingtontimes.com/news/2010/jul/7/investigation-clears-climategate-participants/ (accessed May 27, 2011).

94. These quotes were obtained from Hollar, "'Climategate' Overshadows Copenhagen."

95. CBS Evening News, December 5, 2010; Hollar, "'Climategate' Overshadows Copenhagen," citing Rick Sanchez, CNN, December 7, 2009.

96. BBC Summary of World Broadcasts, "Q&A."

97. *New York Post*, "The EPA's Climate Con," editorial, February 22, 2010.

98. Media Matters for America, "*WSJ* Column Falsely Claims Phil Jones 'Said There Was More Warming in the Medieval Period,'" *Media Matters for America*, February 22, 2010, http://mediamatters.org/research/201002220009 (accessed May 31, 2011); "*NY Post* Distorts Facts to Claim Climate Change Science Is 'Unraveling,'" Media Matters for America, February 22, 2010, http://mediamatters.org/research/201002220003 (accessed May 31, 2011).

99. PEW Research Center's Project for Excellence in Journalism, "'Climate-Gate' Re-ignites the Blogosphere Debate," February 15–19, 2010, http://pewresearch .org/pubs/1507/bloggers-focus-again-climate-gate-controversy (accessed May 31, 2011).

100. *The Australian*, "Boycott Copenhagen: Palin—Copenhagen Summit," December 11, 2009. Palin's remarks were covered in the *Toronto Starr*, the *Irish Times*, and the Guardian; *Washington Post*, December 9, 2009; Petti Fong, "Campus Break-Ins Target Leading Researcher: Real Issue Is 'Harassment of Climate Scientists,' Prof Says," *Toronto Star*, December 11, 2009; Tim Rutten, "Close This Climate 'Gate,'" *Los Angeles Times*, December 12, 2009.

101. BBC News, "'No Malpractice' by Climate Unit," April 14, 2010; Penn State Office of the Vice President for Research, "Investigation of Climate Scientist at Penn State Completed," Penn State Office press release, July 1, 2010; Richard Black, "Dutch Review Backs UN Climate Panel Report," BBC News, July 5, 2010.

102. Rush Limbaugh, February 17, 2010, archived at Media Matters for America.

103. Ibid.

104. Ibid.

105. Rush Limbaugh, January 29, 2010, archived at Media Matters for America.

106. Glenn Beck, Fox News, April 23, 2010, archived at Media Matters for America.

107. Cited in Center for Excellence in Journalism (CEJ). Blog is "Common Folk Using Common Sense."

108. Project for Excellence in Journalism, "Minarets, Climate Controversies Online," December 10, 2009, http://pewresearch.org/pubs/1436/blogs-swiss-ban-minarets-climate gate (accessed May 27, 2011).

109. Justin Gillis, "In Weather Chaos, a Case for Global Warming," *New York Times*, August 14, 2010; McCarthy, "End of Alaotra Grebe Is Further Evidence of Sixth Great Extinction."

110. Oxfam, e-mail alert, 2010.

111. Jim Witkin, "Biodiversity in Peril, the UN Warns," *New York Times*, Green Blog, May 24, 2010, http://green.blogs.nytimes.com/2010/05/24/biodiversity-in-peril-the-u-n-warns/ (accessed May 20, 2011); Karl Ritter, "Gigantic Ice Island Adrift in Arctic," *San Francisco Chronicle*, August 11, 2010.

112. Matthew Knight, "Oceans Failing the Acid Test, U.N. Says," CNN, December 2, 2010, accessed through "Global Warming: Heated Denials—The Organized Effort to Cast Doubt on Climate Change," by Lisa Chiu, Center for Public Integrity, iWatch-News, October 1, 2008, http://www.publicintegrity.org/articles/entry/731/ (accessed May 20, 2011).

113. Eric Pooley, "How Much Would You Pay to Save the Planet?" American Press and the Economics of Climate Change (Discussion Paper D-49, Joan Shorenstein Center on the Press, Politics, and Public Policy, Harvard University, President and Fellows of Harvard College, Cambridge, MA, 2009).

114. Neela Banerjee, "Climate Scientists Plan Campaign against Global Warming Skeptics," *Chicago Tribune*, November 8, 2010.

Chapter 12: The Sounds of Silence

1. Philip Zimbardo, *The Lucifer Effect: Understanding How Good People Turn Evil* (New York: Random House, 2007).

2. Ibid.

3. Ibid.

4. V. Murphy-Berman and J. Berman, *Nebraska Symposium on Motivation: Cross-Cultural Differences in Perspectives on Self* (Lincoln: University of Nebraska Press, 2003).

5. Soloman Asch, "Opinions and Social Pressure," *Scientific American* 193, no. 5 (1955): 31–35; Soloman Asch, "Studies of Independence and Conformity: A Minority of One against the Unanimous Majority," *Psychological Monographs* 70, no. 416 (1951); Muzafer Sherif, "A Study of Some Social Factors in Perception," *Archives of Psychology* 27 (1935): 210–11.

6. Irving Janis, *Groupthink: Psychological Studies of Policy Decisions and Fiascoes* (New York: Houghton Mifflin, 1983).

7. There are exceptions with support for ingroups versus outgroups, which depend on a variety of factors such as power, need for consistency, and belief in a "just world." There is a very large body of work on the psychology of group behavior, which includes Muzafer Sherif and C. I. Hovland, *Social Judgment: Assimilation and Contrast Effects in Communication and Attitude Change* (New Haven, CT: Yale University Press, 1961); James Sidanius, "The Psychology of Group Conflict and Dynamics of Oppression: A Social Dominance Perspective," in *Explorations in Political Psychology*, ed. Shanto Iyengar and William McGuire (Durham, NC: Duke University Press, 1993); Henry Tajfel, *Social Identity and Intergroup Relations* (London: Cambridge University Press, 1978/1982); Muzafer Sherif, "An Experimental Approach to the Study of Attitudes," *Sociometry*: 90–98; Asch, "Opinions and Social Pressure"; Donald Green, Bradley Palmquist, and Eric Schickler, *Partisan Hearts and Minds: Political Parties and the Social Identities of Voters* (New Haven, CT: Yale University Press, 2002); Daniel Bar-Tal, Eran Halperin, and Joseph de Rivera, "Collective Emotions in Conflict Situations: Societal Implications," *Journal of Social Issues* 63, no. 2 (2007): 441–60; W. G. Stephan and C. W. Stephan, "An Integrated Theory of Prejudice," in *Reducing Prejudice and Discrimination*, ed. S. Oskamp (Hillsdale, NJ: Erlbaum, 2000); Eliot R. Smith, "Social Identity and Social Emotions: Toward a New Conceptualization of Prejudice," in *Affect, Cognition, and Stereotyping: Interactive Processes in Group Perception*, ed. Diane M. Mackie and David L. Hamilton (San Diego, CA: Academic Press, 1993); Diane M. Mackie, T. Devos, and Eliot R. Smith, "Intergroup Emotions: Explaining Offensive Action Tendencies in an Intergroup Context," *Journal of Personality and Social Psychology* 79 (2000): 602–16; Cialdini et al., "Basking in Reflected Glory: Three (Football) Field Studies," *Journal of Personality and Social Psychology* 34, no. 3 (September 1976): 366–75; John Jost, Mahzarin R. Banaji, and Brian A. Nosek, "A Decade of System Justification Theory: Accumulated Evidence of Unconscious Bolstering of the Status Quo," *Political Psychology* 25, no. 6 (December 2004): 881–919.

8. Sidanius, "Psychology of Group Conflict and the Dynamics of Oppression," p. 187, citing 1961 experiment from M. Sherif and C. I. Hovland, *Social Judgment: Assimilation and Contrast Effects in Communication and Attitude Change* (1961; repr., Westport, CT: Greenwood Press, 1980).

9. Benedict Anderson, *Imagined Communities: Reflections on the Origins and Spread of Nationalism* (New York: Verso, 2006). For an interesting discussion on group identity and group formation, see also Dipak K. Gupta, *Understanding Terrorism and Political Violence: The Life Cycle of Birth, Growth, Transformation, and Demise* (New York: Routledge, 2008).

10. Alain Destexhe, *Rwanda and Genocide in the Twentieth Century* (New York: New York University Press, 1995).

11. Gupta, *Understanding Terrorism and Political Violence*.

12. Sabrina Ramet, *The Three Yugoslavias: State-Building and Legitimation, 1918–2005* (Washington, DC: Woodrow Wilson Center Press, 2006); Joel M. Halpern and David A. Kideckel, *Neighbors at War: Anthropological Perspectives on Yugoslavia Ethnicity, Culture, and History* (University Park: Pennsylvania State University); Norman Naimark, *Fires of Hatred: Ethnic Cleansing in Twentieth-Century Europe* (Cambridge, MA: Harvard University Press, 2001).

13. Anderson, *Imagined Communities*.

14. See previous citations for psychology of group behavior (esp. notes 7 and 8).

15. Elisabeth Noelle-Neumann, *The Spiral of Silence: Public Opinion—Our Social Skin* (Chicago: University of Chicago Press, 1984), p. x; John Locke, *Essay Concerning Human Understanding*; Alexis de Tocqueville, *Democracy in America*, 1948. See previous references for social psychologists.

16. There is a large body on social construction, which includes William Gamson, David Croteau, William Hoynes, and Theodore Sasson, "Media Images and the Social Construction of Reality," *Annual Review of Sociology* 18 (1992): 373–93; Nicholas Greenwood Onuf, *World of Our Making: Rules and Rule in Social Theory and International Relations* (Columbia: University of South Carolina Press, 1989); Murray Edelman, *Politics as Symbolic Action: Mass Arousal and Quiescence* (Chicago: Markham Publishing, 1971); Stuart Kaufman, *Modern Hatreds: The Symbolic Politics of Ethnic War* (Ithaca, NY: Cornell University Press, 2001); Russell Neuman, Marion R. Just, and Ann N. Crigler, *Common Knowledge: News and the Construction of Political Meaning* (Chicago: University of Chicago Press, 1992); Ann N. Crigler, "Making Sense of Politics: Constructing Political Messages and Meanings," in *The Psychology of Political Communication*, ed. Ann N. Crigler (Ann Arbor: University of Michigan Press, 1998).

17. Craig Nelson, *Thomas Paine: Enlightenment, Revolution, and the Birth of Modern Nations* (New York: Penguin Group, 2006), pp. 82–85.

18. Kaufman, *Modern Hatreds*, pp. 4–5; Tim Allen and Jean Seaton, introduction to *The Media of Conflict: War Reporting and Representations of Ethnic Violence* (New York: St. Martin's Press, 1999).

19. Jean Seaton, "The New 'Ethnic' Wars and the Media," in *The Media of Conflict: War Reporting and Representations of Ethnic Violence*, by Tim Allen and Jean Seaton (New York: St. Martin's Press, 1999); James D, Fearon and David D. Laitin, "Violence and the Social Construction of Ethnic Identity," in*ternational Organization* 54, no. 4 (2000): 845–77.

20. Seaton, "New 'Ethnic' Wars and the Media."

21. For meaning-making and the construction of realities, see Edelman, *Politics as Symbolic Action*; George Mead, *Mind, Self, and Society: From the Standpoint of a Social Behaviorist* (Chicago: University of Chicago Press, 1934); Neophytos Loizides, "Majority-Group Crisis Behavior: Restraint vs. Confrontation" (PhD diss., University of Toronto, 2005).

22. Seaton, "New 'Ethnic' Wars and the Media"; John Marks, interview with the author, 2010.

23. A large body of literature exists on stereotypes, which includes Walter Lippman,

Public Opinion (New York: Free Press, 1922); Edward Said, *Orientalism* (New York: Penguin, 2003).

24. Marks, interview; Graham Spencer, *The Media and Peace: From Vietnam to the "War on Terror"* (New York: Palgrave MacMillan, 2005).

25. Seaton, "New 'Ethnic' Wars and the Media."

26. James Druckman, "On the Limits of Framing Effects: Who Can Frame?" *Journal of Politics* 63, no. 4 (2001): 1041–66; Thomas E. Nelson, Rosalee A. Clawson, and Zoe M. Oxley, "Media Framing of a Civil Liberties Conflict and Its Effect on Tolerance," *American Political Science Review* 91, no. 3 (September 1997): 567–83.

27. There is a very large body of work on framing. On the role of "adversarial" frames around grievances and opportunities, see Loizides, "Majority-Group Crisis Behavior."

28. Richard Lazarus, *Emotion and Adaptation* (New York: Oxford University Press, 1991); Robert Sternberg, "Understanding and Combating Hate," in *The Psychology of Hate*, ed. Robert J. Sternberg (Washington, DC: American Psychological Association, 2005); Aaron Beck and James Pretzer, "A Cognitive Perspective on Hate and Violence," in *The Psychology of Hate*, ed. Robert J. Sternberg (Washington, DC: American Psychological Association, 2005); Kaufman, *Modern Hatreds.*

29. Jean Seaton, "New 'Ethnic' Wars and the Media"; Pippa Norris, Montague Kern, and Marion Just, *Framing Terrorism: The News Media, the Government and the Public* (New York: Routledge, 2003).

30. Please see respective chapters for citations.

31. Please see chapter 7 on Chile for citations.

32. One example of this is how the media caricatured political candidates, K. Jamieson and P. Waldman, *The Press Effect: Politicians, Journalists and the Stories That Shape the Political World* (New York: Oxford University Press, 2002).

33. Todd Gitlin, *The Whole World Is Watching* (Berkeley: University of California Press, 1980); Ange-Marie Hancock, *The Politics of Disgust: The Public Identity of the Welfare Queen* (New York: New York University Press, 2004); D. M. Taylor and F. M. Moghaddam, *Theories of Intergroup Relations: International Social Psychological Perspectives* (Westport, CT: Praeger, 1994).

34. On the "patriotic" and war-related firings, see Glenn Greenwald, "Octavia Nasr's Firing and What the Liberal Media Allows," *Salon*, July 8, 2010; for the firing of the Fox News reporters, see Liane Casten, "The Media Can Legally Lie," Project Censored, 2003, http://www.projectcensored.org/top-stories/articles/11-the-media-can-legally-lie/ (accessed May 31, 2011).

35. W. Lance Bennett, *News: The Politics of Illusion*, 6th ed. (New York: Pearson Longman, 2007).

36. There are various news sources reporting these, which are aggregated in the legal article by Yochai Benkler, "A Free Irresponsible Press: WikiLeaks and the Battle over the Soul of the Networked Fourth Estate," *Harvard Civil Rights–Civil Liberties Law Review* (forthcoming), see http://blogs.forbes.com/andygreenberg/2011/02/22/harvard-law-prof-amazons-wikileaks-shutdown-set-dangerous-precedent/.

37. For gatekeeping, see Bennett, *News*; W. Lance Bennett and John D. Klockner,

"The Psychology of Mass-Mediated Politics," in *The Psychology of Political Communication*, ed. Ann N. Crigler (Ann Arbor: University of Michigan Press, 1998); Doris Graber, *Mass Media and Politics* (Washington, DC: CQ Press, 2006); for framing, see William A. Gamson, *Talking Politics* (Cambridge: Cambridge University Press, 1992); Robert Entman, "Framing Bias: Media in the Distribution of Power," *Journal of Communication* 57 (March 2007): 163–73; George Lakoff, *Moral Politics: How Liberals and Conservatives Think* (Chicago: University of Chicago Press, 2002).

38. Edward S. Herman and Noam Chomsky, *Manufacturing Consent: The Political Economy of the Mass Media* (New York: Pantheon Books,1988); Bennett, *News*; Wayne Wanta, Guy Golan, and Cheolhan Lee, "Agenda Setting and International News: Media Influence on Public Perceptions of Foreign Nations," *Journalism and Mass Communication Quarterly* 81, no.2 (2004): 364.

39. Noelle-Neumann, *Spiral of Silence*, p. 4.

40. Bennett, *News*.

41. Noelle-Neumann, *Spiral of Silence*, p. 4.

42. Ibid., p. ix.

43. Ibid., p. 38.

44. Seaton, "New 'Ethnic' Wars and the Media"; Noelle-Neumann, *Spiral of Silence*; for excluding and silencing minority opinions, see Hancock, *Politics of Disgust*; Iris Marion Young, *Justice and the Politics of Difference* (Princeton, NJ: Princeton University Press, 1990).

45. Bennett, *News*.

46. Antonio Gramsci, *The Prison Notebooks of Antonio Gramsci*, ed. Quinton Hoare and Geoffrey Nowell Smith (New York: International Publishers, 2005).

47. Maxwell E. McCombs and Donald L. Shaw, "The Agenda-Setting Function of Mass Media," *Public Opinion Quarterly* 36, no. 2 (1972): 176–87; Maxwell McCombs, *Setting the Agenda: The Mass Media and Public Opinion* (Cambridge: Polity Press, 2004).

48. Gamson et al., "Media Images and the Social Construction of Reality"; Robert Entman, "Framing: Toward Clarification of a Fractured Paradigm," *Journal of Communication* 43 (1993); Lakoff, *Moral Politics*; Robert Entman, "Framing: Toward Clarification of a Fractured Paradigm," *Journal of Communications* 43, no. 4 (1993): 51–58; Baldwin van Gorp, "The Constructionist Approach to Framing: Bringing Culture Back," *Journal of Communication* 57, no. 1 (2007): 60–78; Neuman et al., *Common Knowledge*; Joseph N. Capella and Kathleen Hall Jamieson, *The Spiral of Cynicism: Press and the Public Good* (New York: Oxford University Press, 1997).

49. Norris et al., *Framing Terrorism*.

50. Gamson et al., "Media Images and the Social Construction of Reality."

51. For citations, please see chapter 11 on climate change.

52. Nico Frijda, *The Emotions* (New York: Cambridge University Press, 1986); Aaron Beck, *Prisoner of Hate: The Cognitive Basis of Anger, Hostility, and Violence* (New York: HarperCollins, 1999); Robert Sternberg, "Understanding and Combating Hate"; Nei Kressel, *Mass Hate: The Global Rise of Genocide Terror* (Boulder, CO: Westview Pres 1999); Joel Halperin, 2007; Kaufman, *Modern Hatreds*; Jerold Post, "When Hatred

Bred in the Bone: Psycho-Cultural Foundations of Contemporary Terrorism," *Political Psychology* 26, no. 4 (2003): 615–35; Marion Just, Ann N. Crigler, and Russell Neuman, "Cognitive and Affective Dimensions of Political Conceptualization," in *The Psychology of Political Communication*, ed. Ann N. Crigler (Ann Arbor: University of Michigan Press, 1998); Rose McDermott, "The Feelings of Rationality: The Meaning of Neuroscientific Advances for Political Science," *Perspectives on Politics* 2, no. 4 (December 2004); Crigler, *Psychology of Political Communication*; Capella and Jamieson, *Spiral of Cynicism*.

53. For hate and intolerance, see Beck, *Prisoner of Hate*; Sternberg, "Understanding and Combating Hate"; Kressel, *Mass Hate*; Eran Halparin, "The Central Role of Group-Based Hatred as an Emotional Antecedent of Political Intolerance: Evidence from Israel," *Political Psychology* 30, no. 1 (2009): 93–111; Eran Halperin, "Group-Based Hatred in Intractable Conflict in Israel," *Journal of Conflict Management* (2008); Kaufman, *Modern Hatreds*; Post, "When Hatred Is Bred in the Bone"; for cynicism, see Capella and Jamieson, *Spiral of Cynicism*.

54. This is based on the work of George Lakoff, including *Moral Politics* and *Thinking Points: A Progressive's Handbook* (New York: Farrar, Straus, and Giroux, 2006) and *The Political Mind: Why You Can't Understand 21st-Century Politics with an 18th Century Mind* (New York: Viking, 2008); John T. Jost et al., "A Decade of System Justification Theory: Accumulated Evidence of Conscious and Unconscious Bolstering of the Status Quo," *Political Psychology* 23, no. 6:881–919 (paper presented at Social Dominance and Intergroup Relations Symposium, December 2004); Drew Westin, *The Political Brain: The Role of Emotion in Deciding the Fate of the Nation* (New York: Public Affairs, 2007).

55. For citations on Burundi, please see chapter 4.

56. For citations on Northern Ireland, please see chapter 5.

57. For citations in this section, please see the respective chapters.

58. For citations, please see the chapter 10 on female genital cutting (FGC) and Senegal.

59. Gramsci, *Prison Notebooks*; Norris et al., *Framing Terrorism*.

60. These resistance groups are noted in their respective chapters. They tended to be small, particularly in Nazi Germany and Rwanda.

61. For science sources, see chapter 11 on climate change; Thomas E. Patterson, *The Mass Media Election: How Americans Choose Their President* (Westport, CT: Praeger, 1980). Lippmann, *Public Opinion*.

62. Maria Armoudian and Ann Crigler, "Constructing the Vote: Media Effects in a Constructionist Model," *Oxford Handbook of American Elections and Political Behavior*, ed. Jane E. Leighley (New York: Oxford University Press, 2010).

Chapter 13: Kill the Messenger

1. Nelson Mandela, *Long Walk to Freedom* (New York: Little, Brown, 1994), p. 509.

2. Nicolas Greenwood Onuf, *World of Our Making: Rules and Rule in Social Theory and International Relations* (Columbia: University of South Carolina Press, 1989); William

A. Gamson, David Croteau, William Hoynes, and Theodore Sasson, "News Images and the Construction of Reality," *Annual Review of Sociology* 18 (1992): 373–93; Murray Edelman, *Politics as Symbolic Action: Mass Arousal and Quiescence* (Chicago: Markham Publishing, 1971); Ann Crigler, "Making Sense of Politics: Constructing Political Messages and Meanings," in *The Psychology of Political Communication*, ed. Ann N. Crigler (Ann Arbor: University of Michigan Press, 1998); W. Russell Neuman, Marion R. Just, and Ann N. Crigler, *Common Knowledge: News and the Construction of Political Meaning* (Chicago: University of Chicago Press, 1992).

3. Dusan Reljic, "The News Media and the Transformation of Ethno-Political Conflicts," Berline Berghof Research Center for Constructive Conflict Management, August 2004, p. 5.

4. Maria Armoudian and Ann N. Crigler, "Constructing the Vote: Media Effects in a Constructionist Model," *Oxford Handbook of American Elections and Political Behavior*, ed. Jane E. Leighley (New York: Oxford University Press, 2010); Andrew Chadwick, *Internet Politics: States, Citizens, and New Communication Technologies* (Oxford: Oxford University Press, 2006); Thomas Patterson, "Creative Destruction: An Exploratory Look at News on the Internet," Joan Shorenstein Center on the Press, Politics, and Public Policy, John F. Kennedy School of Government, Harvard University, August 2007, http://www.hks.harvard.edu/presspol/research/carnegie-knight/creative_destruction_2007.pdf (accessed May 20, 2011).

5. Anders Østergaard, *Burma VJ*, documentary film, 2009, http://www.burmavjmovie.com (accessed May 31, 2011); BBC Summary of World Broadcasts, "Internet Brings Events in Iran to Life," June 15, 2009.

6. Jo Tuckman, "Twitter Feeds and Blogs Tell Hidden Story of Mexico's Drug Wars," *Guardian*, September 26, 2010.

7. Alexis Madrigal, "The Inside Story of How Facebook Responded to Tunisian Hacks," *Atlantic*, January 24, 2011, http://www.theatlantic.com/technology/archive/2011/01/the-inside-story-of-how-facebook-responded-to-tunisian-hacks/70044/ (accessed May 22, 2011).

8. BBC News "Egypt Internet Comes Back Online," Technology, February 2, 2011, http://www.bbc.co.uk/news/technology-12346929 (accessed May 22, 2011); Matt Richtel, "Egypt Cuts Off Most Internet and Cell Service," *New York Times*, January 28, 2011; Mike Giglio, "The Cyberactivists Who Helped Topple a Dictator," *Newsweek*, January 15, 2011.

9. Margaret E. Keck and Kathryn Sikkink, *Activists beyond Borders* (Ithaca, NY: Cornell University Press, 1998); Armoudian and Crigler, "Constructing the Vote."

10. One example is in Peter Dreier's "How Acorn Was Framed," *Perspectives on Politics*, 2010; Peter Dreier, interview on the *Insighters* on KPFK and WPRR, 2010. Another doctored video misconstrued National Public Radio executives' comments in an ostensible effort to damage them, David Folkenflick, "Elements of NPR Gotcha Video Taken out of Context," NPR, March 14, 2011, http://www.npr.org/2011/03/14/ 134525412/Segments-Of-NPR-Gotcha-Video-Taken-Out-Of-Context (accessed May 22, 2011).

11. For the Echo Chamber, see Kathleen Hall Jamieson and Joseph N. Capella, *Echo

Chamber: Rush Limbaugh and the Conservative Media Establishment (New York: Oxford University Press, 2008).

12. George Herbert Mead, *Mind, Self, and Society: From the Standpoint of a Social Behaviorist* (Chicago: University of Chicago, Press, 1934).

13. Stephen M. Younger, *Endangered Species: Mass Violence and the Future of Humanity* (New York: HarperCollins, 2007).

14. Ibid., p. xi.

15. Ibid.

16. Abraham Maslow, *The Farther Reaches of Human Nature* (New York: Penguin, 1971).

17. Gamson et al., "News Images and the Construction of Reality"; G. Tuchman, *Making News* (New York: Free Press, 1978); L. V. Sigal, *Reporters and Officials* (Lexington, MA: Heath, 1978); W. Lance Bennett, *News: The Politics of Illusion*, 6th ed. (New York: Pearson Longman, 2007).

18. Armoudian and Crigler, "Constructing the Vote."

19. Erving Goffman, *Frame Analysis: An Essay on the Organization of Experience* (Cambridge, MA: Harvard University Press, 1974); William A. Gamson, *Talking Politics* (New York: Cambridge University Press, 1992); Robert Entman, "Framing: Toward Clarification of a Fractured Paradigm," *Journal of Communication* 43 (1993); Robert Entman, "Framing Bias: Media in the Distribution of Power," *Journal of Communication* 57 (2007): 163–73; Lakoff, *Moral Politics*.

20. Herbert Gans, *Deciding What's News: A Study of CBS Evening News, NBC Nightly News, Newsweek, and Time* (New York: Vintage Books), p. 40; Mathew Robert Kerbel, *If It Bleeds, It Leads: An Anatomy of Television News* (Boulder, CO: Westview Press, 1980); Bennett, *News*; Entman, "Framing"; Shanto Iyengar and Donald Kinder, *News That Matters: Television and American Public Opinion* (Chicago: University of Chicago Press, 1987); Shanto Iyengar, *Is Anyone Responsible? How Television Frames Political Issues* (Chicago: University of Chicago Press, 1991); E. Barbara Phillips, "What Is News? Novelty without Change," *Journal of Communication* 26, no. 4 (1976): 87–92; P. Bourdieu, *On Television and Journalism* (London: Pluto Press, 1998).

21. Bennett, *News*.

22. On the role of expectations, see Mead, *Mind, Self, and Society*; and Richard Lazarus, *Emotion and Adaptation* (New York: Oxford University Press, 1991).

23. Quote is attributed to Confucius, but this captures the basic idea behind the theory of Abraham Maslow's hierarchy of needs. The concept is contested by some contemporary psychologists.

24. For references here, please see chapter 10 on the tipping point.

25. For agenda setting, see Maxwell McCombs and Donald L. Shaw, "The Agenda-Setting Function of Mass Media," *Public Opinion Quarterly* 36, no. 2 (1972): 176–87; Maxwell McCombs, *Setting the Agenda: The Mass Media and Public Opinion* (Cambridge: Polity Press, 2004); for priming, see Iyengar and Kinder, *News That Matters*; Shanto Iyengar, M. Peters, and D. Kinder, "Experimental Demonstrations of the 'Not So Minimal' Consequences of TV News Programs," *American Political Science Review* 76 (1982):

848–58; David Weaver, "Issue Salience and Public Opinion: Are There Consequences of Agenda-Setting?" *International Journal of Public Opinion Research* 3 (1991): 53–68; David Domke, Dhavan V. Shah, and Daniel B. Wackman, "Media Priming Effects: Accessibility, Association, and Activation," *International Journal of Public Opinion* (1998); Kimberly Gross, "Framing Persuasive Appeals: Episodic and Thematic Framing, Emotional Responses and Policy Opinion," *Political Psychology* 29, no. 2 (2008): 169–92.

26. A large body on meanings and frames exist, including Gamson, *Talking Politics*; see also Bennett, *News*; W. Lance Bennett, *When the Press Fails: Political Power and the News Media from Iraq to Katrina* (Chicago: University of Chicago Press, 2007); Robert McChesney and John Nichols, *The Death and Life of American Journalism: The Media Revolution That Will Begin the World Again* (New York: Nation Books, 2010); Entman, "Framing."

27. Zimbardo, *Lucifer Effect*; Mead, *Mind, Self, and Society*; S. E. Asch, "Studies of Independence and Conformity: A Minority of One against a Unanimous Majority, *Psychological Monographs* 70 (1955); R. F. Baumeister and M. R. Lary, "Opinions and Social Pressure," *Scientific American* (November 1995): 31–35; R. F. Baumeister and M. R. Lary, "The Need to Belong: Desire for Interpersonal Attachments as a Fundamental Human Motivation," *Psychological Bulletin* 117 (May 1995):427–529; S. Moscovici, "Social Influence and Conformity," in *The Handbook of Social Psychology*, 3rd ed., ed. G. Lindzey and E. Aronson (New York: Random House, 1985), pp. 347–412.

28. For a study of peaceful societies, see Doug Fry, *Beyond War: The Human Potential for Peace* (New York: Oxford University Press, 2007).

29. Doris Graber, *Mass Media and Politics* (Washington, DC: CQ Press, 2007); Bennett, *When the Press Fails*.

30. For discussion about how the future creates the present, see Mead, *Mind, Self, and Society*.

31. Sternberg, "Understanding and Combating Hate," in *The Psychology of Hate*, ed. Robert J. Sternberg (Washington, DC: American Psychological Association, 2005).

32. There is a body of literature on actualizing human potential that includes Abraham Maslow and philosophers such as Aristotle (in his *Metaphysics*).

33. Mark Z. Jacobson and Mark A. Delucchi, "A Path to Sustainable Energy by 2030," *Scientific American* (November 2009): 58–65.

34. David Callahan, *Fortunes of Change: The Rise of the Liberal Rich and the Remaking of America* (Hoboken, NJ: John Wiley and Sons, 2010).

35. Rupert Murdoch, News Corporation, http://www.newscorp.com/energy/ (accessed May 31, 2011).

36. The idea that journalists in the for-profit media are not "free" is discussed in other texts, including Edward S. Herman and Noam Chomsky, *Manufacturing Consent* (New York: Pantheon Books, 1988).

37. Bennett, *News*; Ben Bagdikian, *The Media Monopoly* (Boston: Beacon Press, 2000); Robert McChesney, Rich Media, Poor Democracy (Chicago: University of Illinois Press, 1999); James T. Hamilton, *All the News That's Fit to Sell: How the Market Transforms Information into News* (Princeton, NJ: Princeton University Press, 2004); James T. Hamilton, "The Market and the Media," in *The Press*, ed. Geneva Overholser and Kath-

leen Hall Jamieson (Oxford: Oxford University Press, 2005); David Croteau and William Hoynes, *The Business of Media: Corporate Media and the Public Interest* (Thousand Oaks, CA: Pine Forge Press, 2001); Robert G. Picard, "Money, Media, and the Public Interest," in *The Press*; Benjamin Compaine and Douglas Gomery, *Who Owns the Media? Competition and Concentration in the Mass Media Industry* (Mahwah, NJ: Lawrence Erlbaum Associates, 2000); John McManus, *Market Driven Journalism: Let the Citizen Beware?* (Thousand Oaks, CA: Sage Publications, 1994).

38. Maria Armoudian, quoting Michael Stipe of musical group R. E. M., *Global Network News* (May 1995).

39. Philip Seib, *Headline Diplomacy: How News Coverage Affects Foreign Policy* (Westport, CT: Greenwood Publishing Group, 1996), p. xvii.

40. Capella and Jamieson, *Spiral of Cynicism*.

41. McChesney and Nichols, *Death and Life of American Journalism*.

42. Jepperson, "Institutions, Institutional Effects, and Institutionalism"; and Roger Friedland and Robert R. Alford, "Bringing Society Back In: Symbols, Practices, and Institutional Contradictions," in *The New Institutionalism in Organizational Analysis*, ed. Walter W. Powell and Paul J. DiMaggio (Chicago: University of Chicago Press, 1991).

43. H. Peyton Young, "The Dynamics of Conformity," in *Social Dynamics*, ed. Steven N. Durlauf and H. Peyton Young (Washington, DC: Brookings Institution, 2001).

44. Associated Press, "PayPal Cuts WikiLeaks from Money Flow," December 4, 2010.

45. David Gardner, "'Ha Ha, I Hit 'Em': Top Secret Video Showing US Helicopter Pilots Gunning Down 12 Civilians in Baghdad Attack Leaked Online," *Daily Mail Online*, April 7, 2010, http://www.dailymail.co.uk/news/worldnews/article-1263822/WikiLeaks-video-Reuters-journalists-civilians-gunned-US-pilots.html.

46. Maha Azzam, "How WikiLeaks Helped Fuel Tunisian Revolution," CNN, January 18, 2011, http://articles.cnn.com/2011-01-18/opinion/tunisia.wikileaks_1_tunisians-wikileaks-regime?_s=PM:OPINION.

47. Amnesty International, "Amnesty Announces Media Awards 2009 Winners," June 2, 2009, http://www.amnesty.org.uk/news_details.asp?NewsID=18229; Eben Harrell, "WikiLeaks Founder Julian Assange," *Time*, July 26, 2010.

48. Armoudian and Crigler, "Constructing the Vote"; Jody Baumgartner and Johnathon S. Morris, "The *Daily Show* Effect," *American Politics Research* 34, no. 3 (2006): 341–67; Geoffrey Baym, "*The Daily Show*: Discursive Integration and the Reinvention of Political Journalism," *Political Communication* 22 (2005): 259–76; Matthew A. Baum, "How Soft News Brings Policy Issues to the Inattentive Public," in *Media Power in Politics*, 5th ed., ed. Doris A. Graber (Washington, DC: CQ Press, 2005) ; Bill Carter and Brian Stelter, "In *Daily Show* Role on 9/11 Bill, Echoes of Murrow," *New York Times*, December 26, 2010.

49. John Marks, interview with the author, 2010.

50. Ibid.

51. Richard Hofstetter, David Barker, James T. Smith, Gina M. Zari, and Thomas A. Ingrassia, "Information, Misinformation on Political Talk Radio," *Political Research Quarterly* 52 (1999): 353–69.

52. Ban Ki Moon, citing UNESCO.

53. Committee to Protect Journalists, http://www.cpj.org/. This number may actually be higher, particularly by the time this book is published.

54. Marcus F. Franda, *Launching into Cyberspace: Internet Development and Politics in Five World Regions* (Boulder, CO: Lynne Rienner Publishers, 2002).

55. Theodore L. Glasser and Max Gunther, "The Legacy of Autonomy in American Journalism," in *The Press*, ed. Geneva Overholser and Kathleen Hall Jamieson (New York: Oxford University Press, 2005); Gans, *Deciding What's News*; Kerbel, *If It Bleeds, It Leads*; Bennett, *News*; Robert Entman; Timothy Cook, *Governing with the News: The News Media as a Political Institution* (Chicago: University of Chicago Press, 1998); David Croteau and William Hoynes, *The Business of Media: Corporate Media and the Public Interest* (Thousand Oaks, CA: Pine Forge Press, 2001); Todd Gitlin, *The Whole World Is Watching* (Berkeley: University of California Press, 1980).

56. Gans, *Deciding What's News*.

57. In addition to references in note 46, see Timothy Crouse, *The Boys on the Bus* (New York: Ballantine Books, 1974); Robert Entman, 1996, 2005; Kerbel, *If It Bleeds, It Leads*; W. Lance Bennett and John D. Klockner, "The Psychology of Mass Mediated Publics," in *The Psychology of Political Communication*, ed. Ann N. Crigler (Ann Arbor: University of Michigan Press, 1998); W. Lance Bennett and Jarol B. Manheim, "The Big Spin: Strategic Communication and the Transformation of Pluralist Democracy," in *Mediated Politics: Communication in the Future of Democracy*, ed. W. Lance Bennett and Robert M. Entman (Cambridge: Cambridge University Press, 2001).

58. Aidan White, *To Tell You the Truth: The Ethical Journalism Initiative* (Brussels: International Federation of Journalists, 2008), p. ii.

59. Ibid.

60. Jack Snyder and Karen Ballentine, "Nationalism and the Marketplace of Ideas," *International Security* 21 (Fall 1996).

61. *Straits Times* (Singapore), November 22, 1996, LexisNexis.